The Psychology of Integrating Content and Language

PSYCHOLOGY OF LANGUAGE LEARNING AND TEACHING
Series Editors: Sarah Mercer, *Universität Graz, Austria* and
Stephen Ryan, *Waseda University, Japan*

This international, interdisciplinary book series explores the exciting, emerging field of Psychology of Language Learning and Teaching. It is a series that aims to bring together works which address a diverse range of psychological constructs from a multitude of empirical and theoretical perspectives, but always with a clear focus on their applications within the domain of language learning and teaching. The field is one that integrates various areas of research that have been traditionally discussed as distinct entities, such as motivation, identity, beliefs, strategies and self-regulation, and it also explores other less familiar concepts for a language education audience, such as emotions, the self and positive psychology approaches. In theoretical terms, the new field represents a dynamic interface between psychology and foreign language education and books in the series draw on work from diverse branches of psychology, while remaining determinedly focused on their pedagogic value. In methodological terms, sociocultural and complexity perspectives have drawn attention to the relationships between individuals and their social worlds, leading to a field now marked by methodological pluralism. In view of this, books encompassing quantitative, qualitative and mixed methods studies are all welcomed.

All books in this series are externally peer-reviewed.

Full details of all the books in this series and of all our other publications can be found on http://www.multilingual-matters.com, or by writing to Multilingual Matters, St Nicholas House, 31-34 High Street, Bristol BS1 2AW, UK.

PSYCHOLOGY OF LANGUAGE LEARNING AND TEACHING: 12

The Psychological Experience of Integrating Content and Language

Edited by
**Kyle Read Talbot, Marie-Theres Gruber
and Rieko Nishida**

MULTILINGUAL MATTERS
Bristol • Blue Ridge Summit

DOI https://doi.org/10.21832/TALBOT4290
Names: Talbot, Kyle Read, 1988- editor. | Gruber, Marie-Theres, 1987- editor.
| Nishida, Rieko, 1972- editor.
Title: The Psychological Experience of Integrating Content and Language/
Kyle Read Talbot, Marie-Theres Gruber, Rieko Nishida.
Description: Bristol, UK; Blue Ridge Summit: Multilingual Matters, 2021. | Series:
Psychology of Language Learning and Teaching: 12 | Includes bibliographical
references and index. | Summary: 'This book explores the psychology of teaching
and learning a subject through a second or other language. It highlights the
challenges and benefits of teaching and learning in integrated content and language
settings and covers themes such as identity, self-concept, cognition, beliefs,
well-being, interventions and professional development' – Provided by publisher.
Identifiers: LCCN 2020043608 (print) | LCCN 2020043609 (ebook) | ISBN
9781788924283 (paperback) | ISBN 9781788924290 (hardback) | ISBN
9781788924306 (pdf) | ISBN 9781788924313 (epub) | ISBN 9781788924320
(kindle edition)
Subjects: LCSH: Language arts – Correlation with content subjects. |
Language and languages – Study and teaching – Foreign speakers. |
Language and languages – Study and teaching – Psychological aspects. |
English language – Study and teaching – Foreign speakers.
Classification: LCC P53.293 .P79 2021 (print) | LCC P53.293 (ebook)
| DDC 418.0071 – dc23
LC record available at https://lccn.loc.gov/2020043608
LC ebook record available at https://lccn.loc.gov/2020043609
Library of Congress Cataloging in Publication Data
A catalog record for this book is available from the Library of Congress.

British Library Cataloguing in Publication Data
A catalogue entry for this book is available from the British Library.

ISBN-13: 978-1-78892-429-0 (hbk)
ISBN-13: 978-1-78892-428-3 (pbk)

Multilingual Matters
UK: St Nicholas House, 31-34 High Street, Bristol BS1 2AW, UK.
USA: NBN, Blue Ridge Summit, PA, USA.

Website: www.multilingual-matters.com
Twitter: Multi_Ling_Mat
Facebook: https://www.facebook.com/multilingualmatters
Blog: www.channelviewpublications.wordpress.com

The policy of Multilingual Matters/Channel View Publications is to use papers that are
natural, renewable and recyclable products, made from wood grown in sustainable forests.
In the manufacturing process of our books, and to further support our policy, preference
is given to printers that have FSC and PEFC Chain of Custody certification. The FSC and/
or PEFC logos will appear on those books where full certification has been granted to the
printer concerned.

Typeset by Riverside Publishing Solutions.
Printed and bound in the UK by the CPI Books Group Ltd.
Printed and bound in the US by NBN.

Contents

Tables and Figures

Tables

Figures

External Reviewers

Ali H. Al-Hoorie, Jubail Industrial College, Saudi Arabia

Marta Aguilar, Universitat Politècnica de Catalunya, Spain

Sonja Babić, University of Graz, Austria

Phil Ball, Federation of Basque Schools and University of the Basque Country, Spain

Kay Bentley, Freelance CLIL Consultant, UK

Barbara Buchholz, University College of Teacher Education Burgenland, Austria

Elizabeth Erling, University of Graz, Austria

Christina Gkonou, University of Essex, UK

Tammy Gregersen, American University of Sharjah, UAE

Ana Halbach, University of Alcalá, Spain

Nobuyuki Hino, Osaka University, Japan

Kay Irie, Gakushuin University, Japan

Paula Kalaja, University of Jyväskylä, Finland

Chengchen Li, Huazhong University of Science and Technology, China

Margaret Lo, The University of Hong Kong, China

Thomas Lockley, Nihon University College of Law, Japan

Ute Massler, University College of Teacher Education Weingarten, Germany

Dennis M. McInerney, Honorary Professor at The Education University of Hong Kong

Christine Muir, University of Nottingham, UK

Tim Murphey, Kanda University of International Studies, Japan

Hima Rawal, Michigan State University, USA

Bill Snyder, Kanda University of International Studies, Japan

Isobel Wang, University of Graz, Austria

Abbreviations

AHS	Allgemeinbildende Höhere Schule
AI	Artificial Intelligence
ANEW	Affective Norms for English Words
BAC	Basque Autonomous Community
BE	Bilingual Education
BFLPE	Big-Fish-Little-Pond Effect
BHS	Berufsbildende Höhere Schule
BICS	Basic Interpersonal Communicative Skills
CALP	Cognitive Academic Language Proficiency
CAP	Certificado de Aptitud Pedagógica, Certificate of Pedagogical Aptitude
CAPA	Contextualisation, Awareness, Practice, Autonomy
CBI	Content-Based Instruction
CBLT	Content-Based Language Teaching
CEFR	Common European Framework of Reference for Languages
CF	Corrective Feedback
CFE	Corrective Feedback Episode
CLIL	Content and Language Integrated Learning
COLT	Communicative Orientation of Language Teaching
CPD	Continuing Professional Development
CT-CL2SL	CLIL Teachers as Confident L2 Subject Languagers
CT-CL2T	CLIL Teachers as Confident L2 Teachers
CT-CL2U	CLIL Teachers as Confident L2 Users
EAP	English for Academic Purposes
ECTS	European Credit Transfer and Accumulation System
EFL	English as a Foreign Language
EFL SC	English as a Foreign Language Self-Concept
EHEA	European Higher Education Area
EL	English Learners
ELA	English Language Arts

ELT	English Language Teaching
EME	English-Medium Education
EMEMUS	English-Medium Education in Multilingual University Settings
EMI	English as a Medium of Instruction
ERASMUS	European Region Action Scheme for the Mobility of University Students
ESL	English as a Second Language
ESP	English for Specific Purposes
ESS	English-Speaking Students
ETSB	Eastern Townships School Board
FL	Foreign Language
FMI	Foreign-Medium Instruction
	Foreign Language Medium of Instruction
G30	Global 30
GALC	Geneva Affect Label Coder
HE	Higher Education
HTL	Austrian upper-secondary colleges of technology
IC	Instructional Conversation
ICL	Integrated Content and Language
ICLHE	Integrating Content and Language in Higher Education
ID	Individual Differences
I/E	Internal/External
IELTE	Initial English Language Teacher Education
IMA	Intrinsic Motivation – Accomplishment
IMK	Intrinsic Motivation – Knowledge
IMS	Intrinsic Motivation – Stimulation
IRE	Initiation-Response-Evaluation
IW	Incidental Welsh
K-12	Kindergarten through high school
KS3	Key stage 3
L1	First Language
L2	Second Language
L2MSS	L2 Motivational Self System
LLOS	Language Learning Orientations Scale
LP	Language Practice
MEXT	Japanese Ministry of Education, Culture, Sports, Science and Technology
NCLB	No Child Left Behind
NMS	Neue Mittelschule
OCF	Oral Corrective Feedback
OPT	The Oxford Placement Test
PD	Professional Development
REM	Reciprocal Effects Model

ROAD-MAPPING	Roles of English (in relation to other languages) (RO), Academic Disciplines (AD), (language) Management (M), Agents (A), Practices and Processes (PP) and Internationalization and Glocalization (ING)
S-A-L-T	Strategic -All languages -Literacies –Target
SDT	Self-determination Theory
SIOP	Sheltered Instruction Observation Protocol
STEM	Science, Technology, Engineering and Mathematics
SWB	Subjective Well-being
TBL	Task-Based Learning
TESOL	Teachers of English to Students of Other Languages
TL	Target Language
WJEC	Welsh Joint Education Committee

Contributors

Editors

Kyle Read Talbot is a language teacher and researcher in Applied Linguistics. He taught ESL at the University of Iowa in the United States before enrolling as a PhD student at the University of Graz in Austria. He holds an MA in TESOL/Applied Linguistics from the University of Northern Iowa, in Cedar Falls, IA. His current research and thinking interests include the psychology of language learning and teaching, well-being, bilingual and multilingual education and CDST and applied complexity science.

Marie-Theres Gruber works at the Private University College of Teacher Education Graz (KPH Graz). Her teaching and research interests are early foreign language learning, lesson planning and CLIL as well as progressive pedagogy (Jenaplan) and diversity management. She has been involved in different CLIL projects and CLIL in German material development for the Austrian language competence centre (ÖSZ).

Rieko Nishida, PhD is an associate professor at Osaka University. Her research interest has been social and educational psychology of second language learning in the Japanese EFL context. She is especially interested in CLIL and the influence of motivation and other psychological factors in language learning among children and Japanese university EFL learners.

Authors

Victor Arshad received his MA in Second Language Education from McGill University, where he has taken on the role of Strategic Initiatives Analyst, focusing on institutional policies and data within the Research and Innovation sector. A former secondary school teacher from Toronto, Victor taught English through Social Sciences content to Arabic speaking students in Abu Dhabi for many years and experienced the needs for stronger professional development for teachers who teach language through content first-hand. He continues to teach English as a Second Language at the YMCA International Language School in Montréal.

Darío Luis Banegas is a lecturer in TESOL at the University of Strathclyde (UK). Darío is also an associate fellow with the University of Warwick (UK) and a visiting lecturer at universities in Latin America particularly in MA programmes which offer modules on content and language integrated learning (CLIL), action research and curriculum development. Between 2001 and 2019, he was a teacher educator and curriculum developer with the Ministry of Education in Chubut, Argentina. He leads professional development opportunities and supervises action research projects in teacher education. In Argentina, he is involved in teacher associations and founded the Argentinian Journal of Applied Linguistics. His main interests are: CLIL, teacher research and initial English language teacher education.

Emma Dafouz is an Associate Professor in the Department of English Studies at Complutense University of Madrid, Spain. For over two decades she has researched on English-medium education in higher education and CLIL. She has published extensively in international journals (e.g. Applied Linguistics, English for Specific Purposes, AILA Review, Language and Education, International Journal of Bilingual Education and Bilingualism). Her most recent publication is an authored book with Ute Smit entitled *ROAD-MAPPING English Medium Education in the Internationalised University* published in 2020 by Palgrave Macmillan. Emma served as Policy Advisor for curricular internationalisation at her university from 2014–2019.

Christiane Dalton-Puffer is Professor of English Linguistics at the University of Vienna and is co-affiliated to the University's Centre of Teacher Education. She has done research on Middle English and morphology, but today her teaching and research interests are mainly in educational linguistics. She is the author of Discourse in CLIL classrooms (Benjamins, 2007) as well numerous articles. Her current research focus is how teachers and students use language to express subject content and work towards curricular learning goals of specialist subjects. Work in this area has given her a special interest in crossing disciplinary borders in order to convince educators of the relevance of language for learning.

María del Pilar García Mayo is Full Professor of English Language and Linguistics at the University of the Basque Country (Spain). She holds a BA in Germanic Philology from the Universidad de Santiago de Compostela (Spain) and an MA and a PhD in Linguistics from the University of Iowa (USA). Her research focuses on the L2/L3 acquisition of English morphosyntax and the study of conversational interaction in EFL. She has published widely in indexed journals and major publishing companies in the field. Prof. García Mayo is the director of the research group Language and Speech (www.laslab.org) and the co-editor of Language Teaching Research.

Erwin M. Gierlinger, PhD, is Professor of Foreign Language Teaching at the University College of Education in Linz, Austria. His research interests are mainly in CLIL teacher pedagogy. His research in this field has led to various publications. He has also participated in a variety of European CLIL teaching programmes and been in charge of several pre- and in-service courses on the teaching of CLIL. He has developed and published a model for the teaching of CLIL in secondary education and presented this at numerous international conferences. He is also the owner of the CLIL blog: https://clilingmesoftly.wordpress.com.

Nicole Hofstadler worked as a research assistant at the University of Graz, Austria, and is currently involved in a project on content and language integrated learning (CLIL). She also teaches English, History and CLIL at a secondary school in Graz as well as English language courses at the Pädagogische Hochschule Graz, a teacher training college for future primary and secondary educators. Her main interests include teacher education, CLIL and teacher SWB.

Julia Hüttner is Professor of English Language Education at the University of Vienna, Austria, having moved there from the University of Southampton in 2018. Her main research interests lie in Content and Language Integrated Learning (CLIL), English Medium Instruction (EMI) and language teacher cognition. She also addresses the use of video resources to foster teacher learning and development. Her publications include a monograph, edited volumes and numerous journal articles.

Antonio Jiménez Muñoz is an Associate Professor of English at the University of Oviedo. His research gauges the evidence-based impact of policy implementations for both learners and lecturers in multilingual contexts, particularly in Higher Education and the field of Economics. He has published in the International Journal of Bilingual Education and Bilingualism, Porta Linguarum and Iberica and contributed to collections for Routledge, Peter Lang, Lexington and McGraw-Hill. Previously, he taught as a teaching fellow at Kent and Hull in the United Kingdom and was a visiting scholar at Oxford and Cambridge.

Jun Jin is currently a post-doctoral fellow at the University of Graz in Austria. After obtaining an MA in Applied Linguistics (Distinction) at the University of Southampton, UK, and earning a PhD in Education at the University of Hong Kong in Hong Kong, P.R. China, she worked as a post-doctoral fellow and an instructor at universities in Hong Kong. She was also a visiting Fellow at the University of Cambridge in the

United Kingdom, with Doris Zimmern HKU-Cambridge Hughes Hall Fellowship. Her research focuses on issues of teaching and learning in different contexts. Specifically, she is analysing the role of silence, technology-mediated interaction, small group settings, identity and wellbeing. She would like to further explore multilevel perspectives on teaching and learning, combining micro (i.e. the use of language) and macro (i.e. social, cultural and political practices) level analysis. The ultimate goal of her research is to improve and enrich teaching and learning experiences in the process of curriculum development.

Anita Lämmerer is a PhD student and English teacher. She teaches both at tertiary level (University of Graz and University College of Teacher Education Styria) and at a secondary school in Graz, where she oversees CLIL projects and a school-university partnership. From 2015 until 2019 she worked as a research assistant at the Department of English Studies at the University of Graz, where she engaged in several research projects on teacher psychology. Her current research interests include teacher education, CLIL and the psychology of language learning and teaching.

Roy Lyster is Professor Emeritus of Second Language Education in the Department of Integrated Studies Education at McGill University in Montreal. His research examines the effects of instructional interventions designed to counterbalance form-focused and content-based approaches. He has a PhD in Applied Linguistics as well as a B.Ed. and M.Ed. from the University of Toronto and an MA from the Université de Paris VII. He is author of a module called *Content-Based Language Teaching* published by Routledge in 2018, and three books: *Learning and Teaching Languages Through Content* published by Benjamins in 2007, *Vers une approche intégrée en immersion* published by CEC Publishing in 2016, and *Scaffolding Language Development in Immersion and Dual Language Classrooms* (with D. J. Tedick) published by Routledge in 2020.

Laura Mahalingappa (PhD, The University of Texas at Austin) is an associate professor of English as a Second Language (ESL) teacher education at Texas State University. Her teaching and research interests include first and second language acquisition, sociolinguistics and teacher education. She has published research on bilingual language acquisition in marginalised language communities, teachers' beliefs about teaching linguistically and culturally diverse populations and the education of Muslim students. She has taught English in the United States, Turkey and the former Soviet Union. Her recent book on multicultural education, with Nihat Polat, is entitled *Supporting Muslim Students: A Guide to Understanding the Diverse Issues of Today's Classrooms* (2017, Rowman & Littlefield).

Katja Mäntylä, PhD, is currently professor of English at the School of Languages and Translation Studies at the University of Turku, Finland where she trains future teachers of English. Earlier, she has studied language proficiency, especially vocabulary learning. Her most recent research focuses on language learners' and teacher trainees' beliefs, multilingual learning environments and on early foreign language learning.

Sarah Mercer is Professor of Foreign Language Teaching at the University of Graz, Austria, where she is Head of ELT methodology. Her research interests include all aspects of the psychology surrounding the foreign language learning experience. She is the author, co-author and co-editor of several books in this area including, *Towards an Understanding of Language Learner Self-Concept, Psychology for Language Learning, Multiple Perspectives on the Self in SLA, New Directions in Language Learning Psychology, Positive Psychology in SLA, Exploring Psychology for Language Teachers* (Winner of the IH Ben Warren Prize) and *Language Teacher Psychology.*

Ruth Milla teaches FL Teaching, Communicative Competence and English for the Pre-primary and Primary classrooms at the Faculty of Education of the University of the Basque Country (Spain). She holds a degree in English Philology from the University of Deusto (Spain) and a MA in Language Acquisition in Multilingual Settings as well as a PhD in English Philology from the University of the Basque Country. Her research focuses on FL teaching, particularly corrective feedback, and has been presented at national and international conferences and published in journals and publishing companies of the field. She is a member of the research group Language and Speech (www.laslab.org).

Sotiria Pappa is a postdoctoral researcher at the University of Helsinki, Finland, and her research interests centre on professional identity and emotions. Her doctoral research focused on Content and Language Integrated Learning (CLIL) teachers, examining resources, challenges, emotions and identity negotiation in CLIL teaching. She has worked for the Role of Emotions in Agentic Learning at Work (REAL) project at the University of Jyväskylä, Finland, where she focused on Finnish language teachers of immigrant pupils. She has further studied professional identity in relation to doctoral researchers and teacher educators.

Nia Mererid Parry following the successful completion of her Master's in Education studies at Bangor in 2015, Nia started her PhD studies within the field of bilingualism. The doctorate, which falls at a vital period in the revitalisation of the Welsh language, concentrates on evaluating the implementation of Incidental Welsh in English medium secondary schools in North Wales. Nia has presented her work in numerous conferences around Europe and has also been involved in additional research projects for organisations such as Educational Consortias in Wales and y Coleg Cymraeg Cenedlaethol (The National Welsh College).

Richard S. Pinner is an associate professor at Sophia University in Tokyo with over 15 years of experience as a language teacher and teacher trainer. He holds a PhD in ELT and Applied Linguistics and has published several articles on language education, most recently in *Language Teaching Research*, *English Today* and *Applied Linguistics Review*. He is the author of three research monographs and is particularly interested in the areas of authenticity and motivation in ELT and Content and Language Integrated Learning.

Nihat Polat (PhD, The University of Texas at Austin) is a professor and chair of the Department of Curriculum and Instruction at Texas State University. He has taught both graduate and undergraduate courses in the areas of L2 learning, teaching and assessment, teacher education and the education of immigrant and minority populations in K-12 schools. He has published two books and over 30 peer-reviewed journal articles among others. His work has appeared in top-tier journals, including *Applied Linguistics*, *TESOL Quarterly*, *Modern Language Journal*, etc. Previously, he served as Associate Dean for Graduate Studies and Research at Duquesne University, while also siting on national panels (e.g. Fulbright National Screening Committee) and serving as a consulting editor for the *Journal of Educational Research*. With Tammy Gregersen and Peter MacIntyre, he also has an edited volume entitled *Research-Driven Pedagogy: Implications of L2A Theory and Research for the Teaching of Language Skills* (2020, Routledge).

Anssi Roiha, PhD, works as a lecturer at the Department of Teacher Education at the University of Turku, Finland. In his doctoral dissertation (University of Jyväskylä, Finland), he investigated former CLIL pupils' perceptions of the long-term effects of CLIL on their lives. His research interests include CLIL, differentiation and intercultural education.

Ute Smit's main research focus is on English used as a classroom language in various educational settings, by combining micro, meso and macro perspectives. Her publications deal with ELF (English as a lingua franca), CLIL (Content and Language Integrated Learning), EMEMUS (English Medium Education in Multilingual University Settings), teacher beliefs and language policy. Recent projects include 'ADiBE', 'CLIL@ HTL' and 'INTE-R.LICA'. She was a co-founding member of the AILA Research Network on CLIL and Immersion Education, and is presently a board member of the ICLHE (Integrating Content and Language in Higher Education) Association.

Enlli Môn Thomas is a Professor of Research in Education and the Director of Research in the School of Education and Human Development, Bangor University, Wales, UK. Her main research interests span psycholinguistic studies of bilingual language acquisition, particularly in relation to children's acquisition of complex structures under conditions of minimal input and educational approaches to language transmission, acquisition and use.

Acknowledgments

We are incredibly grateful to have had the opportunity to publish this edited collection with Multilingual Matters as part of the Psychology of Language Learning and Teaching series. We would like to thank the series editors Sarah Mercer and Stephen Ryan for helping us find a home for this collection of papers. Particularly, Sarah's support and guidance while developing this volume was essential to its success. We also would like to extend our heartfelt thanks to Laura Longworth of Multilingual Matters for trusting in us and guiding us through this process. This collection simply would not have been possible without a generous grant from the Austrian National Bank (ÖNB) ('Selbstbild & professionelles Wohlbefinden von CLIL Lehrenden', 17136) and the terrific research team we collaborated with along the way. Furthermore, we would like to thank the chapter authors and commend them for their wonderful contributions and for choosing this volume to house their exemplary scholarship. We also would like to recognize and thank the external and internal reviewers for their feedback they provided on the individual chapters as well as the external reviewer for the feedback on the manuscript. Undoubtedly, the astute feedback from the reviewers improved the quality of the papers and the manuscript as a whole.

1 Introduction

Kyle Read Talbot and Marie-Theres Gruber

The Growth and Spread of Content and Language Integrated Programmes

The integration of content and language is not a new phenomenon in education. Coyle (2007: 543) writes that 'being educated in a language other than one's mother tongue has been around for over 5000 years'. In Canada, French immersion programmes have existed since the 1960s (Cenoz *et al.*, 2014). However, recent years have seen an increase in the implementation of programmes where content classes, such as, history, biology, etc., are taught through a language that is typically not the learners', or teachers' first language (L1). It is worth reflecting on how quickly integrated content and language (ICL) programmes are spreading internationally. Since the 2000s, English-medium instruction (EMI) programmes have increased by over 1000% in Europe (Wächter & Maiworm, 2014). In 2016, StudyPortals reported that 'the top 1,000 universities offer over 72,500 full-degree study options taught in English, are located in over 700 cities, and cover over 200 disciplines and sub-disciplines' (Neghina, 2016). The implementation of such programmes, in various languages, but most frequently in English (Dalton-Puffer, 2011), is occurring at all 'phases of education, pre-school, primary, secondary and tertiary as well as many specially designed classes for particular groups of students (e.g. migrants)' (Macaro *et al.*, 2018: 37).

The growth and spread of ICL settings have profound implications for teachers and learners in these contexts. Such programmes are not identical to either language-focused programmes or settings in which content is taught through the L1, as such, it is worth exploring how the experiences and perceptions of teachers and learners in ICL programmes may be dissimilar to teachers and learners in other settings. Some of the differences between teachers and learners' experiences relate to explicit educational policies and other external factors, however, many relevant aspects that shape their educational experiences are internal and relate to the psychologies of teachers and learners. Borg (2019a: 2) suggests, for example, that there is a 'hidden mass' of 'unseen forces' that powerfully influence teacher behaviour which in some cases are 'internal to the teacher, such as their beliefs knowledge, feelings, perceptions, attitudes, and thoughts'. These same internal factors impact on students' behaviours too. Learner beliefs and mindsets, for instance, are related to how students approach their learning and their goals (Mercer & Ryan, 2010). Arguably, investigating the psychological experiences of teachers and learners in ICL contexts is especially critical, given that the effects of the individuals in these roles remain underexplored.

Definitional Issues in Integrated Content and Language Settings

First, we wanted to touch briefly on issues of labelling and definition. Programmes integrating content and language are referred to by various names in the literature. Terms include, but are not limited to, immersion, content-based instruction (CBI), bilingual education (BE), content-based language teaching (CBLT), content and language integrated learning (CLIL), integrating content and language in higher education (ICLHE), foreign-medium instruction (FMI), English-medium instruction (EMI) and English-medium education in multilingual university settings (EMEMUS). These terms refer to forms of integration which can vary in degrees of immersion, spanning from total immersion to language-focused classes with content involved for language practice (Airey, 2016; Met, 1998). They also differ in terms of their implementation, whether enforced through government or policy initiative, or by a bottom-up decentralised push by teachers.

With such variation, attempting to label, and to distinguish between the classification and aims of such programmes is challenging (see, Airey, 2016; Cenoz *et al.*, 2014; Fenton-Smith *et al.*, 2017; Macaro *et al.*, 2018). In respect to CLIL, Cenoz *et al.* (2014: 247) argue that, in general, 'the scope of CLIL is not clear-cut, and as a consequence, its core features cannot be clearly identified'. Marsh (2008: 233) suggests that, 'applications of CLIL are multifarious depending on educational level, environment and the specific approach adopted'. Similarly, Hüttner and Smit (2014: 163) explain that the implementation of CLIL depends on local needs and context and is therefore likely to vary substantially across contexts:

> [T]here is no unified CLIL pedagogy and even less a CLIL method. CLIL practice is informed by local realisations of language teaching methodologies (often with at least a nod to communicative language teaching, itself an approach that encompasses a range of practices) and, most importantly of all, a host of content subjects.

The ways in which CLIL has been conceptualised illustrates this problem. One definition of CLIL offered by Coyle *et al.* (2010: 1) defines it as, 'a dual-focused educational approach in which an additional language is used for the learning and teaching of both content and language'. Though this is referred to as a singular educational approach by Coyle *et al.* (2010), Mehisto *et al.* (2008: 12) refer to it as 'an umbrella term covering a dozen or more educational approaches'. What seems to be generally accepted with CLIL is a dual-focus on content and language learning; however, the proportion as to how the focus is dedicated is not exactly straightforward (Marsh, 2002). In addition to definitional concerns, there are also labelling concerns. To take EMI as an example, Macaro *et al.* (2018: 46), explain that 'labels given to the phenomenon of EMI and their definition are inconsistent and problematic' and often seem to lack sufficient justification for their use. In other words, similar problems plague EMI in terms of how it is defined and labelled.

When the editors first proposed this volume, initial feedback warned of the 'terminological minefield' into which we were entering. With such definitional and labelling concerns in mind, Macaro *et al.* (2018: 37) admitted that 'the overall global picture ... is extremely complex and sometimes confusing'. In recognition of this complexity, we deliberately take a broad understanding of the notion of the integration of content and language and include a wide range of chapters that use distinct terminology to refer to this. We have chosen to refer to 'integrating content and language' in the title of this edited volume, and integrated content and language (ICL) programme when referring to a particular setting or context rather than selecting an existing umbrella term to represent different variations of this. Rather than trying to navigate this terminological minefield alone, we have asked the chapter authors to define and describe how the integration of content and language should be understood considering each of their respective contributions and the appropriacy of terms used in their specific settings.

Integrated Content and Language Programmes as Educational Innovations

Hüttner *et al.* (2013) suggest that the beliefs of teachers and learners might explain the diverse acceptance and success of CLIL in Austria. They referred to CLIL as 'one of the most dynamic pedagogic trends in language teaching in Europe' and as a 'pedagogic innovation'. Indeed, one lens through which to view CLIL and other ICL programmes is as a type of educational innovation, change or reform. Fullan (1994: 20) points out that educational innovations typically fail when initiated through a top-down or bottom-up fashion. He explains, 'In such situations, top-down strategies result in conflict and/or superficial compliance. Expecting local units to flourish through *laissez faire* decentralization leads to drift, *ad hocness*, and/or inertia'. In lieu of either a top-down or bottom-up approach, Fullan (1994) suggests productive connections and coordinated action between centralised and de-centralised agents, in other words, ongoing and facilitative interactions between policymakers, educational managers and classroom stakeholders. Yet, despite being defining in terms of the success or failure of educational change (Day, 2007), stakeholders are often not consulted about the spread of such programmes or how fast they are implemented. For instance, Macaro *et al.* (2018: 50) were surprised to find that none of the studies they reviewed on teacher and student beliefs in EMI contexts described having consulted teachers or learners about which subjects to implement EMI in or how quickly to do this. Though Macaro *et al.* (2018) refer explicitly to EMI in higher education, they speak to a reality in which key stakeholders often are not consulted about the spread of ICL programmes in their local contexts.

Even though teachers and learners may not be consulted about the implementation of ICL programmes in some cases, they are significantly impacted by such innovations or reforms. Day (2007: 598) points out that despite differences in the 'content, direction and pace' of educational reforms or innovations, they often can affect teachers in similar ways, for instance, he suggests that they can challenge teachers' practices 'resulting in periods of at least temporary destabilisation'. Furthermore, he suggests that such reforms often result in higher workloads for teachers and that educational reforms are typically implemented in a way that ignores teachers' identities, which he explains is central to teachers' 'motivation efficacy, commitment, job satisfaction and effectiveness' (Day, 2007: 598). Arguably, some of the same destabilisation and identity challenges that Day (2007) suggests can occur with teachers would also impact the way students perceive and adjust to pedagogic innovations. As stakeholders are central to the success or failure of ICL programmes (Fullan, 1994) and are significantly affected by educational reforms (Day, 2007), we believe that recognising how they react and adapt or are otherwise affected by these settings warrants further attention in the research community.

The Importance of Stakeholder Perspectives

Several research contributions have explored how ICL programmes are implemented at the conceptual, curricular and assessment levels (Dalton-Puffer, 2011; Lasagabaster & Ruiz de Zarobe, 2010; Lin, 2016; Nikula *et al.*, 2016; Wannagat, 2007). Much of this empirical work has focused on the nature of these programmes and their implementation, with comparatively fewer studies focusing on the perspectives and experiences of key stakeholders (for notable exceptions, see: Codó & Patiño-Santos, 2018; Dearden & Macaro, 2016; Doiz *et al.*, 2014a; Doiz & Lasagabaster, 2018; Hessel *et al.*, 2020; Hüttner *et al.*, 2013; Moate, 2011; Pappa *et al.*, 2017). Briefly, we reflect on why we view gathering such perspectives as important, beginning with learners, and then considering teacher perspectives.

In many ICL settings, learners have tended to report positive attitudes (e.g. Massler, 2012; Roiha & Mäntylä, this volume; Seikkula-Leino, 2007;

Vazquez *et al.*, 2014). For example, Doiz *et al.* (2014b) found that students enjoyed the challenge that accompanied CLIL classes and felt positive emotion when reflecting on their accomplishments. In another CLIL study, De Smet *et al.* (2018) found that for a sample of Belgian primary and secondary learners, CLIL learners tended to experience less foreign language classroom anxiety than their non-CLIL counterparts, but similar levels of foreign language enjoyment. More pragmatic attitudes towards toward ICL classes have also been reported (Dalton-Puffer *et al.*, this volume; Hüttner *et al.*, 2013). Hüttner *et al.* (2013: 275) suggested that students in a professionally oriented secondary school in Austria tended to view interactions in CLIL courses 'as closer to the reality of their future profession'. Students also revealed pragmatic attitudes towards CLIL programmes in Bozdoğan and Karlıdağ (2013: 9) qualitative interview study in Turkey. Each of the 15 student participants reported that they perceived advantages in studying through English in terms of future job prospects and greater access to the 'outer world'. Yet, despite perceiving advantages to learning in English, the majority of participants also reported discomfort in class ($n = 14$) and all the participants perceived the subject matter to be more challenging to understand in English. In the EMI context, Doiz and Lasagabaster (2018: 676) reported that learners and teachers both can experience vulnerability in EMI settings, but that 'the EMI experience provides them some productive immunity mechanisms that help them overcome their fears and stress'. In this study, students in particular felt internal and external pressure (i.e. parents, societal expectations, etc.) to take EMI courses because they 'fear the consequences that may ensue if they do not become proficient in English' (Doiz & Lasagabaster, 2018: 670). Though a major aim of ICL programmes is to assist students in developing their language proficiency alongside content knowledge, in many cases both learners and teachers tend to evaluate student proficiency as insufficient (Borg, 2016; Bozdoğan & Karlıdağ, 2013; Macaro *et al.*, 2018; cf. Yeh, 2014). For some students, this can engender feelings of linguistic insecurity and a hesitancy to speak in class (Islam, 2013; Kang & Park, 2005).

As with learners, understanding the psychologies of teachers in ICL contexts is also important. Teachers are fundamentally important to the ecology of classrooms settings (Mercer & Kostoulas, 2018). Research supports the idea that their perceptions and beliefs influence their teaching behaviour and senses of professional integrity (Barcelos & Kalaja, 2012; Borg, 2003, 2019b; Moate, 2011) which also impacts their learners (Reyes *et al.*, 2012). Simply put, teachers have an outsized influence on student learning (Hattie, 2009), including in terms of their achievement (Sammons *et al.*, 2007); if teachers believe in the efficacy of ICL programmes, and if they feel they are supported in enacting these programmes, they are more likely to be successful (Massler, 2012; Wegner, 2012). In contrast, if teachers feel less involved or committed to ICL programmes, implementations are less likely to be successful and teachers are more likely to feel destabilised or as if they are lacking support in their teaching roles (cf. Gruber, 2017; Gruber *et al.*, 2020; Massler, 2012; Wegner, 2012).

Not only can ICL settings position teachers outside of their comfort zones as subject or language specialists, they are also expected to have expertise in both language and subject domains (Bovellan, 2014). Indeed, teachers in ICL contexts may find themselves teaching in situations that may involve a wider scope of responsibilities (e.g. responsible for content and language learning) with an expanded range of roles (e.g. assessment in two languages) which can affect them in various ways. For instance, these settings may engender feelings of linguistic insecurity for some teachers and may also pose threats to their professional integrity (Gierlinger, this volume; Jiménez Muñoz, this volume; Moate, 2011). In some cases, teachers may also perceive these settings as affecting how they perceive their workload negatively (Aguilar, 2017; Dafouz, this volume; Talbot *et al.*, this volume). Yet, despite the existence of significant challenges, Moate (2011: 334) argues that these can be viewed as sites of growth. Specifically, she points out that, 'if challenge however leads to successful adaptation of practice, restored confidence and refined practice, the potential for increasing job satisfaction and improving the learning experience is greater'.

What to Expect from this Volume?

The authors of each chapter have been asked to follow certain guidelines to ensure a degree of continuity across the book. As mentioned above, we have specifically requested that each author explains the nature of the ICL setting featured in their chapter. Secondly, each chapter contains a section dedicated to 'implications for policy and practice' to provide relevant practical considerations for readers. These considerations are relevant for teachers' practice and include suggestions for policy and professional development.

The collection includes perspectives from both teachers and learners and covers one chapter that features voices from pre-service teachers (Chapter 15). Student perspectives are represented in Chapters 4, 6, 7 and 15. Perhaps surprisingly, most of the chapters in this volume, relate to teacher perspectives (Chapters 2, 3, 5, 8, 9, 10, 11, 12, 13 & 15). The general trend in research related to the psychology of language learning (PLL) has been to focus on the learner, yet in the submissions for this volume, we notice a different trend as reflected in the number of contributions focused on teacher perspectives. One possible reason for is a recent call to 'redress the imbalance' between studies focusing on learners and teachers in PLL (Mercer, 2018; Mercer & Kostoulas, 2018). Specifically, in integrated content and language settings, there may also be a tendency to focus on the teacher as several studies have pointed to the challenges that teachers might face in such contexts (e.g. Bovellan, 2014; Gierlinger, 2007; Griva *et al.*, 2014; Gruber *et al.*, 2020).

In addition to a range of stakeholder perspectives, and given that the spread of programmes that integrate content and language is truly a global phenomenon, this volume includes a wide spread of geographical settings including Argentina (Chapter 15), Austria (Chapters 3, 9 & 11), Canada (Chapter 13), Finland (Chapters 2 & 4), Spain (Chapters 7 & 8), Japan (Chapter 14), the United States (Chapter 5) and Wales (Chapter 12).

The collection also addresses various educational levels including perspectives from primary, secondary and tertiary settings. The primary level is represented by Chapters 2, 9 and 13, secondary by Chapters 5, 6, 7, 9, 11, 12 and 13 and tertiary by Chapters 3, 8, 9, 10, 11, 14 and 15. There are also chapters comparing educational levels (Chapter 9) and educational contexts (Chapter 7), as well as one chapter that draws on teacher participants from the primary and secondary levels (Chapter 13).

In terms of conceptual organisation, the chapters in this edited volume have been organised into four general groups. First, issues of identity and self-concept of teachers and learners in language and integrated contexts are investigated (Chapters 2–4). Next, Chapters 5 through 8 delve into teacher cognition and teacher and learner beliefs. Chapters 9–11 look at the challenges and opportunities presented by content and language integrated settings and how these are connected to the broader psychologies of teachers in these settings, including their well-being and confidence. The final grouping of chapters covers professional development, classroom implementations, interventions and teacher research (Chapters 12–15). Finally, the concluding chapter synthesises the main lessons and insights from the collection of papers and proposes an agenda for future research.

The Chapters at a Glance

Following this introductory chapter, Sotiria Pappa draws on two qualitative studies involving Finnish primary teachers. In her reflections, she focuses on CLIL teachers' identity negotiation as they navigate their CLIL settings. Specifically, she details the relationships between socio-contextual and individual influences on these teachers' CLIL practices, as well as how these teachers' emotional experiences influence the ways in which they negotiate their identities. In her discussion, she suggests that teacher identity can be viewed as tool for emerging teachers and that teachers should attempt to reflect how their identities have shaped their teaching and pedagogies. Further, she advises that teachers should consider emotions as fundamental to their teaching and suggests that regulating them is important.

Next, Jun Jin, Kyle Talbot and Sarah Mercer report on a qualitative interview study examining the identities and reported practices of EMI teachers working in HE in Austria. They reflect on the complexities of language use in the EMI context and discuss the need to understand how teaching through another language implies both linguistic and subject-area competence and how this is related to whether these teachers embrace or resist their roles as EMI teachers. The authors find that these teachers generally reported having multiple identities that were at times congruent but at other times the site of tensions. They also discuss how these teachers seemed to resist a language teaching role and seemed to instead understand English through its perception as the international language of science and as a lingua franca and pragmatic reality of their academic careers.

In the fourth chapter, Anssi Roiha and Katja Mäntylä reflect on the English language self-concept and experiences of one former CLIL student in Finland throughout his life course. This study takes an approach that begins with this student's experience with CLIL in primary school and traces his experiences with English from that point till he became a doctor years later. The authors conclude that for this student, CLIL played foundational role in helping to form his strong English language self-concept even though this oscillated over time. They also reflect on how their study is in line with previous studies that suggest it is possible to consider distinct self-concepts for different languages.

Transitioning from the first section pertaining to identity and self-concept, we move to teacher and learner beliefs and teacher cognition in integrated content and language settings. Chapter 5 features Nihat Polat and Laura Mahalingappa discussing the beliefs of teachers about what challenges and opportunities presented by the Sheltered Instruction Observational Protocol (SIOP). The SIOP is an instructional protocol and observational model that, when implemented by teachers, promotes an inclusive education that houses English learners (EL) in the United States, the largest cohort of second language (L2) worldwide, in the same classrooms as English speaking students (ESS). The authors suggest that in order to prepare content-area teachers for the reality of working with ELs and ESS simultaneously, that researchers need to attempt to identify and understand the psychological processes of these teachers who may have limited experience working with ELs. They find that, for the teachers in their study, the SIOP presented both general and discipline-specific challenges, but also specific opportunities related to SIOP features that called for separate listings of content and language objectives. They conclude by calling for more studies on the psychologies of teachers as they are vital in helping to understand what teachers do in classrooms.

Next, in Chapter 6, Christiane Dalton-Puffer, Julia Hüttner and Ute Smit examine CLIL settings in Austrian upper secondary technical colleges (HTL). In the chapter, they report that these secondary-level colleges initially implemented CLIL on a voluntary basis, but in 2011 a shift in national policy mandated a certain number of CLIL hours at HTL schools. As such, the authors investigate how this shift language management policy affected the beliefs teachers and students in these settings by drawing on two data sets, one preceding the change (i.e. 2007/08), and one after the change had been implemented (i.e. 2015/16). In their discussion, they report how participants see CLIL as an acceptable response to what they perceive as the dominant position of English in internationalised workplaces; thus, the acceptance of mandatory CLIL seems to only work because it is in English. Further, the authors reflect on the relative stability in teacher and learner beliefs between the two studies and describe the implications of this.

Chapter 7 has Ruth Milla and María del Pilar García Mayo extending the discussion about teacher and learner beliefs. Specifically, they investigate participants' beliefs about corrective feedback in the Spanish secondary context. Through a mixed methods design including questionnaires and classroom observations, they compare the beliefs of CLIL and English as a Foreign Language (EFL) teachers hold about oral corrective feedback (OCF) and question whether these beliefs correspond to these teachers' actual classroom practices. Next, they examine learners' beliefs; the learners in this study were shared by the CLIL and EFL teacher participants, and, as such, had experience learning in both contexts. Finally, they examined whether these learners' beliefs overlap or differ from CLIL and EFL teachers' beliefs. They find that both CLIL and EFL teachers hold generally positive beliefs about OCF and that the differences between their beliefs were small and not statistically significant, however, despite a lack of marked difference between their beliefs, corrections were more frequent and more varied in EFL classrooms. Finally, in comparing the beliefs of their teachers and learners, the authors found that their population of learners had more positive beliefs about OCF than their teachers did, which the authors point out is in line with previous research. The authors conclude by discussing the mismatch between CLIL and EFL teachers' beliefs and actual classroom practices.

The last chapter in this section, Chapter 8, examines the beliefs of physics lecturers about the integration of content and language in EMEMUS settings in the Basque region of Spain. The author, Dafouz, cites the exponential increase in the implementation of EMI and similar programmes as a central reason that researchers are revisiting stakeholder beliefs about practices and pedagogies considering teaching environments where the language of instruction is different than the local participants L1s. In the findings, Dafouz highlights how the physics lecturers in her sample were aware of the roles that language played in their teaching and explained that they used scaffolding strategies for this reason. For instance, she notes how translanguaging was discussed as a pedagogical strategy that these lecturers employed as means to try to reduce students' language anxiety. One point of agreement among the EMEMUS lecturers was that having students with different levels of English in their classes made their teaching more complex. These teachers also discussed feeling pressured to maintain parallel progress in their EMEMUS and Spanish courses. She concludes by suggesting that support for these teachers is vital for these teachers to build their self-efficacy.

The next section explores how the psychologies of teachers in content and language integrated settings are affected considering the challenges and opportunities these settings present. In the first chapter in this section, Chapter 9, Kyle Talbot, Marie-Theres Gruber, Anita Lämmerer, Nicole Hofstadler and Sarah Mercer compare CLIL/EMI teacher well-being at the primary, secondary and tertiary levels in Austria. The study employs the notion of subjective well-being (SWB) in order to understand the well-being of the teachers in these contexts which consists of individual's cognitive judgments of their own satisfaction with their lives as well as their affective experiences. To contextualise this comparison among educational levels, the authors reviewed CLIL implementation at the primary and secondary levels and how EMI was implemented at the tertiary level in Austria. Findings are organised into contextual factors and teacher-related factors affecting these teachers SWB and notable similarities and differences emerged in comparing the settings. Generally, the findings in this study suggest that the SWB of secondary CLIL teachers may be more at risk than teachers at the primary or tertiary level. The authors suggest that navigating the balance between clearer guidelines about CLIL while simultaneously promoting teacher autonomy in the implementation of CLIL/EMI is essential.

Antonio Jiménez Muñoz in Chapter 10 discusses EMI as a possible 'perfect storm for psychological distress' for its teachers. To learn more about which potential factors may be ailing this population, he asked a global population of EMI lecturers to reflect on their experiences, motivation, beliefs and confidence after having taught EMI for five years. He employs a quantitative-qualitative analysis and, in addition, introduced a novel reflection exercise that asked participating lecturers to write a note to their former selves about the psychological and pedagogical aspects they wish they would have known before beginning their EMI teaching. Findings indicate that sources of anxiety remained for these experienced EMI teachers, but encouragingly, experience seemed to alleviate these lecturers' concerns. Jiménez Muñoz suggests that the heavy emphasis on positive aspects in the findings may be indicative of these participants current psychological well-being. In his discussion, he suggests that one-size-fits-all professional development is not enough to account for the diversity of experiences and contextual influences these lecturers experience in their daily realities as EMI teachers. Instead, he suggests a developmental professional approach for

EMI teaching which would include EMI-specific teaching microskills, participant reflection, collaboration and the introduction of aspects of linguistic description for these lecturers.

In Chapter 11, Erwin M. Gierlinger examines how teachers experience the transition to CLIL and how this affects their linguistic and self-confidence. Gierlinger questions how CLIL environments, which he suggests may take teachers out of their linguistic and pedagogical comfort zones, can possibly threaten teaching confidence. Through a longitudinal design including interviews and observational data, he explores CLIL teacher confidence in terms of their ability to use the L2 to teach their subject, to use the L2 generally and to use the L2 deliberately and explicitly to teach L2 pedagogy. Findings revealed tensions for the CLIL teachers along these three domains. Gierlinger suggests that the notion of L2 confidence emerged as a complex and unstable phenomenon that was heavily influenced by contextual factors. He recommends that any intervention to bolster CLIL teachers linguistic and self-confidence should not only address their confidence in the target language (TL) but also their pedagogical confidence in CLIL and their well-being.

The last section of the book focuses on professional development (PD), interventions and teacher classroom research and how these affect the psychologies of the stakeholders. For instance, in the first chapter in this section, Chapter 12, Nia Mererid Parry and Enlli Môn Thomas examine teacher confidence in light of the implementation of Incidental Welsh (IW) in secondary schools in Wales. IW is a model that aims to normalise the use of Welsh in English-medium secondary schools and is one mode of integrating content and language for the purposes of linguistic vitality. Not only does this chapter examine current practices of IW in secondary schools across the country, it also evaluates the effectiveness of a pilot programme of Welsh language support that was designed to support teachers with minimal knowledge or are lacking confidence in using Welsh. Through a mixed methods design including questionnaires, class observations and focus groups, the authors find that a reluctance to use Welsh was related to low levels of confidence. Rather encouragingly, Parry and Thomas also find that an intervention consisting of Welsh support lessons over the course of six weeks seemed to bolster these teachers' senses of linguistic confidence and willingness to engage with IW. They conclude by suggesting that even short interventions can positively impact teachers' confidence.

Next in Chapter 13, authors Victor Arshad and Roy Lyster explore the lived experiences of eight teachers at the primary and secondary levels in Québec who were teaching social studies in French to primarily to ESS. The study reflects on the teachers' affective trajectories and how they responded to support in the first year of a three-year PD partnership, during which they designed curricular units with a language focus that were implemented in their classrooms.

Through questionnaires, interviews, and classroom observations during the PD, the authors uncovered six core constituents that defined the teachers' experiences: enthusiasm, enlightenment, confusion, collaboration, satisfaction, and reservation. Furthermore, they identified four main aspects that were most satisfying for the teachers; these included an integrated approach to CBI, a visual and sequential model, support from colleagues, and an implementation phase of the instructional units the teachers had designed.

Chapter 14 features Rieko Nishida reflecting on a specific variation of CLIL: Soft-CLIL. Nishida describes how Soft-CLIL involves teaching certain topics in the curriculum within a language course and that it has specific linguistic outcomes. She explores whether a Soft-CLIL implementation within an EFL course influences tertiary-level Japanese students' motivation levels, perceptions of group dynamics and perceived language competency. To investigate this, she reports on one phase of a larger study. In this phase, questionnaires are provided at three intervals throughout the course of one semester; one additional open-ended question at the end of the questionnaire gathered qualitative data. While motivation and perceived competence seemed to increase over the three intervals, students' perceptions of group dynamics remained stable. In her discussion, Nishida reflects on how the learners in this context seemed to respond well to the Soft-CLIL implementation. She also describes how the qualitative data collected suggested that students enjoyed their experience in the classes and that there are reasons to be optimistic about this approach for tertiary level learners in Japan.

The last contribution, Chapter 15, features Darío Luis Banegas and Richard Pinner discussing the impact of a CLIL informed sociolinguistics module on pre-service English language teachers in Argentina. The authors, through a teacher research perspective, explored how this module impacted the motivation and self-confidence of the cohort of pre-service teachers. Data sources were wide-ranging and included instances of pair work, interviews, exams, assignments, feedback on group presentations, a whole class discussion at the end of the module and the teacher's own journal entries. The authors noted that a motivational synergy emerged between the pre-service teachers and their teacher educator in this context. The authors conclude by inviting others to implement a CLIL framework that would include pre-service teacher perceptions and expectations as well as visions of their professional future selves in order to energise their teaching practices.

We have been inspired by the diversity and quality of the contributions we have received for this collection and hope that this volume provides an initial step to inspire others to research stakeholder perspectives in diverse integrated content and language settings. Though we have done our best to represent some of the diversity that exists in integrated content and language settings, it would be impossible to house the many contexts, perspectives, empirical designs, programme types and languages within a single volume. Nevertheless, we hope the reader will find relevant and transferable insights to be gleaned from the chapters, and that this volume overall will inspire teachers to reflect on their own practice and for educational researchers to consider researching in these domains.

References

Aguilar, M. (2017) Engineering lecturers' views on CLIL and EMI. *International Journal of Bilingual Education and Bilingualism* 20 (6), 722–735.

Airey, J. (2016) EAP, EMI or CLIL. In K. Hyland and P. Shaw (eds) *Routledge Handbook of English for Academic Purposes* (pp. 71–83). Abingdon, VA: Routledge.

Barcelos, A.M. and Kalaja, P. (2012) Beliefs in second language acquisition: Teacher. In C.A. Chapelle (ed.) *The Encyclopedia of Applied Linguistics* (pp. 1–6). Blackwell Publishing Ltd.

Borg, S. (2003) Teacher cognition in language teaching: A review of research on what language teachers think, know, believe, and do. *Language Teaching* 36 (2), 81–109.

Borg, S. (2016) *English Medium Instruction in Iraqi Kurdistan.* London: British Council.

Borg, S. (2019a) Language teacher cognition: Perspectives and debates. In J. Voogt, G. Knezek, R. Christensen and K.-W. Lai (eds) *Second Handbook of Information Technology in Primary and Secondary Education* (pp. 1–23). Cham: Springer International Publishing.

Borg, S. (2019b) Language teacher cognition: Perspectives and debates. In X. Gao (ed.) *Second Handbook of English Language Teaching.* Cham: Springer International Handbooks of Education.

Bovellan, E. (2014) Teachers' beliefs about learning and language as reflected in their views of teaching materials for content and language integrated learning (CLIL). Unpublished PhD thesis, University of Jyväskylä.

Bozdoğan, D. and Karlıdağ, B. (2013) A case of CLIL practice in the Turkish context: Lending an ear to students. *Asian EFL Journal* 15 (4), 1–22.

Cenoz, J., Genesee, F. and Gorter, D. (2014) Critical analysis of CLIL: Taking stock and looking forward. *Applied Linguistics* 35 (3), 243–262.

Codó, E. and Patiño-Santos, A. (2018) CLIL, unequal working conditions and neoliberal subjectivities in a state secondary school. *Language Policy* 17 (4), 479–499.

Coyle, D. (2007) Content and language integrated learning: Towards a connected research agenda for CLIL pedagogies. *International Journal of Bilingual Education and Bilingualism* 10 (5), 543–562.

Coyle, D., Hood, P. and Marsh, D. (2010) *CLIL: Content and Language Integrated Learning.* Cambridge: Cambridge University Press.

Dalton-Puffer, C. (2011) Content-and-language integrated learning: From practice to principles? *Annual Review of Applied Linguistics* 31, 182–204.

Day, C. (2007) School reform and transitions in teacher professionalism and identity. In T. Townsend and R. Bates (eds) *Handbook of Teacher Education: Globalization, Standards and Professionalism in Times of Change* (pp. 597–612). Dordrecht: Springer.

Dearden, J. and Macaro, E. (2016) Higher education teachers' attitudes towards English medium instruction: A three-country comparison. *Studies in Second Language Learning and Teaching* 6 (3), 455–486.

De Smet, A., Mettewie, L., Galand, B., Hiligsmann, P. and Van Mensel, L. (2018) Classroom anxiety and enjoyment in CLIL and non-CLIL: Does the target language matter? *Studies in Second Language Learning and Teaching* 8 (1), 47–71.

Doiz, A. and Lasagabaster, D. (2018) Teachers' and students' second language motivational self system in English-medium instruction: A qualitative approach. *TESOL Quarterly* 52 (3), 657–679.

Doiz, A., Lasagabaster, D. and Sierra, J.M. (2014a) CLIL and motivation: The effect of individual and contextual variables. *The Language Learning Journal* 42 (2), 209–224.

Doiz, A., Lasagabaster, D. and Sierra, J.M. (2014b) Giving voice to the students: What (de)motivates them in CLIL classes? In D. Lasagabaster, A. Doiz and J.M. Sierra (eds) *Motivation and Foreign Language Learning: From Theory to Practice* (pp. 117–138). Amsterdam: John Benjamins.

Fenton-Smith, B., Humphreys, P. and Walkinshaw, I. (eds) (2017) *English Medium Instruction in Higher Education in Asia-Pacific: From Policy to Pedagogy* (Vol. 21). Cham: Springer International Publishing.

Fullan, M.G. (1994) Coordinating top-down and bottom-up strategies for educational reform. In R.J. Anson (ed.) *Coordinating Top-Down and Bottom-Up Strategies for Educational Reform.* https://eric.ed.gov/?id=ED376557.

Griva, E., Chostelidou, D. and Panteli, P. (2014) Insider views of CLIL in primary education: challenges and experiences of EFL teachers. *International Journal for Innovation Education and Research* 2, 31–53.

Gierlinger, E.M. (2007) Modular CLIL in lower secondary education: some insights from a research project in Austria. In C. Dalton-Puffer and U. Smit (eds) *Empirical Perspectives on Classroom Discourse* (pp. 79–118). Frankfurt: Peter Lang.

Gruber, M.-T. (2017) PrimA-CLIL: Multiple Stakeholders' Perceptions of CLIL and its Implementation at the Primary School Level in Austria. Unpublished PhD thesis, University of Graz, Austria.

Gruber, M.T., Lämmerer, A., Hofstadler, N. and Mercer, S. (2020) Flourishing or floundering: Factors contributing to CLIL primary teachers' wellbeing in Austria. *CLIL Journal of Innovation and Research in Plurilingual and Pluricultural Education* 3 (1), 19–34.

Hattie, J.A.C. (2009) *Visible Learning. A Synthesis of Over 800 Metaanalyses Relating to Achievement.* London: Routledge.

Hessel, G., Talbot, K., Gruber, M.-T. and Mercer, S. (2020) The well-being and job satisfaction of secondary CLIL and tertiary EMI teachers. *Journal for the Psychology of Language Learning* 2 (2), 73–91.

Hüttner, J., Dalton-Puffer, C. and Smit, U. (2013) The power of beliefs: Lay theories and their influence on the implementation of CLIL programmed. *International Journal of Bilingual Education and Bilingualism* 16 (3), 267–284.

Hüttner, J. and Smit, U. (2014) CLIL (Content and Language Integrated Learning): The bigger picture. A response to: A. Bruton. 2013. CLIL: Some of the reasons why … and why not. System 41 (2013): 587–597. *System* 44, 160–167.

Islam, M.M. (2013) English medium instruction in the private universities in Bangladesh. *Indonesian Journal of Applied* Linguistics 1 (3), 126–137.

Kang, S. and Park, H. (2005) English as the medium of instruction in Korean engineering education. *Korean Journal of Applied Linguistics* 21 (1), 155–174.

Lasagabaster, D. and Ruiz de Zarobe, Y. (eds) (2010) *CLIL in Spain: Implementation, Results and Teacher Training.* Newcastle: Cambridge Scholars Publishing.

Lin, A. (2016) *Language Across the Curriculum & CLIL in English as an Additional Language (EAL) Contexts: Theory and Practice.* Singapore: Springer.

Macaro, E., Curle, S., Pun, J., An, J. and Dearden, J. (2018) A systematic review of English medium instruction in higher education. *Language Teaching* 51 (1), 36–76.

Marsh, D. (ed) (2002) *CLIL/EMILE. The European Dimension: Actions, Trends and Foresight Potential.* University of Jyväskylä.

Massler, U. (2012) Primary CLIL and its stakeholders: What children, parents and teachers think of the potential merits and pitfalls of CLIL modules in primary teaching. *International CLIL Research Journal* 1 (4), 36–46. See http://www.icrj.eu/14/article4. html (accessed May 2017).

Marsh, D. (2008) Language awareness and CLIL. In J. Cenoz and N. Hornberger (eds) *Encyclopaedia of Language and Education (Vol 6): Knowledge about Language* (pp. 233–246). New York & Berlin: Springer.

Mehisto, P., Marsh, D. and Frigols, M.J. (2008) *Uncovering CLIL*. Oxford: Macmillan Publisher Limited.

Mercer, S. (2018) Psychology for language learning: Spare a thought for the teacher. *Language Teaching* 51 (4), 504–525.

Mercer, S. and Ryan, S. (2010) A mindset for EFL: Learners' beliefs about the role of natural talent. *ELT Journal* 64 (4), 436–444.

Mercer, S. and Kostoulas, A. (2018) *Language Teacher Psychology*. Bristol: Multilingual Matters.

Met, M. (1998) Curriculum decision-making in content-based language teaching. In J. Cenoz and F. Genesee (eds) *Beyond Bilingualism: Multilingualism and Multilingual Education* (pp. 35–63). Clevedon: Multilingual Matters.

Moate, J.M. (2011) The impact of foreign language mediated teaching on teachers' sense of professional integrity in the CLIL classroom. *European Journal of Teacher Education* 34 (3), 333–346.

Neghina, C. (2016) Mapping English-taught programmes, Studyportals. See https://studyportals.com/intelligence/mapping-english-taught-programmes-at-the-top-1000-universities-2/ (accessed January 2020).

Nikula, T., Dafouz, E., Moore, P. and Smit, U. (eds) (2016) *Conceptualising Integration in CLIL and Multilingual Education*. Bristol: Multilingual Matters.

Pappa, S., Moate, J., Ruohotie-Lyhty, M. and Eteläpelto, A. (2017) Teacher agency within the Finnish CLIL context: Tensions and resources. *International Journal of Bilingual Education and Bilingualism*, 1–21.

Reyes, M.R., Brackett, M.A., Rivers, S.E., White, M. and Salovey, P. (2012) Classroom emotional climate, student engagement, and academic achievement. *Journal of Educational Psychology* 104 (3), 700–712.

Sammons, P., Day, C., Kington, A., Gu, Q., Stobart, G. and Smees, R. (2007) Exploring variations in teachers' work, lives and their effects on pupils: Key findings and implications from a longitudinal mixed method study. *British Educational Research Journal* 33 (5), 681–701.

Seikkula-Leino, J. (2007) CLIL learning: Achievement level and affective factors. *Language and Education* 21 (4), 328–341. See http://www.scribd.com/doc/13539167/CLIL-Learning-Affective-Factors (accessed May 2017).

Vazquez, V.P., Prieto Molina, M. and Avila Lopez, F.J. (2014) Perceptions of teachers and students of the promotion of interaction through task-based activities in CLIL. *Porta Linguarum* 23, 75–91.

Wächter, B. and Maiworm, F. (eds) (2014) *English-taught Programmes in European Higher Education: The State of Play in 2014*. Bonn: Lemmens Medien.

Wannagat, U. (2008) Learning through L2 – Content and language integrated learning (CLIL) and English as medium of instruction (EMI). *International Journal of Bilingual Education and Bilingualism* 10 (5), 663–682.

Wegner, A. (2012) Seeing the bigger picture: What students and teachers think about CLIL. *International CLIL Research Journal* 1 (4), 29–34.

Yeh, C.-C. (2014) Taiwanese students' experiences and attitudes towards English-medium courses in tertiary education. *RELC Journal* 45 (3), 305–319.

2 Identity and Emotions in Teaching CLIL: The Case of Primary School Teachers in Finland

Sotiria Pappa

Introduction

Drawing on bi/multilingualism and second language acquisition (Cenoz, 2013), CLIL is commonly characterised as 'a dual-focused educational approach in which an additional language is used for the learning and teaching of content and language with the objective of promoting both content and language mastery to pre-defined levels' (Marsh *et al.*, 2012: 11). This understanding of CLIL as a language-enriching teaching method has been expanded to include 'a wide range of educational practices provided that these practices are conducted through the medium of an additional language' (Cenoz *et al.*, 2014: 244). Its main principles of 'every teacher is a language teacher', 'language learning is language use' and 'language learning is a cognitive and social activity' (see Dalton-Puffer, 2011; Moate, 2011) are reflected in the recent Finnish national curriculum, which recognizes the importance of language integration, multilingual and cultural orientation and sensitivity towards language and its use in educational settings (Bergroth, 2016; FNBE, 2014). However, the new curriculum does not define bilingual education in any specific terms, connecting bilingual to general language education (Bergroth, 2016). This lack of definition may not strictly direct teacher action and allows for teacher autonomy regarding CLIL implementation, yet it also allows for variation of extent, degree and quality in CLIL (see also Chapter 6).

The changes of the new curriculum concerning bilingual education, including CLIL, imply that teachers should draw on characteristics and principles of foreign and second language teaching and social constructivism. In turn, these highlight the role of language in relation to content and suggest shifting teachers' understandings of the role. These changes come at a time when CLIL continues to be a grassroots initiative on the part of Finnish teachers. Such initiatives continue, despite the decrease in schools providing CLIL instruction and the persistence of challenges that teachers deemed responsible for the considerable decline in enthusiasm for CLIL within a decade after its introduction to Finnish schools in the mid-90s (Lehti *et al.*, 2006; Pappa, 2018). CLIL teachers' enduring motivation and participation in CLIL programmes indicate a willingness to go beyond the roles and responsibilities of language and non-language subject teachers, while CLIL itself introduces teachers to novel aspects within otherwise familiar instructional conditions. Hence, how CLIL teachers experience their work and their sense of self as professionals (e.g. pedagogue, subject expert, language user) through CLIL may be subject to change (see also Chapters 9 & 11). Such a change will need to be negotiated taking into account resources, challenges and ways of expressing oneself as a teacher through individual and collegial action. If this negotiation gives rise to a positive sense of identity, teachers' self-esteem and self-efficacy may be enhanced (Ruohotie-Lyhty, 2013), thus supporting their motivation and perseverance. With these circumstances in mind as well as the paucity of research on how Finnish CLIL teachers negotiate themselves as educational professionals and colleagues (e.g. Bovellan, 2014; Moate, 2011, 2014), this chapter addresses the identity negotiation of teachers in this context.

This chapter focuses on thirteen teachers doing CLIL in Finnish primary schools and draws on two qualitative studies on CLIL teachers' identity negotiation to address two aspects of their work (Pappa *et al.*, 2017a, 2017b). The first concerns the synergy between social and individual influences in CLIL teaching and the second addresses how emotional experiences at work are involved in CLIL teachers' identity negotiation. After presenting an overview of the findings, the chapter discusses CLIL teachers' professional identity negotiation first in terms of synergy between social and individual influences and, second, in terms of their emotional experiences at the workplace. The chapter argues for the central role of the individual in identity negotiation, as it agentically interprets socio-cultural aspects in lived contexts and selectively responds to the various social affordances in the professional environment. Furthermore, it argues that the process of (re)defining and shaping one's professional identity is an emotional one. The theoretical premise of this chapter is described in the following section.

Theoretical Background

Teacher identity

Teachers' professional identity, or teacher identity, can be understood as an individual's ongoing process of formation and transformation. This process involves personal understandings of oneself as a professional, based on biography, current and envisioned career trajectories, professional relationships, identification at work, belief systems and ethical standards (Eteläpelto *et al.*, 2014). Such personal understandings involve self-directed representation within social contexts and suggestions therein by responding to prescribed identities and roles and by adapting to subjectively interpreted feedback from others (Day *et al.*, 2006; Taylor & Littleton, 2006). As such, professional identity formation becomes a discursive process (Zembylas, 2005), in which a person's self-image is related to others' perceptions, characteristics and group classifications, as well as socially condoned values and beliefs guiding behaviour and action (Pennington & Richards, 2016). Teacher identity is a fluid concept facilitating a continuous examination of the work, tensions and societal roles of 'being a teacher' (Martin & Strom, 2016).

In this chapter, teacher identity is understood as a continuous process in which teachers construct an internal interpretive system for themselves. This may be used as a resource or mediational tool in agentically positioning or contesting themselves within the socio-cultural, historical and discursive contexts that frame their professional action (Flores & Day, 2006). Comprised of organizing principles meaningful to the individual teacher (Flores & Day, 2006), it may also be used to navigate tensions arising from various identities (Beauchamp & Thomas, 2009; Day *et al.*, 2006; see also Chapter 3). Teacher identity is not only a life project that is emotional, shifting, volatile and fragmented (Beijaard *et al.*, 2000; Pinho & Andrade, 2015), but also a lived experience of participation (Bukor, 2015). To achieve a sense of internal consistency among different contextual and temporal positionings and to become agents in shaping their professional identity and direct their professional learning (Emirbayer & Mische, 1998; Eteläpelto *et al.*, 2015), teachers exercise *identity agency*.

Identity agency is the form of professional agency employed in actively shaping the professional self by framing one's experiences according to prior beliefs and self-understandings and intentionally making meaning of situated interactions (Eteläpelto *et al.*, 2015; Ruohotie-Lyhty & Moate, 2016). *Identity agency* is exercised in CLIL teachers' negotiation of their pedagogical and relational identities (Pappa *et al.*, 2017a). Pedagogical identity refers to CLIL teachers' self-understanding as pedagogues and educators in the classroom and its negotiation entails, among other factors, personality traits, pedagogical beliefs and tools, potential courses of action, practices and tensions. Relational identity refers to CLIL teachers' self-understandings as colleagues or members of a teacher community and its negotiation involves learning to become a member of a particular teacher community through its concomitant expectations, shaping discourses, traditions, rules and norms. *Identity agency* is further exercised in negotiating between pedagogical and relational identities to give rise to a sense of professional identity that draws on individual action and dialogic interaction with peers. While dentity negotiation is a a cognitive and relational process, but it is also an emotional one.

Emotion

Despite their conceptual elusiveness (Van Veen & Sleegers, 2006), it can be argued that emotions are embodied experiences with behavioural, psychological and physiological manifestations, but also socially and discursively constructed phenomena (Benesch, 2018; Cross & Hong, 2012). Emotions are subjective experiences in response to social and interactional stimuli (Golombek & Doran, 2014), preceded by stratified experiential states taking place on a pre-personal and pre-discursive level (Kenway & Youdell, 2011). These states are physiological or biological, and become meaningful when evaluated through the prism of the individual's personality, beliefs, preferences, goals, internalised socio-cultural influences and norms (Cross & Hong, 2012). Rather than instrumentally negative or positive to be suppressed and enhanced respectively, all emotions can be seen as signals in evaluating conditions and guides in collective action and change (Benesch, 2018). Emotions are important to guiding teacher action, becoming sites of resistance and self-transformation, as they are situated, involve self-knowledge and are interlaced with identities subject to power structures and agency (Zembylas, 2003).

Emotion and cognition become mutually constitutive and connected in identity negotiation involving communication between individual and collective realities (Geijsel & Meijers, 2005; Meijers, 2002). For instance, language teachers' attention to emotion has been argued to provide a firm foundation for learning, and to facilitate language learners' identity development and cognitive learning process (Arnold, 2011). In applied linguistics and foreign language teaching, the importance of teachers' emotions is increasingly being stressed, with research examining how language teachers' emotions are constructed from a sociological and psychological perspective as well as how their emotions are embedded in power relations, social ecologies, beliefs and practices (Martínez Agudo, 2018). However, the theoretical tensions between the social and the individual in applied linguistics and their empirical resolution often emphasize the social and the language learner (Benson & Cooker, 2013), with the individual and the language teacher remaining under-addressed.

According to Meijers (2002), identity negotiation is a cyclical learning process prompted by negative emotions arising from an experience bringing new circumstances and concomitant exigencies that one's currently held self-concept cannot fully identify with (see also Chapter 4). Geijsel and Meijers (2005; see also Meijers, 2002) posit that the emotional, rather than cognitive, problem of reconfiguring one's identity is resolved by developing a reflexive consciousness through two complementary processes. The first is intuitive sense-giving, an intrapersonal dialogue that draws on concepts shared by others and selected in light of one's life history, so as to render the subjective emotional experience meaningful. The interpersonal dialogue allows for mutual understanding, shared meanings and communally espoused values. The second is discursive meaning giving, the interpersonal dialogue that aims at restoring balance between emotions and cognitions through existing discourses. Within these discourses, the individual identifies concepts suitable for such balance to occur and uses them heuristically in collaboration with others. Such collaboration renders the shared concepts emotionally and rationally explanatory in a way that is meaningful within the interactions supporting this collaboration. This interpersonal dialogue allows for mutual under-standing, shared meanings and communally espoused values.

Research Questions

In addressing the identity negotiation of Finnish primary school teachers involved in CLIL, this chapter is guided by two research questions:

(1) What is the synergy between social and individual influences in CLIL teachers' professional identity negotiation?
(2) How are emotional experiences at work involved in CLIL teachers' identity negotiation?

Methodology

Participants

From five different Finnish primary schools, thirteen CLIL teachers participated in this study. All participants were Finnish, apart from one who came from another European country, and all of them were fluent in English, the language used as a medium of instruction in their CLIL classes. These teachers had completed university-level courses in English, CLIL or bilingual instruction, while one had learned how to teach CLIL from her colleagues. They had come into contact with CLIL through an internship, work abroad or a change of school, where a CLIL programme was followed. Four participants were in the beginning of their teaching career (1–6 years), two in the middle (13 and 16 years) and seven at a later stage (20–30 years). One participant had been teaching special education classes for 12 years before teaching CLIL, while another taught them parallel to CLIL classes. Three participants had taught abroad. All participants seemed to perceive CLIL as a welcome challenge in their teaching, with three of them reporting following the school's policy on CLIL.

The studies

The chapter draws on two studies (Pappa *et al.*, 2017a, 2017b) for a metasynthesis of their findings (Sandelowski & Barroso, 2006). The studies themselves draw on interview data averaging 34 minutes, collected between October and December 2015 and transcribed into a total of 184 pages (Times New Roman, font 12, single line spacing with a break between each speaking turn). Both studies used Thematic Analysis (Braun & Clarke, 2006), although Study 2 further used the concepts of emotion talk and emotional talk (Bednarek, 2009). Emotion talk is an explicit reference to an emotion, such as 'I got really angry with all these changes and I felt that it was honest to let the school head know about how I feel and how this affects my work' (Teacher 3, anger). Emotional talk is an implicit reference to an emotion, such as 'And when you can see their faces … when you can see how kids enjoy learning things and … they are, kind of, the best parts of our daily job' (Teacher 10, joy). Emotion and emotional talk represented participants' discursive strategies in constructing a social reality, rather than their internal affective state (Bednarek, 2009; Golombek & Doran, 2014). A detailed description of the epistemological underpinnings, participant recruitment, data collection process and data analysis can be found at Pappa (2018), while examples of how Thematic Analysis was used and excerpts highlighting the findings of Study 1 and Study 2 may be respectively found in Pappa *et al.* (2017a) and Pappa *et al.* (2017b).

Overview of Findings

This section provides a summary of the main findings of the two studies being considered in this chapter.

Study 1 - Pappa *et al.* (2017a): Pedagogical and relational identity negotiation

CLIL teachers' pedagogical identity, the aspect of professional identity enacted within classroom settings, is predicated, on the one hand, on their personal investment in their work and, on the other hand, on the constant negotiation between personal and professional resources available to them. Rather than separating the latter, participants drew on both. These resources, in conjunction with certain considerations (e.g. methodological choices, views of CLIL and its role within education, language affecting the expression of the teacher self), helped participants become more self-aware and use past experiences as an interpretive lens for making sense of their present conditions and future courses of action. In doing so, participants also made connections across physical and temporal professional contexts and their corresponding principles. The foreign language used as the medium of instruction (here, English) mediated the negotiation between professional and relational aspects in the classroom.

CLIL teachers' relational identity, the aspect of professional identity expressed within the teacher community, but also between teacher and pupils, strongly involved active membership in shared collegiality. Its negotiation entailed agency and individual willingness to partake in shared collegiality, effected principally through acts of sharing and participation. These acts served as a means of bonding over challenges or tensions affecting their classroom, pedagogical tasks, themselves and the teacher community, but also of using colleagues as recourses and prompting proactive responses to the need for collective activity. Such acts seemed to originate in the individual teacher aiming at the collective, while collegiality originated from the wider social and immediate professional environment, affording the individual teacher legitimate membership, connectedness and support. The validation of teachers' relational identity enabled professional guidance and sense making regarding individual and collegial roles in improving CLIL education at their school by way of peer advice and freedom to express their thoughts. CLIL teachers' relational identity further involved reflective autonomy regarding profession-related considerations, i.e. feeling autonomous at work and consciously thinking about work, its meaning, one's performance, and available resources.

Identity negotiation between participants' pedagogical and relational identities was reciprocal. Provided the participants' work environment was one of affordance rather than constraint in the present study, such identity negotiation served as a supportive and structuring resource. However, it depended on the participants' ability to and interest in taking advantage of opportunities for development. Participants' personalities, beliefs and perceptions stemming from their personal biographies helped interpret circumstances and events in their professional lives, rendering them meaningful and informing their actions in the classroom. By allowing individual interpretations to take place through the prism of past experiences and by drawing on themselves as the main resource in identity negotiation, participants developed, reinforced or questioned their sense of self as CLIL teachers. Through interacting with their relational identity, pedagogical identity became embedded in collegial relationships that, in this study, afforded participants support, guidance, collaboration and encouragement. In addition to pedagogical identity being expressed in participants' autonomous action in the classroom, participants' particular social settings at their workplace resulted in creating a sense of belonging and purpose through shared activities for the implementation of a CLIL programme. It could be argued that autonomous action in the classroom was partly mirrored in autonomous action on a collegial level, as teachers jointly took initiatives in CLIL implementation, thus supporting individual teachers' career-based continuums. Finally, considerations, responsibilities and roles in CLIL teaching ceased to be solely individually negotiated in the classroom by participants. Their importance for practice and participants' beliefs about being a CLIL teacher helped participants position themselves in their web of collegial relationships.

Study 2 - Pappa *et al.* (2017a): Emotional experiences in identity negotiation

This study did not strictly distinguish between positive and negative emotions, but rather explored CLIL teachers' emotional experiences at their workplace. Negatively accented emotional experiences stemmed principally from the curriculum and issues of time management or availability (see also Chapters 5, 7, 10 & 13). These affected preparation time, which increases in CLIL teaching, as well as time invested in collegial relationships. On a secondary level, negatively accented emotional experiences stemmed from questioning one's competence as a teacher and from certain negativity toward CLIL. These further manifested as stress, pressure, confusion and feeling overwhelmed. A sense of hurriedness and frustration were found to be the most prevalent negatively accented emotional experiences. In addition, feelings of regret or chagrin for the state or inalterability of certain situations were expressed by some participants (7/13). Others exhibited self-doubt, anxiety and vulnerability connected to their teaching through a foreign language, while a few expressed loneliness in CLIL teaching, due to insufficient collegial support.

Positively accented emotional experiences primarily derived from CLIL and pupils' involvement and, secondarily, from the participants themselves when exercising their profession. The most prevalent positively accented emotional experiences were contentment and empowerment. Other such experiences included feeling efficacious and satisfied with one's work, taking pride in one's work, feeling able to influence one's work environment and practice; maintaining a hopeful outlook and inspiration regarding CLIL and its potential and feeling joy at pupils' learning and enjoyment of CLIL. Teachers' own professional development, in particular, seemed to make participants feel rewarded and enhance confidence in and excitement about their work (see also Chapters 12, 13 & 15). While positive emotional experiences may not pose a threat to identity negotiation, negatively accented ones could create tensions. Yet, the latter hold potential for professional development, should they be understood and meaningfully incorporated into one's sense of teacherhood.

Participants made use of both intrapersonal and interpersonal dialogues to acknowledge emotions at work and render them meaningful for their teacher identity. In their intrapersonal dialogue (i.e. intuitive sense giving), participants used reasoning, self-reliance, resilience and empathy. For instance, participants rationalized challenging events in the classroom, showed persistence in the face of difficulties, relied on themselves as a resource and built their confidence, and were compassionate towards pupils who struggled or were reluctant in CLIL lessons. A few participants were inquisitive about CLIL as a methodology and how the foreign language affects teacher behaviour, while others were defensive in response to external demands from the school, parents and the curriculum. Some of these participants indirectly self-regulated their negative attitudinal responses by drawing their attention to positively accented emotional experiences of the past that rendered their teaching meaningful.

In their interpersonal dialogue (i.e. discursive meaning-giving), participants drew on the complementary concepts of the autonomous employee and the CLIL team, the relationship of which can be seen from the synergistic interdependence between pedagogical and relational identities in the study summarised in the previous sub-section. According to the former concept, the autonomous teacher belongs to a shared school culture and is able to make pedagogical decisions based their own beliefs and ethical principles, without adhering too strictly to curricular guidelines. Such a teacher is supported by stakeholders' enthusiasm and trust as well as a sense of safety from school management and colleagues. The latter concept involved acknowledging peers' work, ideas and potential, but also connectedness with colleagues (see also Chapters 12 & 13), which all participants experienced. Participants found collegial collaboration to be particularly important for coping with negatively accented emotional experiences and positioning themselves as teachers in their professional community.

Discussion

Drawing together the findings of the two studies presented in this chapter, two main conclusions can be suggested. The first is that pedagogical and relational identities may give rise to a more meaningful and less tensioned sense of professional identity when there is synergy between these aspects. This synergy underlies the individual and relational influences comprising one's professional identity, whose negotiation depends on various temporal, emotional, institutional and sociocultural resources (e.g. Beauchamp & Thomas, 2009; Eteläpelto et al., 2015). The second conclusion is that emotions are an integral aspect of CLIL teachers' professional lives and are involved in an identity negotiation process supported and aided by the surrounding collegial community (Cross & Hong, 2012; Geijsel & Meijers, 2005; Meijers,

2002). However, as part of professional learning, negotiating emotions at work in light of one's identity is not solely an individual task, but also a collective one. These conclusions are discussed in more detail in this section in light of the research questions.

The individual and the collective in identity negotiation

Responding to a call for change in one's pedagogical and relational identity, i.e. identity (re)negotiation, requires the exercise of agency, yet such a response is contingent on both individual and contextual conditions. These conditions can be seen in the power invested in Finnish teachers and how the teachers partake of that power. The concept of the autonomous employee reflects the trust and esteem Finnish society has for its teachers. Participants were able to implement CLIL programmes by varying their methodological approaches, working according to their ethical principles, developing their own materials and negotiating curricular goals at the school and local level. At the same time, the concept of the CLIL team implies the use of unofficial power at school to create a self-regulating teacher community that directs the goals of their CLIL instruction and develops materials that support their initiatives. Identity negotiation does not only necessitate a self-reliant and reflective teacher, but also official and unofficial power that enables teachers' *identity agency* to follow governmental guidelines and take actions that affect teachers' day-to-day professional activity. Identity negotiation, then, might not be restricted to pedagogical views of professionalism, but remain fluid by encompassing a broader activity range and involvement (e.g. Akkerman & Meijer, 2011; Beijaard *et al.*, 2000; Edwards, 2015).

The social meeting the individual, and *vice versa*, can further be seen in discursive resources. Across the interview data of the two studies, participants used similar words and ways to refer to doing CLIL and what that means to them in terms of practices and interpersonal relationships. Moreover, they positioned themselves as enthusiastic, determined and sensitive CLIL teachers, albeit wary of idealised notions of CLIL. Using discourses shared by the school and wider professional community becomes part of how CLIL teachers use their professional identity as an interpretive lens, helping them align with or depart from aims and expectations in CLIL teaching (e.g. Eteläpelto *et al.*, 2013; Hökkä *et al.*, 2012). Additionally, it helps them frame and understand emotional experiences at work. Participants used willingness and perseverance to intrapersonally make sense of professional situations and conceptual tools afforded by workplace relationships to facilitate their sense-making and establish shared values. By negotiating emotions at work in light of their identity, participants could sustain autonomy, validate such experiences for themselves and others, enhance rapport and membership, and maintain well-being. Such negotiation highlights the subjectivity of the individual teacher in positioning herself within the community and interpreting its discursive preconditions (Akkerman & Meijer, 2011; Biesta & Tedder, 2007; Eteläpelto *et al.*, 2013; Geijsel & Meijers, 2005; Meijers, 2002; Zembylas, 2003), but also highlights the subjectivity of the community in dialectically co-creating a physical, psychological and cultural space that promotes collective development and well-being at work.

Beside discursive resources, social influences on the individual can be seen in the synergistic space afforded by collegial relationships. Participants' experiences in CLIL varied, yet this was not a limitation in these studies. Rather than imply a hierarchical position of teachers in terms of experience, it helped to underline how colleagues can become a supportive resource for others by means of pedagogical thinking and expertise (see also Moate, 2014). Sharing, being an activity very important to the participants, allowed individual professional trajectories to create shared ideas, advice and materials. In this act of sharing, the individual teacher invested their own professional and relational orientations, sense of purpose and commitment, and they actively attempted to establish a connection with others. This holds potential for creating learning opportunities for a more profound understanding of foreign language mediated teaching, as synergy in collective action affords teachers with values, beliefs and local reality (e.g. Edwards, 2007), which they individually act upon according to their own inclinations.

The social and individual influences on identity negotiation can also be seen in temporal continuums. Teachers' biographies and professional trajectories link the past to the present, while the available professional resources and teacher-pupil relationships constitute a link between the present and future. These complementary temporal frames are bracketed by collegial relationships. Thus, teacher identity negotiation entails a socio-cultural reality and professional circumstances to which the individual teacher responds. These provide the building blocks for identity negotiation in the form of discourses, values and other social affordances (Eteläpelto *et al.*, 2015; Lemke, 2008), which teachers filter and dynamically incorporate into their identity (Akkerman & Meijer, 2011; Coward *et al.*, 2015; Pennington & Richards, 2016). Teachers' responses to socially embedded temporal continuums are given in light of beliefs, orientations and commitments developed throughout their professional careers, and in a manner that may have both short- and long-term effects. Therefore, while separate in analysis, the individual and the social are intricately interconnected, and neither can be given primacy over the other. Yet, the individual plays a central role in identity negotiation, agentically interpreting sociocultural affordances in lived contexts and selectively responding to them within professional environments.

Emotions

Emotions of both positive and negative valence hold potential for development. For instance, hurry and frustration may discourage teachers from seeing CLIL as learning-enhancing and decrease well-being at work. Yet, countered by a persistent interest in teaching through a foreign language, CLIL becomes a sustained part of pedagogical identity and underlines how collegial interaction and influence are important for relational identity. Moreover, doubting one's efficacy as a CLIL teacher may prove detrimental in the long run if not mitigated by colleagues' positive influences, but it can also become a lens through which to re-examine one's pedagogical identity and become more aware, self-reflective and sensitive in enacting it. With pupils being one of their primary sources followed by teachers themselves, positively accented emotional experiences can enhance the perception of CLIL methodology as a teacher's tool to more diversified instruction, deeper learning and curricular aims. At the same time, they can strengthen one's pedagogical identity, due to positive outcomes, and direct it towards higher goals for themselves and pupils alike. Positively accented emotional experiences can also make pedagogical identity amenable to change, methodological initiatives and professional training. This might affect relational identity by prompting professional learning through sharing expertise and creating shared teaching practices.

Especially regarding negatively accented ones, emotional experiences become part of CLIL teachers' identities when understood and rendered meaningful through available conceptual and discursive tools (Meijers, 2002). Intrapersonally, making sense of emotions arising from tensions to CLIL teachers' self-concept highlighted the subjectivity of felt experiences at work, in which emotion ceases to be abstract and is negotiated by personal resources (e.g. Zembylas, 2003). Interpersonally, such sense making was complemented by discursive conditions afforded by others, helping the intuitive become explicit, and offering a safe environment for expressing and accepting negative emotions. Participants came to see such emotions as valid experiences and acknowledged by colleagues. For pedagogical identity, intrapersonal and interpersonal sense making may translate into a sense of normality, empowerment and contentment at work (e.g. Day & Kington, 2008), as well as an emotionally present practitioner. Consequently, emotions can enhance motivation in continuing CLIL, but also reduce feelings of loneliness, frustration and rush. For relational identity, they may translate into moderating emotional dissonance for others through words of understanding or practical advice, active membership in the collegial community, and the shared mentality of challenging, yet jointly manageable, conditions in CLIL teaching. This may co-create shared viewpoints, meanings and principles (e.g. Geijsel & Meijers, 2005), promote autonomy in the classroom, and enhance rapport between colleagues.

Emotions go beyond the individually felt and embodied experience, and become interpersonally negotiated social events (Cross & Hong, 2012; Golombek & Doran, 2014). In the case of the interviewed Finnish teachers, negatively accented emotional experiences were not ignored, but endorsed as a normal aspect of their profession. Moreover, these experiences did not necessarily negatively impact on these teachers' identity negotiation, while some were explained through positively accented ones. The context under examination indicates that positive emotions should be sustained, and negative ones supported. Once supporting emotions at the workplace is seen as a shared responsibility, rather than merely an individual response, opportunities for mutual and communal transformation may arise. In addition to countering detrimental long-term effects of negative emotions (e.g. Beauchamp & Thomas, 2009), addressing emotions collectively can render them a valuable tool for community and individual teacher alike to review past and present future conditions and envision future trajectories.

Implications for Policy and Practice

CLIL is a complex endeavour and teachers choosing to incorporate CLIL into their teaching should be supported. University and school partnership for in-service CLIL teacher training should be strengthened and made available to teachers regardless of work experience. Moreover, CLIL teachers should be supported at school level by collegial CLIL teams whose expected collaboration is not additional to, but included in their work plans. This will help construct socially embedded temporal continuums for teacher identity negotiation that promote effective CLIL teaching over time, a joint sense of professional direction and a space where emotions in CLIL teaching can be constructively addressed by peers.

When it comes to teacher education, teacher identity becomes an academic and discursive tool for prospective teachers. While in training, student teachers should become aware of how personal biographies have shaped currently held convictions and assumptions concerning teacher roles and behaviours. Moreover, courses or modules should train teachers to be self-reflective based on the theoretical background of educational sciences. This would help them to create a re-evaluated belief system about teaching and learning, help them become self-reliant and knowledgeable, and to cultivate an inclination toward educated self-discovery within the profession. Teacher education should also offer opportunities for developing CLIL-appropriate instructional materials and a more conscious, sensitive use and modelling of language in teaching. This will prepare student teachers for responsibilities as material designers and teachers of both content and language. More importantly, however, it will emphasize the role of the foreign language as the medium of instruction and pupils' learning, as well as its role in shaping their pedagogical identity.

Concerning emotions in their identity negotiation, student teachers should learn to see emotions as an integral part of teaching, but also learn ways to constructively regulate emotions for a more profound understanding of themselves and reasons for doing CLIL. Teacher education could benefit from courses explicitly addressing emotions in the teaching profession (e.g. reflective diaries, interdisciplinary syllabus), to make teachers aware of lived realities in teaching without, however, dampening their enthusiasm for it. During the practicum, a student teacher-mentor relationship should encourage and support the expression of emotion in discussing classroom events, irrespective of positive or negative valence. This can further be supported by student teachers sharing their practice experiences in seminars and learning how to draw on others' intellectual and emotional resources through cooperative or project-oriented units. Such actions will help prospective teachers accept negative emotions as a natural part of their professional experience and receive advice that will help them navigate and understand their embodied experiences better. Moreover, it can teach young teachers how emotions can be a shared resource enhancing collective agency, and become a means to membership, recognition and legitimisation within the collegial community. Learning how to foster positive workplace environments through others and having attitudes toward collaborative work can, in the short term, lay foundations for teachers' relational identity and, in the long term, help create synergistic, rather than isolated, teacher cultures in future school environments.

Conclusion

The studies discussed in this chapter helped draw a broad picture of how CLIL teachers in Finnish primary education view themselves as educators and colleagues and how engagement with a teacher community that is sensitive to and accepting of emotional complexities in CLIL teaching can shape that view. To enrich that picture, the way CLIL teachers experience, express and meaningfully interpret their perceived emotional responses can be examined in settings that constrain agency or participation in the local collegial community or agency, impose rules on emotional expression and entail challenging classroom conditions. In addition, research approaches could vary their timeframe (e.g. longitudinal), combine methods (e.g. questionnaires, physiological data, classroom observations, stimulated recall interviews), and focus on in-service CLIL teaching.

Acknowledgements

The author would like to thank Dr Päivi Hökkä and the external reviewers for their insightful feedback on earlier versions of the manuscript.

References

Akkerman, S.F. and Meijer, P.C. (2011) A dialogical approach to conceptualizing teacher identity. *Teaching and Teacher Education* 27, 308–319.

Arnold, J. (2011) Attention to affect in language learning. *Anglistik. International Journal of English* Studies 22 (1), 11–22.

Beauchamp, C. and Thomas, L. (2009) Understanding teacher identity: An overview of issues in the literature and implications for teacher education. *Cambridge Journal of Education* 39 (2), 175–189.

Bednarek, M. (2009) Emotion talk and emotional talk: Cognitive and discursive perspectives. In H. Pishwa (ed.) *Language and Social Cognition: Expression of the Social Mind* (pp. 395–431). Berlin: Mouton de Gruyter.

Beijaard, D., Meijer, P.C. and Verloop, N. (2000) Teachers' perceptions of professional identity: An exploratory study from a personal knowledge perspective. *Teaching and Teacher Education* 16, 749–764.

Benesch, S. (2018) Emotions as agency: Feeling rules, emotion labor, and English language teachers' decision-making. *System* 79, 60–69.

Benson, P. and Cooker, L. (eds) (2013) *The Applied Linguistic Individual: Sociocultural Approaches to Identity, Agency and Autonomy*. Sheffield: Equinox Publishing.

Bergroth, M. (2016) Reforming the national core curriculum for bilingual education in Finland. *Journal of Immersion and Content-Based Language Education* 4 (1), 86–107.

Biesta, G. and Tedder, M. (2007) Agency and learning in the lifecourse: Towards an ecological perspective. *Studies in the Education of Adults* 39 (2), 132–149.

Bovellan, E. (2014) Teachers' beliefs about learning and language as reflected in their views of teaching materials for Content and Language Integrated Learning (CLIL). Unpublished Master's thesis, University of Jyväskylä.

Braun, V. and Clarke, V. (2006) Using thematic analysis in psychology. *Qualitative Research in Psychology* 3 (2), 77–101.

Bukor, E. (2015) Exploring teacher identity from a holistic perspective: Reconstructing and reconnecting personal and professional selves. *Teachers and Teaching* 21 (3), 305–327.

Cenoz, J. (2013) Discussion: Towards an educational perspective in CLIL language policy and pedagogical practice. *International Journal of Bilingual Education and Bilingualism* 16 (3), 389–394.

Cenoz, J., Genesee, F. and Gorter, D. (2014) Critical analysis of CLIL: Taking stock and looking forward. *Applied Linguistics* 35 (3), 243–262.

Coward, F.L., Hamman, D., Johnson, L., Lambert, M., John, I. and Zhou, L. (2015) Centrality of enactive experiences, framing, and motivation to student teachers' emerging professional identity. *Teaching Education* 26 (2), 196–221.

Cross, D.I. and Hong, J.Y. (2012) An ecological examination of teachers' emotions in the school context. *Teaching and Teacher Education* 28 (7), 957–967.

Dalton-Puffer, C. (2011) Content-and-Language Integrated Learning: From practice to principles? *Annual Review of Applied Linguistics* 31, 182–204.

Day, C. and Kington, A. (2008) Identity, wellbeing and effectiveness: The emotional contexts of teaching. *Pedagogy, Culture & Society* 16 (1), 7–23.

Day, C., Kington, A., Stobart, G. and Sammons, P. (2006) The personal and professional selves of teachers: Stable and unstable identities. *British Educational Research Journal* 32 (4), 601–616.

Edwards, A. (2007) Relational agency in professional practice: A CHAT analysis. *Actio: An International Journal of Human Activity Theory* 1, 1–17.

Edwards, A. (2015) Recognising and realising teachers' professional agency. *Teachers and Teaching* 21 (6), 779–784.

Emirbayer, M. and Mische, A. (1998) What is agency? *The American Journal of Sociology* 103 (4), 962–1023.

Eteläpelto, A., Vähäsantanen, K. and Hökkä, P. (2015) How do novice teachers in Finland perceive their professional agency? *Teachers and Teaching* 21 (6), 660–680.

Eteläpelto, A., Vähäsantanen, K., Hökkä, P. and Paloniemi, S. (2013) What is Agency? Conceptualizing professional agency at work. *Educational Research Review* 10, 45–65.

Eteläpelto, A., Vähäsantanen, K., Hökka, P. and Paloniemi, S. (2014) Identity and agency in professional learning. In S. Billett, C. Harteis and H. Gruber (eds) *International Handbook of Research in Professional and Practice-based Learning* (pp. 645–672). Dordrecht: Springer.

Flores, M.A. and Day, C. (2006) Contexts which shape and reshape new teachers' identities: A multi-perspective study. *Teaching and Teacher Education* 22, 219–232.

FNBE (Finnish National Board of Education). (2014) Core Curriculum for Basic Education 2014. See www.oph.fi/english/curricula_and_qualifications/basic_education (accessed January 2018).

Geijsel, F. and Meijers, F. (2005) Identity learning: The core process of educational change. *Educational Studies* 31 (4), 419–430.

Golombek, P. and Doran, M. (2014) Unifying cognition, emotion, and activity in language teacher professional development. *Teaching and Teacher Education* 39, 102–111.

Hökkä, P., Eteläpelto, A. and Rasku-Puttonen, H. (2012) The professional agency of teacher educators amid academic discourses. *Journal of Education for Teaching: International Research and Pedagogy* 38 (1), 83–102.

Kenway, J. and Youdell, D. (2011) The emotional geographies of education: Beginning a conversation. *Emotion, Space and Society* 4, 131–136.

Lehti, L., Järvinen, H.-M. and Suomela-Salmi, E. (2006) Kartoitus vieraskielisen opetuksen tarjonnasta peruskouluissa ja lukioissa [Mapping FL learning in comprehensive and high schools]. In P. Pietilä, P. Lintunen and H.-M. Järvinen (eds) *Kielenoppija tänään–Language Learners of Today* (pp. 293–313). Jyväskylä, FI: Suomen Soveltavan kielentutkimuksen keskus.

Lemke, J.L. (2008) Identity, development and desire: Critical questions. In C.R. Caldas-Coulthard and R. Iedema (eds) *Identity Trouble* (pp. 17–42). Basingstoke: Palgrave Macmillan.

Marsh, D., Mehisto, P., Wolff, D. and Martín, M.J.F. (2012) European Framework for CLIL Teacher Education. See https://www.unifg.it/sites/default/files/allegatiparagrafo/20-01-2014/european_framework_for_clil_teacher_education.pdf (accessed January 2018).

Martin, A.D. and Strom, K.J. (2016) Toward a linguistically responsive teacher identity: An empirical review of the literature. *International Multilingual Research Journal* 10 (4), 239–253.

Martínez Agudo, J. de D. (ed.) (2018) *Emotions in Second Language Teaching*. Cham: Springer.

Meijers, F. (2002) Career learning in a changing world: The role of emotions. *International Journal for Advancement of Counselling* 24 (3), 149–167.

Moate, J. (2011) Reconceptualising the role of talk in CLIL. *APPLES – Journal of Applied Language Studies* 5 (2), 17–35.

Moate, J. (2014) A narrative account of a teacher community. *Teacher Development: An International Journal of Teachers' Professional Development* 18 (3), 384–402.

Pappa, S. (2018) 'You've got the color, but you don't have the shades': Primary education CLIL teachers' identity negotiation within the Finnish context. Unpublished PhD thesis, University of Jyväskylä.

Pappa, S., Moate, J., Ruohotie-Lyhty, M. and Eteläpelto, A. (2017a) Teachers' pedagogical and relational identity negotiation in the Finnish CLIL context. *Teaching and Teacher Education* 65, 61–70.

Pappa, S., Moate, J., Ruohotie-Lyhty, M. and Eteläpelto, A. (2017b) CLIL teachers in Finland: The role of emotions in professional identity negotiation. *APPLES – Journal of Applied Language Studies* 11 (4), 79–99.

Pennington, M.C. and Richards, J.C. (2016) Teacher identity in language teaching: Integrating personal, contextual, and professional factors. *RELC Journal* 47 (1), 5–23.

Pinho, A.S. and Andrade, A.I. (2015) Redefining professional identity: The voice of a language teacher in a context of collaborative learning. *European Journal of Teacher Education* 38 (1), 21–40.

Ruohotie-Lyhty, M. (2013) Struggling for a professional identity: Two newly qualified language teachers' identity narratives during the first years at work. *Teaching and Teacher Education* 30, 120–129.

Ruohotie-Lyhty, M. and Moate, J. (2016) Who and how? Preservice teachers as active agents developing professional identities. *Teaching and Teacher Education* 55, 318–327.

Sandelowski, M. and Barroso, J. (2006) *Handbook for Synthesizing Qualitative Research.* New York, NY: Springer.

Taylor, S. and Littleton, K. (2006) Biographies in talk: A narrative-discursive research approach. *Qualitative Sociology Review* 2 (1), 22–38.

Van Veen, K. and Sleegers, P. (2006) How does it feel? Teachers' emotions in a context of change. *Journal of Curriculum Studies* 38 (1), 85–111.

Zembylas, M. (2003) Emotions and teacher identity: A poststructural perspective. *Teachers and Teaching* 9 (3), 213–238.

Zembylas, M. (2005) Discursive practices, genealogies, and emotional rules: A poststructuralist view on emotion and identity in teaching. *Teaching and Teacher Education* 21 (8), 935–948.

3 EMI Teacher Identity, Language Use and Reported Behaviours in Austrian Higher Education

Jun Jin, Kyle Read Talbot and Sarah Mercer

Introduction

While English has always been the medium of instruction in English-dominant countries, using English as the medium of instruction (EMI) in tertiary education in non-English-dominant countries has expanded recently, particularly in both Asia (Kirkpatrick, 2014) and Europe (Coleman, 2006; Dearden, 2015; Phillipson, 2006), including Austria (Dalton-Puffer *et al.*, 2019). This has been due, in part, to the increasing internationalisation of higher education (Altbach & Knight, 2007). This development can be viewed as providing both opportunities and challenges (Aguilar, 2017; Moate, 2011). For some, the use of English as a Lingua Franca represents a form of linguistic capital that facilitates travel and interaction across diverse cultural and linguistic landscapes (Haidar, 2017; Tollefson & Tsui, 2004). Yet, for others, the growth of EMI is viewed as threatening the learning and professional use of local languages and discourses, reinforcing the dominance of English at the cost of other languages (Martinez, 2016). The growth of EMI in Austrian higher education has resulted in more multilingual classrooms (Dalton-Puffer *et al.*, 2019). As a result of these developments, the concept of translanguaging has also gained attention in these contexts (Creese & Blackledge, 2015; Wei & Lin, 2019). We thus seek to understand the complexities of language use in EMI classroom practice in Austria.

Teacher identity is central to understanding how teachers behave and act within their classrooms (Cohen, 2010; Day *et al.*, 2006; Hargreaves & Dawe, 1990; see also Chapter 2). Within language teaching specifically, research has emphasised the importance of teacher identity for teacher agency (Tao & Gao, 2017), self-esteem (Motallebzadeh & Kazemi, 2018) and teacher professional development and transformation (Johnson & Golombek, 2016; Yazan, 2017). Teachers working in EMI contexts are of particular interest because of the potential challenges teaching in English may pose for their professional identities and linguistic confidence. Teaching a subject through another language implies competence in the subject and the language. Bovellan (2014: 32) explains, 'teachers are confronted with a double role with a demand of mastering both content and language and expected to meet high requirements in both'. This feature is vital to understand in investigating how EMI teachers may embrace or resist the roles of an EMI educator (Aguilar, 2017; Dearden & Macaro, 2016). At the university level, teachers may also have additional professional roles and responsibilities including academic work, research, publishing and securing funding. EMI teachers in Higher Education (HE) thus take on multiple roles and identities which may complement each other but which may also be in conflict. In this paper, we report on a study examining the identities, language use and reported practices of EMI teachers working in HE in Austria.

Literature Review

The spread of EMI in higher education

The teaching of content through an additional language is increasingly common across educational levels and contexts (Dearden, 2015). However, it is most prevalent at the tertiary level (Fenton-Smith *et al.*, 2017) where it is commonly referred to as English Medium Instruction (EMI). In this chapter, we define EMI following Dearden (2015: 2) as, 'the use of English language to teach academic subjects (other than English itself) in countries or jurisdictions where the first language (L1) of the majority of the population is not English'. Whereas CLIL has been referred to as a 'dual-focused educational approach' (Coyle *et al.*, 2010: 1) that emphasises both language and content learning, EMI, according to Dearden and Macaro (2016: 456), is, 'arguably an umbrella term for academic subjects taught through English, one making no direct reference to the aim of improving students' English'. EMI, rather than CLIL, reflects more closely the understandings of the practices of the tertiary-level teachers we interviewed.

Reasons for the spread of EMI are various and include a wish on the part of universities to internationalise (Knight, 2013), to attract international students, to raise university prestige and because of the role of English as a lingua franca (Macaro *et al.*, 2018). Austria is no exception to this internationalisation trend. In a survey of 28 countries in Europe, Austria ranked 10th in terms of the number of programmes taught in English at the tertiary level, 9th in terms of the number of institutions offering English teaching programmes and 11th in terms of how many students were enrolled in these programmes (Wächter & Maiworm, 2014). As in other European contexts, actual EMI implementation in Austria tends to be dynamic and depend on local needs (Smit & Dafouz, 2012), and other factors such as those highlighted in Dafouz and Smit's (2016: 403) dynamic conceptual framework for EMI (which they refer to as EMEMUS; see also Chapter 8), ROAD-MAPPING, an acronym representing '*Roles of English* (in relation to other languages), *Academic Disciplines, (language) Management, Agents, Practices and Processes*, and *Internationalization and Glocalization*' (emphasis in the original).

Though some have been critical of the spread of English in HE (see, for example, Kirkpatrick, 2011; Phillipson, 2009), including in Austria (Unterberger & Wilhelmer, 2011), Dearden and Macaro (2016: 477) found that EMI teachers largely accept that, 'EMI is here to stay and set to increase, and therefore they have to make the best of it'. As it appears that EMI is indeed likely to continue spreading (Dearden, 2015), we are interested in how this affects EMI teachers' professional identities, how they 'make the best of it' and how language use may affect their identities.

Teacher identity

Teacher identities are defining in terms of their practices and professional well-being (Day, 2017; Varghese *et al.*, 2005). Day *et al.* (2006: 613) explain that, 'identities are a shifting amalgam of personal biography, culture, social influence and institutional values which may change according to role and circumstance'. The unique context of EMI offers a fascinating setting for understanding the nature of EMI educators' identities and how these are enacted depending on factors such as their own linguistic confidence, the institutional expectations and support offered as well as the specific demands of their professional roles (see also Chapters 8, 9 & 10). Soren (2013) examined the identities of lecturers in the natural sciences in an EMI context in Danish tertiary education. She produced a model that showed their identities comprised three main elements: professional identity, personal identity and institutional identity (Soren, 2013). Encouragingly, her findings showed that the challenges of teaching in EMI classrooms did not affect the lecturers' personal sense of teacher identity. In another study by Trent (2017), examining the identities of economics and finance university faculty teaching EMI courses, he found that academic staff negotiated multiple identities, including 'academic economist', 'researcher' and 'teacher'. However, his findings revealed that academic staff did experience challenges in constructing their preferred identities in an EMI environment, but he showed how they negotiated such challenges by exercising their agency in various ways (Trent, 2017).

To investigate teacher identity in the specific context of EMI in HE, we draw upon Wenger's (1998) theory of identity formation in practice.

This suggests that identity formation is a dual process of identification and negotiability (Wenger, 1998) which is never completed and is always ongoing and dynamic (Cohen, 2010; Hall & Gay, 1996). Identities are constructed in respect to specific contextual demands and constraints and in mediation with other identities. In this study, we specifically examine how EMI teachers at the tertiary level negotiate the constraints and demands of their roles and how they accommodate their diverse current identities in synthesis with their other past, present and imagined personal and professional identities. Additionally, we seek to understand how their teacher identities are realised and enacted in relation to their language use and professional practices.

Translanguaging

Possible identity conflicts and tensions between policies and practices in EMI classrooms involving multilingual learners and teachers exist (Creese & Blackledge, 2015). One significant decision and possible tension is whether EMI courses are to be taught fully in English only or whether the full linguistic repertoires of the classroom communities will be utilised. This is a decision that is affected by a variety of reasons including local contexts, educational policy and the teachers' and learners' beliefs and preferences. As such, the notion of translanguaging and its utility as a pedagogical practice has recently attracted researchers' attention (Creese & Blackledge, 2015; Wei & Lin, 2019). Following Otheguy *et al.* (2015: 297), 'translanguaging refers to *using ones's idiolect, that is, one's linguistic repertoire, without regard for socially and politically defined language labels or boundaries*' (emphasis in the original). Translanguaging 'empowers both the learner and the teacher, transforms the power relations, and focuses the process of teaching and learning on making meaning, enhancing experience, and developing identity' (Wei & Lin, 2019: 211; see also Chapters 6, 8 & 9). As EMI is likely to continue spreading (Dearden, 2015), we are interested in exploring the relationship between EMI teachers' professional identities and their professional practices, including their language use.

Methodology

In this study, the primary research questions are:

(1) What kinds of identities are held by EMI teachers at the tertiary level in Austria?
(2) What factors appear to contribute to the development of these identities?
(3) How do these identities seem to be reflected in their practice, including language use?

To investigate the complexities of teacher identity and behaviours in EMI contexts, a qualitative study of in-depth interviews was conducted with 10 EMI teachers working in Austrian tertiary institutions.

Interviews

The data in this study were generated through semi-structured interviews. Ten tertiary-level EMI instructors who, at the time of the study, were teaching one or more classes in English volunteered to take part through an opt-in procedure following an open call for participation. The exploratory nature of the study lent itself well to semi-structured interviews. Such interviews allow the researchers to maintain a clear overview of topics to be covered, while still allowing for the dialogue to move in unexpected yet informative directions (Richards, 2009). The interview protocol was comprised of four sections which included information about each teacher's respective professional histories and identities, their approaches and implementation to teaching courses in English, contextual conditions for EMI and their sense of well-being and work-life balance in relation to their profession roles. The interviews, which took place between October 2017 and January 2018, were conducted by three members of the extended research team. Each interview lasted approximately 45 minutes on average and generated a corpus of 75,046 words in total.

Procedures

Before the interviews were conducted, an information sheet and consent form were signed by both a member of the research team and the interviewee, and copies were kept by both parties. Participants were made aware that they were free to withdraw their participation at any time up until the point of publication. All were volunteers. Interviews were conducted with teachers from across Austria. For pragmatic reasons, six of the interviews were conducted online via Skype, the others were carried out face-to-face. In line with Deakin and Wakefield (2014), the research team did not notice a difference in the quality or content between online and in-person interviews. The participants were given the choice of whether to hold the interviews in English or German. Nine of the participants chose to conduct the interviews in English, while one teacher preferred to do it in German. Only relevant extracts from the interview in German were translated into English by a member of the research team who is a bilingual German and English speaker. These interviews were transcribed by the research team for content analysis. This means that typical speech markers and grammatical errors were not transcribed. Silence, laughter and pauses were attended to when deemed significant to meaning. The transcriptions were anonymised at the point of transcription using pseudonyms and removing any identifying markers. A small gift and note of thanks were sent to each participant as a form of reciprocity.

Participants

All volunteers were recruited via email by the research team and were found through online searches of higher education institutions across Austria that offered classes or degree programmes in English. In recruiting these participants, we did not target a specific discipline or university. We aimed to interview as many EMI teachers as possible across Austria; however, we only managed to recruit 10 interviewees. In this chapter, we will explicitly refer to these participants, regardless of their academic appointments, as teachers. The defining selection criteria was that all teachers were teaching at least one EMI class at the time of the study. Three of the teachers were female and seven were male. Two teachers had explicit language training backgrounds. One, Monica (all names are pseudonyms), was an experienced English for Specific Purposes (ESP) instructor who was teaching one EMI course. The other, Gerlinde, had a background in translation. The other teachers had varying levels of experience with the English language but no explicit language teacher training experience. The teachers' experience ranged from 1 to 28 years, with a mean of 15.3 years. The mean was lower when it came to courses taught in English at 8.3 years. Volunteers spanned from 26 to 60 years old with an average of 45.3 years. For more detailed information about the participants, refer to Table 3.1.

Data analysis

Data were coded following thematic analysis procedures outlined in Braun and Clark (2006). The researchers were first acquainted with the data through transcription and repeated readings of the texts. Individual participant vignettes were created by the research team, which allowed the team to further familiarise themselves with the data and participants. Several members of the team went through the data doing extensive memoing and co-discussion before coding began. Initial coding was conducted line-by-line with a focus on identity, dynamics, language use and professional role. Following discussion and synthesis of the initial code list, several researchers alternated in multiple waves of coding. Data were coded using Atlas.ti.

Findings

Identity

Multiple identities

The EMI teachers in this study described having multiple identities (e.g. as a teacher, as a researcher, as a professor, as mother/father/son/daughter, etc.). Sometimes these identities were congruent and, at other times, these identities conflicted. For example, two teachers, Iris and

Table 3.1 Participant biodata

Pseudonym	Gender	Age	Years of teaching experience	Years of teaching experience in English	Subject	Volunteered or forced to teach in English	Interview language
Theo	Male	36	8.5	'difficult to say … the last year it became more frequent'	Finance	'Mixture'	English
Clemens	Male	39	4.5	4.5	Business	Both	English
Monica	Female	57	28	4	English in Medicine	Suggested by department head	English
Amadeus	Male	43	18	10	Biology	Volunteered	English
Iris	Female	50	25	More than 20 years	Biochemistry	Both	English
Paul	Male	26	1	1	Marketing	Volunteered	English
Conrad	Male	60	23	8	Engineering	Volunteered	English
Patrick	Male	51	15	9	IT	Forced	German
Gerlinde	Female	50	NA	NA	HR Management, Organisational Development, Qualitative Research, Social Skills	NA	English
Jacob	Male	41	15	10	Business	Volunteered	English

Clemens, described enjoying having multiple identities. These teachers felt it added positively to their well-being because they liked fulfilling multiple roles. Clemens explained:

> I like to wear different hats, so I like to be a researcher, I like to be teaching, I think a 100% teaching can get also boring, or not boring, but one-dimensional, so I use a lot of examples when I speak about project management, I can use a lot of experiences from the projects ... for example, we have been doing there, I also give when I have to work on examples I anonymise a lot of documents from the projects so they can work on real stuff. (Clemens)

This excerpt illustrates how his 'different hats', or multiple identities, are harmonious and not in conflict. His experiences in one domain act as personal resources that he can draw upon and transfer to other domains when they are needed. He engages and enacts his identity in various domains which seemingly keeps him energised in the profession. At the same time, he uses his experiences as a transferable resources that he can draw upon and apply in other domains.

Oftentimes, multiple identities can coexist and complement each other as in the case of Clemens above. However, sometimes an identity in one domain may dominate or seem stronger than in other domains. This can be attributed to various factors such a person's personality, background and/or social context. An example from this study can be found with Iris. At her university, research was considered of primary importance and teaching was somewhat of an afterthought. She explained:

> ... at the medical university the main focus was really on research. So ... it was also, actually, like one had to do teaching but it was not very welcome or like the boss didn't really appreciate it that much if one was doing too much teaching. (Iris)

Her identities were situated within her social context where her research role was more esteemed. When asked directly if she feels more like a teacher or researcher, she described, 'I think I would say, still from my background, still I feel more like a researcher (laughs) ... In my person'. The above excerpt highlights how her past experience in a context where teaching was considered a secondary concern seemingly boosted her vision of herself as a researcher and, subsequently, her research identity.

In addition to social contexts, a person's identities are influenced by their past and present experiences as well as their ambitions and visions for the future. One teacher, Conrad, had 15 years of industry experience as an engineer. This significantly impacted his EMI teacher identity and what he believed this role entails, as demonstrated in the extract below:

> Well I worked for 15 years for an international company. Travelling through-out the world, and then I switched to be a teacher, and my main motivation is to instruct person in the job, how they could do that job better. (Conrad)

Of course, the social context and needs of the students also affected this emphasis in his teaching. Conrad explained, 'So, we, our job is to make them ready for their job. Not ready for scientific career'. In this sense, his previous engineering experience and belief about preparing students for the job market rather than a scientific career helped shape the way he perceives his responsibilities and subsequent identity as an EMI teacher.

The role of English in EMI teacher identity construction

While taking up various identities, these participants represented a diversity of English language experiences, which seem to have positively influenced their understandings of themselves as EMI teachers. Iris and Jacob both had working experience in English-speaking countries, Monica and Gerlinde have linguistic-related backgrounds, Conrad worked for an international company and travelled around the world, with substantial English language exposure and Paul had international educational and working experiences. All participants in our study reported feeling confident about their English language ability. Theo, for instance, explained:

> My feeling is that I have, that I have the English abilities to, to get the main message over to the students, and that what's important for me, and I also have, it's my impression that I have the ability to express, a specific topic in different words so that students might get different approaches to a problem. (Theo)

Following the reform of the bachelor programme at his university, Theo positioned himself as a teacher willing to teach Finance through English, since other professors refused to teach in English. While some of his colleagues resisted the change, Theo's willingness to embrace change has helped him to develop his identity of being an EMI teacher, as shown below,

> I think, it's a good ability to, to keep my, my English active. So, when you don't have the possibilities to talk English, you somehow lose all the vocabulary. And these courses are, are a chance for me to refresh that, and to keep my English active, and of course it's an advantage if you apply for a job and you can make the statement that you taught English in other, I taught courses in English, and I don't have a problem in that. I guess that's an ability and a skill that will be required more in the future. (Theo)

His belief in the present and future value of the English language as a skill and resource seemingly influenced his decision to teach EMI courses. More importantly, it shows his comfort in this new role.

Another teacher, Jacob also described his comfort and willingness to teach business courses in English. This contrasts with his descriptions of some of his colleagues who he described as being more reluctant to embrace EMI teaching:

> … there's some different degree of embracement [sic] towards English, so , I'm definitely more on the embracing side. I like teaching in English, I like to be consistent with my English teaching materials, there are also other colleagues who are a little bit more reluctant to move into English, or to, to do courses in English. So, for me it's that I'm, I feel comfortable in teaching in English, so for me this is not a problem. (Jacob)

Jacob's comparison of his positive attitude towards EMI with his colleagues' reluctant attitudes in this excerpt indicates that he positions himself as a confident EMI teacher among his colleagues. His previous experience abroad was a key factor in empowering him with the confidence to embrace the role and identity of an EMI instructor. Iris shared a similar experience. She too referred to the value of her post-doctoral working experience in an English-speaking country. In her experience, this seemed to prepare and embolden her to teach in English later in life.

For other participants, the role of English as a key language used in research and international academic discourses seemingly made the transition to EMI teaching easier (Clemens, Paul, Iris, Jacob, Monica). Iris explained:

> And then first of course before you do it the first time, you think, oh god, now three hours in English! But then, it really was not, it was relatively easy, also because as we, as I come from research, so there I am used to give presentations in English. (Iris)

This extract illustrates how Iris' previous experience using English professionally eased her transition from a subject teaching role to that of an EMI teacher. In this extract she also compares the anticipation of teaching in English to the reality of teaching in English and finds that the anticipation was worse than the experience of teaching itself. She drew on her past professional experience using English and found that this was sufficient. She also expressed in the interview how teaching in English became even easier as she developed more experience in this role. A confident EMI teacher identity is constructed through her experience of EMI practice.

Another teacher, Paul, indicated how courses taught through English are considered prestigious and respected more within his institution. For the teachers in his department, identities are not only shaped by their appointments at the university, but also as a result of the types of courses that they are assigned to teach.

> Because the, typically the English-speaking classes are also kind of more prestigious, I would say, on average. I mean looking at the general trends of course, because there are prestigious courses that everyone respects and so on, but not like people disrespect any courses, but you know what I mean, who'd be entirely in German. You know, typically, if you're teaching something in English it would mean that you're teaching at the MBA, master's or PhD levels, so that kind of implies if you're teaching some more advanced courses, and of course, as a lecturer you want to teach these more advanced courses because they're a lot more fun, number one, they're a lot less effort and they're more stimulating for you as a lecturer. (Paul)

Even though all participants expressed generally positive feelings towards teaching in English, two teachers, Gerlinde and Iris, acknowledged that their experience is not universal. Gerlinde explained:

> I know that for some lecturers it's really, it had been a challenge and sometimes it still is, because the students are very strict, because often the English is one of the competences they feel, or they perceive themselves to be better than the lecturers. Whenever they realise that probably the teachers are a little bit insecure or they make mistakes, then they have problems in seeing this teacher as a competent expert in his field or her field. (Gerlinde)

From Gerlinde's perspective, the English competence of teachers is a part of their professional profiles and affects how they are perceived in their roles by students, who in some cases may have higher levels of English proficiency than the teachers. As such, the dual identities for teachers in EMI classes may pose a threat to some teachers' professional senses of self. Even if they are highly competent in their subject, if their linguistic competence is not sufficient, the lecturers' legitimacy and credibility may be challenged. Paul expanded on this view. He explained, 'nobody would ever admit to not feeling comfortable with English, even though some people don't, uhm, but you know so they always, it's kind of, yeah it's nothing that anybody would be willing to admit'. When asked why teachers would be hesitant to admit they were not comfortable teaching through English, Paul responded:

> … all our research has to be conducted in English, right? So, if they admit to not being good at it, they basically saying they're not good at the job, I think. So, it's a prerequisite, you know, it's, I don't know. If you wanted to join the marines and you're afraid of swimming, so, it's not main task, it's not the main thing that we're paid to do, but if you don't have it you're, it excludes you. (Paul)

The above extract highlights how the use of English to teach seemingly creates an in- and out-group based on those who are comfortable with this and those who are not. This also may enforce a scenario when those who may not feel as comfortable teaching through English but remain subject experts are not able to get the help they may want or need.

Conflicts and tensions

A significant challenge for teachers in terms of their identity perceptions can be created when there are conflicts or tensions between roles. One reported tension between differing roles and identities was reported by Gerlinde. She reflected on the increasing pressures in higher education to meet certain criteria that emphasise publishing and university rankings with a subsequent decrease in the value given to teaching, as well as the effect this might have locally:

> Because we are a university of applied sciences and only three or four years ago the focus really was on teaching, but now given all the competition amongst the business school or the universities in general, it's more and more important to also have certain certificates, or accreditations, and you are listed in rankings and so, the academic part including publishing and research is increasing and I think often if we play the game, this international game, there is no benefit for the [local] environment or for the social context where our university is located, or very little. (Gerlinde)

Like Monica, Gerlinde questioned whether the internationalisation of higher education, including the role of English in this, was beneficial for the local community. Another tension noted by three other participants (Amadeus, Patrick, Theo) drew attention to the perceived negative perceptions of the teaching profession in society. This affected the way two of the participants, Amadeus and Theo, felt about their identities as teachers. Amadeus explained:

> Teaching as a career is of course in the natural science field not really accepted as a, at least here in Austria, doesn't feel to be really an acceptable career. So, it's ok to teaching, to get additional money, or to support yourself, but it's not, the career doesn't, you have to teach, but it's not like you have to be, there's no support in a sense that you get a really good teacher, so you don't get really a reward for that, and there are some prizes, of course, but they're not really, doesn't really reflect, is not really reflected in the career steps or something like that. (Amadeus)

Theo also emphasised the frequent misunderstandings about the teaching role of his job in society and expressed some frustration:

> So most of my relatives always ask me when I'm currently on holiday, so they always think that when students are on holidays it's also the

teachers that are on holidays and I always explain them that it's not the case, that it's the five weeks of vacation that every other employee has and that if I'm not teaching I'm rather preparing for the classes or doing research. (Theo)

Perhaps the most notable conflicts and tensions were centred on how EMI teachers enacted their roles and identities as language users. For example, one participant, Monica, normally teaches English for Specific Purposes Courses (ESP) in the field of medicine. However, she also teaches an EMI course in presentation techniques. These courses have different linguistic aims for the learners and sometimes she felt the crossover and role transition was a challenge:

Because in this only one seminar that I have once a year which is always in the winter term, presentation skills, I force myself not to listen to the mistakes that the students make when they talk, and I take the fear off them and say 'this is not the English course, so please feel free to use the language'. But I notice that I keep record of the wrong pronunciation, because I teach the same students, I teach them the pronunciation in a different course, in a different semester. Yeah and I feel forced to tell them, yeah, look, by the way this is not how it's [pronounced], it's different. (Monica)

Monica also expressed concerns about the tensions between her professional identity as an ESP teacher and how EMI teaching and the English language affect the status and future of the German language in Austria:

I mean I like English and I like teaching English, I like speaking English, but I do not see why university classes should be taught in English only, in Austria. Yeah, and that's what my friends from abroad say, like [my] Australian friend, 'we would never ever offer a course in another language, or a study program' ... EMI, as I said would kill ESP. It's I think, I feel that the language is going down as well, the German language, yeah, and there have been, there has been, there is proof, countries of the Far East, or, you know, where the education is in English, and, or, like Singapore, for example. (Monica)

While there is unceasing global debate on English as the international lingua franca, Monica viewed EMI cautiously as a phenomenon that could kill ESP. She constructs an identity of a linguistic expert with an international perspective to reflect the language issues in Austria, Australia and Singapore. Monica has a strong sense of preserving the local language and ESP programmes in Austria, which causes tension and conflict between her EMI practice and her professional beliefs.

Another related issue concerns these EMI teachers' translingual attitudes and identities, especially concerning the use of German and multilingual practices.

> Some teachers they just, they just teach them in German. So that basically especially in the seminars and then they act in a more informal way, and then they just speak German. And this is probably not really the idea, I think, of course on the other hand, and also I remember that one, in my immunology, I had a lab course on immunology and then also one student said, and so I was explaining, and one student said, please speak in German we are anyway all native (laughs), so she really wanted that. Then I thought oh what. Then I did for a short while, and then I thought nah. That's actually not the idea, even though maybe several things would be easier to explain. (Iris)

Iris' reflection reveals how teachers negotiate their identities in the dynamics of language use. When one of her students suggested speaking in German among all German-speaking students, she emphasised her identity of an L1 German speaker situated in a predominately German-speaking context more strongly than her identity as an EMI teacher. However, this conflicted with her idea of she believed an EMI class should be like. Thus, she subsequently reverted back to German. These dynamics between students and teachers reflect a negotiating process of multilingual identity.

Reported teacher behaviours

Translanguaging

Translanguaging is often an explicit behavioural expression of the existence of multiple linguistic identities. Three of the teachers (Clemens, Theo, Jacob) reported some translanguaging in their classrooms albeit only to a limited extent. Some reasons they provided for translanguaging were to provide a specific vocabulary item to German L1 speakers if there was confusion or to sustain the flow of the class in the case of misunderstandings. Interestingly, one of the teachers claimed that building rapport with students was another reason for switching between English and German. Theo explained:

> … from my side, it's 100% English, except that from time to time I provide students with German expressions for a specific term, uhm, but that's it from my side, I also try to keep communication via email in English but if students approach me in German in an individual communication then I do not switch to English. (Theo)

For Clemens, there was a practical reason for switching between English and German from time to time. Due to the nature of his discipline (e.g. entrepreneurship and international business broadly defined), they often had external customers to his university for different projects. As such, the localised setting and the customers facilitated translanguaging in his context. He explained:

> It's a bit artificial if everybody speaks German in the audience and also the customer, maybe he's not so, has not that good command of English language so then we say ok, let's have the presentation in English but switch in the discussion to German. (Clemens)

Interestingly, one teacher discussed how German vocabulary was sometimes forgotten by students in EMI contexts. She explained, 'what happens actually is that sometimes they know all the expert vocabulary in English, but they don't know what that is in German'. Another teacher, Jacob explains that while most all of the content expressed in his courses is through English, he and his colleagues sometimes try to promote and teach German vocabulary. He reports that this 'feels even unnatural' and that 'definitely English is the dominant language here in our research domain'. Nevertheless, Jacob explains that he and others continue to explicitly teach German terminology, which reveals the perceived pragmatic utility of students knowing key terms in their field in both English and German in this context.

Linguistically, English was the predominant language for 6 of the teachers who reported trying to speak in English all of the time or very close to it (Paul, Conrad, Monica, Gerlinde, Iris, Amadeus). Paul, for example, explained that, 'usually when you start a course in English, you just stick to it, there's no transition period or something'. However, three teachers (Monica, Amadeus, Gerlinde) described how their students would frequently switch between English and German, more often than they themselves would. This suggests a possible discrepancy between the translingual identities of the instructors, which may not be reflected in learner identities and shared linguistic practices.

Pedagogical decisions

The teaching as well as linguistic identities of these EMI instructors were reflected through specific pedagogical decisions set against the backdrop of the tensions outlined above and various contextual factors such as programme design, colleagues or student population, the available literature and materials, teacher preferences and the specific discipline of the instructors or topic of the lesson. For example, the role of internationalisation in higher education means that many programmes included international students and so English was used pragmatically as a *lingua franca*. Theo explained, 'this is even an international programme, so we have international students coming here, so we have to teach in English anyway'. Internationalisation was not limited to the student populations referred to in the data. Jacob and Clemens both reported that English was largely used as a lingua franca among colleagues in their departments. Jacob explained:

> ... our subject area is mainly in English, therefore it's quite natural to stay, well let's say, in the language of the academic discourse. It's also that we have several colleagues here in my, in my research group who are not, who are not from Germany, not from Austria, so they are less comfortable with German, so that makes it also easier for us to stay on equal terms with every, with all the members of our research team, and that makes it more flexible also to staff different persons into the courses. If it was German it would be uhm, more restricted because not everybody is on a level to teach in German here.

Other factors also impacted these teachers' decisions to teach in English. For instance, Jacob preferred teaching in English because, pragmatically, all of his materials were in English. In fact, all of the teachers explained that English is the international language of science and that there is, therefore, an abundance of available materials in English.

Balancing content and language

In our data, there was very little balancing of content and language as would have been more typical in a CLIL setting at other educational levels. Content was favoured almost exclusively by all of the participants. Theo explained, 'We're not defining each of the courses as an, a content class plus an English class, but rather as a content class'. He continued:

> There, there are no actual measures that I have to find out whether people fall behind with respect to their English, so that's something that's entirely left over to the students, they have to, or, it's in their responsibility to understand what's going on in the course, and I receive very limited feedback that they have problems with that, so if there would be more feedback, I'd probably respond on that, but we have a very strong focus on content in this courses, and assume that uhm, English is just a, the language of, of conduct that we decided on. (Theo)

Gerlinde expressed a similar sentiment, explaining that, 'English is simply our uhm, yeah, means of transport'. However, Gerlinde suggests that this approach is not always easy for the students who in her view, come from error-focused or more punitive language learning backgrounds and are not used to the mistakes that they hear from their instructors. In her programme, they attempt to emphasise to their students beforehand that it is not a language university:

> [W]e try to prepare the students to the fact that we are not a language university but sometimes that's still, I think for some of the students

that's still difficult yeah, and of course they come, or their socialisation with learning a language has been different, because, maybe for eight or ten years they always were criticised when they made mistakes and whenever they got feedback from teachers it was on mistakes and never on what was good or how well they managed to communicate, so I think that's probably part of this little battle yeah, that whenever they find mistakes they think that's a no-go.

Interestingly, the majority of mentions of language learning by these teachers were centred on vocabulary. Six of the teachers in this study explicitly mentioned vocabulary or vocabulary instruction, almost as if a proxy for language instruction more generally.

Discussion

These EMI teachers negotiate multiple identities as academics, researchers, educators, multilinguals and as EMI instructors specifically. The most notable feature of these identities is how they relate and reflect tensions from the ecologies of their practice. It is striking that none of these educators really perceive their role in this context as language instructors. English represents the mode of instruction but also reflects the international role of English as the language of science and as a *lingua franca* among individuals of diverse linguistic backgrounds. English is clearly seen in this context as a form of linguistic capital (Bourdieu, 1977, 1991; Heller, 1995) that may be tied to the ability to better one's opportunities and career prospects.

In this study, all participants reported feeling confident about their English language abilities and perceived English to be an important teaching competence. Interestingly, two teachers, Paul and Iris, explicitly described a subset of teachers who did not feel as comfortable teaching EMI courses. Unfortunately, we were not able to reach those teachers who might identify as part of that particular subset. Pennington and Richard (2016) suggest that teachers, who use a second or additional language as the medium of instruction, might perceive their non-native status and have concerns about their language competence. Though it seems that this did not affect the teachers in this study in a significant way, it is notable that these other teachers who may not transition, or desire to transition, into an EMI role so seamlessly were described by our participants.

In this study, the complexities of teacher multilingual identities (e.g. professional identity, personal identity, linguistic identity, imagined identity) resulted in varying levels of acceptance or resistance of EMI teaching. The findings in this study show that ten participants embraced their roles in EMI courses in different ways (e.g. voluntarily, forced and both), and adopted comfortably an identity of a university EMI lecturer, while some of their colleagues were described as being more critical of this approach. This echoes Soren's (2013) argument that the imposed need to teach in English might be a challenge or a threat to a professor's academic identity and depends on the individual's personal biography and role expectations. For the teachers in this study, their backgrounds, linguistic competences, localised contexts and professional experiences of using English seemed to be key factors in handling the challenges of being an EMI teacher and flourishing professionally. A similar finding was found in Pappa *et al.* (2017: 64), who described how teachers' beliefs and past experiences can be, 'interwoven into the profession and affect its enactment'. In the context of this study, the beliefs and experiences of the teachers impacted their ability to negotiate their identity in the present as well as their pedagogical decisions and classroom practices.

The most notable identity tension in this study concerns the perception of teaching as one role among others in a tertiary-educators' role repertoire. As noted in van Lankveld *et al.* (2017: 331), 'the undervaluation of teaching compared to research led to tensions in the academics' identity as teachers and to feelings of insecurity and reduced self-esteem'. For these educators, even those who were more dedicated to their teaching responsibilities, the prestige and status of the teaching role in HE is considerably lower than that assigned to researching and publishing. However, an exception to this could be EMI as indicated by Paul. Interestingly, those who are selected to or who choose to teach the EMI classes may possibly be afforded a higher status teaching identity than those who teach in their L1, in this case German. This reflects an interesting potential role for EMI in the context of HE, which could allow some educators to embrace an EMI teaching identity more readily than a regular teaching identity in the tertiary context.

Implications for Policy and Practice

Findings in this study provide educational policymakers and EMI teaching staff with useful information about identity, language use and reported behaviours in Austrian EMI classrooms. Three major implications were identified in this chapter: (1) the need for a greater awareness of the multiple identities that EMI teachers embody, (2) the need for clearer guidelines for EMI implementation and (3) the potential of translanguaging as a pedagogical tool within EMI classrooms.

First, educational policymakers and other interested stakeholders should be aware of EMI teachers' multiple identities in Austrian higher education. This could possibly help avoid unnecessary conflicts and tensions among professional identity, personal identity and EMI teacher identity. As evinced from the data, participants in this study described how some of their colleagues, who may have strong German-speaking professional identities, were often more reluctant to teach EMI courses.

It implies the importance of offering language support programmes for those who may wish to develop their competences in another language, but serves as a caution against making teaching in a foreign language compulsory for all staff. Indeed, the analysis also showed how two teachers, Monica and Gerlinde, were at least somewhat concerned with the current situation of EMI implementation in Austrian universities because of how it affects local contexts and existing educational programmes such as ESP. Therefore, it is important to consider how EMI approaches can be integrated alongside and in cooperation with local resources and existing programmes. It also implies the benefits of raising awareness among staff and policy makers that academic staff may negotiate potentially conflicting identities when they teach EMI courses. Explicit reflection on multiple roles and identities within professional development programmes could help staff harmoniously manage their diverse identities. The findings also suggest the value of tertiary institutions taking concrete steps to explicitly esteem and value educators' teaching roles in HE.

Second, clearer guidelines for EMI implementation need to be considered. A key linguistic tension exists between teaching in English and the expectations and needs of EMI learners, who themselves are typically a diverse population comprised of local and international students. Seeking to meet all these needs in one class often leads to tensions in perceptions about language use and language instruction. It may be advisable in some cases to take steps such as those found at Gerlinde's institution which explicitly aimed to communicate to students that they were not at a language institution, but rather a setting where language is used as a vehicle for content. There is a need for explicitness in EMI provisions and clear guidelines for EMI implementation, which simultaneously help teachers to feel support while providing them the adequate autonomy and flexibility to express their linguistic creativity and tap into their broader language repertoires.

Third, translanguaging seems to be a reality for many of these educators in Austrian EMI classrooms. For some, this is a normal part of their multilingual identity, whereas for others, there seems to be more of a perceived tension against the background of supposed 'ought-to' practice regarding specific language in use. Encouraging educators to see themselves and their learners as translinguals may relieve some of the tensions in identity construction and enactment, engage learners through identity investment and transform relations of power between teachers and students in a positive way (Creese & Blackledge, 2015). As argued by Wei (2018), translanguaging has been shown to be an effective pedagogical practice in different educational contexts that helped to maximise both teachers and students' linguistic resources in the process of problem solving and knowledge construction, this may especially be the case in EMI contexts. As such, it is necessary to consider the language policies of

EMI programmes in Austrian HE contexts in order to 'encourage bi- and multilingualism within the university' (Kirkpatrick, 2014: 4).

Conclusion

To conclude, in this paper, we have explored the identities of EMI instructors at tertiary level in Austria. We have noted the linguistic and pedagogical tensions associated with this role but also revealed the potential benefits for those able and willing to embrace an EMI and translingual identity. The study does not seek to resolve the debate around the conflicting findings outlined in other studies about the potential for the EMI role to be a challenge or a professional enrichment. Instead, the findings highlight the uniqueness and highly individual nature of identity construction and enactment, which is bounded by personal trajectories and contextual constraints and affordances. Some educators flourish in this role, some resist the role and some merely accept the role without any seeming emotional or identity investment. The data suggest to us the benefits of ensuring explicit discussions in EMI contexts about role expectations and the role of language, especially the linguistic potential offered by an acceptance of translanguaging practices for teachers and learners. We feel it is important for teachers to be able to enact their agency in constructing their own notion of the EMI role and, ideally, to take this role voluntarily, rather than have it imposed upon them. In future research, we are interested in taking a longitudinal view of identity development over time following teachers from their first encounters with EMI as they develop their practices and understandings of that role. EMI seems here to stay in HE for the foreseeable future. As such, it would seem important to ensure that educators who take on an EMI role are supported in their institutions in ways which facilitate their pedagogy, esteem their teaching role and enable them to construct positive and harmonious identities as EMI instructors among their plethora of multiple professional identities as HE professionals.

References

Aguilar, M. (2017) Engineering lecturers' views on CLIL and EMI. *International Journal of Bilingual Education and Bilingualism* 20 (6), 722–735.

Altbach, P.G. and Knight, J. (2007) The Internationalization of higher education: Motivations and realities. *Journal of Studies in International Education* 11 (3–4), 290–305.

Bourdieu, P. (1977) The economics of linguistic exchanges. *Social Science Information* 16, 645–668.

Bourdieu, P. (1991) *Language and Symbolic Power*. Cambridge, MA: Harvard University Press.

Bovellan, E. (2014) Teachers' beliefs about learning and language as reflected in their views of teaching materials for content and language integrated learning (CLIL). Unpublished PhD thesis, University of Jyväskylä.

Braun, V. and Clarke, V. (2006) Using thematic analysis in psychology. *Qualitative Research in Psychology* 3 (2), 77–101.

Cohen, J. (2010) Getting recognised: Teachers negotiating professional identities as learners through talk. *Teaching and Teacher Education* 26, 473–481.

Coleman, J.A. (2006) English-medium teaching in European higher education. *Language Teaching* 39 (1), 1–14.

Coyle, D., Hood, P. and Marsh, D. (2010) *CLIL: Content and Language Integrated Learning.* Cambridge: Cambridge University Press.

Creese, A. and Blackledge, A. (2015) Translanguaging and identity in educational settings. *Annual Review of Applied Linguistics* 35, 20–35.

Dafouz, E. and Smit, U. (2016) Towards a dynamic conceptual framework for English-medium education in multilingual university settings. *Applied Linguistics* 37 (3), 397–415.

Dalton-Puffer, C., Boeckmann, K.-B. and Hinger, B. (2019) Research in language teaching and learning in Austria (2011–2017). *Language Teaching* 52 (2), 201–230.

Day, C. (2017) *Teachers' Worlds and Work: Understanding Complexity, Building Quality.* Abingdon: Routledge.

Day, C., Kington, A., Stobart, G. and Sammons, P. (2006) The personal and professional selves of teachers: Stable and unstable identities. *British Educational Research Journal* 32 (4), 601–616.

Deakin, H. and Wakefield, K. (2014) Skype interviewing: Reflections of two PhD researchers. *Qualitative Research* 14 (5), 603–616.

Dearden, J. (2015) *English as a Medium of Instruction - A Growing Global Phenomenon.* London: British Council.

Dearden, J. and Macaro, E. (2016) Higher education teachers' attitudes towards English medium instruction: A three-country comparison. *Studies in Second Language Learning and Teaching* 6 (3), 455.

Fenton-Smith, B., Humphreys, P. and Walkinshaw, I. (eds) (2017) *English Medium Instruction in Higher Education in Asia-Pacific.* Cham, Switzerland: Springer International Publishing.

Hall, S. and Gay, P.D. (1996) *Questions of Cultural Identity.* London: Sage.

Haidar, S. (2017) Access to English in Pakistan: inculcating prestige and leadership through instruction in elite schools. *International Journal of Bilingual Education and Bilingualism* 1–16.

Hargreaves, A. and Dawe, R. (1990) Paths of professional development: Contrived collegiality, collaborative culture, and the case of peer coaching. *Teaching and Teacher Education* 6 (3), 227–241.

Heller, M. (1995) Language choice, social institutions, and symbolic domination. *Language in Society* 24, 373–405.

Johnson, K. and Golombek, P.R. (2016) *Mindful L2 Teacher Education A Sociocultural Perspective on Cultivating Teachers' Professional Development.* New York, NY: Routledge.

Kirkpatrick, A. (2011) English as an Asian lingua franca and the multilingual model of ELT. *Language Teaching* 44 (2), 212–224.

Kirkpatrick, A. (2014) The language(s) of HE: EMI and/or ELF and/or multilingualism? *The Asian Journal of Applied Linguistics* 1 (1), 4–15.

Knight, J. (2013) The changing landscape of higher education internationalisation – for better or worse? *Perspectives: Policy and Practice in Higher Education* 17 (3), 84–90.

Macaro, E., Curle, S., Pun, J., An, J. and Dearden, J. (2018) A systematic review of English medium instruction in higher education. *Language Teaching* 51 (1), 36–76.

Martinez, R. (2016) English as a Medium of Instruction (EMI) in Brazilian higher education: Challenges and opportunities. In K.R. Finardi (ed.) *English in Brazil: Views, Policies and Programs* (pp. 191–230). Londrina, Brazil: Eduel.

Moate, J.M. (2011) The impact of foreign language mediated teaching on teachers' sense of professional integrity in the CLIL classroom. *European Journal of Teacher Education*, 34 (3), 333–346.

Motallebzadeh, K. and Kazemi, B. (2018) The relationship between EFL teachers' professional identity and their self-esteem. *Cogent Education* 5 (1).

Otheguy, R., García, O. and Reid, W. (2015) Clarifying translanguaging and deconstructing named languages: A perspective from linguistics. *Applied Linguistics Review* 6 (3), 281–307.

Pappa, S., Moate, J., Ruohotie-Lyhty, M. and Eteläpelto, A. (2017) Teachers' pedagogical and relational identity negotiation in the Finnish CLIL context. *Teaching and Teacher Education* 65, 61–70.

Pennington, M. and Richard, J.C. (2016) Teacher identity in language teaching: Integrating personal, contextual, and professional factors. *RELC Journal* 47 (1), 5–23.

Phillipson, R. (2006) English, a cuckoo in the European higher education nest of languages? *European Journal of English Studies* 10 (1), 13–32.

Phillipson, R. (2009) *Linguistic Imperialism Continued*. New York, NY: Routledge.

Richards, K. (2009) Interviews. In J. Heigham and R.A. Croker (eds) *Qualitative Research in Applied Linguistics: A Practical Introduction*. Basingstoke: Palgrave Macmillan.

Smit, U. and Dafouz, E. (2012) Integrating content and language in higher education. An introduction to English-medium policies, conceptual issues and research practices across Europe. *AILA Review* 25, 1–12.

Soren, J.K. (2013) Teacher identity in English-medium instruction: Teacher cognitions from a Danish tertiary education. Unpublished PhD thesis, University of Copenhagen.

Tao, J. and Gao, X. (2017) Teacher agency and identity commitment in curricular reform. *Teaching and Teacher Education* 63, 346–355.

Tollefson, J.W. and Tsui, A.B.M. (2004) The centrality of medium-of-instruction policy in socio-political processes. In J.W. Tollefson and A.B.M. Tsui (eds) *Medium of instruction policies: Which agenda? Whose agenda?* (pp. 1–27). Mahwah, NJ: Lawrence Erlbaum.

Trent, J. (2017) Being a professor and doing EMI properly isn't easy: An identity-theoretic investigation of content teachers' attitudes towards EMI at a university in Hong Kong. In B. Fenton-Smith, P. Humphreys and I. Walkinshaw (eds) *English Medium Instruction in Higher Education in Asia-Pacific Multilingual Education* (pp. 212–232). Cham: Springer.

Unterberger, B. and Wilhelmer, N. (2011) English-medium education in economics and business studies: Capturing the status quo at Austrian universities. *International Journal of Applied Linguistics* 161, 90–110.

van Lankveld, T., Schoonenboom, J., Volman, M., Croiset, G. and Beishuizen, J. (2017) Developing a teacher identity in the university context: A systematic review of the literature. *Higher Education Research & Development* 36 (2), 325–342.

Varghese, M., Morgan, B., Johnston, B. and Johnson, K.A. (2005) Theorizing language teacher identity: Three perspectives and beyond. *Journal of Language, Identity, and Education* 4 (1), 21–44.

Wächter, B. and Maiworm, F. (eds) (2014) *English-taught Programmes in European Higher Education: The State of Play in 2014*. Bonn: Lemmens Medien.

Wei, L. (2018) Translanguaging as a practical theory of language. *Applied Linguistics* 39 (1), 9–30.

Wei, L. and Lin, A.M.Y. (2019) Translanguaging classroom discourse: Pushing limits, breaking boundaries. *Classroom Discourse* 10 (3–4), 209–215.

Wenger, E. (1998) Communities of practice: Learning as a social system. *Systems Thinker* 9 (5), 2–3.

Yazan, B. (2017) 'It just made me look at language in a different way:' ESOL teacher candidates' identity negotiation through teacher education coursework. *Linguistics and Education* 40, 38–49.

4 CLIL as a Vehicle for a Positive English Self-concept: An Analysis of One Former Student's Life Course

Anssi Roiha and Katja Mäntylä

Introduction

The interplay between multiple factors such as learners' ages, aptitudes, attitudes, self-perceptions, personality, motivation or learning strategies has an effect on how successful one is in learning a second or foreign language. Of particular interest to our study are both affective factors and self-beliefs as we examine the effect of early CLIL on English language self-concept. Self-concept is an important but not often mentioned psychological construct in language learning. Particularly in CLIL research, the investigation of this construct has remained rare. In this chapter, CLIL is defined as an educational approach in which content is partly taught through a foreign language (Coyle et al., 2010). In Finland (i.e. the context of the study) CLIL started in 1991 and has, throughout the years, established its place in the Finnish education system. It was particularly popular in the beginning as in 1996 approximately 10% of schools reported implementing CLIL at basic education level (Nikula & Marsh, 1996). In the early 2000s, the number of schools providing CLIL had dropped to approximately 5% (Lehti et al., 2006). However, a recent municipal-level survey reveals that the implementation of CLIL has again increased in many municipalities. The survey also indicates that most CLIL programmes in Finland are relatively small scale (i.e. less than 25% of all teaching) (Peltoniemi et al., 2018). The predominant CLIL language in Finland has been English throughout the existence of this teaching approach (Nikula & Marsh, 1996; Peltoniemi et al., 2018). The Finnish national core curriculum for basic education allows all schools to employ CLIL so long as the content objectives are met in all the subjects (Finnish National Board of Education, 2014).

This chapter draws on empirical data from a case study that investigated 24 former students' experiences of CLIL (Content and Language Integrated Learning) and its effects on their English language self-concept (Roiha & Mäntylä, 2019). More specifically, in this chapter, we focus on one participant, Kimmo, and how his English self-concept manifests throughout the course of his life. We rely on the theoretical underpinnings of self-concept as a dynamic and multidimensional psychological construct that reflects people's self-perceptions (e.g. Mercer, 2011). Initially, we will review how self-concept has been defined and how it has been previously investigated within CLIL contexts. We will then move on to a detailed analysis of Kimmo's interview. The results of the study indicate that early CLIL can be an effective approach in forming the foundation of strong target language self-concept. Furthermore, the findings support the views of foreign language self-concept being a situational construct that can oscillate throughout the years. The findings also suggest that foreign language self-concept is constantly constructed in social situations and interactions with interlocutors (see also Chapter 2). The data are in line with earlier studies that suggest it is more reasonable to consider separate self-concepts for different foreign languages. Moreover, the data suggest dividing foreign language self-concept into even more domain-specific self-concepts within a language, such as English writing, speaking or reading self-concept (see also Laine & Pihko, 1991; Mercer, 2011; Walker, 2015). Finally, the practical implications for foreign language and CLIL education based on this study will be discussed.

Self-concept

Conceptualising self-concept

Self-concept, which has been extensively studied in psychology, is generally seen as a multidimensional and hierarchical construct that represents a person's self-perceptions in various domains (e.g. Marsh *et al.*, 1988; Marsh & Shavelson, 1985; Shavelson *et al.*, 1976). Although most scholars have focused on the cognitive dimension of self-concept, it is also considered to include an affective evaluative component (e.g. Pihko, 2007), which some empirical studies have supported (e.g. Arens *et al.*, 2011; Tracey *et al.*, 2014). According to Shavelson *et al.* (1976: 411), self-concept is 'organized, multifaceted, hierarchical, stable, developmental, evaluative, differentiable'. These many dimensions of self-concept show in different models depicting it. For instance, Shavelson *et al.* (1976) have divided the global self-concept into academic and non-academic self-concepts. Marsh *et al.* (1988) have further separated the academic self-concept into math self-concept and verbal self-concept, which incorporates a holistic foreign language self-concept.

Self-concept has been further conceptualised as having a relatively stable core that is formed early on and several less stable domain-specific self-concepts. School itself constitutes an important venue regarding the formation of one's academic self-concept as students' educational outcomes have been shown to influence it (e.g. Marsh & Craven, 2006; Valentine *et al.*, 2004). Additionally, parents' and teachers' beliefs about students' abilities can have an impact on their self-concept (e.g. Frome & Eccles, 1998; Pesu, 2017). Marsh *et al.* (2018) have created an integrated academic self-concept model for the formation and development of academic self-concept. Their model comprises the internal/external (I/E) frame of reference model, reciprocal effects model (REM) and the big-fish-little-pond effect (BFLPE) model. According to the I/E model, students juxtapose their math and verbal self-concepts, and the assumed difference will further increase the domain-specific self-concept that they perceive to be stronger. The external frame of reference refers to people comparing their own perceived self-concept to other people's self-concepts which correspondingly affects the nature of their own self-concept (Marsh, 1986). The REM model, in turn, refers to academic self-concept and students' achievement being both the causes and effects of each other (Marsh, 1990). The BFLPE model assumes that students' academic self-concepts are influenced by their peers. Therefore, a student who is in a class with more abled students is likely to have a lower academic self-concept than an equally able student with less abled peers (Marsh & Seaton, 2015). The above models are also applicable to foreign language learning which we will discuss in more detail as follows.

Self-concept in foreign languages

Relying on Marsh *et al.*'s (1988) structure of self-concept, Mercer (2011) has defined the foreign language self-concept as 'an individual's self-descriptions of competence and evaluative feelings about themselves as a Foreign Language (FL) learner' (Mercer, 2011: 14). For the sake of operationalising, Pihko (2007) has further separated the foreign language self-concept into three smaller components: (1) real/actual self which refers to learners' subjective perceptions of themselves in a language, (2) ideal self which stands for learners' wishes and desires of language learning (i.e. the level of competence in a given language one aspires to achieve) and (3) self-esteem/self-worth in language learning which she considers as the most important component. Pihko's (2007) conceptualisation bears similarities to

Dörnyei's (2005) L2 Motivational Self System (L2MSS) which highlights the Ideal L2 Self (i.e. the L2 user one aspires to become) as the paramount component of motivation. Thus, for Pihko (2007) self-esteem weighs more in self-concept whereas in Dörnyei's (2005) model one's aspirations are emphasised more.

Many studies have approached foreign language self-concept as a holistic construct that encompasses all foreign languages. However, for instance, Mercer (2011) has raised the need to acknowledge distinct self-concepts in different languages and domains within languages. Similarly, Laine and Pihko (1991) regard foreign language self-concept as a hierarchical structure that includes global, specific and task levels. The global level refers to learners' perceptions of themselves as a foreign language learner whereas the specific level designates learners' self-perceptions in a specific language. The task level, in turn, relates to learners' perceptions of their abilities in specific language skills such as speaking or writing, thus somewhat resembling self-efficacy (e.g. Bong & Skaalvik, 2003). In support of this, Yeung and Wong (2004) found that teachers (n = 437) had distinct self-concepts in different languages. Moreover, Lau et al.'s (1999) findings imply the need to separate a foreign language self-concept into even more microscopic self-concepts within the language such as listening, speaking, reading or writing self-concept (see also Walker, 2015).

Akin to global self-concept, foreign language self-concept is also believed to be affected by internal and external factors. For instance, Mercer (2011) adheres to Marsh's (1986) I/E model. When applying the I/E theory to language learning, Mercer (2011) has suggested that learners make comparisons more broadly across several subjects or various foreign languages. Other internal factors according to Mercer (2011) are beliefs about foreign language learning and specific languages as well as affect. External factors comprise social comparisons, feedback from significant others, perceived experiences of success and failure and past experiences with the language (Mercer, 2011). Pihko (2007), in turn, proposes that learners' language self-concept is formed gradually through their learning experiences. Positive language situations help create a strong language self-concept while negative experiences are likely to have an adverse effect. In addition, Pihko (2007) emphasises the role of feedback from peers and teachers.

In this study, we approach the data through a specific English (as a foreign language) self-concept which we regard as a subcomponent of the global foreign languages self-concept (e.g. Marsh et al., 1988). We adhere to the conceptualisations by Mercer (2011) who defines it broadly as people's beliefs and evaluative feelings of themselves as English language learners and users. Similarly, we believe that English self-concept has both cognitive and affective components (e.g. Pihko, 2007).

Prior studies on self-concept in CLIL

To the best of our knowledge, few studies have examined self-concept in CLIL contexts. Some have used Dörnyei's (2005) Second Language Motivational Self System (L2MSS) to compare CLIL students' motivation to that of non-CLIL students and found that CLIL students tend to have a stronger Ideal L2 Self, although often already at the outset of CLIL (e.g. Mearns *et al.*, 2017; Sylvén & Thompson, 2015). In Finland, Seikkula-Leino (2002) compared the foreign language self-concept of 101 non-CLIL and 116 CLIL students in years 5 and 6. The data were collected using a Likert-scale, in which the self-concept indicator was an adjusted version of Laine and Pihko (1991). She found that the CLIL students' foreign language self-concept was significantly weaker than the non-CLIL students'. The CLIL students perceived themselves as weaker learners of English in general, and specifically in reading, writing, speaking and comprehension. This is an interesting result considering that the CLIL students were factually better at English based on their higher school grades. Similar results have also been found by, for instance, Mercer (2011). According to Seikkula-Leino (2002), this can be the result of CLIL, as in CLIL lessons, the students are being exposed to foreign language which may be harder to bear on an affective level than learning through one's L1.

Pihko (2007) investigated the foreign language self-concept of 209 CLIL and 181 non-CLIL Finnish secondary students. Contrary to Seikkula-Leino's (2002) results, she found that the CLIL students' foreign language self-concept was more positive than their non-CLIL peers'. The survey examined the students' real/actual self in general, and specifically in reading, speaking, pronunciation, writing, listening, vocabulary and grammar. The results showed that the CLIL students' real/actual self was significantly higher in all the domains. Interestingly, both groups assessed reading, listening and pronunciation as their strongest domains respectively. Furthermore, the CLIL students' self-esteem/self-worth was also significantly higher than the non-CLIL students'. Ideal self, in turn, was high in both groups, although still slightly higher among the CLIL students. Pihko (2007) deduces that CLIL classes are a potential environment for developing one's positive target language self-concept as CLIL students are constantly using the language in meaningful ways. As a limitation, Pihko's (2007) study did not take *a priori* differences into account.

Rumlich (2016), in turn, investigated the English as a foreign language self-concept (EFL SC) in a German CLIL context. His study examined the change in 321 CLIL students', 221 non-CLIL students' (i.e. students from CLIL schools who did not receive CLIL) and 134 regular students' (i.e. students from non-CLIL schools) EFL SC during a two-year period (years 6-8). Rumlich (2016) took *a priori* differences into account and found that the CLIL students had an initially higher EFL SC. This notwithstanding, the CLIL students' EFL SC slightly increased during the two-year period whereas for regular students it remained the same and for non-CLIL peers slightly decreased. Rumlich (2016) emphasises that the results regarding the effect of CLIL on students' self-concept should be interpreted with caution as the CLIL students' initially higher EFL SC seems to explain most of the increase.

Dallinger *et al.* (2016) studied the effect of CLIL on students' English and History learning. Their sample included 1281 students from 54 classrooms, out of which 483 were CLIL students, 354 non-CLIL students from CLIL schools and 444 non-CLIL students from schools without a CLIL programme. In addition to academic achievement, the study touched upon self-concept and showed that the CLIL students' English self-concept was substantially higher compared to the non-CLIL students.

Most previous studies on self-concept in CLIL have been quantitative and focused on students currently enrolled in CLIL. With this study, we aimed to fill an important research gap by qualitatively examining the effect of CLIL on students' target language self-concept in the long-term. Contrary to the above studies, we did not endeavour to measure the participants' self-concept but rather describe how it was expressed in their narratives. For instance, according to Zimmerman (2000), it can be problematic to measure *de facto* self-concept. This may also partly explain the discrepancies between the aforementioned studies.

Overview of the Study

Although the focus of this chapter is on one participant, Kimmo, we will first briefly outline the larger study from which this case study is drawn (for more details see Roiha & Mäntylä, 2019). The participants (n = 24) commenced their schooling in 1992. The CLIL programme in the target school had started a year before during the onset of CLIL programmes in Finland. The applicants were not pre-tested, but priority was given to students who already had some experience of English. The participation in the programme was voluntary. CLIL was implemented in most subjects and at the primary level, 25% of all teaching was in English. In the 1st and 2nd years, CLIL was mostly carried out through class routines, songs, rhymes and games rather than teaching content. From the 3rd year onwards, the amount of CLIL teaching increased and the participants also started to receive formal English teaching alongside CLIL. CLIL continued in lower secondary school but was less extensive than in primary school. Author 1 had been a student himself in the target class the entire 9-year comprehensive school. This position and the earlier relationship with the participants also added a distinctive character to the data collection and analysis (Garton & Copland, 2010).

Knowing the participants and sharing school experiences with them naturally had both advantages and disadvantages. First of all, due to the shared experience, the researcher had a thorough understanding of the phenomenon being studied. Moreover, the common history may have made the participants more open in the interviews. However, some of the participants may have also been inclined to overemphasise their English language self-concept as they were interviewed by their former classmate.

The study aimed to investigate how the participants' English language self-concept is expressed and what role the participants assign to CLIL in the forming of their English self-concept. The data were collected through individual life course interviews which were recorded, transcribed verbatim and analysed inductively using theory-oriented thematic analysis (Braun & Clarke, 2006; Eskola, 2018). That is, the data coding was guided by theory and prior studies of self-concept, but the final coding was based on what emerged from the data. For instance, the definition of English self-concept as a multidimensional, dynamic and situational construct guided the analysis. All the data excerpts that concerned the participants' perceptions of themselves as language learners and users were coded. The labels used to code the data (e.g. language anxiety, self-confidence, social comparisons, limitations in English skills etc.) were combined and sorted into several subthemes (i.e. robust self-concept, dynamic self-concept, multidimensional self-concept, the significance of early CLIL and social comparisons). The analysis led to two overarching themes (i.e. expression of English language self-concept and perception of factors influencing English language self-concept).

The data used specifically for this chapter (i.e. Kimmo's interview) are approximately 9000 words of transcribed text. In addition to the thematic analysis that was carried out with the overall data on self-concept, we relied on narrative analysis to analyse Kimmo's life history (Polkinghorne, 1995). For that, we created the following framework, which was inspired by Kuronen (2010):

(1) Introduction: deals with Kimmo's comprehensive school times. In it, Kimmo reflects on his past CLIL education and its nature.
(2) Episodes: focuses on Kimmo's entire post-CLIL life course and his life events related to English language (either positive or negative).
(3) Evaluation: covers Kimmo's micro-level assessments of his life events in relation to his English self-concept formed by CLIL.
(4) Conclusion: summarises the significance of CLIL education in Kimmo's life. He makes a macro-level assessment of his CLIL experience and its role in constructing his life course thus far.

Combining both methods of analysis (i.e. thematic analysis and narrative analysis) enabled us to look at the data from several perspectives.

Kimmo's life course and English self-concept[1]

In this section, we will focus on Kimmo's life course. We have divided the section into three parts corresponding to the relevant time periods: (1) CLIL years, (2) upper secondary school and (3) university and the present time. At first, we will provide a brief synopsis of Kimmo's life to help contextualise and relate the results to his life trajectory.

Kimmo attended the CLIL programme for the entire nine years. He had no prior experience of English. Following the CLIL comprehensive school, he completed upper secondary school with the highest grade in the English language matriculation examination. Kimmo entered university in Finland and completed a master's degree in mathematics in Finnish, apart from a few courses and course materials in English. After graduation, Kimmo continued with a doctoral programme for a while before moving to Estonia to obtain a Doctor of Medicine degree. The first two years of his studies were in English and the remaining four in Estonian. After receiving his diploma, Kimmo returned to Finland and at the time of the interview, was working as a doctor in a hospital while simultaneously writing his Doctor of Medical Science dissertation in English.

CLIL years

In general, Kimmo reflected on his past CLIL times in a highly positive way, appreciating both the teaching and the class as a community. He considered that as a result of CLIL, he had learnt English imperceptibly and had been completely comfortable with the use of English. He stated that at the time, he had not perceived CLIL as anything special or extraordinary or something that would be more beneficial for him than mainstream education, which is often the case with CLIL students (e.g. Pladevall-Ballester, 2015).

> It was totally normal and natural ... somehow I thought that others also studied like this.

Kimmo's interview implies that the fact that CLIL started already in year 1 made it a natural and taken-for-granted teaching approach for him. It can also be interpreted that due to the gradual start with CLIL and the relatively moderate amount of it, instruction in English did not feel overwhelming. Kimmo articulated that, at the time, he had been satisfied with only 25% of the overall teaching being CLIL. However, when reflecting on the issue in retrospect, he contemplated that there could have been even more lessons and subjects taught in English to gain a more extensive vocabulary.

A fairly prevalent theme in Kimmo's interview was the reciprocal relation between his strong English self-concept and his language using experiences. Kimmo mentioned how his English skills had enabled him to participate in international forums on the internet, which was quite exceptional for a young student back then:

> It was very motivating to study it [= English] because I was using it in computer things and when browsing the internet ... I have these memories that I have been in some chat rooms and I have written in English and then when I have told them that I come from Finland and ... that I am like quite young ... then I have gotten praises that wow you are totally fluent in this ... it was somehow surprising because they were making quite bad spelling mistakes.

It appears that the early English proficiency had encouraged Kimmo to use the language for real communication. The positive recognition from the environment had reciprocally reinforced his high English self-concept while also influencing his motivation to study English. It seems that age was an important factor for Kimmo as he presumably was under the impression that his interlocutors were older than he was. The fact that they were nonetheless making errors in their writing appeared to be somewhat remarkable for Kimmo. This coincides with the views of Mercer (2011) and Pihko (2007) who have proposed that self-concept is constructed in language using situations and social interactions.

Self-concept is considered to be a situational, dynamic and fluid construct (e.g. Mercer, 2011). We identified traces of this also in Kimmo's interview. Although generally speaking Kimmo's English self-concept seemed to have been very strong during his CLIL years, the time period also included moments when his self-concept had oscillated slightly. One illustration of this is the language anxiety he had experienced in English. This was mostly during primary school when he was speaking with native English speakers while visiting his sister who lived in the United Kingdom. Kimmo elaborated on the issue as follows:

> Everyone is probably more or less at the same level [in the CLIL class] ... whereas the natives ... they speak fast ... fluently ... and they might laugh and I have been very sensitive to that.

Kimmo stressed that he never experienced language anxiety in CLIL lessons, which can be seen as a testimony of a safe learning environment and feeling of achievement in class. Kimmo's quotation further exemplifies how self-concept is formed in relation to social comparisons (Marsh, 1986; Mercer, 2011). The native speakers appeared to be a significant frame of reference for him. Kimmo had previously communicated orally mostly with other non-native speakers and fully engaging with native speakers for the first time provided him with a new frame of reference. The external comparisons he made therefore plausibly resulted in a momentarily decline in his self-concept. There is evidence showing that in general it seems to be easier and more comfortable for Finns to speak a foreign language with other non-natives than with natives (Leppänen *et al.*, 2011). Kimmo felt language anxiety only outside the CLIL class. However, Pihko (2007) found that, despite their high self-concept, CLIL students also experienced some language anxiety in class, although to a much lesser extent than their non-CLIL peers.

Upper secondary school

Entering upper secondary school (age 16–19) was a period when Kimmo became more conscious of his language skills and started to notice some differences to others. There the CLIL students were merged with non-CLIL students in formal English lessons which offered Kimmo a natural venue to compare his language skills to those of other students. Consequently, this seemed to positively affect his English self-concept which is in line with the big-fish-little-pond effect model (Marsh & Seaton, 2015). In general, as Kimmo got older, he began to view his language skills more analytically:

> I started to be aware of it [= English skills] more because I was able to complete the courses just by taking the exams. ... For me Finnish essays were always like this that I had to sit down and it was always a bit hard to inflect the sentences.. but in English already the starting point was that this is relaxed.. that I just sit in front of the computer and start typing.. and that some nice text just comes. ... Writing in English was considerably easier for me.. it could be because I was relatively better at English and I got better grades.. in that way it was more rewarding.

A few interesting issues can be analysed from the above quotation. Firstly, the high grades Kimmo received in English seemed to work as a frame of reference that reinforced his English self-concept. In general, school attainment has been shown to be one influencing factor to academic self-concept (e.g. Marsh & Craven, 2006; Valentine *et al.*, 2004). Secondly, the quotation illustrates how Kimmo juxtaposes his Finnish and English self-concepts. Somewhat remarkable, is that at that period of Kimmo's life, his English self-concept seemed to have been described even more positively than his Finnish self-concept. It can be interpreted that the internal comparisons between his Finnish and English self-concepts had further reinforced the latter one. This could partly be a reflection of different teaching methods as the Finnish lessons often focus more on form and are more analytical, for instance, in terms of syntax and grammar. The CLIL lessons, in turn, tend to be more meaning-focused and the emphasis is often more on content. Thirdly, despite his more positive English self-concept, factually Kimmo's proficiency in Finnish had been higher than in English. This demonstrates how self-concept represents one's self-beliefs rather than the actual level of ability (e.g. Mercer, 2011). Finally, the quotation suggests, following the conceptualisation by Laine and Pihko (1991), that Kimmo's task self-concept (i.e. writing) had affected his specific (i.e. Finnish) self-concept. Since he had received low grades in writing tasks in Finnish, he had started to perceive his overall ability in Finnish more negatively.

Upper secondary school was also a time for Kimmo when his language anxiety seemed to vanish, which further highlights the dynamic nature of self-concept. Kimmo associated this with ample exposure to oral communication situations when visiting his sister. This is in accordance, for instance, with Pavlenko (2013) and Pihko (2007) who propose that authentic language use helps to create a positive self-concept.

> There were just so many of those situations [where I have used English] so it became somehow normal ... and [sister's name omitted] friends are very kind and nice that they don't think badly ... so that way it has been a safe environment to use the language.

Kimmo's quotation demonstrates how the environment has a central role in developing and influencing one's self-concept. It is interesting to contemplate whether negative feedback from his interlocutors would have had an adverse effect on his self-concept and consequently to his subsequent English using situations.

In general, self-concept is considered to have a relatively stable core and domain-specific parts which are more subject to change. It is suggested that the domain-specific self-concepts which one regards as important can positively affect one's global self-concept (e.g. Hardy & Moriarty, 2006). This appeared to be the case for Kimmo for whom being proficient in English was highly important. Thus, his overtly positive English self-concept seemed to have had a direct bearing on his more global self-perceptions. The following quotation also illustrates the affective dimension of self-concept:

> It was a very important thing to me [= being good at English] ... and it probably relates to the fact that I had a better vocabulary or something ... but for my self-esteem it was a very big thing.

Overall, Kimmo's linguistic repertoire consisted of Finnish, English, German, Swedish and Estonian. For instance, Mercer (2011), based on her data, has contemplated whether it would be feasible to break the foreign language self-concept into language-specific self-concepts, such as English or Italian as a foreign language self-concept. In accordance with this, Kimmo's self-concept was portrayed differently in different languages, although to a lesser extent than with some of the other participants (see Roiha & Mäntylä, 2019). For instance, Kimmo compared studying the different foreign languages as follows:

> For me, Swedish felt always like English ... it felt like many things go like in English and it felt easier ... then German, in turn, was 'from another planet' [says it in English] ... that it felt strange and ... like I didn't ... I ran out of motivation with it.

In general, out of all the foreign languages Kimmo had studied, English self-concept arose by far as the most positive one for him. The issue appeared to be somewhat dependent on the specific language as Kimmo seemed to analyse various languages based on their perceived similarity or difference to English. He had clearly enjoyed the ease of learning a language where he could detect similarities to English. Again, this issue could also be partly connected to the varied teaching approaches. That is, many of the participants reported how English was implicitly acquired in CLIL lessons, whereas the teaching of German, for instance, was more form-focused.

There seemed to be some discrepancy between Kimmo's task level self-concepts (e.g. Laine & Pihko, 1991) within his English self-concept. One example of this is his occasionally low speaking self-concept which was manifested in his language anxiety. Comparably, his writing self-concept was portrayed as high and stable as he emphasised that writing in English had always been very effortless for him, even more so than in Finnish. Similarly, in Pihko's (2007) study, the CLIL students assessed their speaking skills as only their fifth strongest domain after reading, listening, pronunciation and writing. However, in contrast to Kimmo, the majority of the participants in the present study perceived that CLIL had enhanced particularly their speaking skills (see Roiha, 2019).

University times and present

Kimmo had experience of university level studies both in Finland and Estonia. Both time periods seemed to be significant for his English self-concept as he again had noticed that he stood out from the cohort and fared better than his peers in English:

> There [= at university in Finland] it was quite clearly noticeable that I was better at English than most. Giving presentations [in English] in some seminars was not a problem ... or reading articles. ... I wasn't anxious because of the language. Mostly about the content because in maths it's quite strict and it's possible you make mistakes in the thinking process so I was more nervous about that than about the language.

In that context, Kimmo was completely comfortable with using English and appeared to have a strong self-concept. The comparisons to his peers arguably increased his strong English self-concept even further. The quotation also reinforces that, at least in this context and time frame, he had shed his language anxiety. He had used English both with native and non-native speakers, and presumably noticed that he manages well with it. These encounters had also provided him with opportunities to compare his English skills to those of others perhaps not as proficient in English as he.

In general, Kimmo considered that as the literature and other materials were in English, the learning at the university partly resembled CLIL, which he was used to and very comfortable with. The foreign language therefore had not played a role in his learning process as it presumably had for some of his peers. This was particularly apparent at the university in Estonia where his courses were in English:

> For instance, when we talked about the ethics of medicine which is already relatively challenging linguistically ... so it was nice when you were able to take a stand on things.. like on those kind of ethical questions where you already need to explain a bit more ... I noticed that the ones for whom the language was not that strong just sat quietly those lessons.

Nowadays, English is still present in Kimmo's life to some extent. For instance, he mentioned using English with his sister's bilingual children. In addition, he occasionally uses English at work when communicating with patients who do not speak Finnish:

> It's quite nice ... nice variation ... I like to speak English ... I don't find it anyway challenging to explain things in English ... I like it ... sometimes I have to find words and it's slower to explain if a patient asks something a bit more challenging ... but then again it's often related to the fact that the patients themselves are not very strong at English so the language you speak has to be quite basic.

Kimmo also used English in his doctoral project in which he collaborated with foreign scholars and regularly communicated with other medical doctors and researchers in international forums online. He emphasised that he was very comfortable with using English and trusted his language skills also in that context. One additional explanation for this could be that professional jargon is often relatively easy to master as it concerns topics one deals with regularly and is a significant element in one's linguistic identity (see also Chapter 11).

In general, Kimmo's self-concept appeared to have gone through some changes throughout his life course:

> I have maybe only started to realise it in recent years that it [= English] is in a way a foreign language and that I don't master it that well. I have had this that this is like my language ... my own language.

The quotation highlights how the affective dimension is strongly present in Kimmo's English self-concept. Overall, his interview revealed that even though as a young student his English self-concept seemed to have been even stronger than his Finnish self-concept, their order had shifted when reaching adulthood. This suggests that the network of self-concepts in different languages can evolve and change throughout the years based on one's experiences with each language. Furthermore, the variations in Kimmo's English self-concept can also be explained by the proposition that self-concept becomes more complex when learners gain proficiency in a language (e.g. Mercer, 2011). Therefore, it could be that as Kimmo has become older and more advanced in English, he has also become more critical about his skills.

In summary, it seemed that at the time of the interview, Kimmo's self-concept was fairly strong yet realistic as he trusted his language skills while acknowledging his perceived shortcomings as an English user. In general, Kimmo perceived CLIL as a highly prominent factor in forming the foundation of his strong English self-concept:

> For real I don't know what ... where I would be if I hadn't been in this kind of ... or if my English skills hadn't been so [good]. ... Well okay you teach English differently from this [= CLIL] but it's like a very big asset to have such strong English because the working life is more and more international.

Kimmo's reflection shows that he sees English as a gateway to knowledge and understanding that he would not have been able to reach only through Finnish. It is also interesting that he does not seem to think that he would have gained equivalent skills in English in a non-CLIL class with only formal English teaching. In the following section, we summarise the findings of the study and discuss their implications.

Conclusion

This chapter investigated one learner's perception of CLIL in creating the foundation of his English language self-concept. Despite some oscillation during Kimmo's life course, his confidence as an English user and strong English self-concept seemed to permeate throughout his reported life trajectory to date. Overall, CLIL had had a significant role in building and developing Kimmo's self-concept. Its role among other internal and external factors influencing this dynamic, situational and multidimensional construct (e.g. Mercer, 2011) is indisputable. For Kimmo, particularly social comparisons with his non-CLIL peers had reinforced his self-concept, whereas interactions with native English speakers had had a temporary adverse effect.

One finding worth addressing is Kimmo's somewhat negative outlook towards other foreign languages. Similarly to him, many participants associated their negative attitude and self-concept in other foreign languages with CLIL (see also Roiha & Sommier, 2018), even though CLIL is claimed to foster a positive attitude towards languages in general (e.g. Marsh, 2000). The juxtaposition of the implicit language learning in CLIL with the focus-on-form approach other foreign languages were taught in was very prominent in the data. The internal comparisons across languages (Marsh, 1986; Mercer, 2011) can be interpreted to have reinforced Kimmo's strong English self-concept and weakened his self-concept in other foreign languages. This result raises the need to pay increasing attention to other languages in CLIL contexts and to reconsider the teaching methods in language education in general. For instance, including learning via language use also in formal language classes can make them more meaningful and motivating.

Finally, a few limitations are worth mentioning. Firstly, in addition to CLIL, formal English lessons seemed to constitute an important context for the development of Kimmo's self-concept (see also Chapter 11). Secondly, besides CLIL, Kimmo's attitudes towards different languages may partly be related to the societal status of languages in Finland (e.g. Leppänen et al., 2011). In general, when interpreting the results, it is important to bear in mind the context and time of the study. In Finland in the 1990s, CLIL was only emerging and generally regarded as more exceptional than today. Therefore, it is highly plausible that the feedback and social comparisons had a more significant impact on Kimmo's self-concept than they would possibly do now. Despite its limitations, the study broadens the scope of research on CLIL by helping to understand how it may contribute to self-concept over a longer period of time. In the future, it would be fruitful to conduct similar research in various CLIL settings across countries. It would also be important to investigate the long-term effects of CLIL with other languages than English that has a unique global role to better uncover the effects of this teaching approach on target language self-concept.

Implications for Policy and Practice

Though the results of the study cannot be generalised, a few tentative suggestions may be made for language teaching. Primarily, the study indicates that, at least for Kimmo, CLIL was a highly beneficial teaching approach for a positive view of the target language self, stemming from the early exposure to CLIL. This coincides with the results from studies on early language learning (Muñoz & Singleton, 2011) that state that starting early seems to create positive attitudes and willingness to communicate and use the foreign language, even though the level of proficiency would not necessarily benefit from an early start. This provides another incentive for the implementation of CLIL already at an early primary stage. For Kimmo, the psychological and social learning environment had been very positive. Therefore, it can be important to create a safe and supportive setting in which students are encouraged to use the language freely without the fear of making mistakes. One salient theme of the present study was the symbiotic relationship between Kimmo's positive English self-concept and language use. That is, using the language in a meaningful way at a young age came up recurrently in the interview. English had been a vehicle for authentic interaction and content learning prompting the implication of incorporating plenty of communicative language situations in CLIL teaching. With the help of contemporary technology, creating these situations, for instance, interactions across countries is relatively feasible and easy to arrange not just in CLIL classes but also in mainstream language education.

Note

(1) The chapter manuscript has been reviewed by Kimmo (pseudonym) to ensure his consent to such a detailed synopsis of his life course.

References

Arens, A.K., Yeung, A.S., Craven, R.G. and Hasselhorn, M. (2011) The twofold multidimensionality of academic self-concept: Domain specificity and separation between competence and affect components. *Journal of Educational Psychology* 103 (4), 970–981.

Bong, M. and Skaalvik, E.M. (2003) Academic self-concept and self-efficacy: How different are they really? *Educational Psychology Review* 15 (1), 1–40.

Braun, V. and Clarke, V. (2006) Using thematic analysis in psychology. *Qualitative Research in Psychology* 3 (2), 77–101.

Coyle, D., Hood, P. and Marsh, D. (2010) *CLIL: Content and Language Integrated Learning*. Cambridge: Cambridge University Press.

Dallinger, S., Jonkmann, K., Hollm, J. and Fiege, C. (2016) The effect of content and language integrated learning on students' English and history competences – Killing two birds with one stone? *Learning and Instruction* 41, 23–31.

Dörnyei, Z. (2005) *The Psychology of the Language Learner: Individual Differences in Second Language Acquisition*. Mahwah, NJ: L. Erlbaum.

Eskola, J. (2018) Laadullisen tutkimuksen juhannustaiat: Laadullisen aineiston analyysi vaihe vaiheelta [Midsummer magic of qualitative research: A step by step analysis of qualitative data]. In R. Valli (ed.) *Ikkunoita tutkimusmetodeihin 2. Näkökulmia aloittelevalle tutkijalle tutkimuksen teoreettisiin lähtökohtiin ja analyysimenetelmiin* [Windows to Research Methods 2. Perspectives for a Novice Researcher on the Theoretical Basis and Analysis Methods of Research] (pp. 209–231). Jyväskylä: PS-kustannus.

Finnish National Board of Education. (2014) National core curriculum for basic education. Helsinki: Finnish National Board of Education. See www.oph.fi/english/curricula_and_qualifications/basic_education (accessed January 2018).

Frome, P.M. and Eccles, J.S. (1998) Parents' influence on children's achievement-related perceptions. *Journal of Personality and Social Psychology* 74 (2), 435–452.

Garton, S. and Copland, F. (2010) 'I like this interview; I get cakes and cats!': The effect of prior relationships on interview talk. *Qualitative Research* 10 (5), 533–551.

Hardy, L. and Moriarty, T. (2006) Shaping self-concept: The elusive importance effect. *Journal of Personality* 74 (2), 77–402.

Kuronen, I. (2010) Peruskoulusta elämänkouluun. Ammatillisesta koulutuksesta syrjäytymisvaarassa olevien nuorten aikuisten tarinoita peruskoulusuhteesta ja elämänkulusta peruskoulun jälkeen [From comprehensive school to the school of life. Narratives of young adults' engagement in basic education and of their life course following comprehensive school are at risk of exclusion from vocational education and training]. Unpublished PhD thesis, University of Jyväskylä.

Laine, E. and Pihko, M.-K. (1991) *Kieliminä ja sen mittaaminen [The Foreign Language Self-Concept and How to Measure It]*. Jyväskylä: University of Jyväskylä.

Lau, I.C., Yeung, A.S., Jin, P. and Low, R. (1999) Toward a hierarchical, multidimensional English self-concept. *Journal of Educational Psychology* 91 (4), 747–755.

Lehti, L., Järvinen, H.-M. and Suomela-Salmi, E. (2006) Kartoitus vieraskielisen opetuksen tarjonnasta peruskouluissa ja lukioissa [An Inquiry about the Status of CLIL Education in Comprehensive and Upper Secondary Schools]. In P. Pietilä, P. Lintunen and H.-M. Järvinen (eds) *Kielenoppija tänään – Language learners of today* (pp. 293–313). AFinLA yearbook 2006. Jyväskylä: The Finnish Association for Applied Linguistics Publications 64.

Leppänen, S., Pitkänen-Huhta, A., Nikula, T., Kytölä, S., Törmäkangas, T., Nissinen, K., Kääntä, L., Räisänen, T., Laitinen, M., Koskela, H., Lähdesmäki, S. and Jousmäki, H. (2011) *National survey on the English language in Finland: Uses, meanings and attitudes*. Helsinki: Varieng. See http://www.helsinki.fi/varieng/series/volumes/05/ (accessed February 2019).

Marsh, D. (2000) Using languages to learn and learning to use languages. Jyväskylä, FI: University of Jyväskylä. See http://archive.ecml.at/mtp2/clilmatrix/pdf/1uk.pdf (accessed February 2019).

Marsh, H.W. (1986) Verbal and math self-concepts: An internal/external frame of reference model. *American Educational Research Journal* 23 (1), 129–149.

Marsh, H.W. (1990) The causal ordering of academic self-concept and academic achievement: A multiwave, longitudinal panel analysis. *Journal of Educational Psychology* 82 (4), 646–656.

Marsh, H.W. and Craven, R.G. (2006) Reciprocal effects of self-concept and performance from a multidimensional perspective: Beyond seductive pleasure and unidimensional perspectives. *Perspectives on Psychological Science* 1 (2), 133–163.

Marsh, H.W. and Seaton, M. (2015) The big-fish-little-pond effect, competence self-perceptions, and relativity: Substantive advances and methodological innovation. In A.J. Elliott (ed.) *Advances in Motivation Science* (pp. 127–184). New York, NY: Elsevier.

Marsh, H.W. and Shavelson, R.J. (1985) Self-concept: Its multifaceted, hierarchical structure. *Educational Psychologists* 20 (3), 107–123.

Marsh, H.W., Byrne, B.M. and Shavelson, R.J. (1988) A multifaceted academic self-concept: Its hierarchical structure and its relation to academic achievement. *Journal of Educational Psychology* 80 (3), 366–380.

Marsh, H.W., Pekrun, R., Murayama, K., Arens, K.A., Parker, P.D., Guo, J. and Dicke, T. (2018) An integrated model of academic self-concept development: Academic self-concept, grades, test scores, and tracking over six years. *Developmental Psychology* 54 (2), 263–280.

Mearns, T., de Graaff, R. and Coyle D. (2017) Motivation for or from bilingual education? A comparative study of learner views in the Netherlands. *International Journal of Bilingual Education and Bilingualism*. Advance online publication.

Mercer, S. (2011) *Towards an Understanding of Language Learner Self-Concept*. Dordrecht: Springer.

Muñoz, C. and Singleton, D. (2011) A critical review of age-related research on L2 ultimate attainment. *Language Teaching* 44 (1), 1–35.

Nikula, T. and Marsh, D. (1996) *Kartoitus vieraskielisen opetuksen tarjonnasta peruskouluissa ja lukioissa [An Inquiry about the Status of CLIL Education in Comprehensive and Upper Secondary Schools]*. Helsinki, FI: Finnish National Agency for Education.

Pavlenko, A. (2013) The affective turn in SLA: From 'affective factors' to 'language desire' and 'commodification of affect'. In D. Gabryś-Barker (ed.) *The Affective Dimension in Second Language Acquisition* (pp. 3–28). Bristol: Multilingual Matters.

Peltoniemi, A., Skinnari, K., Mård-Miettinen, K. and Sjöberg, S. (2018) *Monella kielellä Suomen kunnissa 2017. Selvitys muun laajamittaisen ja suppeamman kaksikielisen varhaiskasvatuksen, esiopetuksen ja perusopetuksen tilanteesta [In Many Languages in Finnish Municipalities 2017. A Report on the State of Other Extensive and Small-scale Bilingual Early Childhood Education, Pre-primary Education and Basic Education].* Jyväskylä, FI: University of Jyväskylä.

Pesu, L. (2017) The role of parents' and teachers' child-related competence beliefs in the development of students' self-concept of ability. Unpublished PhD thesis, University of Jyväskylä.

Pihko, M.-K. (2007) *Minä, koulu ja englanti. Vertaileva tutkimus englanninkielisen sisällönopetuksen ja perinteisen englannin opetuksen affektiivisista tuloksista [Me, School and English. A Comparative Study of the Affective Outcomes of English Teaching in Content and Language Integrated (CLIL) Classes and in Traditional Foreign Language Classes].* Jyväskylä, FI: University of Jyväskylä.

Pladevall-Ballester, E. (2015) Exploring primary school CLIL perceptions in Catalonia: Students', teachers' and parents' opinions and expectations. *International Journal of Bilingual Education and Bilingualism* 18 (1), 45–59.

Polkinghorne, D.E. (1995) Narrative configuration in qualitative analysis. *International Journal of Qualitative Studies in Education* 8 (1), 5–23.

Roiha, A. (2019) Investigating former pupils' experiences and perceptions of CLIL in Finland: A retrospective analysis. *Nordic Journal of Studies in Educational Policy* 5 (2), 92–103.

Roiha, A. and Mäntylä, K. (2019) 'It has given me this kind of courage...': The significance of CLIL in forming a positive target language self-concept. *International Journal of Bilingual Education and Bilingualism.* Advance online publication.

Roiha, A. and Sommier, M. (2018) Viewing CLIL through the eyes of former pupils: Insights into foreign language and intercultural attitudes. *Language and Intercultural Communication* 18 (6), 631–647.

Rumlich, D. (2016) *Evaluating Bilingual Education in Germany: CLIL Students' General English Proficiency, EFL Self-Concept and Interest.* Frankfurt am Main, DE: Peter Lang.

Seikkula-Leino, J. (2002) Miten oppilaat oppivat vieraskielisessä opetuksessa? Oppilaiden suoriutumistasot, itsetunto ja motivaatio vieraskielisessä opetuksessa [How pupils achieve in Content and Language Integrated Learning (CLIL)? Pupils' achievement levels, self-esteem and motivation in CLIL]. Unpublished PhD thesis, University of Turku.

Shavelson, R.J., Hubner, J.J. and Stanton, G.C. (1976) Validation of construct interpretations. *Review of Educational Research* 46 (3), 407–441.

Sylvén, L.K. and Thompson, A. (2015) Language learning motivation and CLIL: Is there a connection? *Journal of Immersion and Content-Based Language Education* 3 (1), 28–50.

Tracey, D., Yeung, A.S., Arens, A.K. and Ng, C. (2014) Young second language learners' competence and affective self-concept. *Asian EFL Journal* 16 (4), 76–95.

Valentine, J.C., DuBois, D.L. and Cooper, H. (2004) The relation between self-beliefs and academic achievement: A meta-analytic review. *Educational Psychologist* 39 (2), 111–133.

Walker, C. (2015) A study of self-concept in reading in a second or foreign language in an academic context. *System* 49, 73–85.

Yeung, A.S. and Wong, E.K.P. (2004) Domain specificity of trilingual teachers' verbal self-concepts. *Journal of Educational Psychology* 26 (2), 360–368.

Zimmerman, B.J. (2000) Self-efficacy: An essential motive to learn. *Contemporary Educational Psychology* 25 (1), 82–91.

5 Teacher Cognition about Challenges and Opportunities of Integrative Language and Content Teaching: The SIOP Example

Nihat Polat and Laura Mahalingappa

Introduction

The education of linguistic minority students is an important issue in today's global world, especially in countries that receive large numbers of immigrants each year such as the United States, Australia, Canada and the European Union. This continuous influx has made schools increasingly responsible for supporting students who are receiving their education in a second or third language. Schools need to provide extra assistance to these students not only for academic achievement, but with language development and sociocultural competence as well, which are all necessary components in building and maintaining a successful life for individuals in their new countries. This responsibility can be perceived by schools and teachers as an opportunity to bring diversity into the classroom, but also as a challenge if appropriate supports for students are not put in place. Unfortunately, lack of such support could result in student underachievement, stunting the possibility of students' long-term success.

English learners (EL) represent the largest population of second language (L2) learners around the world. For example, in US schools alone, there are approximately 5 million ELs (National Center for Education Statistics [NCES], 2020), constituting around 10% of the total K-12 (Kindergarten through high school) population. Unfortunately, by a number of measures, the US K-12 system has not been very successful in helping ELs meet the aforementioned goals, for example, in national reading and math tests, ELs have been reported to consistently underperform compared to their non-EL peers (Polat *et al.*, 2016). While there may be political (e.g. laws, policies,) and social (e.g. socioeconomic status) reasons for the achievement gap between ELs and English-speaking students (ESS), arguably one of the most important is the schooling system itself (Crawford, 2004). For example, in the US context, the most common programme option for ELs is pullout programmes, which have been found to be the least effective option because of a lack of focus on academic language proficiency, academic content learning and opportunities of integration with their native-speaking peers (Crawford, 2004). Thus, most educators now argue that we can no longer continue to offer ELs this form of education in self-contained ecologies (pullout programmes) with lowered linguistic and academic demands (Echevarría *et al.*, 2011). Hence, a sense of urgency for a just, equitable and inclusive education for ELs is necessary (Buxton *et al.*, 2008).

To ensure that ELs learn English effectively and build solid sociocultural competence, and, at the same time, succeed in their content-area studies (e.g. math, science), schools need to utilize effective instructional models that focus on both academic achievement and general and academic language development (Cummins, 1984) in an integrative approach. Further, such instruction needs to be offered in inclusive classrooms with ESSs to maximize the opportunity for ELs to acquire critical cultural perspectives and practices through authentic socialization with their peers (Hawkins, 2004). A well-known model of this sort, particularly in the US context, is the Sheltered Instruction Observation Protocol (SIOP) (Echevarría *et al.*, 2008, 2010; Echevarría *et al.*, 2011; Short *et al.*, 2010; Vogt *et al.*, 2009). The What Works Clearinghouse (WWC) defines SIOP as 'a framework for planning and delivering instruction in content areas such as science, history, and mathematics to English language learners as well as other students', with the purpose of assisting teachers to 'integrate academic language development into their lessons, allowing students to learn and practice English as it is used in the context of school, including the vocabulary used in textbooks and lectures in each academic discipline' (WWC, 2020). It claims to help ELs improve their English language skills while they also learn content in the same classroom as their English-speaking peers (Echevarría *et al.*, 2011).

To explore the effectiveness of this model (described below) in the K-12 US context, this study explores beliefs of two content-area teachers about what the SIOP (see Echevarria *et al.*, 2008, 2010) offers them in their classes with ELs. Specifically, we address the following research question: What are K-12 science and ELA teachers' beliefs about the challenges and opportunities the SIOP poses to the implementation of integrative language and content teaching? In so doing, we use the SIOP instructional materials and qualitative data from both teachers, who had been certified and trained in both their content specialization and English as a second language (ESL).

Literature Review

Teacher cognition

Research suggests that classroom tasks that involve higher cognitive and analytic skills (e.g. synthesizing, evaluating) and promote academic language proficiency that grants access to content knowledge (Reyes & Vallone, 2007; Zwiers, 2014) constitute the core elements that can potentially help educators narrow and hopefully close the achievement gap between ELs and their non-EL counterparts. To address this achievement 'debt', the federal No Child Left Behind (NCLB) act designated responsibility (Crawford, 2004; Polat, 2010) for mainstream teachers to receive further training to help ELs in inclusive content-area classrooms (Buxton *et al.*, 2008). Indeed, currently many teacher educators and school districts are exploring opportunities to help content-area teachers become more prepared for classrooms with ELs. Such attempts have been followed up by several new pedagogical models and textbooks aimed at helping teachers support ELs in mainstream classes (Short *et al.*, 2010).

To help content-area teachers become better prepared for ELs, we need to identify how they approach their work and the psychological processes through which they make sense of their profession. One construct that has been commonly used to understand the psychology of teachers is cognition (Borg, 2003; see also Chapters 6, 7 & 8). Borg (2003: 81) describes teacher cognition as 'the unobservable cognitive dimension of teaching – what teachers know, believe, and think'. In a more recent study, Borg and Alshumaimeri (2019: 30) expanded this definition by stating, '... we feel it is more productive to think of teachers' cognitions as being characterized by systems of competing forces which vie for implementational supremacy (i.e. in shaping teachers' actions)'. Pajares (1992) characterized cognition as teachers' self-reflection, beliefs and knowledge about teaching, students and content and awareness of problem-solving strategies essential to classroom teaching. Pedagogical beliefs are a key component of the construct of cognition and are interconnected with teacher preparation and practice (Borg, 2003; Polat, 2011).

In fact, the adaptive function of belief systems help teachers define and understand their professional responsibilities, students and context (Coady *et al.*, 2016; Coulter & Smith, 2006; Pajares, 1992). Explorations of such aspects of cognition, such as beliefs, play a critical role in understanding how teachers think, what they do with new information and if training can have any impact on shaping and developing new pedagogical belief systems. Indeed, teachers' pedagogical beliefs systems have been explored in many areas of educational research (e.g. Arnett & Turnbull, 2007; Barcelos, 2003; Pajares, 1992). Some of this work has reported a significant amount of variation in mainstream teachers' beliefs about various aspects of ELs' education (e.g. Coady *et al.*, 2016; Polat & Mahalingappa, 2013; Reeves, 2006). Others studied how teachers' pedagogical beliefs manifest themselves in their instructional practices (Gibbons, 2002; Richardson, 1996), both in facilitating and debilitating ways, influencing student learning outcomes (Karabenick & Noda, 2004).

This study uses teacher cognition as a framework to examine the ways teachers think about instructional models to support ELs in content-area classrooms. We adopt this conceptual framework because we acknowledge that teachers' knowledge and beliefs systems are intertwined dimensions of the underlying psyche structures that inform teacher-thinking and decision-making (Borg, 2003). In other words, according to this framework, teachers' knowledge informs their pedagogical belief systems, attitudes, etc., while also being informed by them (Borg, 2003). Moreover, some research and theory have linked teacher cognition to classroom practices because teacher cognition and classroom practices exist in 'symbiotic relationships' (Borg, 2003: 19). For a review of such work, please see Borg (2003) and Borg and Alshumaimeri (2019).

The SIOP

The SIOP is a model of sheltered instruction and observational protocol that champions the integrative teaching of language and content (Echevarría *et al.*, 2008). Hence, it focuses on different aspects and elements of educational planning, delivery and assessment related to several dual-focused approaches covered in this edited volume, including Content and Language Integrated Learning (CLIL), Foreign Language Medium of Instruction (FMI), bilingual education (BE), etc. For example, CLIL offers a set of integrated parameters (cognition, culture, content and communication) where learning outcomes (content) are targeted in the context of varying levels of cognitive demands (cognition) and language is used as a facilitative meaning making and negotiation tool (communication) in culturally relevant (culture) ways (Coyle *et al.*, 2010). Likewise, using eight main components (*preparation, building background, comprehensible input, strategies, interaction, practice and application, lesson delivery* and *review and assessment*), the SIOP builds on a broad range of theories and research around issues of integrative curriculum and instruction. It advocates for the integrative education of content and academic language skills because research has documented strong correlations between academic success and academic language proficiency in CLIL, SIOP and BE contexts (Bailey, 2007; Coyle *et al.*, 2010; Hawkins, 2004; Zwiers, 2014). This is primarily because such models offer meaningful, context-embedded and authentic instruction where learners engage in theme-based activities and cognitively guided and demanding tasks that provide collaborative scaffolding opportunities for learners of varying strengths and needs (Echevarría *et al.*, 2011; Short *et al.*, 2010; see also Chapters 8 & 11). Note that there has also been research that has challenged the effectiveness of these models or offered counter arguments (e.g. Bruton, 2011; Daniel & Conlin, 2015; Polat & Cepik, 2016).

The SIOP aims to provide content-based instruction to both ESSs and ELs. As argued by Echevarría *et al.* (2008) this approach utilizes numerous developmentally appropriate strategies that make dense academic language and content comprehensible to ELs while also increasing student participation and engagement for all students. Indeed, contrary to pull-out programmes that keep ELs in self-contained classrooms for English instruction, this model supports inclusive classrooms where ELs and ESSs are educated together (Echevarría *et al.*, 2010; Echevarría *et al.*, 2011). This way, ELs achieve all three main goals set for the education of linguistically and culturally diverse students: language learning and development, academic achievement and sociocultural competence.

Hoping to address these three goals, the SIOP is structured around eight components with 30 features that are listed under them. It includes *preparation* (6 features), *building background* (3 features), *comprehensible input* (3 features), *strategies* (3 features), *interaction* (4 features), *practice and application* (3 features), *lesson delivery* (4 features) and *review and assessment* (4 features) (Echevarría *et al.*, 2008). The first component of the model is *preparation*, which involves separate listings of both the content and language objectives on the lesson plan while also explicitly preparing for specific classroom practices related to content concepts, materials, etc. Next is *building background* that focuses on the key vocabulary and links between new and past learning and EL' background.

Comprehensible input highlights the rate of teachers' speech, clarity of explanations and uses of instructional techniques. The *strategies* component includes learning techniques (e.g. scaffolding) and strategies of varying levels, whereas *interaction* underscores interactions between the teacher and students. *Practice and application* concerns the application of language and content knowledge integratively and *lesson delivery* highlights aspects of instructional practice, including achieving the lesson objectives. The last component, *review and assessment*, ensures that the learning of key vocabulary and concepts has occurred, and students' learning outcomes are explicitly considered (Echevarría *et al.*, 2008, 2010).

This study

Despite its common use in L2 teaching in the United States and around the world, the current structure of the SIOP has been criticized by some researchers for the organization of its measures, its primary instructional focus, its factorial validity and certain implementation difficulties (Daniel & Conlin, 2015; Polat & Cepik, 2016). For more information about the factor structure and validation of the SIOP, see the Polat and Cepik study (2016). To unravel some of the difficulties and benefits that surround the model, this study explores teacher beliefs about challenges and opportunities the SIOP offers to two different content-area teachers. Specifically, we ask the following research questions: what are K-12 science teachers' beliefs about the challenges and opportunities the SIOP poses to the implementation of integrative language and content teaching?

Method

Participants and context

Participants included one K-12 (specifically, grades 6 through 8) science teacher and one English Language Arts (ELA) teacher, both of whom were employed in a public-school district in a large city in the Eastern United States. These two participants were selected because they met several sampling requirements (to reduce effect of possible intervening variables), including (comparable) educational backgrounds, years of teaching experience, age, gender, etc. Both teachers self-identified as White, non-Hispanic women who had grown up in the same city. Each teacher was certified in their respective middle-level content areas (6 through 8 grades). At the time of data collection, they were both pursuing an ESL specialist certificate as an addition to their existing teaching credentials. The science teacher, Ms June (age = 28), had 4 years of K-12 teaching experience whereas Ms Rose (age = 30) was in her fifth year of teaching ELA. Both teachers reported little international travel and very limited exposure to ELs until their district received a large number of children from refugee families. Both had studied Spanish but had limited proficiency in the language.

As part of their State ESL specialist certificate requirements and programme accreditation demands, the participants had completed a curriculum that included 19 competencies structured around five TESOL domains of (1) language and language acquisition, (2) culture, (3) planning, implementing and managing instruction, (4) assessment and (5) professional responsibilities. The programme also required a 60-hour ESL practicum. As part of this programme, the participants had also taken a course entitled 'Integrated Literacy in the Content Areas' that focused only on the SIOP. As part of this SIOP course, all students were required to develop units and lessons for content-area classes with ELs. Using the main SIOP textbook (Echevarria et al., 2008, 2010), they were trained to be able to identify and rate (i.e. how well each feature was used in class) each of the 30 SIOP features appropriately. In such class activities, these teachers also analysed and rated sample SIOP features (based on examples in the SIOP textbooks) and received feedback from their classmates and the course instructor (i.e. the first author). In those rated features, SIOP instruction was rated based on a 1-to-5 Likert scale where 1 meant the feature was least evident and 5 meant it was most evident in the lesson.

The lessons

As part of the project, both teachers taught a SIOP lesson to their own students. To ensure adherence to all eight components and 30 features of the model, these science and ELA lessons were developed by two separate groups of teachers led by Ms June and Ms Rose specifically for their classes. Group members were teachers certified in their content areas and were going through the same ESL teacher certification programme. In addition, to ascertain fidelity to the model, both lessons were adapted from the SIOP textbooks and online materials for different grade levels and content areas (Echevarría *et al.*, 2008, 2010; Short *et al.*, 2010).

In line with SIOP components and features, each lesson included separately listed language and content objectives, key concepts and vocabulary, building background (links to past learning and student backgrounds) and comprehensible input activities (e.g. rate of speech), interactive and integrative teaching strategies (e.g. group work) and review and assessment activities (e.g. review of objectives). Finally, preparation efforts and educational materials for each lesson also involved specific accommodations to modify the whole instructional delivery to the specific needs of ELs who needed additional support.

After the lessons and instructional materials were finalized by the respective groups and verified by the course instructor, each teacher taught the lesson to their own class in a 40-minute session. Both lessons were videotaped for further analyses by the researchers. In Ms Rose's sixth-grade ELA class were 21 ESSs and five ELs. In her sixth-grade science class, Ms June had 23 students, six of whom were ELs.

For both lessons, to ensure fidelity to the SIOP and its uniqueness as an instructional model, they chose lesson plans from the SIOP textbooks entitled *The SIOP Model for Teaching English Language-Arts to English Learners* (Vogt *et al.*, 2009) and *The SIOP Model for Teaching Science to English Learners* for grades 6 through 8 (Short *et al.*, 2010). Ms Rose's ELA lesson was about 'strategy use in identifying the main purpose of a text'. As per her SIOP lesson plan, Ms Rose had her objectives, different instructional activities and materials and a list of strategies. She also had a few specific modifications (e.g. a graphic organizer) for ELs to make the content more accessible and to make sure they learned the content as well as the ESSs. Ms June's lesson was about 'the geology of our planet: earth'. Following the same SIOP lesson format as Ms Rose, she also had her SIOP objectives, activities and instructional materials as well as a few modifications for the ELs ready. She also had a couple of geological maps and a YouTube video about earth's geology to show her students in class.

Data collection and analysis

Data sources were twofold: three forms of teacher responses to the SIOP and individual interviews. The SIOP-response data included (a) teachers' self-reported SIOP ratings, (b) and the researcher's (the first author) observation ratings of teachers' instructional planning and (c) the videotaped lessons. Data from the SIOP was used for two purposes. Firstly, it was used by the two teachers to provide narrative accounts (beliefs) about challenges and opportunities of each of the 30 SIOP features in their teaching. For example, for the feature 'content objectives clearly defined, displayed and reviewed with students', feature 1 listed under the *preparation* component, the teachers provided separate comments about 'challenges' and 'opportunities' they encountered while incorporating this feature in their lesson plan and delivery. While they were encouraged to provide such comments for all 30 features, the teachers focused on certain features and the length of their narratives varied from just a few sentences to a few paragraphs. Secondly, the instructor (first author) also used the protocol as an observation tool to document 'challenges' and 'opportunities' the two teachers experienced (in their groups) while preparing the lesson plans and materials prior to teaching. Finally, the instructor watched the video of each lesson to observe if and how a teacher struggled with or utilized certain opportunities afforded by the model to teach the content more effectively. This exercise was particularly focused on the areas of 'challenges' and 'opportunities' that were reported (narratives) by the two teachers.

The second source of data included the individual interviews, which were conducted within a week of the teaching of each class to benefit from recall of information. The researcher (first author) conducted 50 to 65-minute-long interviews with each teacher to discuss more in-depth the 'challenges' and 'opportunities' the protocol posed to their teaching. To make the interviews more focused and effective, the researcher focused only on the features for which the teachers had provided narrative accounts. However, each teacher was given the opportunity at the end of the interview to offer comments about any feature they wished. For consistency and triangulation purposes, the basic interview question was adapted from the same directive question on the protocol. Basically, we asked: 'You provided in the protocol that you experienced some challenges and/or opportunities posed by this individual feature (name of the feature) to your efforts as you were preparing for the lesson, planning your lesson, and/or teaching it? Can you elaborate how? For example, you said (reading from their narrative), can you elaborate on what you mean by that? We also asked a few questions based on our review of the teaching video in conjunction with particular features. For example, we asked 'I noticed in the video when you were making connections to students' prior knowledge, you struggled a little. How does that relate to what you're saying now'?

We analysed our data by identifying themes around beliefs about the challenges and opportunities provided by each teacher in their interviews and narrative account in the protocol. Aware of our own possible biases and socioculturally situated interpretations, particularly in interview data (Clandinin & Connelly, 2000), we tried to focus on how each thematic narrative constitutes a coherent picture as triangulated by other sources of evidence, including our observation and video review notes. As each teacher specializes in a different content area (science versus ELA) and the settings and student demographics are never the same, rather than only engaging in cross-case analyses, we focused on each case in its unique context and entirety (Clandinin & Connelly, 2000). Basically, as we conducted multiple iterations of reviews of the interview data and the narrative accounts, we tried to focus on the meaning intended by the teacher rather than our positionality and general personal judgements about the protocol to determine our selection of excepts and or interpretations.

Findings and Discussion

Beliefs about challenges

Ms Rose reported several beliefs pertaining to challenges, three of which seemed to consistently recur in all three data sources (narratives, observation and interviews). These three challenges included features 1, 2 (*preparation*), 13 (*strategies*), 16 (*interaction*) and the use of quantifying adjectives in nine different features (4, 13–14, 16, 18–19, 27–29: see Echevarria *et al.*, 2013). In addition to identifying these challenges related to the use of quantifying adjectives inherent in the descriptions, Ms June reported beliefs related to difficulties with SIOP features 15 (a variety of questions or tasks that promote higher-order thinking skills), 19 (ample opportunities for students to clarify key concepts in L1 as needed with aide, peer, of L1 text) and 26 (pacing of the lesson appropriate to students' ability level). Of the multiple challenges-related beliefs Ms June reported, two were recurring themes in the narrative accounts, observation notes and interviews.

First, in Ms Rose's case, she identified two *preparation* component features, namely 1 (content objectives) and 2 (language objectives clearly defined, displayed and reviewed with students) as challenges the SIOP poses for ELA teachers. She reported to believe that it is hard to 'clearly' distinguish between language and content objectives in language arts classrooms. She emphasized the domain-specific (ELA) nature of this challenge. The same challenge was highlighted in her interview and the observation notes also documented that both Ms Rose and her group struggled with this notion while calibrating the lesson plan. On her protocol, she wrote:

> I can't imagine how it's possible to clearly distinguish what is 'language' and what is 'content' [emphasis hers] in language arts. Maybe for mathematics teachers this is easy. For language arts teachers the teaching of a group of nouns and identifying the content these nouns represent are the same skills. In mathematics, teaching the word divide can be part of language objective and learning how to do division can be a content objective. In language arts teaching a word is a language skill and teaching them how to identify the main idea, like we did for this lesson, is also a language skill.

The second challenges-related belief Ms Rose reported was about the *strategies* feature 'ample opportunities provided for students to use learning strategies' (13) and the *interaction* feature 'frequent opportunities for interaction and discussion between teacher/student and among students' (16). In short, she reported to believe in the interview and her narrative that *opportunities for interaction* and *learning strategies* 'are almost the same things' and it was hard for her to think of these features as two separate features, especially in practice. The observation notes also indicated that she raised this point in the group discussions when they were calibrating the lesson for her to teach. She said, 'I still think these two are the same things'. In her protocol narrative, she commented:

> These two items (features) are confusing. I know we went through multiple examples in class to see how each item (feature) is different but when you do it in class it seems like they are almost the same things. When I think about strategies to use in my lesson, I focus on interactive activities, which is what SIOP tells us to do. In my opinion, when one creates opportunities for interaction in class, all kinds of strategies happen together.

We offer two points of discussion of these results. First, unfortunately, most teaching practices, even in multilingual classrooms, have not historically explicitly considered ELs' language development as an instructional goal (Crawford, 2004; Vogt *et al.*, 2009). This may be partially due to two reasons. First, many teacher education programmes in the United States do not have specific training requirements for content-area teachers who work with ELs in mainstream classes. Therefore, many teachers lack facilitating pedagogical beliefs (Daniel & Peercy, 2014; Polat & Mahalingappa, 2013) and dispositions (Strom *et al.*, 2019) about supporting ELs' academic achievement and language development in such classrooms. Second, many of these teachers also lack exposure to ELs at their schools (due to demographics) and/or meaningful social interactions with ELs as part of their practicum or field experiences as part of their pre-service teacher education (Hughes

& Mahalingappa, 2018; Mahalingappa *et al.*, 2018; Polat *et al.*, 2019b). Therefore, it is rather promising that an ELA teacher underscores the importance of the explicit listing of language objectives on content lesson plans. This will, at least, increase the awareness of content-area teachers and heighten their sense of responsibility to support EL's language development as part of their regular classroom instruction, for which many studies have advocated (e.g. Pettit, 2011; Platt *et al.*, 2003; Polat, 2010; Polat & Mahalingappa, 2013).

In her beliefs, Ms June reported to experience particular difficulty with the use of different questions and tasks that specifically promote higher levels of thinking and learning (feature 15) by ELs. In her protocol she underscored how hard it is to 'not water down the task' while making level-appropriate linguistic modifications. Quite interestingly, she also discussed this feature in connection with the 'pacing of the lesson' (feature 26: pacing of the lesson appropriate to students' ability level). She commented that she believed she could do better in engaging ELs in higher-levels of learning if she had more time to move along with the whole class. She said in her interview:

> I guess one of my biggest struggles is about, like how to push my ELs to learn at high levels, like my other students. I mean 'not water down the task'. It's just hard, like, to get them to understand, especially students like Mary [pseudonym] with low levels. As I was trying to challenge my ELs to engage in deeper thinking, learning you know, I had to simplify my questions and explanations. It took me a long time, and by the time I was done, some of my other students started to chat. I had to rush and by the end, I don't know how much challenge was left there [laughs].

Ms June also, both in her interview and the protocol narrative, described the difficulty she faced with the use of the EL's L1 and peers to help make the key concepts clear for ELs (feature 19: ample opportunities for students to clarify key concepts in the L1 as needed with aide, peer, or L1 text). For example, in her narrative she stated:

> After 510 [i.e. a graduate course in SLA] and this class, I now appreciate better how important it is to use ELs' L1 during the class. I could do this either by finding bilingual materials or helping them in class myself. My district doesn't have bilingual materials. Since I speak very little Spanish and only one of my ELs is Spanish speaker, it took me a lot of time to deal with this feature. Having ELs receive help from peers, like sitting together, helps when you have speakers of the same language. I don't have this in my class now!

To understand these results we turn to current research on issues related to these features. First, the most direct comparison we can make here relates to the Polat and Cepik (2016) study on the factorial structure of the SIOP. In their study, Polat and Cepik (2016: 837) found that of the eight components of the current SIOP structure only four seemed to measure 'distinguishably stable performance evaluation factors in determining teaching effectiveness that is specifically characterized as sheltered instruction'. It is quite interesting that three of these features (15: a variety of questions or tasks that promote higher-order thinking skills; 19: ample opportunities for students to clarify key concepts in L1 as needed with aide, peer, of L1 text; and 26: pacing of the lesson appropriate to students' ability level) were among those features that did not load on any of the four factor solutions reported in this study. This implies that the challenge could have been due to the use of adjectives or, alternatively, a possible problem with the overall structure of each feature (confounding effect). We believe this may be true, especially for features 15 (a variety of questions or tasks that promote higher-order thinking skills) and 26 (pacing of the lesson appropriate to students' ability level), because Ms June consistently discussed these two features together as if she could not think of them as two independent features. This adds to current research about need for a reconsideration of the structure of this model (Daniel & Conlin, 2015; Polat & Cepik, 2016).

Second, another reason why she reported to believe that these features were challenging may be because science, as an inherently demanding subject, could be particularly harder for ELs at lower proficiency levels (Buxton et al., 2008). The use of L1 in clarifying complex concepts to make content more comprehensible could be essential (De La Campa & Nassaji, 2009; Lin, 2006; Polat, 2016). Whether due to the nature of inquiry (science) (Buxton et al., 2008) or teachers' lack of readiness in making instructional accommodations for ELs (Villegas, 2018), it is clear that teacher education programmes need to increase their efforts in helping content-area teachers become more competent in helping ELs in inclusive environments (Daniel & Peercy, 2014; Polat, 2010). Experiencing this very reality in her own classroom, Ms June reported her struggle with engaging ELs in higher order thinking and science learning while also maintaining the expected pace appropriate to the whole class. Such instructional challenges in multilingual classrooms, especially in absence of L1 support, have been reported in previous research as well (Rosebery & Warren, 2008).

Third, the challenges-related beliefs that both Ms Rose and June listed included the use of adjectives in these certain features that created some vagueness since the adjectives acted as benchmarks to determine not if, but *how well* they included these features in their teaching. They argued that, while it was relatively easy to determine if a feature was present or absent in a SIOP lesson, adjectives/phrases like high degree (feature 4), ample (13, 19), consistently (14), frequent (16), sufficient (18) and regular (29) are too ambiguous to make a judgement about it in a real mainstream class. In her interview Ms Rose argued:

> Ok, this one is tricky. Let me show you (showing protocol). See, I under-
> lined all these words. See, ample, frequent, sufficient. Somehow all the

evaluations we did in the SIOP book (the main SIOP book offers scenarios), there was nothing about how much is ample or sufficient. For example, look at feature 16. It says (reading from the protocol) 'Frequent opportunities for interaction and discussion between teacher/student and etc.'. What does frequent mean? Like how many times? This was a challenge when we were planning the lesson and I kept thinking, like, if I was doing this 'frequently' enough.

In her interview Ms June relayed:

In the group [when they were working on lessons], we had discussions about what 'to a high degree' means in using supplemental materials [i.e. feature 4: supplementary materials used to a high degree, making the lesson clear and meaningful]. As part of other SIOP features, we already use these … We use modifications. The examples for this item (feature) were 'visuals, 'graphs', etc. So, if I use one YouTube video, or a volcano picture, I'm good? Or, how many. No one in the group had a good answer, you know. You were there too [i.e. the first author].

Both the observation notes and narrative accounts confirmed these interview data. For example, the observation notes suggested that both groups had the longest discussion and disagreement about what the use of these adjectives implied in these features. There were also disagreements among group members about what the term 'comprehensive' meant in features 27 (comprehensive review of key vocabulary) and 28 (comprehensive review of key content concepts).

The fact that teachers from two content areas consistently identified the use of adjectives/quantifiers (e.g. *ample, sufficient*) in nine different SIOP features as a source of challenge advises a re-examination of these features to improve the effectiveness of this model. This finding aligns with previous results critiquing the factorial structure and other aspects of the model (Daniel & Conlin, 2015; Polat & Cepik, 2016). For example, Daniel and Conlin (2015) reported that the SIOP concentrates more heavily on the teacher actions than those of the students. Some of these features were among those features that did not seem to belong to any of the four factor structures in Polat and Cepik's (2016) study, the only factorial validity examination of the SIOP. For example, these features included features such as 4: Supplementary materials used to a high degree, making the lesson clear and meaningful; 14: Scaffolding techniques consistently used assisting and supporting student understanding; 19: Ample opportunities for students to clarify key concepts in L1 as needed with aide, peer, of L1 txt; 29: Regular feedback provided to students on their output. Therefore, it seems that these adjectives are causing real challenges for teachers.

Beliefs about opportunities

In her belief account about SIOP opportunities, Ms Rose emphasized three SIOP features she found to be particularly effective. These included features 6 (meaningful activities that integrate lesson concepts), 21 (activities provided for students to apply content and language knowledge in the classroom) and 22 (activities integrate all language skills). Feature 6 is from the *preparation* component while 21 and 22 are from *practice and application* components. Our analyses also suggest that a SIOP-unique opportunity to which both Ms Rose and June referred was the separate listing of language and content objectives (features 1 and 2).

In describing these two features (i.e. 1 and 2) as unique SIOP opportunities that support ELs' education, Ms Rose made two interesting observations. First, in her belief narrative and interview, she underscored the importance of integrating the learning of content and L2 skills through meaningful activities. For example, as also documented in the observation notes, she discussed integrative instruction both in terms of language and content and the language skills. Second, she also discussed this point consistently in the context of content area teachers' responsibility for ELs' education. This point was a recurring theme in group discussions (observation notes) during lesson preparation activities. In her interview she argued:

> This feature (feature 6: meaningful activities that integrate lesson con-
> cepts) is awesome! I think for ELs, integrating content areas with English
> skills makes learning more real and meaningful. This way ELs can use
> stuff they learn in social studies in language arts too. This will also push
> content teachers to think about ELs education and talk to ESL teachers
> to help them ... Integrating language skills, like speaking and reading. It
> is more natural this way, also, to make language use more meaningful.

As for feature 21 (activities provided for students to apply content and language knowledge in the classroom), from the *practice and application* component, Ms Rose emphasized the use of instructional modes, like this feature, that go beyond knowledge and comprehension level and engage students in learning through application. She noted in her narrative:

> This feature is unique in lots of ways. We learned in Bloom's taxonomy
> that deeper learning happens if the students get to apply the information
> they learn. This way they understand better and remember better. As a
> teacher can tell more easily if an EL doesn't understand when she has
> difficulty to apply the new information. This happens a lot.

Ms June's overall impression of the model was mixed; however, she reported to believe that this model 'offers a lot of good qualities' (her protocol). Although she mentioned several opportunities the SIOP offers, she consistently emphasized features 27 (comprehensive review of key vocabulary), 28 (comprehensive review of key content concepts) and 30 (assessment of student comprehension and learning of all lesson objectives throughout the lesson as opportunities) as opportunities. Further, like Ms Rose, she also considered the separate listing of language and content objectives (*preparation* component), which we discussed under Ms Rose's case, as the most unique aspect of this model.

Interestingly, all of these three features she listed as offering opportunities for effective instruction are from the *review and assessment* component. Nevertheless, in discussing why and how these features offered unique opportunities for effective instruction, she made connections to other features as well. For example, she made multiple references to feature 9 (key vocabulary emphasized) as she considered feature 27. This is interesting as some content-area teachers may consider vocabulary instruction as the basis for language instruction (Creese, 2005). In other words, feature 27 was an opportunity because of feature 9. In her own words, 'you can *review the key vocabulary* all you want, but without listing them and teaching them, you won't get much from the students' (interview). She also wrote on her protocol:

> This feature [i.e. 27] definitely offers unique opportunities, but not on its own. Together with feature 9, this feature can be very helpful for teachers to meet the vocabulary teaching goals.

Ms June also discussed feature 28 (comprehensive review of key content concepts) to be an opportunity for effective instructional practice in science classrooms. Once again, however, she took a relational approach, rather than a stand-alone one, both in her interview and narrative data. She reported to believe that feature 28 (comprehensive review of key content concepts) can be a unique opportunity because content concepts are emphasized in features 3 (content concepts appropriate for age and educational background level) and 12, which encourages the use of various techniques to make content concepts clear. In her interview she argued:

> One of my favourites [opportunities] is the review of key concepts [i.e. feature 28]. You know, in science, everything is like a concept. When they don't know academic language, ELs can't handle science content, which is dense ... I think this feature is very useful because it's consistent with some other ones. Like, this one and this [showing feature 3 and 12 on the protocol]. These are all related to each other.

One other feature Ms June considered a unique strength of the SIOP was Assessment of student comprehension and learning of all lesson objectives (feature 30). Although, in different belief accounts she made references to this feature as a 'strategy not unique to the SIOP' that all classroom teachers do, she did underscore the critical value in explicitly including it on the lesson plan. She claimed in her belief narrative that 'having review of objectives as a goal, basically, explicitly writing it on the lesson plan will increase my efforts to actually do it. Because I have to mark my plan'.

We can situate these results in current research in a number of different ways. First, it appears that Ms Rose considered features 6 (meaningful activities that integrate lesson concepts) and 22 (activities integrate all language skills) to be highly inter-related features. This is an interesting finding because it corroborates the result by Polat and Cepik (2016) who found these two SIOP features to be highly correlated with each other ($r = 0.42$), constituting, with a few other features, one of the four reliable factor structures (for details, see Polat & Cepik 2016). Second, her understanding of integrated literacies in multilingual classrooms is in line with current research on the role of such practices on ELs' education (Short *et al.*, 2010). Undoubtedly, these reported beliefs, whether challenges or opportunity-related, could be different if the two content-area teachers did not also have training in ESL instruction.

In addition to making references to Bloom's taxonomy and higher levels of student engagement as she discussed this feature (6), this excerpt shows that Ms Rose also considered this feature for review and assessment purposes. Withstanding some previous research that have questioned the effectiveness of some integrative models (e.g. Bruton, 2011; Daniel & Conlin, 2015; Polat & Cepik, 2016), overall this finding also supports research that has underscored the critical role of meaningful and context-embedded education in learning language and content knowledge and skills (Bailey, 2007; Coyle *et al.*, 2010; Hawkins, 2004; Vogt *et al.*, 2009; Zwiers, 2014). Finally, Ms Rose's focus on integrative education also offers hope for the involvement of content-area teachers in the education of ELs (Daniel & Peercy, 2014), especially in the context of some research that has found a lack of responsibility for EL's education by some content-area teachers (Hughes & Mahalingappa, 2018; Mahalingappa *et al.*, 2018; Pettit, 2011; Platt *et al.*, 2003; Polat, 2010; Polat & Mahalingappa, 2013; Polat *et al.*, 2019b).

Taken together, Ms June's narrative accounts are in line with previous research that has reported that such instructional modes facilitate academic language proficiency and ELs' access to content-area knowledge (Short *et al.*, 2010; Zwiers, 2008). It seems that Ms June considered the whole review and assessment component as a strength of the SIOP. More importantly, despite leaving out feature 29 (feedback), she made references to the coherence and consistency among these SIOP features. This result also corroborates the finding of Polat and Cepik (2016), who reported that of the eight SIOP components, the review and assessment was the most reliable factor.

Another interesting finding here is how Ms June characterized two of these three features as SIOP-unique strengths because of their relations to other features, not due to their individual merit. She considered feature 27 (review the key vocabulary) as an opportunity only in relation with features 9 and 28 in relation with feature 3. Such a relational perspective could be interpreted as an overall positive trait of the SIOP as an effective instructional model.

Conclusion

Based on our results, we present the following conclusions about these two teachers' beliefs pertaining to the challenges and opportunities the SIOP offered them in their teaching. First, both of these teachers reported several challenges and opportunities-related beliefs that they claimed were SIOP-specific. Nonetheless, some of these opportunities and challenges seemed to be about the model itself and their beliefs about it, whereas others were due to the application of the model to science and ELA fields and how their beliefs affected this. Second, beyond a dichotomous identification of these SIOP features, both teachers reported some features to be opportunities that also posed challenges (e.g. features 1: content objectives, and 2: language objectives) in implementation. Finally, the reported opportunities or challenges involved features in all eight SIOP components, sometimes with the uniqueness of one feature depending on its relation with another one.

Implications for Policy and Practice

Taken together, these conclusions offer several pedagogical implications, though we caution our readers not to generalize our results to all multilingual classrooms where these content areas are taught. First, it appears that, despite its highly common use, the SIOP poses some general and some discipline-specific challenges for content-area teachers. In fact, while beyond the scope of this study, it is not far-fetched to expect complications in the implementation of this model in different settings due to the interaction of general (i.e. emanating from the factorial structure of the model) versus area-specific (e.g. lessons based on math versus social science content) challenges. Therefore, more research, particularly qualitative work on SIOP instruction in different content areas is warranted, particularly since the model now has specific textbooks for almost all content areas in different grade levels (e.g. Short et al., 2010). For example, explorations of challenges and opportunities the model offers in social studies, a content-area with a heavy language load, could be very useful.

Third, results of this study also indicate that, when used as a teacher performance evaluation tool (e.g. in merit raises or tenure cases) in content-focused language teaching settings, this model should be used with caution, paying special attention to the unique nature of the content area (e.g. math, science). In other words, the level of challenge or opportunity posed by the model may vary depending on if the observed lesson is based on, for instance, science versus ELA. Otherwise, due to inherent biases emanating from the structure of the SIOP, some content-area teachers could be evaluated unfairly. Based on the results of the two cases here, for example, we could imagine ELA teachers facing greater challenge than science teachers in implementing SIOP features 1 and 2 (objectives). This also implies that when we train teachers to use this model as a unique instructional model or the professionals (officials) to utilize it as a performance evaluation tool, we must consider discipline-related particularities (challenges and opportunities).

Fourth, studies like this one are particularly important as the same protocol is used across all content areas and grade levels without any field-specific adaptations. Indeed, in light of current work on the implications of theory and research for additional language education (Polat *et al.*, 2019a), this somewhat 'one-size-fits-all' approach may be fundamentally flawed. This kind of work can also improve the model's current factorial structure and effectiveness in line with some recent research that has raised serious questions (Daniel & Conlin, 2015; Polat & Cepik, 2016).

Fifth, as these are only two cases in different content areas, this study could be replicated in other contexts and with more teachers to offer more robust suggestions for similar contexts where science and ELA are taught in multilingual classrooms. Finally, regardless of the strength of the association between teacher beliefs and practices, the symbiotic relationship between the two or even the yet-to-be examined possible causal effects beliefs and practices have on each other, there are lessons (or pedagogical implications) to be learned from the findings of this study. Again, without making generalizations, we learn from this study that the selection of the curriculum and instruction requires utmost attention because, no matter how well (opportunities) a curriculum may work for a teacher in one particular content area, it also comes with unique challenges. Some of these opportunities or challenges may be peculiar to the instructional model itself, while others may emanate from implementation related-factors such as teacher preparation and qualifications, student characteristics and so forth. Thus, explorations of this sort that look into the psychology of teachers can prove vital in helping teacher educators understand why teachers do what they do. Based on these teachers reported beliefs about their own implementation of the SIOP in their respective content areas, it also seems not too farfetched to expect connections between their cognition and some aspects of their instructional practices. This assumption is warranted, particularly, because it is well acknowledged in the field that beliefs systems are intertwined dimensions of teachers' underlying psyche structures that inform their decision-making in the presence of many competing forces (Borg, 2003; Borg & Alshumaimeri, 2019).

References

Arnett, K. and Turnbull, M. (2007) Teacher beliefs in second and foreign language teaching: A state-of-the-art review. In H.J. Siskin (ed.) *From Thought to Action: Exploring Beliefs and Outcomes in the Foreign Language Program* (pp. 9–28). Boston, MA: Thomson & Heinle.

Bailey, A.L. (ed.) (2007) *The Language Demands of School: Putting Academic English to the Test*. New Haven, CT: Yale University Press.

Barcelos, A.M.F. (2003) Researching beliefs about SLA: A critical review. In P. Kalaja and A.M.F. Barcelos (eds) *Beliefs about SLA: New Research Approaches* (pp. 7–33). Dordrecht: Kluwer Academic Publishers.

Borg, S. (2003) Teacher cognition in language teaching: A review of research on what language teachers think, know, believe, and do. *Language Teaching* 36, 81–109.

Borg, S. and Alshumaimeri, Y. (2019) Language learner autonomy in a tertiary context: Teachers' beliefs and practices. *Language Teaching Research* 23, 9–38.

Bruton, A. (2011) Is CLIL so beneficial, or just selective? Re-evaluating some of the research. *System* 39, 523–532.

Buxton, C., Lee, O. and Santau, A. (2008) Promoting science among English language learners: Professional development for today's culturally and linguistically diverse classrooms. *Journal of Science Teacher Education* 19, 495–511.

Clandinin, D.J. and Connelly, F.M. (2000) *Narrative Inquiry*. San Francisco, CA: Jossey-Bass.

Coady, M., Harper, C. and de Jong, E. (2016) Aiming for equity: Preparing mainstream teachers for inclusion or inclusive classrooms? *TESOL Quarterly* 50, 340–368.

Coyle, D., Hood, P. and Marsh, D. (2010) *CLIL: Content and Language Integrated Learning*. Cambridge: Cambridge University Press.

Coulter, C. and Smith, M. (2006) English language learners in a comprehensive high school. *Bilingual Research Journal* 30, 309–335.

Crawford, J. (2004) *Educating English learners: Language Diversity in the Classroom*. Los Angeles, CA: Bilingual Education Services.

Creese, A. (2005) Is this content-based language teaching? *Linguistics and Education* 16, 188–204.

Cummins, J. (1984) *Bilingualism and Special Education: Issues in Assessment and Pedagogy*. Clevedon: Multilingual Matters.

Daniel, S. and Conlin, L. (2015) Shifting attention back to students within the sheltered instruction observation protocol (SIOP). *TESOL Quarterly* 49, 169–187.

Daniel, S. and Peercy, M. (2014) Expanding roles: Teacher educators' perspectives on educating English learners. *Action in Teacher Education* 36, 100–116.

De La Campa, J. and Nassaji, H. (2009) The amount, purpose, and reasons for using L1 in L2 classrooms. *Foreign Language Annals* 42, 742–759.

Echevarría, J., Vogt, M.E. and Short, D.J. (2008, 2010, 2013) *Making Content Comprehensible for Elementary English Learners: The SIOP Model*. Boston, MA: Pearson.

Echevarría, J., Richards-Tutor, C., Canges, R. and Francis, D. (2011) Using the SIOP model to promote the acquisition of language and science concepts with English learners. *Bilingual Research Journal* 34, 334–351.

Gibbons, P. (2002) *Scaffolding Language, Scaffolding Learning: Teaching Second Language Learners in the Mainstream Classroom*. Portsmouth, NH: Heinemann.

Hawkins, M. (2004) Researching English language and literacy development in schools. *Educational Researcher* 33, 365–384.

Hughes, E. and Mahalingappa, L. (2018) Experiences and perceived benefits of an electronic pen pal experience on preservice teachers' preparation for working with English learners. *Action in Teacher Education* 40, 253–271.

Lin, A. (2006) Beyond linguistic purism in language-in-education policy and practice: Exploring bilingual pedagogies in a Hong Kong science classroom. *Language and Education* 20, 287–305.

Karabenick, S.A. and Noda, P.A.C. (2004) Professional development implications for teachers' beliefs and attitudes toward English language learners. *Bilingual Research Journal* 28, 55–76.

Mahalingappa, L., Hughes, E. and Polat, N. (2018) Developing preservice teachers' self-efficacy and knowledge through online experiences with English language learners. *Language and Education* 32, 127–146.

National Center for Education Statistics (NCES) (2020) *English Language Learners in Public Schools*. https://nces.ed.gov/programs/coe/indicator_cgf.asp. Accessed November 13, 2020.

Pajares, M.F. (1992) Teachers' beliefs and educational research: Cleaning up a messy construct. *Review of Educational Research* 62, 307–332.

Pettit, S.K. (2011) Teachers' beliefs about English language learners in the mainstream classroom: A review of the literature. *International Multilingual Research Journal* 5, 123–147.

Platt, E., Harper, C. and Mendoza, M.B. (2003) Dueling philosophies: Inclusion or separation for Florida's ELLs. *TESOL Quarterly* 37, 105–133.

Polat, N. (2010) A comparative analysis of pre-and in-service teacher beliefs about readiness and self-competency: Revisiting teacher education for ELLs. *System* 38, 228–244.

Polat, N. (2011) Pedagogical treatment and change in preservice teacher beliefs: An experimental study. *International Journal of Educational Research* 49, 195–209.

Polat, N. (2016) *L2 Learning, Teaching, and Assessment: A Comprehensible Input Perspective*. Bristol: Multilingual Matters.

Polat, N. and Cepik, S. (2016) An exploratory factor analysis of the sheltered instruction observation protocol as a teacher performance evaluation tool. *TESOL Quarterly* 50, 817–843.

Polat, N. and Mahalingappa, L. (2013) Pre- and in-service teachers' beliefs about ELLs in content area classes: A case for inclusion, responsibility, and instructional support. *Teaching Education* 24, 58–83.

Polat, N., Gregersen, T. and MacIntyre, P. (eds) (2019a) *Research-driven Pedagogy: Implications of L2A Theory and Research for the Teaching of Language Skills*. New York, NY: Routledge.

Polat, N., Mahalingappa, L., Hughes, E. and Karayigit, C. (2019b) Change in preservice teacher beliefs about inclusion, responsibility, and culturally responsive pedagogy for English learners. *International Multilingual Research Journal* 13, 222–238.

Polat, N., Zarecky-Hodge, A. and Schreiber, J. (2016) Academic growth trajectories of ELLs in NAEP data: The Case of fourth- and eighth-grade ELLs and non-ELLs on mathematics and reading tests. *The Journal of Educational Research* 109, 541–553.

Reeves, J. (2006) Secondary teacher attitudes toward including English language learners in mainstream classrooms. *The Journal of Educational Research* 99, 131–142.

Reyes, S.A. and Vallone, T.L. (2007) *Constructivist Strategies for Teaching English Language Learners*. Thousand Oaks, CA: Corwin Press.

Richardson, V. (1996) The role of attitudes and beliefs in learning to teach. In J. Sikula (ed.) *Handbook of Research on Teacher Education* (pp. 102–119). New York, NY: Macmillan.

Rosebery, A.S. and Warren, B. (2008) *Teaching Science to English Language Learners: Building on Students' Strengths*. Arlington, VA: National Science Teachers Association.

Short, D., Vogt, M. and Echevarría, J. (2010) *The SIOP Model for Teaching Science to English Learners*. Boston, MA: Pearson Education.

Strom, K., Margolis, J. and Polat, N. (2019) Teacher professional dispositions: Much assemblage required. *Teachers College Records* 121, 1–28.

Villegas, A.M. (2018) Introduction to 'Preparation and development of mainstream teachers for today's linguistically diverse classrooms'. *The Educational Forum* 82, 131–137.

Vogt, M., Echevarría, J. and Short, D. (2009) *The SIOP Model for Teaching English Language-Arts to English Learners*. Boston, MA: Pearson Education.

What Works Clearinghouse (2020) *The Sheltered Instruction Observation Protocol*. See https://ies.ed.gov/ncee/wwc/Intervention/504 (accessed June 2020).

Zwiers, J. (2008) *Building Academic Language: Essential Practices for Content Classrooms, Grades 5–12*. San Francisco, CA: Jossey-Bass.

Zwiers, J. (2014) *Building Academic Language: Meeting Common Core Standards Across Disciplines, Grades 5–12*. Hoboken, NJ: John Wiley & Sons.

6 From Voluntary to Obligatory CLIL in Upper Secondary Technical Colleges: Teacher and Student Voices from a Diverse Landscape

Christiane Dalton-Puffer, Julia Hüttner
and Ute Smit

Introduction

Since its beginnings more than 20 years ago, Content and Language Integrated Learning (CLIL)[1] and its related research have been accompanied by a mixture of unbridled enthusiasm and scathing criticism. With the coming of age of CLIL, a more even-handed and differentiated evaluation of its potential is sought in line with some stock taking of how the programmatic proposals of the mid-1990s have panned out in the variety of European educational landscapes (see, e.g. Perez Cañado, 2017; Hüttner & Smit, 2013).

Following the conceptualisation of CLIL as local responses to the (perceived) global importance of English, we will be considering one very specific context here, i.e. Austrian upper-secondary colleges of technology (HTL). This type of school is characterised by its focus on engineering and technology and dual focus on preparing students for high-level entry into the world of work and academic preparation for those wishing to pursue higher education. Unlike other professionally oriented schools, the HTL are prestigious and sought-after educational choices.

With the future workspace of students conceptualised as international, CLIL was taken up by some of these colleges fairly early on. However, while early CLIL was voluntary in that students could choose whether or not to join their school's CLIL strand, a certain amount of CLIL was made obligatory in 2011. Given the criticism on CLIL research of dealing with (self-)selected groups of learners (Bruton, 2013; Paran, 2013), this change in external organisation is not trivial and does, we argue, merit a closer look.

The angle of research we are focusing on here is that of investigating the effect of this change in language management structure on the psychological experiences of CLIL as verbalised by participants, i.e. teachers and students. The importance of perceptions and beliefs in teaching and learning is well established (see, e.g. Borg, 2018, 2019; Kalaja et al., 2018 for overviews), but it is very unusual to have access to long-term data from the same institution during such a period of change. The first study, HTL Study 1, was conducted in 2007/8 and the second one, HTL Study 2, in 2015/16.[2] In the following, the effect of language management changes on participant cognitions regarding CLIL will be outlined, thus showing the influences of a move from innovation into mainstream.

Language policy

In view of the focus of this paper on how teachers and students experience a particular type of CLIL and its development over time, we are interested in the changing designs of CLIL, their implementations and how they have been socially constructed. As argued in Hüttner et al. (2013), the resulting interrelationship of elements is well captured in the tripartite model of language policy, developed by Spolsky (2004, 2009) and expanded by Shohamy (2006).

Taking a sociolinguistic view, this model conceptualises language policies as consisting of three diverse, yet equally relevant components, each of which is multi-layered in itself: (a) language management, i.e. the explicit and implicit regulations that are provided top-down to influence language practices; (b) language practices, i.e. which varieties are used by whom, for what purpose and when; and (c) language beliefs, i.e. the evaluations and expectations social agents have about language choice (Spolsky, 2004: 5–14). By elaborating on the discontinuities between the three components and their internal structuring, Shohamy (2006: 45) urges researchers to deal critically with the contested nature of policy mechanisms behind 'organizing, managing and manipulating language behaviours'. 'In other words, when dealing with a specific language practice (LP), researchers need to pay attention to all three components - what is done, what should be done and what is believed to be done – as well as their complementary or conflicting interdependence' (Hüttner et al., 2013: 269).

In terms of the CLIL policies at stake here, the expanded tripartite model foregrounds that the regulations, practices and participant beliefs stand in a complex and potentially contradictory relationship to one another; a relationship that requires concerted research attention at any point in time and, particularly, in a long-term perspective.

Experiencing educational change: Teacher and learner cognitions

The starting point of our study in terms of extended language policy model lies in the study of what Spolsky terms 'language beliefs'. We, however, consider the use of the term 'belief' as limiting when targeting a broad representation of the mental lives of teachers and students and so, for the purposes of this chapter, will use the term 'teacher and learner cognition' (see also Chapters 5, 7 & 8). We are thus expanding the concept introduced by Borg (2003, 2006, 2012) for second language teachers to refer to the knowledge, beliefs and thoughts of both learner and teacher participants in an institutional, educational endeavour, as well as having an affective and identity dimension.

We acknowledge that this is an extremely broad umbrella term, which does not do justice to some, arguably highly important, distinctions, such as those between beliefs and knowledge, especially pedagogical content knowledge (Shulman, 1986), between cognition and emotion or between belief and ideology. Adopting one concept for both teachers and students also bridges the usually separate strands of research, on the one hand, into learners, mostly under the heading of 'learner beliefs' (see, e.g. Kalaja *et al.*, 2018 for an overview), and, on the other hand, into teachers, which tends to come under the heading of either 'teacher beliefs' or 'teacher cognition' (see, e.g. Borg, 2006, 2019; Fives & Buehl, 2012; Kubanyiova & Feryok, 2015 for overviews). Given the focus of this chapter and the constraints of space, a full argumentation of our conceptualisation is not possible here, but some key features are given below.

Thus, for us, teacher and learner cognitions are dynamic, contextual, discursively constructed and stand in a complex, non-linear relationship to actions, emotions and experiences. In applying these identifying features, we align with research into learner beliefs, especially in what has been grouped under 'contextual approaches' (see, Kalaja *et al.*, 2018); and in relation to emotions suggested in the so-called 'affective turn' in learner beliefs (see, e.g. Aragão, 2011, Dufva, 2003), as well as the expansion to include emotion and identity as elements of teacher cognition (Borg, 2012).

The focal area for us in this paper lies on the contextual nature of participant cognitions and in this, importantly, on the interaction between contextual change (in the sense of language management change) and participant cognitions. The importance of addressing this interaction in the context of educational changes, for instance the introduction of English as a (new) medium of instruction, has been established (Baker & Hüttner, 2017; Hüttner *et al.*, 2013; Jenkins, 2014) and will be discussed in greater detail with reference to CLIL below.

We feel that by using an encompassing concept for both learners and teachers, we can draw a more coherent picture of the mental lives of all participants in an educational change.

Literature review: Research on participant cognitions in CLIL

The research gap in CLIL with regard to participant cognitions observed by Dalton-Puffer and Smit (2013) has been rapidly narrowing since, with over 50 publications dating from 2016 to 2019 (Dalton-Puffer, 2019). The majority of the research originates from Spain but also from The Netherlands, Sweden, Finland, Poland, Germany, Belgium and Austria. Studies frequently compare CLIL and non-CLIL participants at either upper primary or secondary school level, and are mostly cross-sectional. Quantitative and qualitative studies have been considered for this brief overview. None of the studies reviewed was carried out in a context where CLIL is obligatory for all learners of a given school type.

In an early qualitative study, Hüttner *et al.* (2013) investigated belief structures of Austrian HTL CLIL teachers and learners interviewed in 2008. Findings suggest that the strength of beliefs with regard to language learning and effects of CLIL, combined with the relative absence of language management result in a construction of CLIL and of CLIL-success that is partly at odds with those of experts or policy-makers, but which is linked directly to local CLIL practices. One other qualitative study (Roiha & Sommier, 2018) retrospectively gauges long-term effects on CLIL-learners' language attitudes. Findings call into doubt the alleged benefits of CLIL on positive attitudes towards languages in general as well as interculturality.

Learner studies generally diagnose positive affectivity connected with CLIL (more motivation, less anxiety, more enjoyment, higher expectations for the future, self-confidence), but several researchers have recently pointed out that this disposition, especially with regard to foreign language learning motivation, actually pre-dates the onset of CLIL-instruction (Broca, 2016; Mearns *et al.*, 2017; Paulsrud, 2018; Rumlich, 2016; Thompson & Sylvén, 2018) and that specific target languages (De Smet *et al.*, 2018) as well as programme intensity (Somers & Linares, 2018) impact on the intensity of affectivity effects. In contrast, Otwinowska and Foryś (2017) found symptoms of negative affectivity and Intellectual Helplessness correlated with primary-level learners' grades in mathematics and science rather than their English grades.

With regard to teachers' cognitions, findings suggest CLIL is experienced as a positive challenge and enhancement of teachers' professional profile (e.g. Oattes *et al.*, 2018; Pavón Vázquez & Méndez García, 2017; Sandberg, 2018) but also to trigger feelings of excessive demand as well as threatening teachers' professional integrity (Gierlinger, 2017; Moate, 2011; Pappa *et al.*, 2017; Sandberg, 2018) as 'teachers often struggle in trying to understand their dual role in CLIL' (Skinnari & Bovellan, 2016: 166), but also appreciate affordances such as increased opportunities for collaboration with colleagues. Two studies from the Netherlands report an enhancement of CLIL-teachers' pedagogical repertoire and increased levels of job satisfaction despite the challenges, also showing the subject discipline of a CLIL-teacher to influence the pedagogical approaches they report using, as well as a notable difference between the kinds of pedagogies reported by CLIL content-teachers and their regular counterparts (Oattes et al., 2018; van Kampen et al., 2018). Comparisons between different groups of stakeholders (Lasagabaster & Doiz, 2017; van Kampen et al., 2017) show divergences between the views of school management teams, CLIL-experts and CLIL-teachers regarding pedagogical principles as well as CLIL-goals.

Context of Study

HTL schools combine two educational foci, i.e. engineering with general pre-university education, and thus enable their alumni to enrol at university or to directly enter professional jobs. Such double qualification makes HTL highly popular, despite their longer duration and heavy workload. The curricula combine theoretical and practical subjects of the school's respective technical specification, for instance, information technology or civil engineering, with traditional school subjects, such as sciences, social sciences, mathematics and German (as a first language). While HTL are thus demanding on various counts, foreign languages traditionally play a relatively minor role. In contrast to other upper secondary school types, the HTL requirements include only a single foreign language, English, with two lessons per week. However, the increasing internationalisation of the engineering industry has positioned English very differently. With most employers expecting their technical staff to be able to work in English, HTL heads and teachers started grassroots initiatives using English as medium of instruction already in the early 1990s.

In view of this development, the Austrian Ministry of Education commissioned a country-wide study in 2007, aiming for a detailed description and evaluation of the status quo of CLIL across HTL (Dalton-Puffer et al., 2008). Questionnaire-based surveys showed that two thirds of all HTL reported some English-medium teaching, mainly in technical subjects, but also in some general academic subjects. Additionally, semi-structured interviews with 28 teachers and 30 students at seven HTL sites highlighted the overall positive evaluation of CLIL teaching. A major motivation for CLIL was to help students improve their readiness and abilities to speak English and so their employability. While the grassroots nature of this CLIL uptake offered individual freedom, it was also criticised for its fragmentary structure, lacking systematicity and hence limited sustainability (Dalton-Puffer et al., 2008).

This situation changed fundamentally in 2011 when the Ministry of Education made CLIL obligatory for all HTL students (BMUF, 2011). More precisely (BMB, 2016), the regulations stipulate that all HTL students take at least 72 CLIL lessons per school year. While these are optional for the first two years, they are mandatory for each of the remaining three years and need to be recorded in the class register. These CLIL lessons can take place in all subjects except for German, English and Religious Instruction, but are recommended for the technical subjects. Details of the actual implementation (e.g. number of lessons, years, subjects) explicitly remains a school-based decision, but a dual focus of CLIL teaching in the sense of integrating language-aware education is stipulated.

Following on this, also internationally unusual, decision to make CLIL obligatory for all students of a school type, the ministry commissioned a second country-wide multi-method study in 2015, aiming to elicit first evaluations of CLIL practices under the new policies (Smit *et al.*, 2016). This was done by combining a quantitative survey conducted in all HTL schools with five case studies of CLIL teaching, including lesson observation and interviews with teachers and student groups. While the overall outcome of the quantitative survey, answered by more than 15,000 students and 650 teachers, revealed a range of responses, most likely reflecting the wide variety of CLIL realisations across the many schools, it is interesting to note that less than 20% of all students reported feeling anxious when having to speak English in CLIL lessons, hinting at generally low levels of fear of speaking English. When it comes to the question of subjectively experienced language improvement, teachers and students reveal the full range of answers, with the tendency to support the potential of CLIL for language learning.

Against this backdrop of large-scale quantitative findings of a rather general nature, a deeper look into the experiences and cognitions of teachers and students is called for.

Research Design

The present, qualitative, study is guided by the following global research questions:

(1) What do the participants' accounts reveal about their cognitions, of the CLIL realities they experience?
(2) To what extent does a change in organisational structures affect these accounts?

Particularly the second question is possible because we can draw on teacher and student cognitions elicited in interviews and focus groups at two points in time: 2007/08, before the introduction of obligatory CLIL (HTL1), and 2015/16, four years after CLIL became obligatory in Austrian HTLs (HTL2). Both studies were commissioned by the Ministry of Education, on a nationwide basis, with the intention of obtaining a comprehensive picture of CLIL provisions in the HTL sector. On both occasions, therefore, the intention of data collection was considerably broader than the focus of the present study. HTL Study 1 involved 28 teachers and 30 students in individual interviews; HTL Study 2 consisted of five teacher interviews and eight focus groups with a total of 29 students. Given the diversity of the participating groups, the teachers were mainly technical content teachers with a few specialising in general academic subjects or English as a foreign language, and the students ranged from 15 to 19 years of age, bringing with them different types and intensities of CLIL experiences.

For the present study, a secondary data analysis was conducted from a qualitative content analysis perspective (Flick, 2018; Kuckartz, 2014). Passages from both datasets were preselected via a first round of coding by interview topic, as well as by selecting topic-based data-summaries and extracts produced for the first study. Content analysis then proceeded with a code set that was developed iteratively, combining deductive and inductive steps, and allowing for multiple categories for the same text passage. Coding was done by all three authors, ensuring that each transcript was read and coded independently by two coders. Disagreements were discussed and led to a reduction of categories. The final set of categories can be grouped into two sub-sets:

(a) Categories foregrounding descriptions of practices:
    Investment Time/Effort, Problem, Plus-Language/Content, Purpose/ Aim and *Enrich* (the last one overlapping with b).
(b) Categories foregrounding evaluations and emotions:
    Confidence, Anxiety, Enjoyment, Interest, Doubt.

In a second round of systematising and summarising the categories and of comparing them across both data sets, we could identify five themes that form the basis of the following description and discussion of our findings.

Findings

To begin with research question 2, the analysis of both datasets revealed remarkable continuities between the two points in time, despite the dramatic change in language management. In other words, the change to compulsory CLIL did not result in markedly different teacher and learner cognitions. At the same time, we could identify a range of new coping-strategies that appear to have developed in order to 'make

CLIL normal' in the context of teaching and learning at HTL. In view of such relatively subtle changes relevant to research question 2, we are presenting the findings in relation to research question 1, pointing out time-dependent differences whenever they were topicalised.

Reasons for doing CLIL in Austrian HTL: 'It's the job, stupid'

The status of English which fosters the spread of CLIL in Europe generally is also at play in the Austrian context. Thus, using English in professional contexts is considered as the unquestioned future reality of these teenagers and CLIL as a means of preparing for this out-of-school pattern of language use. More precisely, participants conceptualise this as lingua franca use, referring to English as 'working language' and 'world language' (see also Chapter 3). The need to engage with speakers of other L1s in international contexts is foregrounded and described, for instance, as needing to answer that 'phone call from China' (HTL2_T) and being able to speak with colleagues 'from the whole world' (HTL2_T). Drawing partly on teachers' own professional experience in industry, the importance of confidence rather than correctness in using English is highlighted.

Both teachers and students express this future perspective of student English use in an emotionally neutral manner and present it as a normal fact of engineering life:

Extract 1:[3]

for us engineers ... English is our second mother tongue our professional language. and this ... has to be lived experience so not something extra, not an exception (HTL2_T)

Extract 2:

so, in general, that you can really in English, well experience how this is and you see what surely is going to be important later in professional life (HTL2_S)

Apart from the positioning of CLIL as a suitable educational response towards this reality of professional English use (see also Chapter 11), software engineers also point towards reasons for doing CLIL related to the English-language dominance in their field. Participants highlight that, given the predominance of English terminology, it is 'easier', 'a small step' or simply 'better' to completely switch to English.

While participants in both studies referred to employability and imagined future lingua franca practices when highlighting the point of doing CLIL, only participants in HTL Study 1 talked about the excitement or challenges of engaging in an educational innovation, partly also in emotionally coloured terms:

Extract 3:

the aim was that we um offer something new in [name of school] (HTL1_T)

Extract 4:

and it is also more interesting, because being taught in German, is not really exciting. So actually it's fun (HTL1_S)

Implementing CLIL in HTLs: 'The devil lies in the detail'

While the normalisation of doing CLIL by the time of HTL Study 2 results in a reduced need to justify doing CLIL as such, views on the requirements for successful CLIL implementations are clearly expressed by participants. The points addressed relate to language and content competences of teachers and students, suitable choices of content areas, time required for CLIL and the role of German in CLIL.

One student perspective that comes across clearly is that teachers need to have sufficient levels of English language proficiency and also benefit from a lack of force of doing CLIL, viz.

Extract 5:

and (.) perhaps not to force certain teachers who can't do this. because I think that's useless (.) that's useless for both students and teachers (HTL2_S)

Students also position their own competence levels, both in terms of English and in terms of the content taught, as reasons against using CLIL. In these statements we frequently find emotionally coloured terms relating to feelings of frustration, such as 'overtaxing students', students being 'at [their] limits already in German' or challenged with 'completely new content – already difficult to understand in German', or as this student summarises:

Extract 6:

and then to discuss things that are new and complicated in English is for sure not a good idea ... it is difficult (HTL2_S)

In general, some subject or content areas are seen as unsuitable due to either their difficulty or their Austrian focus. Students also point towards the need for more time to allow for the extra challenge of learning through English, saying that CLIL 'won't work' otherwise.

In sum, while using English at HTL is accepted, the challenges of the actual implementation are seen in a varied and partly emotionally coloured way. Participants have notions about what constitutes a suitable level of additional demand and so might be motivational, and what is too challenging and hence induces anxiety.

Adapting to language management demands: 'Toning down the pressure from above'

Teachers' readiness is key to any CLIL implementation, as their attitudes will be decisive not only for the spirit in which CLIL happens in the classroom but also whether it is done at all. In both studies, teachers stress the positive aspect of voluntariness and the negativity of force and obligation. In HTL Study 1, this position was formulated with particular urgency, pointing out the joy that arises from doing something out of the box, something which lies in one's own autonomous decision:

Extract 7:

I'd really grant the schools the autonomy that they can design that how it fits them best and obviously the more is directed from above and how things have to be done, the less pleasure it is for the people and the students ... the future lies in the autonomy and in the self-determination and the creativity of the schools themselves, in my opinion (HTL1_T)

Unsurprisingly, in HTL Study 2, the introduction of obligatory CLIL is seen critically. In sum, however, the killjoy effect of the top-down regulation is topicalised less often and less vehemently than one might have expected, presumably because schools leave teachers and departments much liberty in how they organise themselves as long as the overall mandate of '72 hours per year' is fulfilled.

What is seen as crucial, however, is a positive attitude on the part of the school management in order to alleviate the pressure felt from above:

Extract 8:

in the sense of, guys that's good we'll do that we can discuss this. Orders, if you want, from the principal because he is the boss (.) that's important (.) if this is being communicated positively to the schools then it can work. and then people will do it ... if it is communicated positively from above (HTL2_T)

In other words, school-level management of CLIL which leaves choices to the teachers can alleviate the pressure of ministerial regulations.

Addressing increased cognitive demands on students: 'Making CLIL manageable'

Working through complex engineering content in a second language increases the cognitive demand on learners. Interestingly, rather than prompting complaints, this circumstance seems to motivate learners to describe more intensive cognitive engagement during lessons, e.g. *'and then with English you reflect more' (HTL2_S)*. In addition, students reported a sense of enrichment through better concentration, and improved ability to remember content because of more intensive engagement.

Extract 9:

because then it is unusual that you listen to English, so you are basically forced to pay attention and ... (HTL2_S)

Students also remark on more learner-centred pedagogy being used in CLIL. They get to read more different texts and do group work where they have to work through materials and get into an exchange with their colleagues about questions of understanding. There is more self-directed learning and more careful sequencing of the material introduced. Most importantly, teachers reportedly explain things better when teaching in English:

Extract 10:

yeah as mentioned before that everything was explained in a better way basically and that yeah also more slowly and in more detail yeah and the teacher tried really to bring it across using easy vocab. (HTL2_S)

All in all learners are positive as long as the right balance of challenge and support is maintained. Perhaps unsurprisingly, students never voice the concern that content is covered less deeply in English than in German, a point that is, however, made by one teacher: *'as mentioned before, in German if I'd only teach this in German, things could be dealt with in (.) er (.) more detail' (HTL2_T)*. This seems to indicate that some teachers try to reduce cognitive complexity of content in order to counterbalance the challenge arising from the use of L2 English so as not to undermine the students' self-confidence.

Just as often, teachers mention taking recourse to German as an explicit means of reducing cognitive challenge *'the less understanding there is from the students' side you automatically switch back to German' (HTL1_T)*. This leads to the reverse conclusion that the announcement of a CLIL lesson in English is a clear indication for students that a technically easy topic is about to be discussed: *'so when*

I then choose to do a lesson in English the students secretly know that the content to come is not really challenging' (HTL2_T).

Interestingly, however, and in contrast to expectations, teachers in Study 2 do not overly emphasise the extra preparation time and effort that comes with teaching their subject in English. This, we think, points to the normalcy which CLIL has acquired in the schools that participated in the second study.

Addressing student negative emotions: 'CLIL without fear'

Challenges are not only associated with the content covered in CLIL teaching, but also with its other central ingredient, i.e. 'language' or, more precisely, with English. Here, students of both studies topicalise language anxiety, especially in the early days of experiencing CLIL when English can appear to be a *'barrier that is fear-inducing and needs to be overcome'* (HTL2_S). Such fears can also taint expectations of CLIL, expecting technical CLIL lessons 'to be much more difficult' (HTL2_S). That language anxiety is an important topic becomes also evident when turning to the teachers' views. Motivated by their personal emotionally tense experiences of having to cope with English in professional contexts, the participating teachers take the student worries seriously and view CLIL as a viable means to lower their anxiety levels when using English: *'the big advantage I see in CLIL is to lower students' fear of the language'* (HTL2_T).

Besides language anxiety, inhibitions of speaking English can also depend on the speed of topic development and turn-taking that leaves some students too little time to formulate their contributions at the level of correctness they are aiming for (Extract 11). The noticeable consequence of such missed opportunities is that students are more quiet than usual; a development that arguably counteracts the aforementioned advantage of CLIL and its generally shared aim of increasing student confidence when using English.

Extract 11:

I wouldn't say it's about daring. I was thinking about it too long and then there was another topic and then it didn't fit the discussion anymore. So that happens that you think about something for too long how to phrase this correctly. You don't want to say anything wrong and then [your comment] doesn't fit the discussion anymore. Then you think right away doesn't matter. (HTL1_S)

Clearly, teachers can take a range of measures to support active student participation, and there are also individual examples in our data set that hint at such pedagogical possibilities, such as the use of online dictionaries to identify technical terminology or of pair work to develop a subject-specific glossary. Apart from such individual activities, however, there is one measure that permeates both studies and characterises in particular the second one: combining English and German to alleviate student difficulties and facilitate their understanding and classroom interaction. Reflecting its widespread use, such pedagogical translanguaging (Lewis *et al.*, 2012; Nikula & Moore, 2019; see also Chapters 3, 8 & 9) comes in various forms, ranging from changing languages on student request via topic-related language choice to bilingual lecturing moving continuously between languages. While not all of these forms of translanguaging meet with unquestioned student appreciation (see also Paulsrud, 2018),

Extract 12:

because then (.) I'm just getting into English and then she always starts using German and then again she says something in English and then it is a bit confusing so I don't know it is easier for me to follow if everything is in English right (HTL2_S)

the deliberate and educationally oriented use of both languages acknowledges that a monolingual English approach could harm the respective content teaching and learning experience (*'yeah totally English is simply partially very hindering, I personally think'* (HTL2_S)). In combination with the widely held lingua franca understanding of their English use (Extract 13), the translanguaging enacted by all participating teachers supports their aims of increasing student confidence in using English for subject-specific purposes (cf. Sandberg, 2018).

Extract 13:

I don't consider everything a problem if someone ... says two three words in German ... I'm also not perfect make hundreds of mistakes and admit that openly (HTL2_T)

Discussion and Implications for Policy and Practice

Our investigation of the psychological experience of teachers and students after the introduction of compulsory CLIL at HTL was guided by two main research questions, i.e.:

(1) What do the participants' accounts reveal about their cognitions of the CLIL realities they experience?
(2) To what extent does a change in organisational structures affect these accounts?

Spolsky's model of extended language policy implies that a change in one of its elements, as in our case language management, might result in a change in (at least) one of the other elements, in our context, language beliefs and/or language practices. With voluntary CLIL in Austria being experienced as a neutral or positive endeavour (Hüttner *et al.*, 2013), one question looming large was whether an obligation of using CLIL would give these cognitions a more negative slant.

What we did find, however, was a strong tendency towards 'normalising CLIL'; thus, all participants embrace the view of internationalisation at the workplace as a suitable reason for doing CLIL and lack any overtly emotionally coloured stance on this. With great acceptance, CLIL is constructed as a suitable response to the dominant position of English in typically envisaged engineering workplaces. In other words, obligatory CLIL works if and only if it is in English, reflecting the sociolinguistic reality of 'globalised bilingualism', which describes widely observed language practices in Austria 'combining German as prime language and English as default additional language' (Smit & Schwarz, 2020). Similar practices are most likely to be found in other European countries, such as Sweden where high school students express a similar stance regarding the 'normalcy' of English next to their main educational language (Paulsrud, 2018).

While there are a range of cognitions regarding what constitutes a successful implementation of CLIL in the micro-context of any specific school, teacher cognitions view CLIL as (ideally) an achievable activity for *all* students within a 'safe' environment for gaining language confidence. In this manner, CLIL is constructed as inclusive of all students, whereas English competence is limited to a desirable extra qualification for future engineers, but not accepted for educational gate-keeping. Students do express emotionally coloured cognitions on CLIL with regard to a number of areas, including cognitive and linguistic challenges, anxiety and details of implementation of practice, but while a range of cognitions are voiced in this area, an expectation of alleviating negative cognitions is strong and initial pressures and insecurities seem to give way to a sense of normality and even confidence, a trajectory which can also be read from interviews with Swedish upper secondary students (Paulsrud, 2018). Thus, what we do find in the reports of all participants in HTL Study 2 is that the implementation practices have changed to reduce various challenges that CLIL might pose to 'the average student' rather than 'the voluntary CLIL student'.

If we consider the participants' tendency to keep the language beliefs aspect rather stable (a stability also reported in a longitudinal study by Thompson & Sylvén, 2018), it is not surprising that the remaining area of language practices experiences changes. Teachers, holding the greatest agency, introduce what may be best described as a range of 'safety nets' for CLIL. The first of these measures addresses the reduction of the extra cognitive challenge of CLIL to acceptable levels; on the content side, this is achieved through choice of subject in terms of perceived difficulty and through adapting pace. This purposeful selection of content seems to be accepted with very few negative cognitions expressed on this matter. In terms of the language practices element, CLIL at HTL is conducted bilingually, whether this policy is explicit or not; students (and teachers) take recourse to German to address or avoid language problems, activating the use of the whole repertoire of languages of education available (cf. Nikula & Moore, 2019; Sandberg, 2018; van Kampen *et al.*, 2018).

The Austrian educational system is characterised by comparatively little external management or control; thus, our findings suggest that teachers are able to take independent professional decisions in a general atmosphere of trust. While not verbalised explicitly in our interview data, this trust seems to permeate the CLIL at HTL enterprise throughout all layers of the educational hierarchy:

- Participants trust that CLIL is a worthwhile endeavour at HTL.
- The Ministry introduced obligatory CLIL, but accompanied this with only minor control mechanisms, implying a trust in the schools of following that directive.
- Head teachers seem overall happy to let their heads of department or individual teachers decide how best to implement CLIL, trusting their judgement.
- Teachers believe that CLIL is or can be made manageable for all students.
- Students share this belief and trust that teachers will (or should) take actions to ensure such achievability.

Thus, at the core of the psychological experience of CLIL at HTL as a positive and achievable addition to engineering education seems to lie the agency of teachers in deciding what to change in their language practices given the change in language management, rather than maintaining the same practices and accepting a change towards a more negative experience in students. In our context, this overriding belief might well lead to changes in the practice of CLIL that are not ideal; thus, while anxiety is clearly limited by reducing cognitive challenge, one might argue that this runs counter to many of the tenets of CLIL of maintaining equal content input and hence challenge. However, what it does achieve is an inclusivity of diverse learner abilities and thus a sustainability of CLIL. Similar degrees of flexibility and adaptation to individual learner groups have been reported in earlier studies focusing on teacher practices (Sandberg, 2018; van Kampen *et al.*, 2018).

One of the limitations of the present study is its being based on secondary data analysis. In other words, data collection at the two points in time, while sharing a large number of common concerns and even concrete questions, was not carried out with the same instrument. We counterbalanced this by involving team members from both studies (HTL1 and HTL2) in the present data analysis and writing of the chapter. A second limitation of the present study in terms of its comparability with earlier research is the fact that it seems to be the first study of its kind carried out in a context that was made CLIL-obligatory through a top-level policy decision between the two points in time.

While we acknowledge that it is difficult to transfer findings from one context to another, we consider a major practical implication of our findings to lie in allowing teachers in the first instance to take agency over the implementation of CLIL, whether voluntary or obligatory (see also Chapter 2, 3 & 9). Our findings suggest that this might well ensure a manageable level of challenge and reduce negative emotions, such as anxiety or fear, and foster an inclusive environment. However, on a more critical note, we would also argue that this cannot be the final stage of a sustainable and effective CLIL practice; some level of systematic feedback from students, both in terms of their cognitions and their educational achievements, as well as feedback from educational researchers needs to be taken into account in order to optimise the potential of CLIL and avoid the risk of having too low expectations of what is achievable. While ensuring that students and teachers consider an educational practice to be achievable and free from anxiety is of utmost importance, the details of what is, in fact, achievable, needs to be established with input from outside the micro-system of a specific classroom.

Notes

(1) By CLIL we mean educational programmes of varying descriptions (from individual modules lasting a few weeks to the delivery of several curriculum subjects over of several years) united by the fact that school-level content subjects are taught and studied in a language which is not the majority language of a given education system and thus a second or foreign language for learners and teachers alike. Dual focus pedagogy is inscribed in the name CLIL but not necessarily a classroom reality. In Europe, CLIL tends to be anchored in subject pedagogy (cf. Dalton-Puffer, 2017).

(2) The two studies are labelled as HTL1 and HTL2 throughout this chapter.

(3) All extracts are the authors' translations from the interviews, which were led in German. The identification of each extract contains the study it is from (HTL1 or HTL2) and whether the utterance was made by a student (S) or a teacher (T).

References

Aragão, R. (2011) Beliefs and emotions in foreign language learning. *System* 39, 302–313.

Baker, W. and Hüttner, J. (2017) English and more: A multisite study of roles and conceptualisations of language in English medium multilingual universities from Europe to Asia. *Journal of Multilingual and Multicultural Development* 38 (6), 501–516.

BMB (2016) CLIL – Content and Language Integrated Learning. Leitfaden zur Umsetzung an HTLs. See https://www.htl.at/htlat/schwerpunktportale/clil-content-and-language-integrated-learning/musterformulare-downloads/ (accessed June 2019).

BMUF (2011) Allgemeines Bildungsziel, schulautonome Lehrplanbestimmungen, didaktische Grundsätze und gemeinsame Unterrichtsgegenstände an den Höheren Technischen und Gewerblichen (einschließlich Kunstgewerblichen) Lehranstalten.

BGBl_II_Nr_300_2011_Anlage 1. See https://www.ris.bka.gv.at/eli/bgbl/II/2011/300 (accessed June 2019).

Borg, S. (2003) Teacher cognition in language teaching: A review of research on what language teachers think, know, believe, and do. *Language Teaching* 36 (2), 81–109.

Borg, S. (2006) *Teacher Cognition and Language Education: Research and Practice*. London: Continuum.

Borg, S. (2012) Current approaches to language teacher cognition research: A methodological analysis. In R. Barnard and A. Burns (eds) *Researching Language Teacher Cognition and Practice: International Case Studies* (pp. 11–29). Bristol: Multilingual Matters.

Borg, S. (2018) Teachers' beliefs and classroom practices. In P. Garrett and J.M. Cots (eds) *The Routledge Handbook of Language Awarenesss* (pp. 75–91). London: Routledge.

Borg, S. (2019) Language teacher cognition: perspectives and debates In Y. Gao (ed.) *Second Handbook of English Language Teaching* (pp. 1–23). Heidelberg: Springer.

Broca, Á. (2016) CLIL and non-CLIL: Differences from the outset. *ELT Journal* 70 (3), 320–331.

Bruton, A. (2013) CLIL: Some of the reasons why … and why not. *System* 41, 587–597.

Cañado, M.L.P. (2017) Stopping the 'pendulum effect' in CLIL research: Finding the balance between Pollyanna and Scrooge. *Applied Linguistics Review* 8 (1), 79–99.

Dalton-Puffer, C. (2017) Same but different: Content and language integrated learning and content-based instruction, In M.A. Snow and D. Brinton (eds) *The Content-Based Classroom* (2nd edn) (pp. 151–164). Ann Arbor, MI: University of Michigan Press ELT.

Dalton-Puffer, C. (2019) What can empirical research tell us about CLIL implementations? Mapping the landscape. Plenary lecture. PASE - Polish Association for the Study of English 2019 Annual Conference, Adam Mickiewicz University, Poznan, 28 June 2019.

Dalton-Puffer, C. and Smit, U. (2013) Thinking allowed: Content and language integrated learning: a research agenda. *Language Teaching* 46 (4), 545–559.

Dalton-Puffer, C., Hüttner, J., Jexenflicker, S., Schindelegger, V. and Smit, U. (2008) *Content and Language Integrated Learning an Österreichs Höheren Technischen Lehranstalten. Forschungsbericht.* Wien, AT: bm: ukk.

De Smet, A., Mettewie, L., Galand, B., Hiligsmann, P. and Van Mensel, L. (2018) Classroom anxiety and enjoyment in CLIL and non-CLIL: Does the target language matter? *Studies in Second Language Learning and Teaching* 8 (1), 47–71.

Dufva, H. (2003) Beliefs in dialogue. In P. Kalaja and A.M.F. Barcelos (eds) *Beliefs about SLA: New Research Approaches* (pp. 87–104). Dordrecht: Kluwer.

Fives, H. and Buehl, M.M. (2012) Spring cleaning for the 'messy' construct of teachers' beliefs: What are they? Which have been examined? What can they tell us? In K.R. Harris, S. Graham, T. Urdan, S. Graham, J.M. Royer and M. Zeidner (eds) *APA Educational Psychology Handbook, Vol 2* (pp. 471–499). Washington, DC: American Psychological Association.

Flick, U. (2018) *An Introduction to Qualitative Research*. Los Angeles, CA: SAGE.

Gierlinger, E.M. (2017) I feel traumatized: Teachers' beliefs on the roles of languages and learning in CLIL. In J. Valcke and R. Wilkinson (eds) *Integrating Content and Language in Higher Education: Perspectives on Professional Practice* (pp. 97–116). Frankfurt am Main: Peter Lang.

Hüttner, J. and Smit, U. (2013) CLIL (content and language integrated learning): The bigger picture. A response to: A. Bruton. 2013. CLIL: Some of the reasons why and why not. *System* 41, 587–597.

Hüttner, J., Dalton-Puffer, C. and Smit, U. (2013) The power of beliefs: Lay theories and their influence on the implementation of CLIL programmes. *International Journal of Bilingual Education and Bilingualism* 16 (3), 267–284.

Jenkins, J. (2014) *English as a Lingua Franca in the International Cniversity: The Politics of Academic English Language Policy*. Abingdon: Routledge.

Kalaja, P., Barcelos, A.M.F. and Aro, M. (2018) Revisiting research on L2 learner beliefs: Looking back and looking forward. In P. Garrett and J.M. Cots (eds) *The Routledge Handbook of Language Awareness* (pp. 222–237). New York, NY: Routledge.

Kuckartz, U. (2014) *Qualitative Text Analysis: A Guide to Methods, Practice & Using Software*. Los Angeles, CA: SAGE.

Kubanyiova, M. and Feryok, A. (2015) Language teacher cognition in applied linguistics research: Revisiting the territory, redrawing the boundaries, reclaiming the relevance. *The Modern Language Journal* 99, 435–449.

Lasagabaster, D. and Doiz, A. (2017) A longitudinal study on the impact of CLIL on affective factors. *Applied Linguistics* 38 (5), 688–712.

Lewis, G., Jones, B. and Baker, C. (2012) Translanguaging: Developing its conceptualization and contextualisation. *Educational Research and Evaluation* 18 (7), 655–670.

Mearns, T., de Graaff, R. and Coyle, D. (2017) Motivation *for* or *from* bilingual education? A comparative study of learner views in the Netherlands. *International Journal of Bilingual Education and Bilingualism*, 1–14.

Moate, J.M. (2011) The impact of foreign language mediated teaching on teachers' sense of professional integrity in the CLIL classroom. *European Journal of Teacher Education* 34 (3), 333–346.

Nikula, T. and Moore, P. (2019) Exploring translanguaging in CLIL. *International Journal of Bilingual Education and Bilingualism* 22 (2), 237–249.

Oattes, H., Oostdam, R., de Graaff, R. and Wilschut, A. (2018) The challenge of balancing content and language: Perceptions of Dutch bilingual education history teachers. *Teaching and Teacher Education* 70, 165–174.

Otwinowska, A. and Foryś, M. (2017) They learn the CLIL way, but do they like it? Affectivity and cognition in upper-primary CLIL classes. *International Journal of Bilingual Education and Bilingualism* 20 (5), 457–480.

Pappa, S., Moate, J., Ruohotie-Lyhty, M. and Eteläpelto, A. (2017) Teacher agency within the Finnish CLIL context: Tensions and resources. *International Journal of Bilingual Education and Bilingualism*, 1–21.

Paran, A. (2013) Content and language integrated learning: Panacea or policy borrowing myth? *Applied Linguistics Review* 4 (2), 317–342.

Paulsrud, B. (2018) Just a little plus: The CLIL student perspective. In L.K. Sylvén (ed.) *Investigating Content and Language Integrated Learning: Insights from Swedish High Schools* (pp. 282–297). Bristol: Multilingual Matters.

Pavón Vázquez, V. and Méndez García, M. del C. (2017) Analysing teachers' roles regarding cross-curricular coordination in content and language integrated learning (CLIL). *Journal of English Studies* 15, 235–260.

Roiha, A. and Sommier, M. (2018) Viewing CLIL through the eyes of former pupils: Insights into foreign language and intercultural attitudes. *Language and Intercultural Communication*, 1–17.

Rumlich, D. (2016) *Evaluating Bilingual Education in Germany: CLIL Students' General English Proficiency, EFL Self-Concept and Interest*. Frankfurt am Main: Peter Lang. (Mehrsprachigkeit in Schule und Unterricht, Band 15).

Sandberg, Y. (2018) Teaching and learning content through two languages: The biology and history teacher perspective. In L.K. Sylvén (ed.) *Investigating Content and Language Integrated Learning: Insights from Swedish High Schools* (pp. 298–314). Bristol: Multilingual Matters.

Shohamy, E. (2006) *Language Policy: Hidden Agendas and New Approaches*. New York, NY: Routledge.

Shulman, L.S. (1986) Those who understand: Knowledge growth in teaching. *Educational Researcher* 15 (2), 4–14.

Skinnari, K. and Bovellan, E. (2016) CLIL teachers' beliefs about integration and about their professional roles: Perspectives from a European context. In T. Nikula, E. Dafouz,

P. Moore and U. Smit (eds) *Conceptualising Integration in CLIL and Multilingual Education* (pp. 145–167). Bristol: Mulitlingual Matters.

Smit, U. and Schwarz, M. (2020) English in Austria: Policies and practices. In R. Hickey (ed.) *English in the German-Speaking World*. Cambridge: Cambridge University Press.

Smit, U., Finker, T., Dalton-Puffer, C., Hüttner, J. and Lechner, C. (2016) *Zur Implementierung von CLIL in den Regelunterricht an HTL: Fragenentwicklung für die Evaluation und Fallstudien zur Unterrichtspraxis: Endbericht des Forschungsprojekts*. Studie im Auftrag des BMB, ausgeführt vom Institut für Anglistik und Amerikanistik der Universität Wien.

Somers, T. and Llinares, A. (2018) Students' motivation for content and language integrated learning and the role of programme intensity. *International Journal of Bilingual Education and Bilingualism*, 1–16.

Spolsky, B. (2004) *Language Policy*. Cambridge: Cambridge University Press.

Spolsky, B. (2009) *Language Management*. Cambridge: Cambridge University Press.

Thompson, A.S. and Sylvén, L.K. (2018) CLIL and motivation revisited: A longitudinal perspective. In L.K. Sylvén (ed.) *Investigating Content and Language Integrated Learning: Insights from Swedish High Schools* (pp. 76–95). Bristol: Multilingual Matters.

van Kampen, E., Admiraal, W. and Berry, A. (2018) Content and language integrated learning in the Netherlands: Teachers' self-reported pedagogical practices. *International Journal of Bilingual Education and Bilingualism* 21 (2), 222–236.

van Kampen, E., Meirink, J., Admiraal, W. and Berry, A. (2017) Do we all share the same goals for content and language integrated learning (CLIL)? Specialist and practitioner perceptions of 'ideal' CLIL pedagogies in the Netherlands. *International Journal of Bilingual Education and Bilingualism*, 1–17.

7 Teachers' and Learners' Beliefs about Corrective Feedback Compared with Teachers' Practices in CLIL and EFL

Ruth Milla and María del Pilar García Mayo

Introduction

The present chapter focuses on secondary teachers' and learners' beliefs about corrective feedback (CF) through a mixed methods study exploring these beliefs. A belief is defined as:

> [A] proposition which may be consciously or unconsciously held, is evaluative in that it is accepted as true by the individual, and is therefore imbued with emotive commitment; further, it serves as a guide to thought and behaviour. (Borg, 2001: 186)

Although there has been previous research on the topic of teachers' and learners' beliefs about CF, the present study examines beliefs about oral corrective feedback (OCF) among teachers and learners in the underexplored content and language integrated learning (CLIL) context and compares those to beliefs of teachers and learners in a mainstream English as a foreign language (EFL) setting.

CF is a teaching technique that has been defined as 'a reactive type of form-focused instruction which is considered to be effective in promoting noticing and thus conducive to learning' (Yang & Lyster, 2010: 237). Example (1) below illustrates a corrective feedback episode (CFE), which is the usual context where OCF takes place:

Example (1) CFE

(1) **Learner:**   ... there ***haven't been** any victims.

   Teacher: there **weren't** any victims. **You are talking about the past, right? There weren't any victims. There weren't any.** What other word do you have for victim?

   Learner: but was today!

   Teacher: yes, but **the tense that you have is past: 'were involved'. It is not: 'there has been an accident' and then you can use the present. No, the past.** Another word for victims?

(Milla, 2017: 307)

In (1) we can see the three typical moves of a CFE. First, the learner produces a grammar error in the error move. In other CFEs, errors can be related to pronunciation, vocabulary or unsolicited first language (L1) use, for example. Second, is the CF move provided by the teacher, which may adopt different forms such as recasts, clarification requests, repetitions, elicitations, metalinguistic information or explicit corrections. These types are themselves classified into two wider categories depending on the information provided: *reformulations* (recasts, explicit correction) are those CF types that present the learner with the target form, whereas *prompts* try to elicit the learner's self-repair. In (1) the CF move consists of a reformulation and some metalinguistic information on the nature of the error. Finally, the third move corresponds to a 'learner's reaction in some way to the teacher's CF' (Lyster & Ranta, 1997: 49), which is referred to as uptake. This move is not always present in the episode, since sometimes the learner ignores the correction or does not react to it. In the cases when CF is recognised, an uptake can take the form of a needs-repair move (Lyster & Ranta, 1997), as in (1), where the learner reacts to the CF but fails to repair the error. In other cases, the learner successfully repairs the error and thus the CF move proves to be effective.

Research on OCF effectiveness has widely investigated the effects of different factors such as learners' age, level of proficiency, teachers' and learners' beliefs or learning context (García Mayo & Milla, 2021). Regarding context, CFEs have been analysed in foreign language (FL) and second language (L2) settings. However, CLIL, an educational approach where 'curricular content is taught through the medium of a FL typically to learners participating in some form of mainstream education at the primary, secondary or tertiary level' (Dalton-Puffer, 2011: 183) has been overlooked regarding CF and teachers' and learners' beliefs about it, particularly in secondary education classrooms (Llinares & Lyster, 2014).

At the secondary level of education, CLIL and EFL teachers normally have different backgrounds. EFL teachers usually have linguistic training, with undergraduate (and sometimes master's degrees) in English Studies. These teachers generally pay more attention to language forms than their CLIL counterparts. On the other hand, CLIL teachers in secondary schools, at least in the context in which the present study has been carried out, are content teachers with an English certificate (Level C1, Common European Framework of Reference; Council of Europe, 2018). Because these teachers take different career paths, there may be differences in these teachers' beliefs about OCF and, subsequently, differences in their classroom practices. Unlike primary school CLIL lessons, secondary and tertiary level CLIL programmes do not typically find a content and language form balance but, rather, are more oriented to content, leaving formal issues aside (Pica, 2002).

The main goal of this chapter is to examine teachers' and learners' beliefs about OCF in both CLIL and mainstream EFL classes in secondary schools of the Basque Autonomous Community (BAC), a region in the north of Spain. Moreover, the connection between teachers' beliefs and their actual classroom practices will also be considered.

Previous research on beliefs about corrective feedback

What teachers and learners believe guides their behaviour in the classroom and, consequently, affects the language learning process. Beliefs are important in order to understand CFEs in two ways: (1) what teachers believe guide their decisions about feedback provision and (2) what learners believe motivates their responses to corrections from the teacher and even whether they notice them.

The following section will briefly review previous research on teachers' and learners' beliefs about OCF in different contexts.

Teachers' beliefs

Whereas Borg (2001) defined beliefs, generally, Basturkmen et al. (2004) specifically define teachers' beliefs as, 'statements teachers ma[k]e about their ideas, thoughts and knowledge that are expressed as evaluations of what "should be done", "should be the case" and "is preferable"' (Basturkmen et al., 2004: 244; see also Chapters 5, 6 & 8). Therefore, teachers' beliefs about CF might guide their corrective behaviour and influence the amount of correction, the CF types used and the error types addressed.

Over the last few decades, researchers have been interested in teachers' beliefs about their own practices, seeking to elucidate which beliefs lead to more successful language teaching (Borg, 2006). Researchers also have become increasingly concerned with specific aspects of language teaching, such as grammar (Schulz, 2001), literacy instruction (Grisham, 2000) and oral feedback provision (Basturkmen et al., 2004; Chavez, 2006; Lyster

& Saito, 2010; Schulz, 2001). The findings of these studies on teachers' beliefs about CF have been mixed.

Some research has reported that teachers held beliefs against providing CF in oral interactions (Basturkmen *et al.*, 2004; Brown, 2009; Lasagabaster & Sierra, 2005). The reluctance to provide feedback when engaged in oral communication was attributed to two concerns: (1) teachers were thought to be afraid of breaking the communicative flow and (2) teachers feared that OCF might cause learner anxiety. However, in most studies on teachers' beliefs, OCF has been found to be necessary and beneficial for L2 learning. Teachers acknowledge that learners expect to be corrected and state the importance of allowing them to self-repair (Farrell & Bennis, 2013).

With the rapid growth of CLIL programmes in Europe (Nikula *et al.*, 2013), one area that has clearly been underexplored is what teachers' and learners' believe about OCF in this setting. Content teachers, or teachers who teach non-linguistic subjects such as history or maths, consider their main goal to be concentrating on the teaching of content, not language (Lo, 2014). Although these teachers might regard linguistic accuracy as important, especially when teaching in CLIL settings, they tend to focus on fluency and content. In CLIL lessons the focus on language is incidental and the attention to form is not provided in an explicit manner (De Graaff *et al.*, 2007), CLIL teachers are less likely to use CF than their language counterparts (Lorenzo *et al.*, 2010)

However, research has found that integrating language and content (i.e. by means of CF or other form-focused techniques) can be beneficial to language learning (Llinares, 2015) because it helps noticing and overcoming classroom limitations (Lightbown & Spada, 1990). Generally speaking, content teaching on its own is not sufficient in immersion settings, as has been found in studies in this type of content-oriented classrooms (García Mayo, 2011; Lightbown, 2014; Swain, 1988). Since some educational contexts are more form-oriented (EFL and ESL), others more meaning-oriented (L2 or immersion) and others, such as CLIL, try to strike a balance between form and content, it would be reasonable to assume that teachers' and learners' beliefs will be influenced by the context they are in and, therefore, methodological decisions will reflect those beliefs.

There are not many studies that have investigated the extent to which teachers' beliefs are materialised in classroom corrective practices and mixed findings have been reported. Some research has found consistency between beliefs and practices (e.g. Chavez, 2006), while others demonstrate that teachers' corrective behaviours do not follow their reported beliefs (e.g. Basturkmen, 2012; Farrell & Yang, 2019) regarding types of feedback and timing (Ölmezer-Öztürk, 2019).

The mismatch between teachers' beliefs and corrective behaviours have been attributed to different reasons (Bao, 2019), for example, some teachers refer to time and curriculum constraints, which lead them to ignore errors and to focus more on content than on accuracy itself (e.g. Yoshida, 2008). In other cases, it seems that the teachers' individual characteristics (such as language proficiency, educational background, learning experience or personality) also mediate between beliefs and teaching practices (Chavez, 2006). In addition, the contexts where teachers are immersed have been argued to affect their beliefs, but also to constrain their classroom practices (Basturkmen, 2012; Borg, 2003; Ölmezer-Öztürk, 2019). Moreover, content teachers (i.e. CLIL teachers) acknowledge the positive effects and necessity of OCF, but they often do not consider themselves to be responsible for providing it to their students (De Graaff et al., 2007). Thus, in this case, their reported beliefs were incongruent with respect to their corrective practices.

All in all, there are relatively few studies on this topic and researchers have called for further investigation on the comparison of CF beliefs and classroom practices (Ellis, 2010; Llinares & Lyster, 2014; Mori, 2011; Roothoft, 2014, 2018; Samar & Shayestefar, 2009). As mentioned above, CLIL contexts are in need of research regarding teachers' and learners' beliefs about CF. Borg (2003, 2006) suggests that research on specific curricular areas and with teachers whose L1 is not the target language should be carried out, and this is precisely one of the main goals of the present study.

Learners' beliefs

Learners' beliefs and their potential effects on CF effectiveness are also under-researched (Katayama, 2007). Findings so far have shown learners' hold positive beliefs about OCF in several contexts. In fact, learners generally seem to demand more CF from their teachers and do not seem to feel anxiety as a result of being corrected (Brown, 2009). Regarding learners' beliefs about OCF types, findings are mixed. Both high-proficiency (Kaivanpanah et al., 2015) and low-proficiency learners (Mohammed, 2006; Yoshida, 2008) have shown preference for OCF types that elicit self-correction, such as prompts (Zhu & Wang, 2019). However, in other studies, advanced learners were reported to prefer corrections by means of recasts (Brown, 2009). These different preferences have been attributed to learners' individual differences (ID) and the influence of the instructional context (García Mayo & Milla, 2021; Lyster et al., 2013).

Several studies have investigated learners' IDs such as motivation or anxiety in CLIL vs. non-CLIL contexts. Findings show that learners involved in CLIL programmes appear to have more positive beliefs about the FL and language learning (Lasagabaster, 2011; Lasagabaster & López Beloqui, 2015) and they seem to have lower rates of anxiety than their non-CLIL counterparts (Thompson & Sylvén, 2015). However, to our knowledge, Sylvén (2015) is the only study that contrasts EFL and CLIL learners' beliefs about language, but it is a case study of only one CLIL and one EFL learner. There do not seem to be any studies on CF beliefs held by CLIL vs. EFL learners.

Mismatch between teachers' and learners' beliefs about OCF

A mismatch has also been found between learners' beliefs and teachers' CF practices (Amrhein & Nassaji, 2010; Lasagabaster & Sierra, 2005; Lee, 2013). Learners generally demand more frequent, immediate and more explicit OCF, preferably in the form of prompts, while teachers advocate for delayed feedback and are afraid of over-correction. Teachers generally try to delay corrections and provide OCF in the form of recasts to a selection of errors. The fact that learners' expectations do not match teachers' behaviour might lead to students' demotivation and a lower effectiveness of teachers' OCF strategies (Schulz, 2001).

More research is clearly needed on how teachers' and learners' beliefs about OCF might vary depending on the learning context, including with CLIL learners and on how those beliefs might potentially influence the learners' responses to OCF practices (Basturkmen *et al.*, 2004; Lyster *et al.*, 2013). Findings from this type of research could contribute to an increase in OCF effectiveness to promote language learning.

The Present Study

The main aim of the present study is to compare teachers' and learners' beliefs in both a CLIL and an EFL setting through a mixed methods design. Our findings will help educational stakeholders to better understand if and how CLIL teachers provide OCF and the main challenges they face in a teaching environment that expects them to strike a balance between content and language.

On the basis of previous research, we entertained the following research questions (RQs) and hypotheses:

(1) What beliefs do CLIL and EFL teachers hold about OCF and its types? Do these beliefs correspond to their actual classroom practices?

We aimed at comparing the beliefs of teachers in the two instructional contexts and to explore whether these beliefs corresponded to the teachers' actual OCF use. The predictions were that CLIL and EFL teachers, being in different contexts and having distinct backgrounds, will show varied beliefs about OCF. Although the use of recasts is predicted to be high in both settings (Lyster & Mori, 2006; Sheen, 2004), it is expected that EFL teachers will be more concerned with accuracy, use a higher percentage of CF moves and will address grammar and pronunciation errors. On the other hand, CLIL teachers will prefer more implicit OCF types, such as recasts, and will probably pay attention to lexical errors since the lessons are more centred on content than EFL lessons (Doiz & Lasagabaster, 2017).

The second research question pertained to students:

(2) What beliefs do learners hold about OCF and its types? Do these beliefs influence their uptake?

As in previous research, learners are expected to hold positive beliefs about CF, demanding extensive correction from the teachers (Schulz, 2001), both in CLIL and EFL contexts. They will probably show more positive beliefs towards more explicit types, such as elicitations, and prompts in general (Kaivanpanah et al., 2015; Yoshida, 2008).

Last, we examined whether there was a mismatch or uniformity to teachers' and students' beliefs in these two instructional settings:

(3) Do learners' beliefs overlap with CLIL and EFL teachers' beliefs?

We hypothesised that learners would hold more positive beliefs about OCF than the teachers as found in previous studies (Kaivanpanah et al., 2015; Yoshida, 2008), and they would report preference for explicit, immediate as well as comprehensive feedback (Lee, 2013).

In order to explore these research questions, we designed a mixed methods study. It consisted of three parts: (1) a teacher beliefs questionnaire sent to CLIL and EFL teachers in the BAC region, (2) teacher observations with one CLIL and one EFL teacher who taught the same cohort of learners and (3) a learner beliefs questionnaire administered to learners from the same school where the teacher observations took place.

Participants and context of study

The context in the present study is a well-known public high school in Bilbao, one of the three major cities in the BAC. The BAC is a bilingual community in the north of Spain with two official languages, Spanish and Basque. Basque is nowadays taught in all public and nearly all private schools, and used as the language of instruction in the vast majority. After the Spanish Education Reform Act in 1990 (LOGSE, 1990), English was established as the official FL from the age of 8 onwards (before that it was 11) but in many Spanish communities EFL teaching starts at 4 or even earlier (García Mayo, 2017). Nowadays, in the BAC more and more schools are implementing trilingual programmes (Merino & Lasagabaster, 2015), using CLIL-like systems for subjects taught through English.

The sample in this study was formed by a group of teachers and a group of learners. A beliefs questionnaire was sent to secondary school CLIL and EFL teachers in the BAC, and a total of 11 CLIL and 20 EFL practitioners completed and returned the questionnaire with their beliefs about OCF. The CLIL teachers were responsible for different subjects taught in English, such as Social Sciences or Economics.

In addition, in order to fill the gap in teachers' and learners' beliefs about OCF in CLIL settings, a high school with a trilingual programme (Spanish, Basque and English) was selected. There, two teachers of the same group of second year post-compulsory education learners ($n = 26$; mean age 17.1), one EFL and one CLIL teacher, volunteered to be observed during their lessons. The EFL teacher was a female who had been teaching English for 26 years. She had a degree in English Studies and had completed different courses to update her knowledge of English. She had a self-reported very advanced level. Moreover, like all teachers in secondary education in Spain, she had completed a postgraduate course on teacher training called Certificate of Pedagogical Aptitude (CAP, *Certificado de Aptitud Pedagógica*), which nowadays is equivalent to an MA degree.

The CLIL teacher was male with a background in Economics and 20 years of teaching experience, during the last seven years of which he had used English as the language of instruction. In Spain, teachers working in CLIL programmes in high schools are required to have the CAP certificate and also a C1 level in the foreign language they use in the classroom. The CLIL teacher had obtained this certificate several years ago and had a self-reported advanced level of English. He taught Economics, Business Studies and Administration and Management Processes, optional subjects in the trilingual programme. As most students (24 out of 26) took Business Studies, that one was the class chosen to be observed.

As mentioned above, the 26 learners (14 female and 12 male) that were shared by the CLIL and EFL teachers belonged to an intact class of second year post-compulsory secondary education. For these students, this was the final year of secondary school before entering university. As mentioned above, their program was trilingual with 30% of the lessons devoted to each of the three languages. In order to be eligible for the programme, the learners had to have shown a sufficient English level by passing an English test or, otherwise, having taken English lessons during secondary education. The Oxford Placement Test (OPT) (Syndicate U.C.L.E., 2001) that the learners completed as part of the present study revealed that they had an intermediate level (B1 = 16 learners, B2 = 10 learners).

The learners' beliefs questionnaire was completed by this second-year learners and another group of first year learners in the same programme ($n = 25$, 3 male and 22 female: mean age = 16). These first-year learners also had an intermediate level (B1 = 18 learners, B2 = 7 learners), according to the OPT (Syndicate U.C.L.E., 2001).

Instruments

In order to explore the potential correspondence between teachers' and learners' beliefs and their classroom behaviours, EFL and CLIL secondary school teachers and learners completed a questionnaire on beliefs about CF (both written and oral, although only items on OCF will be analysed for the present study) and grammar teaching and learning. The data were triangulated with the transcription of the audio-recordings of the teachers' classroom observations, as is standard in studies on OCF (Basturkmen *et al.*, 2004; Lyster & Mori, 2006; Llinares & Lyster, 2014).

Both questionnaires were adapted from Schulz's (1996) questionnaire investigating teachers' beliefs about error correction and grammar teaching. Some items were added to Schulz's (1996) version and some others were removed to adapt the questions to the specific aims of the present study, such as items on beliefs about CF types, or the need for CLIL teachers to correct oral errors. In the questionnaire, the teachers were asked about their general beliefs about OCF and their opinions about the different types as well as their beliefs about the need for CF to be provided by EFL and CLIL teachers (see the Appendix). The questionnaire consisted of 33 items: 5 background questions, 27 closed questions with a 5-point Likert scale ranging from (Completely disagree (1) to Completely agree (5)) with an open-ended question at the end. Twelve of the closed questions were related to OCF and findings regarding those items will be reported in the present chapter. The items in the teachers' questionnaire were tested for reliability and the value of Cronbach's alpha obtained was 0.792. In addition, a parallel questionnaire was designed for learners with items about the same issues (not included in the appendices due to space constraints). In example (2) the first item in the teachers' and the learners' questionnaires, asking about their beliefs about OCF, are illustrated:

Example (2)

Teachers' questionnaire:

 (6) When learners make errors in speaking a second language, teachers should correct them.

Learners' questionnaire:

(14) When I make errors in speaking a second language, I like my teacher to correct them.

As for the classroom observation procedure, 15 CLIL and 12 EFL lessons were audio-recorded and their contents were transcribed and codified by the first author. CFEs were codified following the conventions in Lyster and Ranta's (1997) seminal study. The second author transcribed and codified 25% of the data. Inter-rater reliability, calculated by a simple agreement rate, resulted in 98%. CFEs used by the two teachers were then tallied. Moreover, the activities, the different teaching techniques and classroom management strategies were analysed using a Communicative Orientation of Language Teaching scheme (COLT) (Spada & Fröhlich, 1995). This scheme has been used in previous comparative studies (Llinares & Lyster, 2014; Lyster & Mori, 2006; Milla & García Mayo, 2014) and has proved to be useful in establishing the predominant orientation of the lessons, whether to meaning or to language form. This information, together with the results of the beliefs questionnaire, was expected to provide a clear picture of what happened in the actual lessons and the possible reasons behind the two teachers' classroom behaviour.

To summarise, the data in this study came from (1) the observation of 15 CLIL and 12 EFL recorded lessons taught by two teachers to a group of 26 second year high-school learners in a CLIL programme, and (2) the beliefs questionnaires completed by CLIL and EFL teachers ($n = 31$) and learners of both first ($n = 25$) and second ($n = 26$) year high-school classes.

Therefore, the data analysis consisted of considering the scores (1 to 5) in the responses to the closed questions and submitting those values to U Mann Whitney tests, comparing first EFL and CLIL teachers' beliefs about OCF (research question 1) and then teachers' and learners' beliefs about OCF (research question 3). Then, in order to answer the second part of research question 1, several aspects of the classroom observation procedure in CLIL and EFL lessons were considered such as the amount of OCF and CF types most frequently used, among others (see below). Items related to aspects related to OCF and CF were selected from the teachers' questionnaire. Finally, a qualitative comparison was carried out between each of the classroom aspects and CLIL teacher's and EFL teacher's respective responses to the related questionnaire items.

Findings

Teachers' beliefs and practices

The first research question aimed at comparing the beliefs of teachers in two instructional contexts and whether or not those beliefs corresponded to their actual practices. The findings show that, in general, both CLIL and EFL teachers' beliefs about OCF were positive

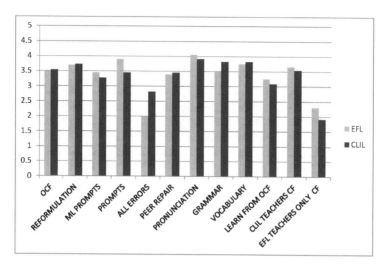

Figure 7.1 Means of EFL and CLIL teachers' responses to the beliefs questionnaire

in the sense that they consider OCF a useful pedagogical tool for learner language development and, although there were slight differences between CLIL and EFL teachers' responses, as Figure 7.1 above illustrates, the U-Mann Whitney test revealed that those differences did not reach significance.

Previous literature did not predict these findings, since content teachers in other studies were reported to have fewer positive beliefs towards OCF than their language teacher counterparts (Doiz & Lasagabaster, 2017; Lo, 2014). Content teachers were also reported to orient their classes to meaning and fluency, rather than to accuracy. Therefore, we did not expect such positive beliefs about the use of prompts on the part of the CLIL teachers.

Regarding the comparison of teachers' beliefs with classroom corrective behaviour, the data analyses from the classroom observation procedure revealed significant differences between the EFL and the CLIL teacher in several aspects. First, the COLT scheme showed a different classroom orientation; CLIL lessons were clearly oriented to meaning whereas EFL lessons were more focused on form, which supported previous studies (Doiz & Lasagabaster, 2017; Lo, 2014). Although the beliefs questionnaire did not reveal significant differences between CLIL and EFL teachers, the COLT scheme indicated that their practices went in separate directions.

Further differences were found regarding the amount of corrections, which were much higher in EFL than in CLIL lessons ($p < 0.01$) and the types of CF, which were more varied in type in EFL than in CLIL ($p < 0.01$), a context in which the teacher predominantly used recasts.

Table 7.1 Number of observations for CFEs and their turns

	EFL	CLIL
CF/CFEs	148	114
Recasts	84	81
Repetitions	4	7
Clarifications	5	7
Elicitations	29	10
Metalinguistic	6	8
Explicit correction	20	1
UPTAKE	91	35

The type of errors corrected were also different ($p < 0.01$); the CLIL teacher reacted mainly to lexical errors and hardly ever to grammar or pronunciation errors, while the EFL teacher provided CF to all types of errors, especially pronunciation. Table 7.1 above displays the CFEs figures in the two settings.

These findings were contrasted with the CLIL and the EFL teachers' responses from the questionnaire regarding the following aspects: (1) the item asking about the need to correct all errors was compared to the amount of OCF provided, (2) the beliefs about reformulations and prompts were compared to the use of these OCF types and (3) the teachers' responses to the items asking about the need to correct different error types (pronunciation, grammar and vocabulary) were compared to the teachers' correction of these types of errors.

When the EFL teacher's beliefs and practices were analysed it could be seen that she had neutral beliefs about OCF and the different CF types ('Neither Agree Nor Disagree') but her provision of CF was rather frequent (e.g. she corrected 78% of the errors and up to 91% of pronunciation errors). Thus, her corrective practices did not exactly match her beliefs. Additionally, in informal conversation with one of the researchers, she stated that she was really in favour of correcting oral errors and she had a strong form-focused orientation that led her pedagogical decisions. Therefore, it seems that the responses to the questionnaire did not reflect her actual beliefs.

Regarding the CLIL teacher's beliefs, they were very positive towards OCF, which did not match his corrective behaviour (e.g. he only corrected about 25% of the learners' errors). Similarly, he rated prompts rather high in the scale, but he used recasts more frequently and prompts only in 40% of the CFEs. Regarding the type of errors, he considered that it was more important to correct pronunciation errors than vocabulary or grammar errors. However, in his classroom practice he addressed vocabulary errors (81% of his CF moves) and ignored pronunciation errors most of the time.

Learners' beliefs

The second research question dealt with learners' beliefs about OCF, whether or not those beliefs had an impact on uptake. When comparing learners' and teachers' beliefs, the results from the U-Mann Whitney tests revealed that significant differences between learners' and teachers' opinions were related to the general beliefs about OCF ($p < 0.01$), CF types (reformulations ($p = 0.028$), metalinguistic prompts ($p < 0.01$), error types (grammar ($p < 0.01$), the benefits of CF for learning ($p < 0.01$), peer correction ($p < 0.01$), the benefits of correcting all errors ($p < 0.01$) and the need for CLIL teachers to correct the learners' oral errors ($p < 0.01$). Learners always conveyed more positive answers with one significant exception, namely, peer correction, which they considered less preferable to teacher's corrections.

Learners' versus teachers' beliefs

Our findings support previous research in EFL or ESL settings, which have also shown that learners' beliefs were more positive than teachers' in most aspects (Amrhein & Nassaji, 2010; Brown, 2009; Lasagabaster & Sierra, 2005; Lee, 2013). These results indicate that learners are willing to be corrected by means of reformulations or prompts and that they generally want to be corrected for any type of error (pronunciation, grammar or vocabulary). They feel that OCF helps them in their learning process and expect that teachers provide them with the highest proportion of correction when involved in oral interaction, both in EFL and in CLIL lessons.

Discussion and Conclusion

This chapter has explored teachers' and learners' beliefs about OCF. Additionally, this chapter has compared teachers' beliefs to their OCF practices in an EFL and a CLIL secondary education classroom in the BAC region. The analysis of the data from a teacher and learner beliefs questionnaire and from the tallying of the CFEs in the recorded oral interaction data from the classroom observation procedure yielded several interesting observations. CLIL and EFL teachers' beliefs were found to be similar but, when beliefs were compared to their actual classroom behaviour, differences were attested. Thus, the EFL teacher was found not to follow her own reported beliefs and the CLIL teacher's beliefs were not in line with his actual CF behaviour, either. This CLIL teacher considers CF necessary for language learning but he does not feel it is his responsibility to pay attention to formal aspects of the language he uses to teach content (as previously reported in other learning settings, such as English medium instruction (Doiz & Lasagabaster, 2017). These beliefs, together with time limitations due to the extensive curriculum required to be covered, led to his increased focus on lexical errors and his disregard for learners' formal or linguistic errors. When these errors were considered by this CLIL teacher, they were addressed by means of indirect CF types such as implicit recasts. Moreover, he did not attend to pronunciation errors.

In spite of the fact that this study was carried out in a CLIL context, a setting not included in previous research on learners' beliefs about OCF, our findings show that these learners seem to have more positive beliefs about OCF in terms of its beneficial effect on their learning than the CLIL and EFL teachers in this study which is in line with previous research (Amrhein & Nassaji, 2010; Lasagabaster & Sierra, 2005; Lee, 2013; Schulz, 2001). In the CLIL context of this secondary school, learners demanded OCF for all error types and through both reformulations and prompts. Learners appear not to be concerned about anxiety or loss of communicative flow, which some teachers have considered as potential reasons to avoid further OCF or the use of explicit CF types, such as prompts.

The origin of teachers' and learners' beliefs might come from different sources, such as their educational background, motivation and from the sociolinguistic context itself. Thus, further research is needed in other contexts and with different CLIL models, either more form-oriented or more balanced (Sylvén, 2013), regarding teachers' beliefs and the correspondence with classroom practices, particularly in the context of CLIL secondary education. In the present study, the main orientation of CLIL and EFL lessons to meaning and to form, respectively, has been found to affect the results. A confirmation of this finding is necessitated and would involve observing additional classrooms in different contexts and with different populations of students. We also recommend that learners' beliefs should be further researched and compared to what teachers believe and what teachers do concerning OCF, in order to create a more complete picture of CLIL teachers' and learners' beliefs and classroom behaviour.

The present study has clear limitations that need to be acknowledged. We only observed one CLIL and one EFL teacher in a secondary school in the BAC. Of course, more observations of this type from more teachers in other schools of the same country and in other parts of the world would be necessary to obtain more robust findings. Furthermore, the learners have an intermediate proficiency level in the target language. In studies with more advanced learners, or beginner learners, it would be necessary to assess whether the same OCF types would be used.

Implications for Policy and Practice

This study has provided information on OCF from the classroom observation of two teachers, one EFL and one CLIL, together with data from questionnaires of high-school teachers in the BAC region. Although the data are limited and restricted to a particular region, we believe several pedagogical implications can be derived from their analysis.

The first is related to the fact that the CLIL teacher's beliefs and practices did not match, and his lessons were not balanced in terms of content and language. Teachers' reflections on their own practices and beliefs as well as the convergence between beliefs and practices are hypothesised to help language teaching (Farrell & Yang, 2019). Teachers should be made aware of their own practices and provided with further training on CLIL and on the importance of OCF in their lessons. For example, teacher training courses for CLIL teachers could include actual video recordings of their behaviour in different content classes in such a way that they could observe the frequency (or lack thereof) with which they use OCF and the most frequent types in their repertoire. Teachers could also be shown how to draw learners' attention to formal aspects of the language by means of implicit OCF moves in such a way that content classes could also include attention to language. Moreover, CLIL and EFL teachers should try to assess what their learners' beliefs about OCF are (Zhu & Wang, 2019). They should try to make them aware of the benefits of this pedagogical tool, explain the major types a teacher could use and perhaps ask their opinions about their favourite types. If learners see their expectations fulfilled, their motivation may increase and better learning results can be obtained (Ellis, 2010).

As just mentioned above, attention to language form in content lessons has been found to be essential for adequate language development (García Mayo, 2011; Lightbown, 2014; Lyster, 2007; Swain, 1988) and OCF could be one way to draw learners' attention to those aspects that usually go unnoticed in content classes. Additionally, collaboration between CLIL and EFL teachers could promote metalinguistic awareness and better results regarding language learning (Lyster *et al.*, 2013).

References

Amrhein, H.R. and Nassaji, H. (2010) Written corrective feedback: What do learners and teachers prefer and why? *Canadian Journal of Applied Linguistics* 13, 95–127.

Bao, R. (2019) Oral corrective feedback in L2 Chinese classes: Teachers' beliefs versus their practices. *System* 82, 140–150.

Basturkmen, H. (2012) Review of research into the correspondence between language teachers' stated beliefs and practices. *System* 40 (2), 282–295.

Basturkmen, H., Loewen, S. and Ellis, R. (2004) Teachers' stated beliefs about incidental focus on form and their classroom practices. *Applied Linguistics* 25 (2), 243–72.

Borg, M. (2001) Teachers' beliefs. *ELT Journal* 55 (2), 186–88.

Borg, S. (2003) Teacher cognition in language teaching: A review of research on what language teachers think, know, believe, and do. *Language Teaching* 36 (2), 81–109.

Borg, S. (2006) *Teacher Cognition and Language Education: Research and Practice*. London: Continuum.

Brown, A. (2009) Learners' and teachers' perceptions of effective foreign language teaching: A comparison of ideals. *The Modern Language Journal* 93 (1), 46–60.

Chavez, M. (2006) Classroom-language use in teacher-led instruction and teachers' self-perceived roles. *International Review of Applied Linguistics* 44, 49–102.

Council of Europe (2018) Common European Framework of Reference for Languages: Learning, Teaching, Assessment (CEFR). Companion Volume with New Descriptors. See https://rm.coe.int/cefr-companion-volume-with-new-descriptors-2018/1680787989 (accessed June 2019).

Dalton-Puffer, C. (2011) Content and language integrated learning: From practice to principles. *Annual Review of Applied Linguistics* 31, 182–204.

De Graaff, R., Koopman, G.J., Anikina, Y. and Westhoff, G. (2007) An observation tool for effective L2 pedagogy in content and language integrated learning (CLIL). *International Journal of Bilingual Education and Bilingualism* 10 (5), 603–624.

Doiz, A. and Lasagabaster, D. (2017) Teachers' beliefs about translanguaging practices. In C.M. Mazak and K.S. Carroll (eds) *Translanguaging in Higher Education: Beyond Monolingual Ideologies* (pp. 157–176). Bristol: Multilingual Matters.

Ellis, R. (2010) A framework for investigating oral and written corrective feedback. *Studies in Second Language Acquisition* 32, 335–349.

Farrell, T.S.C. and Bennis, K. (2013) Reflecting on ELT teacher beliefs and classroom practices: A case study. *RELC Journal* 44 (2), 163–176.

Farrell, T.S.C. and Yang, D. (2019) Exploring an EAP teacher's beliefs and practices in teaching L2 speaking: A case study. *RELC Journal* 50 (1), 104–117.

García Mayo, M.P. (2011) The relevance of attention to form in communicative classroom contexts. *ELIA - Estudios de Lingüística Inglesa Aplicada* 11, 11–45.

García Mayo, M.P. (2017) *Learning Foreign Languages in Primary School: Research Insights*. Bristol: Multilingual Matters.

García Mayo, M.P. and Milla, R. (2021) Corrective feedback in second vs. foreign language contexts. In H. Nassaji and E. Kartchava (eds) *The Cambridge Handbook of Corrective Feedback* (pp. 471–493). Cambridge: Cambridge University Press.

Grisham, D.L. (2000) Connecting theoretical conceptions of reading to practice: A longitudinal study of elementary school teachers. *Reading Psychology* 21 (2), 145–170.

Kaivanpanah, S., Alavi, S., and Sepehrinia, S. (2015) Preferences for interactional feedback: Differences between learners and teachers. *The Language Teaching Journal* 43 (1), 74–93.

Katayama, A. (2007) Learners' perceptions toward corrective feedback to oral errors. *Asian EFL Journal* 9 (4), 289–305.

Lasagabaster, D. (2011) English achievement and student motivation in CLIL and EFL settings. *Innovations in Language Learning and Teaching* 5 (1), 3–18.

Lasagabaster, D. and López Beloqui, R. (2015) The impact of type of approach (CLIL versus EFL) and methodology (book-based versus project work) on motivation. *Porta Linguarum* 23, 41–57.

Lasagabaster, D. and Sierra, J.M. (2005) Error correction: Learners' versus teachers' perceptions. *Language Awareness* 14, 112–127.

Lee, E. (2013) Corrective feedback preferences and learner repair among advanced ESL learners. *System* 41, 217–230.

Lightbown, P.M. (2014) *Focus on Content-based Language Teaching*. Oxford: Oxford University Press.

Lightbown, P.M. and Spada, N. (1990) Focus on form and corrective feedback in communicative language teaching: Effects on second language learning. *Studies in Second Language Acquisition* 12 (4), 429–448.

Llinares, A. (2015) Integration in CLIL: A proposal to inform research and successful pedagogy. *Language, Culture and Curriculum* 28 (1), 58–73.

Llinares, A. and Lyster, R. (2014) The influence of context on patterns of corrective feedback and learner uptake: a comparison of CLIL and immersion classrooms. *The Language Learning Journal* 42 (2), 181–194.

Lo, Y.Y. (2014) Collaboration between L2 and content subject teachers in CBI: Contrasting beliefs and attitudes. *RELC Journal* 45 (2), 181–196.

LOGSE (1990) *Ley Orgánica de Ordenación del Sistema Educativo.* BOE núm. 238. See http://www.boe.es/boe/dias/1990/10/04/pdfs/A28927-28942.pdf.

Lorenzo, F., Casal, S. and Moore, P. (2010) The effects of content and language integrated learning in European education: Key findings from the Andalusian bilingual sections evaluation project. *Applied Linguistics* 31 (3), 418–442

Lyster, R. (2007) *Learning and Teaching Languages Through Content. A Counterbalanced Approach.* Amsterdam: John Benjamins.

Lyster, R. and H. Mori (2006) Interactional feedback and instructional counterbalance. *Studies in Second Language Acquisition* 28 (2), 269–300.

Lyster, R. and Ranta, L. (1997) Corrective feedback and learner uptake: Negotiation of form in communicative classrooms. *Studies in Second Language Acquisition* 19, 37–66.

Lyster, R. and Saito, K. (2010) Oral feedback in classroom SLA. A meta-analysis. *Studies in Second Language Acquisition* 32, 265–302.

Lyster, R., Quiroga, J. and Ballinger, S. (2013) The effect of biliteracy instruction on morphological awareness. *Journal of Immersion and Content-Based Language Education* 1 (2), 169–197.

Lyster, R., Saito, K. and Sato, M. (2013) Oral corrective feedback. *Language Teaching* 46 (1), 1–40.

Merino, J.A. and Lasagabaster, D. (2015) CLIL as a way to multilingualism. *International Journal of Bilingual Education and Bilingualism,* 1–16.

Milla, R. (2017) Corrective feedback episodes in CLIL vs. EFL classrooms: Teachers' and learners' beliefs and classroom behaviour. Unpublished PhD thesis, University of the Basque Country.

Milla, R. and García Mayo, M.P. (2014) Corrective feedback episodes in oral interaction: A comparison of a CLIL and an EFL classroom. *International Journal of English Studies* 14 (1), 1–20.

Mohammed, N. (2006) An exploratory study of the interplay between the teachers' beliefs, instructional practices, and professional development. Unpublished PhD thesis, University of Auckland.

Mori, R. (2011) Teacher cognition in corrective feedback in Japan. *System* 39, 451–467.

Nikula, T., Dalton-Puffer, C. and Llinares García, A. (2013) European research on CLIL classroom discourse. *Journal of Immersion and Content-Based Language Education,* 70–100.

Ölmezer-Öztürk, E. (2019) Beliefs and practices of Turkish EFL teachers regarding oral corrective feedback: A small-scale classroom research study. *The Language Learning Journal* 47 (2), 219–228.

Pica, T. (2002) Subject-matter content: How does it assist the interactional and linguistic needs of classroom language learners? *The Modern Language Journal* 86 (1), 1–19.

Roothoft, H. (2014) The relationship between adult EFL teachers' oral feedback practices and beliefs. *System* 46, 65–79.

Roothoft, H. (2018) Teachers' beliefs about oral corrective feedback: A comparison of secondary and adult education. *Huarte de San Juan. Filología y Didáctica de la Lengua* 18, 151–176.

Samar, G.R. and Shayestefar, P. (2009) Corrective feedback in EFL classrooms: Learner negotiation strategies and uptake. *Journal of English Language Teaching and Learning* 212, 107–134.

Schulz, R.A. (1996) Focus on form in the foreign language classroom: learners' and teachers' views on error correction and the role of grammar. *Foreign Language Annals* 29, 343–364.

Schulz, R.A. (2001) Cultural differences in learner and teacher perceptions concerning the role of grammar instruction and corrective feedback. *The Modern Language Journal* 85, 244–258.

Sheen, Y. (2004) Corrective feedback and learner uptake in communicative classrooms across instructional settings. *Language Teaching Research* 8 (3), 263–300.

Spada, N. and Fröhlich, M. (1995) *COLT. Communicative Orientation of Language Teaching Observation Scheme: Coding Conventions and Applications.* Sydney, AU: National Centre for English Language Teaching and Research.

Swain, M. (1988) Manipulating and complementing content teaching to maximize second language learning. *TESL Canada Journal* 6 (1), 68–83.

Syndicate, U.C.L.E (2001) *Quick Placement Test.* Oxford: Oxford University Press.

Sylvén, L.K. (2013) CLIL in Sweden-Why does it not work? A metaperspective on CLIL across contexts in Europe. *International Journal of Bilingual Education and Bilingualism* 16 (3), 301–320.

Sylvén, L.K. (2015) CLIL and non-CLIL students' beliefs about language. *Studies in Second Language Learning and Teaching* 5 (2), 251–272.

Thompson, A.S. and Sylvén, L.K. (2015) 'Does English make you nervous?' Anxiety profiles of CLIL and non-CLIL students in Sweden. *Apples-Journal of Applied Language Studies* 9 (2), 1–23.

Yang, Y. and Lyster, R. (2010) Effects of form-focused practice and feedback on Chinese EFL learners' acquisition of regular and irregular past tense forms. *Studies in Second Language Acquisition* 32, 235–263.

Yoshida, R. (2008) Teachers' choice and learners' preference of corrective-feedback types. *Language Awareness* 17, 78–93.

Zhu, Y. and Wang, B. (2019) Investigating English language learners' beliefs about oral corrective feedback at Chinese universities: A large scale study. *Language Awareness* 28 (2), 139–161.

Appendix

Teachers' questionnaire

Dear teacher,

This questionnaire aims to find out about your beliefs and concerns regarding error feedback and grammar teaching. All your answers will be treated confidentially

1. Name: _____
2. School: _____
3. Subjects taught: _____
4. Years of teaching experience: _____
5. English level: Advanced   Very Advanced   Bilingual
   Express your opinion about the following statements:
6. When learners make errors in speaking a second language, teachers should correct them. _____

Strongly agree	Agree	Neither agree nor disagree	Disagree	Strongly disagree

7. Teachers should correct oral errors by providing learners with the correct form.

Strongly agree	Agree	Neither agree nor disagree	Disagree	Strongly disagree

8. Teachers should correct learners' oral errors by providing explanations as to why what they say is incorrect.

Strongly agree	Agree	Neither agree nor disagree	Disagree	Strongly disagree

9. Teachers should help learners to self-correct their oral errors instead of providing them with the right form.

Strongly agree	Agree	Neither agree nor disagree	Disagree	Strongly disagree

10. Teachers should allow other learners to correct oral errors.

Strongly agree	Agree	Neither agree nor disagree	Disagree	Strongly disagree

11. Teachers should correct pronunciation errors.

Strongly agree	Agree	Neither agree nor disagree	Disagree	Strongly disagree

12. Teachers should correct oral grammar errors.

Strongly agree	Agree	Neither agree nor disagree	Disagree	Strongly disagree

13. Teachers should correct oral vocabulary errors.

Strongly agree	Agree	Neither agree nor disagree	Disagree	Strongly disagree

14. Teachers should correct all oral errors.

Strongly agree	Agree	Neither agree nor disagree	Disagree	Strongly disagree

15. Learners learn more when teachers correct their oral errors.

Strongly agree	Agree	Neither agree nor disagree	Disagree	Strongly disagree

16. When learners make errors in writing, teachers should correct them.

Strongly agree	Agree	Neither agree nor disagree	Disagree	Strongly disagree

17. Teachers should correct written errors by just drawing attention to them (with a mark, underlining them…).

Strongly agree	Agree	Neither agree nor disagree	Disagree	Strongly disagree

18. Teachers should provide learners with the target form to their written errors.

Strongly agree	Agree	Neither agree nor disagree	Disagree	Strongly disagree

19. Teachers should help learners obtain the correct form for their written errors rather than giving it to them.

Strongly agree	Agree	Neither agree nor disagree	Disagree	Strongly disagree

20. Teachers should correct all written errors.

Strongly agree	Agree	Neither agree nor disagree	Disagree	Strongly disagree

21. Teachers should correct spelling or punctuation errors.

Strongly agree	Agree	Neither agree nor disagree	Disagree	Strongly disagree

22. Teachers should correct learners' written grammatical errors in writing.

Strongly agree	Agree	Neither agree nor disagree	Disagree	Strongly disagree

23. Teachers should correct written vocabulary errors.

Strongly agree	Agree	Neither agree nor disagree	Disagree	Strongly disagree

24. Learners learn more when the teacher corrects their written errors.

Strongly agree	Agree	Neither agree nor disagree	Disagree	Strongly disagree

25. The teachers of subjects taught in English should also correct language errors.

Strongly agree	Agree	Neither agree nor disagree	Disagree	Strongly disagree

26. Only the English teacher should correct language errors.

Strongly agree	Agree	Neither agree nor disagree	Disagree	Strongly disagree

27. It is more important to practice a language in real-life situations than to study and practise grammatical structures.

Strongly agree	Agree	Neither agree nor disagree	Disagree	Strongly disagree

28. Learners should keep grammar rules in mind when they write in English or read what they have written.

Strongly agree	Agree	Neither agree nor disagree	Disagree	Strongly disagree

29. There should be more formal study of grammar in English lessons.

Strongly agree	Agree	Neither agree nor disagree	Disagree	Strongly disagree

30. There should be more formal study of grammar in the lessons of the subjects taught in English.

Strongly agree	Agree	Neither agree nor disagree	Disagree	Strongly disagree

31. Studying grammar helps the learning of a foreign/language.

Strongly agree	Agree	Neither agree nor disagree	Disagree	Strongly disagree

32. Generally speaking, learners' communicative ability improves most quickly if they study and practice the grammar of a language.

Strongly agree	Agree	Neither agree nor disagree	Disagree	Strongly disagree

33. Is there anything you would like to comment about teaching grammar and/or error correction, etc.?

8 'So, after a Week, I Became a Teacher of English': Physics Lecturers' Beliefs on the Integration of Content and Language in English-Medium Higher Education

Emma Dafouz

Introduction

As a result of the internationalisation of higher education, English-medium instruction (EMI) has grown exponentially in European universities at an increase of over 1000% since the 2000s (Wächter & Maiworm, 2014). This educational change has led researchers and practitioners to revisit participant beliefs with regards to long-standing teaching and learning practices and pedagogies, now that the language of instruction is no longer the stakeholders' first language (L1).

While EMI is a widespread term, there is still much debate about how it differs from other related labels (Smit & Dafouz, 2012), such as CLIL (Content and Language Integrated Learning) or ICLHE (Integrating Content and Language in Higher Education). Put simply, EMI principally refers to the teaching and learning of an academic subject through English, very often without an explicit focus on language learning or specific language aims and is typically implemented at the tertiary level (Dafouz, 2017: 170). Given that the EMI acronym falls short of describing some of the defining features of the context (i.e. tertiary education, and the use of other languages in relation to English), the label EMEMUS or 'English-medium education in multilingual university settings' will be used hereafter (see Dafouz & Smit, 2016). The EMEMUS label addresses

133

more explicitly the multilingual nature of many higher education settings where English, together with other linguistic repertoires, are represented. Moreover, EMEMUS uses the term 'education' instead of 'instruction' to view teaching and learning as much more interactive and learner centred. In other words, EMEMUS represents more accurately and comprehensively this growing phenomenon.

In the case of Spain, where this research is based, the shift to EMEMUS has raised questions regarding the role of other national languages (e.g. Catalan or Basque) in education (Doiz *et al.*, 2013) and to what extent the quality of teaching and learning is affected in these settings (Dafouz *et al.*, 2014). As for lecturers, early studies focused on their personal views and attitudes towards such a substantial change in their teaching habits (Dafouz *et al.*, 2016). However, preliminary investigations often portrayed content lecturers, or lecturers who teach non-linguistic subjects, as a uniform and homogenous group and usually failed to examine possible disciplinary differences in their conceptualisation of language-related issues.

In view of this gap, this paper sets out to explore the psychological beliefs on the integration of content and language of a concrete set of professionals, in this case physics lecturers, who have largely been under-researched in the literature (but see Airey, 2012). Two main reasons guide the choice of participants. First, the focus is on a disciplinary area, physics, which according to European surveys (see e.g. Wächter & Maiworm, 2014) is less prone to EMEMUS, even though English is known to be the language of research and science. In this respect, Kuteeva and Airey (2014: 534) noted that '[a]lthough the impact of disciplinary differences on teaching and learning has been widely discussed in educational research …, little research has explored this issue in relation to English-medium instruction in Europe'. Second, in the institutional context where this research is based, science degrees have not usually taken the lead in the implementation of EMEMUS programmes. In addition to these disciplinary reasons, by choosing in-service lecturers rather than pre-service, a research gap is filled. As noticed in the literature, much of the work on teachers' psychological beliefs focuses on pre-service professionals, while in-service lecturers 'are a vitally important population to understand in terms of their unique psychological situations and the specific challenges they face' (Mercer & Kostoulas, 2018: 6).

Structurally, the chapter will unfold as follows: first, the theoretical anchoring will be explained by examining different perspectives on content and language integration and then by focusing more specifically on teacher beliefs and the role of disciplinary culture in the construction of such beliefs; second, the methods and dataset used in this study will be described and third, the findings will be discussed. The chapter will conclude with reference to pedagogical implications for teacher education programmes and directions for future research.

Theoretical Anchoring

Different perspectives on the integration of content and language

Integration is a 'shared concern for all forms of education that have simultaneous content and language learning objectives' (Nikula *et al.*, 2016: 1). Nevertheless, language and content have been on the agenda of educationalists, sociologists and linguists for decades. More recently, the advent of EMEMUS and other approaches to education where an L2 is used as medium of instruction (e.g. bilingual education, immersion programmes, content-based instruction and CLIL) have triggered enormous interest in the effectiveness of the integration of content and language.

Drawing principally on the work produced by the ConCLIL project,[1] three different perspectives have been adopted to approach the integration of content and language, and are briefly described in the following lines.

The first perspective conceptualises integration from the point of view of curriculum and pedagogy planning. It is concerned, therefore, with the institutional level of planning curricula and pedagogies where decisions are made regarding what will be integrated and how this will be done. Typically, curricula are documents containing learning goals that include what learners should know at the end of the year, term or degree and usually describe how the goals should be achieved. The onset of EMEMUS (but most particularly CLIL in primary and secondary education), have somewhat challenged the strict separation of content and language subjects and advocated an 'integrated curriculum' where 'the linguistic nature of subjects or the subjects as represented in language are more visible' (Nikula *et al.*, 2016: 10). Given, the traditional

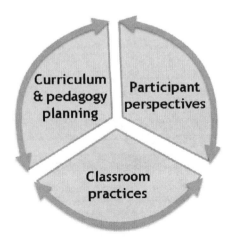

Figure 8.1 Three perspectives on integration (Nikula *et al.*, 2016: 9)

design of curricular and pedagogical planning in most countries and institutions, truly integrated curricula are still hard to find (but see Lorenzo, 2013). In university settings more specifically, streamlining a dense curriculum and the use of accessible models to guide content lecturers to make sense of content and language integration, are two of the main needs most frequently mentioned. The results section will revisit these issues in the light of our findings.

The second perspective views integration from the participant side, that is, the side connected to stakeholder perceptions and beliefs, whether explicit or implicit, of integration in content learning. As this study has taken the stakeholder perspective as an entry point to the notion of integration, I will address this matter in more detail later when referring to teacher beliefs.

The third perspective describes integration from the view of classroom practices. In other words, it focuses on the local level where classroom practices implement *in situ* language and content integration. The way teachers integrate content and language in their actual classroom discourse, or how materials are scaffolded to accommodate to disciplinary and language difficulties are some of the issues dealt within this perspective. In CLIL settings, and also EMEMUS, considerable attention has been paid to the ways in which lecturers can make their language more salient and thus support students in their understanding of complex lectures, lengthy texts or subject-specific language. Also, given that classroom discourse can be understood as a co-constructed accomplishment by lectures and students (Dafouz & Smit, 2016), it is of interest to explore integration from the point of view of interaction. In this respect, attention to the performance of specific academic discourse functions (e.g. explaining, defining, etc.) or the use of the participants' L1 in the classroom (i.e. translanguaging) to scaffold content learning attracts interest too. Finally, assessment deserves serious consideration in the integration of content and language at the classroom level, as very often university lecturers, not being language experts themselves, complain that they cannot (and/or wish not to) attend to language issues when evaluating student performance (Aguilar, 2017). Generally speaking, therefore, much research concludes that lecturers, who are L2 users themselves, do not systematically 'make subject-relevant language use a salient focus' (Nikula *et al.*, 2016: 19). In light of this, it is thus a major objective of teacher educational programmes in EMEMUS to address such issues in an explicit and systematic manner (Dafouz, 2018).

Despite this tripartite classification, integration is a 'truly multidimensional phenomenon' (Nikula *et al*, 2016: 3) and thus, the three-fold distinction, while enabling us to address this complex notion in an orderly manner, inevitably cuts across all three perspectives. The focus on the participant view somewhat bridges the gap between all three perspectives, since the way individuals perceive the integration of content and language is 'an important mediating phase between content and language integration as articulated in curricula, pedagogical plans and guidelines, on the one hand, and, as translated into pedagogical practice, on the other hand' (Nikula *et al.*, 2016: 14).

Teacher beliefs on content and language integration: The notion of self-efficacy

Even though there might not be a direct *causal* relationship between teacher beliefs and action, beliefs are thought to greatly influence classroom practice and, most importantly, to play a major role in supporting or hindering change in teacher learning and development (Mercer & Kostoulas, 2018; see also Chapters 5, 6 & 7). Conceptually, beliefs can be defined as a complex set of psychological variables based on attitudes, experiences and expectations. Borg (2001: 186) describes a belief as a 'proposition which may be consciously or unconsciously held, … evaluative in that it is accepted as true by the individual, and therefore imbued with emotive commitment; further, it serves as a guide to thought and behaviour'. At the same time, beliefs can be understood as 'dynamic and emergent, socially constructed and contextually situated, experiential, mediated, paradoxical and contradictory' (Kalaja & Barcelos, 2003: 232–233).

In EMEMUS contexts, where an L2 is used as instructional tool, research has brought to consciousness the need to attend to 'language work' in content subjects (Nikula *et al*, 2016). In other words, in addition to knowledge of language in their respective content areas, teachers also need to apply this knowledge in the planning stages as well as actively engage students in exploring language and content. This concern is strongly dependent on the notion of self-efficacy, that is, the positive self-belief in one's own competence to successfully achieve a particular task (Bandura, 2008; see also Chapters 11, 12 & 15). In the case of lecturers who often do not teach through their L1, self-efficacy is even more important as these professionals are not always believed to have threshold levels of English proficiency (Tsui, 2018). Thus, self-efficacy is closely related 'to the amount of efforts teachers are willing to invest, the expectations they hold, and their perseverance against setbacks' (Tsui, 2018: 106). Extensive research on self-efficacy has explored how teachers perceive their sense of efficacy when exposed to new teaching and learning situations (e.g. Hoy & Spero, 2005; Wyatt, 2016), generally concluding that teachers with a strong sense of efficacy tend to be 'more open to new ideas and innovations, more willing to experiment with new teaching methods, [and] better in meeting the needs of their students' (Blonder *et al.*, 2014: 8).

Work by Bandura (1997, 2008) identified four different ways to develop self-efficacy. The first and arguably most effective one is mastery of experiences. Although experiencing success boosts self-efficacy, undergoing failure contributes to its strengthening by means of learning how to overcome difficulties through effort and resilience. The second way of building self-efficacy involves social modelling. By observing people considered to be similar to ourselves succeed in their endeavours, our conception of self-efficacy is also heightened. Third, social persuasion suggests that being induced to believe in ourselves by people who are influential in our lives encourages sustained self-improvement. Finally, our physical and emotional states will also impact our sense of efficacy and thus this impact will be positive if an effort is put into reducing anxiety and turning negatives beliefs into constructive ones. Accordingly, examining teachers' perceptions of their self-efficacy in EMEMUS and their beliefs on language and content integration will provide critical insights that will help us to support other lecturers and design language-sensitive teacher education programmes.

Disciplinary cultures and integration: The case of physics

As argued earlier, differences in lecturers' beliefs across disciplines can be interpreted as evidence of existing disciplinary cultures. Each discipline has its own set of characteristics and qualities which are not solely epistemological, but also the product of cultural phenomena, embodied in collections of like-minded people, each with their own codes of conduct, sets of values and distinctive intellectual tasks (Becher, 1987). Disciplinary cultures thus can be described as the common set of assumptions, attitudes, conceptualisations, epistemologies and values held by members of a specific discipline (see also Chapters 3, 5 & 11).

Educational research has claimed for decades that students often do not appropriately understand the disciplinary language that they are exposed to, for instance, in lectures and that they later need to use themselves (Neumann & Becher, 2002). Thus, analysing the causes of problems in students' understanding, with a view towards making the discourse of the disciplines more accessible and transparent, is paramount.

In physics, even without the added complication of an L2, language issues 'may be particularly acute due to the experienced complexity and abstractness inherent in learning science' (Airey, 2009: 27). Bernstein (1999, quoted in Airey, 2012: 69) 'singled out physics as the discipline with the most hierarchical knowledge structure', this means that it 'develops by adding more and more phenomena into the same explanatory system'. Learning physics then strongly depends on mastering previous levels or layers of knowledge. From an EMEMUS perspective, Airey (2012: 73) argues that 'moving between languages may entail loss of precision – terms may not exist or have slightly different meanings in another language' thus the paramount importance of using physics terms in an accurate and precise way.

In this regard, if by examining physics teachers' beliefs in EMEMUS we are able to identify specific literacy practices, then lecturers' could elaborate more language-sensitive pedagogies, and students, in turn, could develop the ability to participate successfully in the communicative practices of the discipline (Kuteeva & Airey, 2014). The following sections will describe how teacher beliefs were investigated in the dataset and the resulting findings.

Methodology

Research context

This study reports on aspects of a larger research project, which focuses on the role of the English language in the internationalisation process of Spanish Higher Education.[2] The onset of English-medium education in Spanish universities dates back to the turn of the millennium when top-down policies such as the European Higher Education Area (EHEA) paved the way to the use of English as a means to favour student and staff mobility across member states (Smit & Dafouz, 2012). In the large state-run university where this study is based, engaging in these English-taught programmes is voluntary for teachers and students alike. Thus, following other pioneering degrees (e.g. Business Studies, Education, Computer Science or Psychology), the Faculty of Physical Sciences opened one English-taught group in 2018 in parallel to three Spanish-taught cohorts as a means to promote international skills amongst regional students and gradually attract international learners in the coming years.

Participants and data collection

The dataset used in this study consist of a carefully selected focus group of four in-service physics content lecturers with Spanish as their first language (L1) and English as their second language (L2). All four lecturers have experience teaching their respective courses in the physics degree programme through their L1. At the time of the focus group, they had just completed teaching equivalent courses through English. More specifically, the courses under scrutiny were Computer Science Laboratory, Physics Foundations I, Mathematics and Chemistry, which were all compulsory courses in the first year of the physics degree. These courses were purposefully chosen to ensure that for all four lecturers this was their first-time teaching through English[3] (see Table 8.1 for a summary of the dataset).

As required by the institution's language policy, the four lecturers had certified their level of English proficiency (C1 level, CEFR) and the students had certified a B2 level (CEFR) upon enrolling in the English group offered in the degree programme.

Table 8.1 Description of participants and their teaching experience

Lecturers	Subject taught	Year and degree	Teaching experience in Physics degree	
			in Spanish	in English
V (female) >40 years old	Computer Science Laboratory	Year 1 – Degree in Physics	2 years	1 year
C (male) >40 years old	Physics Foundations I	Year 1 – Degree in Physics	5 years	1 year
G (male) >50 years old	Mathematics	Year 1 – Degree in Physics	around 30 years	1 year
F (male) ≤ 40 years old	Chemistry	Year 1 – Degree in Physics	3 years	1 year

For the focus group, which took place in February 2019, a protocol consisting of 20 questions was designed to guide a semi-structured interview with the participants. The questions first addressed lecturers' personal teaching backgrounds and aimed at creating a relaxed atmosphere. Drawing on previous work conducted on teacher beliefs (see Dafouz *et al.*, 2016), another set of questions on participants' views and experiences on teaching and learning in English-medium education followed, together with specific queries on the integration of content and language in their respective subjects. The focus group was planned to allow for a flexible question order to favour interaction. The focus group was conducted in the lecturers' L1, that is Spanish, to facilitate communication and make the situation more comfortable since, except for two of the lecturers who had met the researcher before in a teacher education course, it was the participants' first encounter.

Research approach and data analysis

A focus group interview, that is, a 'carefully planned discussion designed to obtain perceptions on a defined area of interest in a permissive non-threatening environment' (Krueger, 1994: 6), was selected as the most appropriate qualitative research tool for analysis. Generally speaking, focus groups facilitate the exploration of complex issues as seen from a variety of perspectives derived from participants' own experiences and conceptualisations of a phenomenon. In addition, they generate a large amount of data quickly, at less cost than individual interviews and with the advantage of triggering interactive group dynamics and meaningful discussion among participants. At the same, they allow immediate opportunities for clarification, follow-up questions and probing responses (Krueger, 1994). The qualitative data gathered was inductive and naturalistic as it was directly recorded and videotaped, after informed consent was granted by the participants. Initially, the audio and video recordings were carefully examined independently by the author of the chapter and another member of the research team. Intensive and close listening led to a focus on details and the subsequent identification of major emerging themes. Such themes were listed by each researcher individually and then examined together. Teacher comments were transcribed over the next weeks in the language of the focus group (i.e. Spanish) and translation into English was undertaken by the researcher when extracts were finally chosen to illustrate participants' beliefs. The data in Spanish were analysed following content analysis, a highly flexible research methodology that enables 'making inferences based on quantified analysis of recurring, easily identifiable aspects of text content' (White & Marsh, 2006: 23). As typical of content analysis, the final list of themes was based on their recurrent presence in teachers' responses (see Lichtman, 2013) and their pertinence with respect to the focus of this study[4], namely physics teachers' beliefs on the integration of content and language in EMEMUS and self-efficacy.

Results and Discussion: Teacher Beliefs on Content and Language Integration

As the development of the focus group turned out to be very dynamic and highly participatory in addition to the original 20 questions mentioned earlier, other questions were asked on the fly to elicit further details of these lecturers' views and beliefs. In order to adjust to the scope of this study, and bearing in mind the aforementioned criteria of recurrence and pertinence, lecturers' comments have been grouped into the three perspectives of integration displayed in the theoretical framework, namely participant perspectives, classroom practices and curriculum and pedagogy planning (see Figure 8.1). The next subsections will discuss these perspectives in detail.

Participant perspectives

From the opinions expressed by our physics lecturers, it can be inferred that their views of EMEMUS, and more specifically, of the roles that language plays in these settings, were clearly presented. To begin with, they immediately reported that an explicit focus on disciplinary language was decisive to cater for their students' needs. In this regard, lecturers collectively commented that the use of English as the language of instruction had foregrounded that these first-year leaners were *novice* to both the disciplinary content and the subject-specific language, as Extract 1 shows:

Extract 1: Lecturer G

The fundamental problem is that they [students] don't know a single mathematical word in English. And that's a serious problem. **English** prepositions for all of us who are not natives are hell, but in mathematics they are a minefield because each one means one thing and does not mean another. So, after a week, I became a teacher of English. As I entered the classroom, I would put 'English for Maths' on the blackboard and I would give them an explanation of the terms we were going to use in that lesson.

The first year at university is crucial in students' acculturation process, as together with the aforementioned difficulties in understanding and using technical vocabulary and comprehending dense lectures, learners also need to meet institutional and disciplinary requirements, which are often not explicitly stated (see Evans & Morrison, 2011). Interestingly, our lecturers also admitted that language concerns were arguably not so evident when teaching their subjects in Spanish as the L1. Lecturer V, for instance, commented that she 'hadn't noticed this problem so much when teaching the Spanish group' and lecturer F, added that 'this was probably happening in all the classes but the fact that English was used simply made it more patent'.

Similarly, research by Cammarata and Tedick (2012: 257) in immersion contexts describes these views as a process of awakening that takes teachers from initially identifying themselves as content experts to ultimately envisioning themselves as partly responsible for teaching the language of their discipline. In this respect, when directly asked during the focus group if they viewed themselves as teachers of English, lecturers unanimously answered 'no' but, concurrently, provided many examples of their multifaceted psychological views of the roles of English in their teaching practices, as Extract 2 below unfolds:

Extract 2: Lecturer C

I've learned a lot of English from my field by having to prepare for class. Because when you speak English, either you are speaking English with a foreigner in a trivial, everyday conversation or you are speaking scientific English in a congress, which is a very closed world. Here [in an EME lesson] **you are between the two worlds and that has forced me to make a great effort.**

In this extract, the lecturer comments on the 'great effort' made to identify the specific linguistic features needed to teach physics in English and to use the appropriate register when addressing novice learners. In other words, the teacher verbalises the necessity to strike a balance between the use of high-stake scientific language required in conference papers and the informal English used in everyday communicative exchanges with 'a foreigner'. It is precisely this intermediate register, this specific classroom discourse, which the teacher describes as situated 'between the two worlds', the one he had to develop more specifically.

However, in the following line, it seems that such initial effort proved successful as the lecturer's interpretation of his own learning experience of classroom English for physics is seen in a positive light ('I have learned a lot of English from my field'). Such positive rendering of his mastery of experience, in Bandura's (2008) terms, seems to have reinforced his perceived self-efficacy to teach in EMEMUS; particularly now that his English language abilities have extended to include other contexts of use and have increased his confidence too.

The next section will examine lecturers' classroom practices and their integration of content and language issues.

(Reported) classroom practices

This section has been called '(reported) classroom practices' as the use of a focus group as a data gathering instrument only allowed the researcher to rely on what the lecturers *said* they did in their classrooms rather than on what they actually did in such settings. The observation of the actual practices reported by the lecturers interviewed is to be followed up in a future study by the research team.

As commented earlier, the change in the language of education was reported to trigger additional teaching roles that, in turn, called for a number of pedagogical adaptations in the classroom, such as more repetition of key terms, slowing down the lecturing pace, use of the blackboard to spell out or write down disciplinary language and the design of bilingual glossaries. Most of these adaptations are linked to our teachers' understanding that these first-year students need very specific conceptual support but also disciplinary language scaffolding to develop complex disciplinary knowledge:

Extract 3: Lecturer C

Scientific-technical language is very precise. And students lack this language.

Extract 4: Lecturer G

The problem is not that they [the students] don't know the mathematical terminology they have to learn. It's just that since they've never heard math in English, they have no idea [...] Ordinary language is much more tolerable to inaccuracies, but it is not so in mathematics. In mathematics an *in, on, off* or *if* changes and the exercise is wrong because it means a completely different thing.

With regards to disciplinary language, all fours lecturers agreed that terminological accuracy is an inherent feature of the sciences, but the mathematics teacher insisted that this is even more particular of this discipline. Correspondingly, teaching practices were reported to be accommodated to develop students' terminology. Such adaptations included, for instance, slowing down the lecturing pace, providing a higher number of illustrations and examples to support their explanations or uploading permanent online materials for student consultation. In addition, domain-specific language challenges often translated into teachers investing more time in covering the stipulated syllabus. As a result, all four lecturers found themselves at the crossroads of needing more time to teach in English and, at the same time, having to cover a vast amount of disciplinary matter. As participant C put it:

Extract 5: Lecturer C

In terms of classroom dynamics, the size of the group was the same as I've always had, so it doesn't make any difference, but there is a big difference. **I am not a native speaker of English, then I can't speak at the same speed in Spanish as I can in English.** But also, if I go at my maximum speed, **I know that there is a third of them** [the students] **that do not follow me.** That is important because our courses **have an extremely extensive syllabus. So, if I slow down, I can't cover it.**

Extract 5 describes a situation which is frequently found in English-medium courses, namely, speech rate reduction. Interestingly, lecturer C initially mentions his non-native speaker condition to explain why he cannot speak faster in English and cover more content. However, immediately after he claims that a slower lecturing pace can benefit students who may have more comprehension problems. In other words, this example shows how self-efficacy may decline when our content teachers feel less secure, particularly in their oral production when their non-nativeness may be more visible. In this regard, Tsui (2018: 113) argues that in English-medium settings, if teachers are thought not to be fluent in English by their learners, their 'content expertise might be questioned as well'. Nevertheless, this extract also shows how mastery of experience is essential to regain one's confidence. Thus, our lecturer, instead of focusing on his self-perceived weaknesses (e.g. speaking more slowly), underscores instead the pedagogical value of talking more slowly as a means to enhance students' learning.

Along similar lines, translanguaging, i.e. the use of the L1 to alleviate and scaffold students' difficulties with disciplinary and linguistic competence (García & Wei, 2014), is rendered as another pedagogical strategy used by our interviewees. Although all four teachers reported to invite students to switch languages when conceptual difficulties arose and/or when English prevented them from communicating (see Extract 6 below), lecturers V and C claimed that, as a general rule, their students did not resort to Spanish. The mathematics teacher (Lecturer G), in contrast, openly encouraged translanguaging practices in his classroom:

Extract 6: Lecturer G

I've had to adapt a lot of material and, moreover, I explained and encouraged them [the students], and they did it continuously, to ask me in the middle of class in Spanish how to say that in English. Their communicative competence in scientific English was terrible.

While the reasons for this are not totally clear, it could be argued that this lecturer's encouragement of student questions in Spanish helped to prevent conceptual confusion and the accurate use of mathematical terminology. Even though recent research views on translanguaging have portrayed this as a pedagogical strategy to scaffold student learning in multilingual settings (see also Chapters 3, 6, & 9), many practising teachers may still perceive this as a sign of low teaching self-efficacy (Dafouz et al., 2016). Teacher F described his view in the following terms:

Extract 7: Lecturer F

I don't use Spanish with my students, although sometimes I feel that it would save lots of time. I mean, concepts need to be explained more slowly in English but if I switch to Spanish then how can I guarantee that students will switch back to English again?

This extract is particularly revealing as lecturer F confesses avoiding translanguaging practices mainly to ensure efficient classroom management. In other words, his concerns are not principally linked to students questioning his English language abilities or his possible need to resort to Spanish to streamline explanations. Rather, the lecturer is reflecting on his capacity to retain English as the language of instruction throughout the course. Self-efficacy here could be more closely connected to teaching experience than to language competence. As lecturer F is the youngest of the four interviewees and the least experienced (see Table 8.1), it could be argued that he cannot rely on prior teaching experience to minimise the anxiety and self-consciousness associated with first-time exposure to EMEMUS. In this vein, the study by Tsui (2018) on teacher self-efficacy in English-medium settings in Taiwan recommends encouraging senior faculty to take the lead in this type of educational contexts so that teaching experience and pedagogical knowledge can counteract possible lower levels of self-efficacy on the part of more inexperienced faculty.

Curriculum and pedagogy planning

With regards to prospective planning, our lecturers agreed that two main factors were to be taken into account when (re)designing the curriculum and pedagogies to be used in their EMEMUS groups:

(1) the heterogeneity of students' proficiency in English and (2) the need to follow parallel study plans in Spanish and English.

In terms of English proficiency, teachers disagreed when it came to evaluating their students' English levels. While two lecturers (V and F) claimed that their students' proficiency levels seemed to have impinged negatively upon the learning process, the other two lecturers (C and G) were more surprised by the heterogeneity in their students' linguistic competence. These two teachers affirmed that students' mixed language levels had limited some of their teaching practices by having to slow down the pace of their teaching and, thus, reduce syllabus coverage. Interestingly, and despite teachers sharing the same cohort of learners, very different perceptions about students' English proficiency emerged. After extended discussion, the lecturers' final conclusion pointed to the importance of students' learning and using subject-specific language, rather than, or in addition to, general English. As described by the participants:

Extract 8: Lecturer F

Some [students] come into university having studied Chemistry in upper high school and that's very advantageous when compared to those [students] who have not.

Extract 9: Lecturer C

I have a kind of a leeway in the sense that some of our subjects are supposed to have been seen, at a lower level, in the second year of high school. **In the case of General Physics. it is much worse because there are years when 40 or 50% of the students in the class have never studied Physics, not even in Spanish.**

From these two comments, it could be argued that while perceived low English competence may impact students' understanding of the content matter negatively, some previous exposure to the discipline, even in the L1, is generally viewed by the lecturers as an asset. Derived from this comes the thought of whether the B2 level (CEFR) commonly required as threshold for students to enrol in EME is actually an accurate indicator of what they really need to successfully engage in the learning of an academic discipline in a L2. It may be the case that general language proficiency should also be supplemented with notions of domain-specific language or at least certain academic skills and discourse. This type of language, however, is not usually covered in the general English courses offered in lower levels of education, nor included in most of the accreditation exams that students take. Thus, questions regarding the *real* language needs of students joining EMEMUS programmes require further investigation.

The second point raised in curriculum planning was the requirement for all student groups to follow a parallel curriculum in Spanish and English. As dictated by the programme, students need to comply with the same study plans to guarantee that there is no loss of content nor quality in the groups taught through English. This situation entails that identical content (sometimes even worksheets and handouts) and, most importantly, exams be designed in the Spanish and English strands by the content teachers involved, as this quotation reflects:

Extract 10: Lecturer C

In the case of physics, **coordination [among Spanish and English strands] is 100%.** It means that, for example, the worksheets are the same in all groups, and there are a series of exercises that have to be done compulsory by all groups [Spanish and English].

Two implications stem from this parallel curriculum policy. First, EMEMUS teachers, at least in this specific university setting, need to invest considerable amounts of time and effort translating and adapting documents and materials into English.[5] Nevertheless, such initial effort pays off as lecturers in this institution have a reduced teaching load so that more time can be invested in materials development and classroom preparation. Moreover, first-year struggles usually wear off in the subsequent years as teachers gradually gain more experience, increase their confidence, capitalise on the time invested planning and adapting materials and ultimately, enhance their international profile (for discussions on this last point see Dafouz, 2018). Second, our teachers' concern with parallel content coverage (English and Spanish) has led them to find useful pedagogical strategies to maximise their lecturing time and to scaffold students' learning process. In this regard, one of the most interesting comments that emerged from the group discussion was lecturer C's explicit reference to the need to use classroom discourse in a more effective way, as Extract 11 summarises:

Extract 11: Lecturer C

There are concepts that are always difficult to explain and even more so in English. There have been topics in a class that would normally take me 20 minutes to cover in Spanish and that I have planned and thought over **for two long days when preparing for the English group** [...]. **In Physics, discourse has to be connected as much as you can with everyday life. It took me twice as long to prepare this subject in English** and I've been teaching it for years! 60% of the reasons is connected to the need to translate a huge amount of material, and 40% is because **I had to think about how to connect and deliver my speech.** [...] **I had to find** a narrative.

This concrete reference to the use of narratives to explain complex content was quite revealing. Although storytelling or narratives are a common discursive technique traditionally embraced by the humanities, in the sciences this type of discourse has been less developed. Pedagogically, narratives seemed to fulfil a three-fold function. First, they facilitate teachers' comprehensive and orderly delivery of disciplinary content, providing lecturers with a discourse sequence of context-dependent events with enough power to hold learners' attention and engage them with complex content (Dahlstrom, 2014). Second, narratives favour the creation of a memorable context for students to anchor new knowledge and make the relevant connections between new and old information that ultimately ease understanding (Easton, 2016). Additionally, narratives may provide an effective added valued to the more traditional logical-scientific way of teaching science (Dahlstrom, 2014).

While only the physics teacher, lecturer C, overtly verbalised the possibility of using narratives as a way to structure his classes more effectively and ultimately speed up lecture preparation, the chemistry teacher, lecturer F, briefly agreed on considering this possibility. In contrast, lecturers G and V, the mathematics and the computer science teacher respectively, commented that their subjects were different and thus narratives were arguably not so relevant. The conclusion section will revisit these reflections when discussing the practical implications for teacher professional development programmes.

Towards the end of the group discussion, lecturer G reinforced the need to put aside time to truly integrate language issues in his subject course so that his students' outcomes were more successful, now that specific language difficulties had been identified. Such a psychological view is fitting with teachers that show a strong sense of self-efficacy since research suggests that these professionals tend to be more organised and generally plan better than those without such a strong sense (Blonder et al., 2014). Extract 12 summarises this teacher's planning strategy to reduce effort and enhance student learning:

Extract 12: Lecturer G

In September **I'm going to 'sacrifice' an entire week to give them a crash course on English math (...) It's going to save me a lot of time and effort.** In fact, I have already prepared it because I have witnessed the linguistic obstacles of my students this year.

Conclusions

The results of this exploratory study of in-service physics lecturers' beliefs on the integration of content and language suggest that these professionals are aware of the multifaceted roles that language plays in their teaching and learning. In this regard, lecturers claimed to have employed certain scaffolding strategies in their classroom strategies, such as slowing down their lecturing pace, using more visuals (graphs and diagrams), practical examples, bilingual glossaries and offering permanent online materials to support novice learners. Additionally, the use of translanguaging as a pedagogical strategy to assist students in alleviating their anxiety when faced with a complex term or a conceptual difficulty in the L2 was also mentioned, especially in the case of the mathematics teacher interviewed.

In terms of curricular and pedagogical planning, all four lecturers agreed that, in spite of having certified a B2 English level upon university entrance, students' mixed ability made teaching more complex. Concurrently, they argued that some previous exposure to the content subject (for example in lower levels of education) had a more positive effect on students' academic performance than higher levels of general English proficiency. It was also suggested that students generally lacked subject-specific language in English to follow the explanations and to resolve problems adequately and that this was something absolutely vital in the physics degree programme and most specifically in the mathematics course (see also Airey, 2012: 75 on this particular point). The hierarchical structure of physics and its accurate and unequivocal terminology also needs to be taken into consideration. Additionally, lecturers commented on the pressure to follow parallel curricula in the Spanish and English strands and consequently their need to maximise their lecturing time to cover the content. In this regard, the physics teacher explicitly proposed the use of narratives as a way to organise classroom discourse and deliver complex disciplinary content more efficiently. By doing this, he claimed to attract students' attention, alleviate their cognitive load and enable them to remember more easily lengthy scientific explanations. While the efficacy of narratives needs to be further explored in this specific research context, such a discursive strategy could indeed be introduced in the custom-made teacher education programmes currently offered at our institution.

As for the use of a focus group, our interviewees remarked that this method had enabled them to tap into certain psychological beliefs and pedagogical concerns that they had not formulated 'out loud before' (Lecturer V). They also observed that it had somewhat 'lifted' them from their in-service disciplinary expert perspective and allowed them to reflect on the rules governing the disciplinary discourse of physics – something that 'they had not reflected upon previously in a conscious way' (Lecturer F).

Implications for Policy and Practice

From a teacher education perspective, providing lecturers with explicit support for EMEMUS can be decisive in determining their chances for building a strong sense of confidence and self-efficacy (see also Chapters 10, 11, 12 & 15). This support, as stated earlier, is vital not only for pre-service teachers, but possibly even more so for in-service professionals, like the ones examined here, as they need to adapt their long-standing teaching practices and psychological beliefs to new realities that may demand different skills and competences. Thus, providing content learning with enhanced and disciplinary specific language attention could go a long way if the language needs and language uses of the different areas were identifiable by the professionals directly involved.

Further research clearly needs to enlarge the dataset and include other disciplines in addition to physics, as well as complement the focus group experience with actual classroom observations. It would be interesting, as well, to investigate whether senior staff, which entails more experience (but in some settings also lower levels of English proficiency), is perceived as more competent pedagogically speaking by EMEMUS students, than junior staff, with lower levels of teaching experience, yet often higher levels of English proficiency. Finally, lecturer psychological beliefs could be compared with student perceptions to identify differences and/or similarities in their views of the integration of content and language in EMEMUS.

Acknowledgements

I would like to thank the lecturers that participated in the focus group without whom the study could not have seen the light. This work is part of the larger research project titled 'The Role of English in the Internationalization of Spanish Higher Education' (Ref. 940940) based at Complutense University of Madrid. A special thanks also goes to Davinia Sánchez García for her assistance during data collection and data transcription of the focus groups. Finally, I thank too the editors and the anonymous reviewers for their constructive comments on earlier drafts of this paper.

Notes

(1) The ConCLIL project (2011–14), led by Tarja Nikula, sought to conceptualise Content and Language Integrated Learning (CLIL) with the collaboration of an international group of scholars from different countries and academic backgrounds.
(2) The project is titled 'The Role of English in the Internationalization of Spanish Higher Education' and is based at Complutense University of Madrid, Spain (see https://clue-project.weebly.com/).
(3) While lecturer G had taught through English for 10 years at a US university, this was also his first-time teaching through English at the current institution.
(4) Another major topic that emerged in the discussion group and was not included in this chapter for reasons of scope and space was institutional policies on teacher language requirements and incentives.
(5) The exception to this rule was the mathematics lecturer who explained that he was using a US textbook as instructional material and that most of the exercises and handouts used in class were taken from this book.

References

Aguilar, M. (2017) Engineering lecturers' views on CLIL and EMI. *International Journal of Bilingual Education and Bilingualism* 20 (6), 722–735.

Airey, J. (2009) Science, language, and literacy: Case studies of learning in Swedish university physics. Acta Universitatis. Uppsala Dissertations from the Faculty of Science and Technology, 81, Uppsala.

Airey, J. (2012) 'I don't teach language': The linguistic attitudes of physics lecturers in Sweden. In U. Smit and E. Dafouz (2012) (eds) Integrating content and language in higher education: Gaining insights into English-medium instruction at European universities. *AILA Review* 25, 64–79.

Bandura, A. (1997) *Self-efficacy. The Exercise of Control.* New York, NY: Freeman.

Bandura, A. (2008) On the functional properties of perceived self-efficacy revisited. In H.W. Marsh, R.G. Craven and D.M. McInerney (eds) *Self-processes, Learning, and Enabling Human Potential* (pp. 15–49). Greenwich, CT: Information Age.

Becher, T. (1987) Disciplinary discourse. *Studies in Higher Education* 12 (3), 261–274.

Bernstein, M. (1999) Vertical and horizontal discourse: An essay. *British Journal of Sociology Education* 20, 157–173.

Blonder, R., Benny, N. and Jones M.G. (2014) Teaching self-efficacy of science teachers. In R. Evans, J. Luft and C. Czerniak (eds) *The Role of Science Teachers' Beliefs in International Classrooms: From Teacher Actions to Student Learning* (pp. 3–15). Rotterdam: Sense Publishers.

Borg, M. (2001) Self-perception in ELT teachers' beliefs. *ELT Journal* 53 (2), 186–188.

Cammarata, L. and Tedick, D. (2012) Balancing content and language in instruction: The experience of immersion teachers. *Modern Language Journal* 96 (2), 251–269.

Dafouz, E. (2017) English-medium instruction in multilingual university settings: An Opportunity for Language Development. In P. Garret and J.M. Cots (eds) *The Routledge Handbook of Language Awareness* (pp. 170–185). New York, NY: Routledge.

Dafouz, E. (2018) English-medium instruction and teacher education programmes in higher education: Ideological forces and imagined identities at work. *International Journal of Bilingual Education and Bilingualism* 21 (5), 540–552.

Dafouz, E. and Smit, U. (2016) Towards a dynamic conceptual framework for English-medium education in multilingual university settings. *Applied Linguistics* 37 (3), 397–415.

Dafouz, E., Camacho, M. and Urquía, E. (2014) 'Surely they can't do as well': A comparison of business students' academic performance in English-medium and Spanish-as-first-language-medium programmes. *Language and Education* 28 (3), 223–236.

Dafouz, E., Huettner, J. and Smit, U. (2016) University teachers' beliefs of language and content integration in English-medium education in multilingual university settings. In T. Nikula, E. Dafouz, P. Moore and U. Smit (eds) *Conceptualising Integration in CLIL and Multilingual Education* (pp. 123–144). Bristol: Multilingual Matters.

Dahlstrom, M.F. (2014) Using narratives and storytelling to communicate science with nonexpert audiences. *Proceedings of the National Academy of Sciences* 111 (Supplement 4), 13614–13620.

Doiz, A., Lasagabaster, D. and Sierra, J.M. (eds) (2013) *English-Medium Instruction at Universities: Global Challenges.* Bristol: Multilingual Matters.

Easton, G. (2016) How medical teachers use narratives in lectures: A qualitative study. *BMC Medical Education* 16 (3). DOI: 10.1186/s12909-015-0498-8.

Evans, S. and Morrison, B. (2011) The student experience of English-medium higher education in Hong Kong, *Language and Education* 25 (2), 147–162.

García, O. and Wei, L. (2014) *Translanguaging: Language, Bilingualism and Education.* New York, NY: Palgrave Macmillan.

Hoy, A.W. and Spero, R.B. (2005) Changes in teacher efficacy during the early years of teaching: A comparison of four measures. *Teaching and Teacher Education* 21, 343–356.

Kalaja, P. and Barcelos, A.M. (eds) (2003) *Beliefs about SLA: New Research Approaches.* Dordrecht: Kluwer Academic Press.

Krueger, R.A. (1994) *Focus Groups: A Practical Guide for Applied Research.* London: SAGE Publications Ltd.

Kuteeva, M. and Airey, J. (2014) Disciplinary differences in the use of English in higher education: Reflections on recent language policy developments. *Higher Education* 67 (5), 533–549.

Lichtman, M. (2013) *Qualitative Research in Education.* Thousand Oaks, CA: Sage.

Lorenzo, F. (2013) Genre-based curricula: Multilingual academic literacy in content and language integrated learning. *International Journal of Bilingual Education and Bilingualism* 16 (3), 375–388.

Mercer, S. and Kostoulas, A. (2018) *Language Teacher Psychology.* Bristol: Multilingual Matters.

Nikula, T., Dalton-Puffer, C., Llinares, A. and Lorenzo, F. (2016) More than content and language: The complexity of integration in CLIL and bilingual education. In T. Nikula, E. Dafouz, P. Moore and U. Smit (eds) *Conceptualising Integration in CLIL and Multilingual Education* (pp. 1–25). Bristol: Multilingual Matters.

Neumann, R. and Becher, T. (2002) Teaching and learning in their disciplinary contexts: A conceptual analysis. *Studies in Higher Education* 27 (49), 405–417.

Smit, U. and Dafouz, E. (eds) (2012) Integrating content and language in higher education: An introduction to English-medium policies, conceptual issues and research practices across Europe. *AILA Review* 25, 64–79.

Tsui, C. (2018) Teacher efficacy: A case study of faculty beliefs in an English-medium instruction teacher training program. *Taiwan Journal of TESOL* 15 (1), 101–128.

Wächter, B. and Maiworm, F. (eds) (2014) *English-taught Programmes in European Higher Education: The State of Play in 2014.* Bonn: Lemmens Medien GmbH.

White, M. and Marsh, E. (2006) Content analysis: A flexible methodology. *Library Trends* 55 (1), 22–45.

Wyatt, M. (2016) 'Are they becoming more reflective and/or efficacious?' A conceptual model mapping how teachers' self-efficacy beliefs might grow. *Educational Review* 68 (1), 114–137.

9 Comparatively Speaking: CLIL/EMI Teacher Well-being at the Primary, Secondary and Tertiary Levels in Austria

Kyle Read Talbot, Marie-Theres Gruber,
Anita Lämmerer, Nicole Hofstadler
and Sarah Mercer

Introduction

This chapter compares the findings of a qualitative study that investigated the subjective well-being (SWB) of Content and Language Integrated Learning (CLIL) teachers at the primary and secondary levels and English Medium Instruction (EMI) instructors at the tertiary level in Austria. The aim of the study was to arrive at a more nuanced understanding of the social, contextual and individual factors that affect how these teachers in Austria experience their roles as CLIL/EMI teachers and how they perceive that this impacts their well-being. It is hoped that the study can cast light on the kinds of support CLIL/EMI teachers would benefit from in order to flourish professionally.

Literature Review

Understanding well-being

To understand the well-being of teachers working as CLIL/EMI educators, we have turned to the notion of SWB. SWB 'refers to people's evaluations of their lives' and includes, 'both cognitive judgments of life satisfaction and affective evaluations of moods and emotions' (Diener & Lucas, 1999: 213). Diener and Lucas (1999: 213) explain that, 'if a person reports that her life is satisfying, that she is experiencing frequent pleasant affect, and that she is infrequently experiencing unpleasant affect, she is said to have high subjective well-being'. With SWB, the affective and cognitive components are distinct and can be measured separately. SWB allows judgments about a person's well-being to emanate from the individual's own perspective and highlights its subjective nature. For instance, a person's life could be judged as poor for well-being from an outside observer; however, if that same individual perceives their life positively, they could be said to have high SWB. SWB represents a personal evaluation of one's circumstances and what it means for the individual, and research methodologies need to accommodate this uniqueness and subjectivity. Evidence suggests that SWB is, 'associated with and precedes numerous successful outcomes, as well as behaviours paralleling success' (Lyubomirsky *et al.*, 2005). These associations include positive mental health, positive attitudes and beliefs, longevity and physical health, high quality social relationships, reduced absenteeism at work and job success and satisfaction (Lyubomirsky *et al.*, 2005).

Teacher well-being

In an analysis of work-related stress across 27 occupations, Smith *et al.* (2000) found that the teaching profession had the highest proportion of individuals located in the high stress category. A similar finding was reported in Johnson *et al.*'s (2005) comparison of occupational stress across 26 professions. In their rankings, teaching was one of the six most stressful jobs and one of only three occupations with worse than average ratings in terms of physical health, psychological well-being and job satisfaction. In their analyses, teaching was rated the second lowest occupation in terms of reported physical health and psychological well-being and sixth lowest in terms of reported job satisfaction. There are various reasons why teaching rates consistently poorly in occupational comparative data. Johnson *et al.* (2005) suggest that the high emotional labour involved in teaching is one possible reason why teachers specifically experience high levels of stress. Ingersoll (2006) suggests that one cause of teacher stress is when teachers feel micro-managed and voiceless. An additional factor leading to higher stress rates in teacher populations include their rapidly evolving roles. Teaching is becoming more pressured and increasingly complex (Day & Gu, 2010). Dealing with changing roles and responsibilities can increase stress for teachers (Travers & Cooper, 1996). Travers (2017: 29) explains that against a backdrop of increasing demands that, 'the rewards of teaching have become increasingly obscured by these demanding work conditions which typify many schools'.

The antithesis of stress and burnout is well-being. As teachers play a critical role in student achievement and learning processes (Hattie, 2009), their well-being is of importance not only for themselves as individuals but also for their learners. Research suggests teachers who have higher well-being are more effective teachers (Barber & Mourshed, 2007; Caprara *et al.*, 2006; Klusmann *et al.*, 2008; Kunter *et al.*, 2013) and positively impact the achievement of their students (Briner & Dewberry, 2007; Caprara *et al.*, 2006; Spilt *et al.*, 2011). Additionally, when teachers experience high well-being it can impact students' motivation for learning and experience of positive emotions in their classrooms (Frenzel *et al.*, 2009; Pekrun *et al.*, 2011). Therefore, it seems to us that it is vitally important for teachers and learners that we understand teacher well-being and what contributes to this, in order to ensure they flourish in their roles as professionals (Mercer *et al.*, 2016; Talbot & Mercer, 2018) and that, subsequently, their learners are thus experiencing the best version of their teachers.

Teacher well-being in CLIL/EMI contexts

CLIL is defined as encompassing 'any activity in which a foreign language is used as a tool in the learning of a non-language subject in which both language and the subject have a joint role' (Marsh, 2002: 58). In comparison, EMI is defined by Macaro *et al.* (2018: 37) as, 'The use of the English language to teach academic subjects (other than English itself) in countries or jurisdictions where the first language of the majority of the population is not English'.

CLIL and EMI settings constitute interesting contexts through which to explore teacher SWB. CLIL and EMI present both challenges and opportunities for teachers (see also Chapters 2, 10 & 11). For example, research suggests that some teachers feel there are benefits to teaching CLIL including the ability to try new teaching methods and to expand students' perspectives (Skinnari & Bovellan, 2016). In one study, Nikula (2010) found that CLIL teaching was associated with positive student teacher relationships. One significant challenge CLIL teachers may face is that their knowledge, pedagogical and linguistic competencies need to extend to both subject and language learning domains (Bovellan, 2014). In particular, Moate (2011) noted that CLIL teaching can engender feelings of linguistic insecurity and thus may pose a threat to language teachers' senses of professional integrity. Yet, in the same study, Moate (2011) found that her teacher participants acclimated to the role over time (3–6 years). In a study examining primary teacher agency within the Finnish CLIL context, Pappa *et al.* (2017; see also Chapter 2) found factors that both constrained teacher agency and resources that enabled it. Factors constraining teacher agency included teaching through English and classroom related tensions, whereas resources promoting teacher agency included autonomy, flexibility and an openness to change. Another challenge noted in the literature is the lack of appropriate teaching materials for CLIL at both the primary (Bovellan, 2014; Pappa *et al.*, 2017) and secondary levels (Banegas, 2012).

Mixed findings can also be found at the tertiary level. In two systematic reviews of EMI both Williams (2015) and Macaro *et al.* (2018) concluded that the implementation of EMI currently creates more challenges than opportunities for tertiary level teachers and students. Despite this, Macaro *et al.* (2018: 68) argue, 'it is hard to see anything but further expansion of EMI in [higher education]'. At the same time, research also suggests that teachers have positive motivations for teaching EMI courses. In the German context, Earls (2016) found that teachers and students believed that for some subjects, teaching in English was more pragmatic. Dearden and Macaro (2016) found in a study comparing the beliefs of EMI teachers is Austria, Italy and Poland that, overall, the teacher participants were in favour of EMI and its expansion because they believed that internationalisation was important and would attract more students. They summarised, 'probably the best way to sum up our respondents' attitudes is that EMI is here to stay and to increase, and therefore they have to make the best of it' (Dearden & Macaro, 2016: 477). In another EMI study, Aguilar (2017: 731–732) found that engineering lecturers perceived EMI as benefitting students and were satisfied with their lecturing in English, but some were 'baffled about the extra workload they inadvertently had on their shoulders'. The same study also revealed that the EMI teachers in the sample perceived EMI as improving their English fluency, which eventually also boosted their confidence in the language. Such mixed findings were also found by Hofstadler *et al.* (2020) who revealed that teachers at secondary schools in Austria perceived CLIL as leading to an increased workload, but they also saw it as a positive opportunity from which to grow and develop as a teacher. These mixed results suggest that the role as a CLIL/EMI educator may bring benefits but may also give rise to increased demands and stressors for educators. As these demands and stressors may be shared or vary across educational levels, we hoped that a comparison would cast light on possible types of support teachers at each level could benefit from.

Methodology

Aim of the study

This study aims to understand teacher perceptions of CLIL/EMI at all educational levels in Austria to see what lessons can be drawn for how teachers' SWB in these roles can best be promoted.

CLIL/EMI contexts in Austria

Primary level

Primary schoolteachers are trained generalists in eight subjects (German, maths, science, music, physical education, wood and needle work, art and modern foreign languages). As a rule, they are not trained specialists in non-German language teaching. Within their primary school teacher education, foreign language teaching plays a minimal role; within a 240-ECTS curriculum (European Credit Transfer and Accumulation System, where one Credit Point stands for approximately 25 to 30 hours of work), six to eight ECTS (depending on the federal state) are allotted to the subject modern foreign languages. Within this small amount of training, the teachers should acquire or improve their individual foreign language skills as well as gain knowledge in foreign language didactics and lesson planning.

In Austria, primary school teachers generally have the autonomy to decide the amount and intensity of foreign language teaching in their own classrooms as long as it reaches at least one hour per week (BMUKK, 2012). Furthermore, the curriculum allows teachers to decide themselves how to integrate language, in which subject and how often, using their own choice of topic from a selection (BMUKK, 2012). Consequently, quality, themes and length of instruction in the foreign language vary across the nation, from teacher to teacher, and from school to school (Dalton-Puffer, 2007; Eurydice, 2006).

Secondary level

Austria generally differentiates between lower and upper secondary level and has several types of state secondary schools. At the lower secondary level, students and parents have a choice between the Neue Mittelschule (NMS) offering four years of lower secondary and general secondary schools (AHS – Allgemeinbildende Höhere Schule) offering eight years and covering both upper and lower secondary. For upper secondary, students also have the choice to attend various vocational schools (BHS – Berufsbildende Höhere Schule, covering four to five years) as well as polytechnic schools/pre-vocational schools (1 year). Both the AHS as well as the BHS prepare students for the Matura, the Austrian centralised school-leaving exam which is a pre-requisite for tertiary education.

Austrian secondary school teachers typically study two subjects. In the context of CLIL, this can mean that some have a dual specialisation in a language and another subject but may have little to no explicit CLIL training. Not all CLIL teachers will necessarily have a language as one of their two subjects. The implementation of CLIL varies extensively among secondary schools. Within the BHS school type, all HTLs (Höhere technische Lehranstalt), a type of vocational school, are required by law to teach CLIL for 72 lessons per school year in every class (BMUKK, 2011). The national curriculum for AHS also mentions CLIL in their curriculum (BMUKK, 2000), although its implementation depends on each individual school and can vary considerably across settings. Given the differences between the AHS and BHS school types, we deliberately chose to interview teachers from both types of schools.

Tertiary level

In Europe, EMI takes various forms and is implemented in ways that depend on what is needed locally (Smit & Dafouz, 2012). Austria ranks 10th in the European Union in terms of the number of programmes in English available at the tertiary level (Wächter & Maiworm, 2014). In 2014, it was estimated that 1.8% of students in Austria are enrolled in programmes that are taught in English. The growth of EMI at the tertiary level has been driven by a slightly different albeit related agenda than that at the secondary or primary levels. In higher education (HE), the decision for EMI is often motivated by perceived or actual benefits that a given university would receive, especially in terms of provisions for international students (Macaro *et al.*, 2018; Naidoo, 2006).

We have chosen to use EMI explicitly when referring to the HE context in this paper. EMI, according to Macaro *et al.* (2018: 37), 'is a term used ubiquitously geographically and, usually but not exclusively, applied to HE'. Apart from being a term more often associated with HE, EMI also is distinct from CLIL in other ways. For instance, according to Dearden (2015), EMI is explicitly related to the English language, whereas CLIL does not specify which target language is to be studied. Furthermore, while CLIL has an explicit goal of both content and language instruction, EMI does not necessarily have the same dual objectives that are typical in many CLIL settings, where language and content are said to be emphasised equally (Dalton-Puffer, 2011).

Participants

Thirty-two teachers participated in the study; six were teaching CLIL in primary schools, 16 in secondary schools and 10 were teaching EMI at the tertiary level. At the time of the interviews, the teachers were employed in Austria, albeit in different federal states (Styria, Vienna, Tyrol and Salzburg). Regarding age, the research group was diverse, ranging from 22 to 61 years. Correspondingly, the amount of experience with CLIL varied greatly among all interviewed teachers, stretching between one to 22 years. A summary of the information can be found in Tables 9.1, 9.2 and 9.3, which include detailed anonymised data of all participants.

Interviews

The data analysed in this paper were collected over a period of two months (November to December 2017) through individual in-depth, semi-structured interviews. Interviews lasted approximately one hour and were conducted at the choice of the interviewee in either English or German with occasional instances of code-switching. Depending on the location of the participants relative to the research team, interviews took place in person or via Skype. The interview protocol was designed to

Table 9.1 Primary teachers

ID	Sex	Age	Teaching Experience (years)	CLIL Teaching Experience (years)	CLIL Hours Taught Per Week (hours)	Volunteered or forced to teach CLIL lessons	Language Used During Interviews
P1	F	29	7	6	5	Volunteered	German
P2	F	28	9	8	5	Volunteered	German
P3	F	29	7	7	5	Volunteered	German
P4	F	27	5	4	3	Volunteered	German
P5	F	35	5	5	3	Volunteered	German
P6	F	35	7	7	6	Volunteered	German

reflect the two main interests of our study with the first section focusing on CLIL teachers' personal experiences, attitudes and beliefs, and the second section examining the interviewees' SWB (e.g. 'How satisfied are you with being a CLIL/EMI teacher at the moment?'). The open-ended questions in the protocol remained largely the same across all educational levels and they were only adapted to suit the specifics of the educational levels as appropriate. The interview data were transcribed including pauses, laughter and silences when meaningful.

Data analysis

The data were analysed using data analysis software QCAMap, Atlas.ti and MAXQDA. The data from each educational level were coded by different sections of the research team and each section of the research team utilised their preferred data analysis programme. In all cases, the data were first memoed and discussed by each respective research group and subsequently, were relayed back to the larger group for consideration. Each data set was then coded multiple times in a reiterative process by different researchers in consultation with each other. The first coding phase was exploratory and subsequent stages were more focused. Each wave of coding was also accompanied by discussions between members of the research team on the emerging code list. The last phase in each case was selective thematic coding in which to bring out the main themes and their subcategories.

Ethics

Teachers were contacted via personal and professional networks. Additionally, some EMI teachers were contacted through email via their university websites. All participants were provided with a participant information sheet outlining the nature of the study as well as a consent sheet, detailing what was expected of them and how their data would be

Table 9.2 Secondary teachers

ID	Sex	Age	Subjects	Teaching Experience (years)	CLIL Teaching Experience (years)	Volunteered or Asked to Teach CLIL	School Type	Language Used During Interviews
S1	M	*	Engineering (BHS)	*	*	Volunteered	BHS (HTL)	English
S2	F	44	Biology, Microbiology	6	2	Volunteered	BHS	English
S3	F	53	Architecture	8	3	Volunteered	BHS (HTL)	English
S4	F	60	English & Geography	35	20	Volunteered	AHS	English
S5	M	58	IT & electrical engineering	30	22	Volunteered	BHS (HTL)	English
S6	F	22	English & Biology	1	1	Volunteered	AHS	English
S7	M	41	'Theory'	7	5	Both	BHS (HTL)	English
S8	F	29	English, History & IT	4	2	Was asked	AHS	English
S9	F	60	English & History	35	15	Volunteered	AHS	English
S10	M	60	IT	20	15	Volunteered	BHS (HTL)	German
S11	F	61	English & French	33	*	Volunteered	BHS (HTL)	English
S12	F	41	English & Math	15	8	Volunteered	BHS (HTL)	English
S13	F	55	Music	27	8	Volunteered	AHS	German
S14	F	48	Accounting, Business Studies & Economics	12	12	Volunteered	BHS	English
S15	F	50	Biology & Chemistry	20	3	Volunteered	BHS (HTL)	English
S16	M	60	IT	20	20	Volunteered	BHS (HTL)	English

*Indicates information not provided or collected.

Table 9.3 Tertiary teachers

ID	Sex	Age	Discipline	Teaching Experience (years)	EMI Teaching Experience (years)	Volunteered or Forced to Teach EMI	Language Used During Interviews
T1	M	36	Accounting, Finance, Research Methods	8.5	'the last year it became more frequent'	'mixture'	English
T2	M	39	Project Management, Entrepreneurship	4.5	4.5	Both	English
T3	F	57	English in Medicine	8	3	Suggested	English
T4	M	43	Microbiology, Molecular Biology	18	4	Volunteered	English
T5	F	50	Biochemistry, Molecular Biology	25	20+	Both	English
T6	M	26	Customer Management, Marketing Research	1	1	Volunteered	English
T7	M	60	Electronics	23	8	Volunteered	English
T8	M	51	IT	15	9	Forced	German
T9	F	50	Organisational Management	*	*	*	English
T10	M	41	Business, Management	15	10	Volunteered	English

*Indicates information not provided or collected.

used, particularly with regards to the protection of their identity. Prior to interviewing, all participants signed a consent form and gave explicit permission to record, transcribe and utilise their data. All names, places and other identifying markers have been anonymised to protect the identity of the participants.

Findings

In this section, we present the factors that appeared to affect the SWB of the teachers working in the different contexts. We have divided these into two main categories – those related to the context and those related to the teacher as an individual.

Context-related factors affecting teachers' SWB

Implementation and policy

A key factor that seems to play a role into how efficacious teachers feel in their roles depends on their sense of agency which is defined to a considerable extent by contextual factors, especially localised educational policy and its implementation (see also Chapter 2). As noted above, in Austria, the implementation of CLIL/EMI tends to vary greatly between educational levels but also within educational levels. In our data set, one commonality across all the educational levels was the teachers' descriptions of a relatively *ad hoc* implementation of CLIL/EMI. Although some reported this as being frustrating, the lack of structure or guidelines was also paradoxically seen as an opportunity for the teachers to explore their creativity and exercise their autonomy (see also Chapter 6).

For example, three of the six primary teachers reported feeling abandoned due to a lack of clarity about how CLIL should be implemented in their setting. Despite this, all primary teachers reported feeling autonomous in their decisions on what subject and content to teach in English. This flexible feeling was expressed as positive for these teachers' SWB. At the secondary level, eight of the 14 teachers, who reported experiencing substantial autonomy in their implementation of CLIL, reported enjoying how the relatively *laissez faire* implementation of CLIL in their schools allowed them to be independent and flexible in their own practices. Yet, at the same time, five other secondary teachers expressed feeling stressed by the lack of any clear guidance as to what they should be doing. As S9 explained, 'everyone is lost'. Specifically, four of the nine HTL teachers expressed some frustration as they were obliged by law to teach 72 CLIL hours per school year, yet what happens in practice was left up to individual teachers with little or no guidance. At the tertiary level, all the teachers also described a relatively *ad hoc* approach to EMI implementation that depended on the goals or aims of specific university departments but all of them reported appreciating the autonomy in how they implemented EMI within their own classrooms.

Stakeholders

Key educational stakeholders also emerged as a contextual variable, which impacted the SWB of the educators. At the primary level, parents were reported by all the teachers as being a stress factor negatively influencing their SWB. Some of their negative experiences that they reported included parents questioning the teacher's authority in terms of their age and LX[1] teacher status. One teacher, P6, expressed frustration about parents who said that they would prefer any CLIL lesson to be taught by L1 speakers of English. P6 explained, 'if you teach CLIL, then the parents' first question is whether one is a native speaker'. Some of the teachers at the secondary level explained that CLIL students often came from higher social backgrounds and that because of this, their parents tended to be more involved and sometimes more demanding. This was not perceived as a negative factor, *per se*, but rather more of a workplace complication. At the tertiary level, parents unsurprisingly did not feature although they were a notable stressor for the other two levels of educators.

The relationship with students also appeared impactful on the teachers' SWB. At the primary level, being part of their pupils' lives and seeing how they developed were the most motivating factors for all interviewees. P1 explained, 'I like being the coach, I find it cool, I find it cool how children change, they develop, achieve their goals, how you notice that you can motivate them'. At the secondary level, student–teacher relationships were mostly described as positively impacting the teachers' SWB. However, three teachers also emphasised the negative side effects that can arise if teachers and students do not 'get along'. Generally, the students appear to play a key role in motivating teachers to engage in CLIL with the teaching experience being described as rewarding by seven teachers. Also, at the tertiary level, the connection with and impact on students was felt to be positive for their SWB. As T4 described:

> I think there are many things rewarding … talking with students about different possibilities … If you get to the level that you can get some connection to the students, and then, and you get of course some impression that they really, once they really pursue you as somebody that wants to help you, every moment is rewarding.

In terms of the tertiary level specifically, a unique aspect of the teacher-student relationship emerged. Only one teacher felt responsible for their students' language learning and otherwise they believed that the responsibility for keeping up with the language was by and large the responsibility of the students themselves. This meant the teachers at the tertiary level did not feel stressed or unduly concerned by their students' language levels or linguistic issues which was positive for these teachers' SWB. T6 explained, 'that's the standard I think, right, you just assume students know the language and if they don't, well tough luck'. The one teacher who did feel responsible for her students' language abilities, T3, is notable because a large part of her professional profile involved teaching an English for Specific Purposes (ESP) course and she only had one EMI class. For her, it was normal to attend to linguistic-related issues and, as such, her role change in her EMI class affected her differently.

Social status and appreciation

The role that teachers hold in society and how they perceived their social status was explicitly mentioned by teachers at all educational levels in this study. At the primary level, five teachers felt that the amount of preparation needed for CLIL lessons was typically overlooked by authorities and not appreciated by head teachers or colleagues. Simultaneously, these teachers described the media as largely perpetuating the idea that teachers work short hours and have unduly long holidays. As P3 discussed, teachers have to cope with discussions in the media implying that they do not work enough as they 'already go home at noon'. She explained that this was 'really annoying' and described how during the summer, 'the newspapers start the miserable discussion of shortening the break'. Two primary teachers and one secondary teacher even described experiencing a lack of appreciation within their own families who did not appreciate the amount of work they do. P6 explained her frustrations, 'I often sat till midnight, and then you have someone telling you that you do not work'.

Feeling a lack of appreciation is not unique to the primary teachers. Most secondary school teachers felt that there was a lack of appreciation (10 out of 16) and lack of support from both federal and institutional authorities. In terms of CLIL specifically, half of the secondary teachers stated that despite CLIL having a prestigious status and being widely requested, their work was neither appreciated nor supported. Seven of these teachers also expressed sensitivity about the social status of their profession generally in Austrian society. S4 explained: 'I have been a teacher for such a long time, and you know that you don't get any support and that you don't get any recognition whatsoever'. Eight of the teachers felt this perceived lack of appreciation and respect from society negatively impacted their SWB. S4 described how routinised it felt to go through the cycle where individuals in society questioned the worth of teachers and how she coped with it: 'At certain times of the year, I don't turn on the radio, I don't turn on the TV'.

The same sensitivity to perceived negative societal perceptions of teachers was not as pronounced among the tertiary-level EMI teachers. However, two teachers did explain that their research roles were viewed as more prestigious and respected than were their teaching roles suggesting a similar lower level of appreciation for the act of teaching within the tertiary sector. T4, for instance, explains:

> In my thinking, teaching and research is always two different heads that I try to incorporate but teaching as a career is of course in the natural science field not really accepted as, at least here in Austria, doesn't feel to be really an acceptable career.

T4 has a particularly unique perspective on this as he, at the time of the study, had recently just started teaching at a secondary school in addition to his university role. He explained how his status at the secondary school is generally higher because students' parents and colleagues know that he is also a university teacher and researcher, which affords him a certain status and respect compared to others who 'only' teach at secondary level.

Teacher-related factors affecting teachers' SWB

Conviction and personal attitudes

SWB can be affected positively when you are convinced of what you do and have a congruence between personal and work values (Li *et al.*, 2015; Sagiv & Schwartz, 2000). Generally, all the interviewees at the primary level expressed positive attitudes towards CLIL and held strong beliefs that young learners benefit from learning English. Two interviewees believed that CLIL was potentially more successful than regular English language teaching and expressed a belief that CLIL is a fun alternative to regular teaching approaches for both students and teachers, describing CLIL as 'something different'.

Similarly, most of the secondary CLIL teachers generally held positive attitudes towards this teaching approach. Only three BHS teachers (S3, S15 & S11), whose schools have obligatory CLIL lessons, were critical about the current CLIL policy emphasising that 'some [students] are good in the language and others are not' (S15). However, the majority of teachers (10 out of 16) were convinced their students benefit from CLIL as one teacher concludes, 'I think it is for everybody' (S16).

In contrast, the tertiary-level teachers simply seemed to accept that their universities were active sites of internationalisation and that EMI was a natural part of this. There was less conviction of the approach and rather simply acceptance of it as a state of practice. Nevertheless, two of the tertiary-level teachers were critical of an EMI approach. T3 questioned how useful it would be for local students to take courses in English rather than German, 'I do not see why university classes should be taught in English only, in Austria'. She also had concerns about the possible long-term effects of EMI instruction on learning and use of the German language.

Balance of content and language

Across the data sets, it became apparent that the balance of content and language instruction varied across educational levels and varied greatly among individual practitioners at each level. At the primary level, all teachers described the focus as being on content exclusively. In order to make this content focus work, all teachers discussed using scaffolding and creating additional materials to aid student comprehension.

At the secondary level, the balance of language and content tended to vary to a much larger extent. Some of this variance appears to be based on the teacher's personal understanding of CLIL ranging from content-based (hard CLIL) to language-based (soft CLIL) or a blend of the two (Ball *et al.*, 2015). However, assessment procedures also seemed to play a role. In CLIL classes at secondary level in Austria, students can elect whether to take their final exams in German or the language that the CLIL course is taught in. This leads some secondary teachers

(S4, S5, S7 & S10) to argue with frustration that there is no need to explicitly teach language as 'it doesn't count. Never ever' (S4). Half of the teachers, who have a teaching degree in both a foreign language and a content subject (S4, S6, S9 & S14), emphasise teaching CLIL in a content-driven manner. 'It's content! I teach content in English' one of them explains (S4). Still, almost half of them (S2, S3, S6, S8 & S9) state that teaching the language within CLIL is important too.

At the tertiary level, content was the unequivocal primary consideration for all the teachers who all felt comfortable with this focus. However, T3, who was primarily an English for Specific Purposes (ESP) teacher, did feel that switching roles between ESP and EMI was 'hard' and despite an active effort, she still found herself keeping track of her students' language, which was a stressor. In her role as an EMI teacher, although she sought to emphasise content, she found ignoring language issues unnatural and uncomfortable. In this EMI class, she had to constantly remind herself that her role was different and not to assess language as she normally would. It was her awareness of language and language teaching that seemed to lead to a sense of stress; an awareness of language issues that the other teachers at this level seemed relatively unconcerned by.

Use of L1/L2

Code-switching was described as occurring most frequently at the secondary level in our data set (14 of 16 participants). Reasons for this were the topic and the teacher's perception of the topic's complexity. It also often depended on the students. Some teachers in the sample expressed concern for their students' well-being as it related to their English use. For instance, S3 explained, 'I don't want to force them to speak English'. Other teachers, like S5, try to avoid code-switching altogether, stating that, 'It is not good, from my point of view'. Many teachers also would freely switch languages when they could not recall a specific vocabulary word. Other reasons for mixing or switching languages were strategic. Often challenging content or specific points the teachers wanted to emphasise were repeated in the students' L1. However, most teachers (12 out of 16) made a deliberate attempt to use English most of the time. They also encouraged their students to speak in English as much as possible.

Whereas the secondary teachers reported significant variance and flexibility in their classroom language use, almost all teacher talk in the tertiary EMI classrooms occurred in English. Three of these teachers did report that code-switching would sometimes occur in their classrooms, but this was reported to be quite limited. Two of the tertiary teachers did question the English-only approach, but for different reasons. T9 questioned the efficacy of teaching only in English in Austria where many of the students will be living and working in a German-speaking country and T3 questioned how effective an English-only approach can be if taught by those lacking English language expertise themselves. She explained, 'If the facilitator or the teacher doesn't know the language quite well, I think the content suffers'. Notably, all the tertiary teachers in our sample were quite comfortable and happy with their ability to teach through English for the most part. Though all teachers were confident in their abilities to teach through English, three teachers (T2, T5 & T9) emphasised how taxing it could be to teach in English all the time. T9, for example, explained that teaching in English is, 'just very energy absorbing while I'm in class'.

At the primary level, the teachers did not discuss code-switching.

Perception of workload

With regards to workload, all the primary teachers perceived this as being high and stressful. Comparing CLIL preparation to other subjects taught in their L1, most interviewees (P1, P2, P4, P5, P6) reported needing more time due to the lack of suitable material for primary level CLIL. As teacher (P1) states, 'in year four to use CLIL on this level … to do English, is crazy, simply because it is massive in preparation, the arrangement, the preparation, the material, in year four … very exhausting …' (P1). In fact, all the participants said that they create their own materials for the subjects they teach in English.

This sentiment was largely shared by teachers at the secondary level. The majority of secondary teachers (10 out of 16) also perceived the workload to be much higher in CLIL compared to teaching regular lessons. However, only four teachers explicitly noted the elevated workload as negatively affecting their SWB. For half of the teachers the possibility to design their own teaching material was seen as positively contributing to their SWB. As one teacher explains, 'I'm just really [by] motivated finding and making my material, my own material that I can use' (S6). Two BHS teachers (S7 & S1) said they did not perceive much of a difference in overall workload.

The tertiary EMI teachers did not report major differences in how they perceived their workloads in EMI courses compared to classes taught in their L1s. Four of the teachers reported it was even less work to teach in English. This was primarily due to the widespread availability of materials for use at the tertiary level and for academic discourse. All of the teachers in this study commented on how the primary language of their academic discipline was English, which made materials easy to find; 'As I come from a research [background], so there I am used to give presentations in English'. This does not mean that there were not high energy costs associated with teaching and conversing in the actual classroom in English. T2, for example, described how teaching in English both challenged and benefitted him, 'of course teaching in English implies more work and a bigger challenge but it also allows me to improve my English'. T5 also described both a benefit and drawback of teaching through English, 'I sort of realised that the first, like the first times just, it was more exhausting than it used to be in German. And sometimes it can actually also be easier and because all the literature is in English'.

Discussion

Comparing the SWB and experiences of teachers involved in CLIL/EMI across the educational levels reveals some interesting and rather telling distinctions. The first rather dispiriting issue concerns the social status of teachers in Austria and the relative status of teaching at school, compared to teaching at a university. The finding in this sample supports what Treiman (1977) and Ganzeboom and Treiman (1996) found while comparing occupational prestige scores among professions; university professors were placed near the top of these rankings, whereas secondary and primary school teachers ranked lower (secondary teachers were ranked slightly higher than were primary teachers). The situation in Austria is complex regarding social status. The OECD (2005: 82) cross-country educational report on teacher retention highlighted that, in Austria, '... two-thirds of teachers are not happy with the image of the teaching profession, and that this is their major source of job dissatisfaction; and yet other information indicates that the social standing of teachers in Austria is relatively high'. What is key here seems to be the teachers' perceptions of their own social status. The issue of perceived status and appreciation was compounded for some teachers who felt the extra work and effort involved in CLIL was not recognised by their colleagues or institutions. Not feeling appreciated at work is a key factor associated with burnout and prolonged stress (Kalimo *et al.*, 2003); the fact that many of these teachers did not perceive the appreciation or status they felt they deserved is a troubling finding.

A second major issue across settings concerns the somewhat paradoxical finding concerning policy and implementation. On the one hand, all the teachers enjoy having the autonomy to design and structure their own teaching content and format. Yet, on the other hand, some teachers also feel disoriented and unclear about what is expected of them. This lack of clarity in terms of guidelines and directions can be frustrating and confusing, especially in the more typically rigidly controlled settings of primary and secondary. The higher degree of autonomy at tertiary level was typically less of a concern (Babi & Talbot, 2019; Davies & Jenkins, 2013). Research suggests that, in general, having autonomy and work schedule flexibility is a positive contributor to reported SWB (Golden *et al.*, 2013). Understanding how to best to support CLIL/EMI teacher autonomy while also considering how a lack of clarity impacts these teachers SWB should be a top priority for educational stakeholders moving forward.

The third major issue concerns the relative roles of language and content in the teaching and how this affects these teachers' SWB. Interestingly and in line with the literature (Aguilar, 2017), tertiary teachers generally do not feel any tension or responsibility to teach English language objectives (see also Chapters 10 & 11). This is merely their mode of communication and their focus and main identities are as content teachers. In contrast, the primary teachers feel a considerable pressure to teach the language and to such an extent that it deters some of them from continuing teaching CLIL (Gruber *et al.*, 2020). In secondary, there is an interesting division according to whether a teacher has language teaching experience or not and school type. In the HTLs, the teachers were more similar to those in tertiary and saw themselves as subject teachers who happened to teach in English. Their focus was also more on the content and they displayed less, or no stress associated with the language teaching dimension which they felt was not really their concern. For those aware of language teaching in their dual roles, typically in AHS secondary schools, they reported feeling more pressure and stress to meet the demands of a dual strand approach attending to both content and language simultaneously and in equal measure. A related effect was the degree of code-switching. For those with less perceived pressure to teach or stay in English, they were more flexible and reported switching between languages more often with less sense of stress. These findings raise interesting questions about EMI and CLIL for teachers' linguistic well-being. It suggests that when the pressure to teach two goals is removed and when an open approach to language use and translanguaging is encouraged, teachers are likely to experience higher SWB in their CLIL/EMI roles. This more open approach to language use and translanguaging has been found to affect well-being in other contexts (Andrews *et al.*, 2018).

Conclusion

This chapter has examined the contextual and personal factors affecting CLIL and EMI teachers' SWB. It has compared the situations across the educational levels and found some striking similarities and notable differences. While many of the beliefs and convictions of CLIL/EMI teachers were comparable across levels, important differences between the educational levels were observed regarding implementation and policy of CLIL/EMI, the balance of content and language within classrooms, stakeholder perceptions, perceived status, teacher workload, how teachers defined and operationalised CLIL/EMI in their own teaching and their respective motivations for teaching in English. Though many of the factors contributing to CLIL/EMI teachers' SWB were also comparable across levels, the results indicate that the SWB of CLIL teachers at the secondary level may be most at risk.

Implications for Policy and Practice

The message for policy makers is that teachers, especially at primary and secondary, would benefit from more support in their professional roles generally and their CLIL roles specifically. Clearer guidelines on expectations and the frameworks for CLIL instruction would be useful, while respecting teacher autonomy as well as a programme of information for parents and other stakeholders about what CLIL involves and appropriate expectations. Recognition of the additional workload involved for teachers at all levels would be an additional vital step in ensuring facilitative conditions for CLIL/EMI educators. For CLIL/EMI teachers, recognising that teacher SWB is not a luxury but instead a key building block for effective practice is an essential first step. One other possible avenue to positively promote teacher SWB through pre-service and in-service training would be to establish a more open approach to translanguaging in the classroom that takes advantage of broader linguistic repertoires. As CLIL and EMI appear to be continuing to expand across all educational levels in many countries in Europe and beyond, more needs to be done to actively engage with teacher perspectives and ensure that their needs are properly understood and that they receive the kinds of support necessary to ensure they flourish as professionals in these roles.

Acknowledgements

Findings are part of a nationwide study funded by the ÖNB in Austria. This project investigates CLIL/EMI teachers' well-being across the primary, secondary and tertiary level in Austria. We want to thank all of the extended research team who contributed to this project entitled: Selbstbild & professionelles Wohlbefinden von CLIL Lehrenden. The project number is 17136. More information can be found by following the link below: https://www.oenb.at/jublfonds/jublfonds/projectsearch?id=6059&action=detailview&origin=resultlist.

Note

(1) '"LX", meaning any foreign language acquired after the age at which the first language(s) was acquired, that is after the age of 3 years, to any level of proficiency' (Dewaele, 2017: 238).

References

Aguilar, M. (2017) Engineering lecturers' views on CLIL and EMI. *International Journal of Bilingual Education and Bilingualism* 20 (6), 722–735.
Andrews, J., Fay, R. and White, R. (2018) What shapes everyday translanguaging? Insights from a global mental health project in Northern Uganda. In G. Mazzaferro (ed.) *Translanguaging as Everyday Practice* (Vol. 28) (pp. 257–273). Cham: Springer.

Babić, S. and Talbot, K.R. (2019) Third-age university teachers in language education: Navigating the boundaries of work-life balance and retirement. In A. Kostoulas (ed.) *Challenging Boundaries in Language Education* (pp. 183–189). Cham: Springer.

Ball, P., Kelly, K. and Clegg, J. (2015) *Putting CLIL into Practice*. Oxford: Oxford University Press.

Banegas, D.L. (2012) CLIL teacher development: Challenges and experiences. *Latin American Journal of Content and Language Integrated Learning* 5 (1), 46–56.

Barber, M. and Mourshed, M. (2007) *How the World's Best-Performing School Systems Come Out on Top*. New York: McKinsey & Company.

Bovellan, E. (2014) Teachers' beliefs about learning and language as reflected in their views of teaching materials for content and language integrated learning (CLIL). Unpublished PhD thesis, University of Jyväskylä.

Briner, R. and Dewberry, C. (2007) *Staff Well-being is Key to School Success*. London: Worklife Support Ltd/Hamilton House.

Bundesministerium für Unterricht, Kunst und Kultur (BMUKK) (2000) *Lehrpläne Lehrpläne der allgemeinbildenden höheren Schulen*. Dokument Nr. 2000_133_2 in der Fassung vom 11. Mai 2000. See https://rdb.manz.at/document/ris.c.BGBL_OS_20000511_2_133 (accessed March 2019).

Bundesministerium für Unterricht, Kunst und Kultur (BMUKK) (2011) *Lehrpläne der Höheren technischen und gewerblichen Lehranstalten*. Dokument Nr. BGBLA_2011_II_300 in der Fassung vom 7. September 2011. See https://www.ris.bka.gv.at/eli/bgbl/II/2011/300 (accessed October 2017).

Bundesministerium für Unterricht, Kunst und Kultur (BMUKK) (2012) *Lehrplan der Volksschule*. BGBl. Nr. 134/1963 in der Fassung BGBl. II Nr. 303/2012 vom 13. September 2012. See https://www.bmbf.gv.at/schulen/unterricht/lp/lp_vs_gesamt_14055.pdf (accessed December 2016).

Caprara, G.V., Barbaranelli, C., Steca, P. and Malone, P.S. (2006) Teachers' self-efficacy beliefs as determinants of job satisfaction and students' academic achievement: A study at the school level. *Journal of School Psychology* 44 (6), 473–490.

Dalton-Puffer, C. (2007) *Discourse in Content and Language Integrated Learning (CLIL) Classrooms*. Amsterdam: John Benjamins Publishing Company.

Dalton-Puffer, C. (2011) Content-and-language integrated learning: From practice to principles? *Annual Review of Applied Linguistics* 31, 182–204.

Davies, E. and Jenkins, A. (2013) The work-to-retirement transition of academic staff: Attitudes and experiences. *Employee Relations* 35 (3), 322–338.

Day, C. and Gu, Q. (2010) *The New Lives of Teachers*. New York, NY: Routledge.

Dearden, J. (2015) English as a medium of instruction: A growing global phenomenon. London: British Council. See https://www.britishcouncil.org/education/ihe/knowledge-centre/english-languagehigher-education/report-english-medium-instruction (accessed August 2016).

Dearden, J. and Macaro, E. (2016) Higher education teachers' attitudes towards English medium instruction: A three-country comparison. *Studies in Second Language Learning and Teaching* 6 (3), 455.

Dewaele, J.-M. (2017) Why the dichotomy 'L1 versus LX user' is better than 'native versus non-native speaker'. *Applied Linguistics* 39 (2), 236–240.

Diener, E. and Lucas, R.E. (1999) Personality and subjective well-being. In D. Kahneman, E. Diener and N. Schwarz (eds) *Well-being: The Foundations of Hedonic Psychology* (pp. 213–229). New York, NY: Russell Sage foundation.

Earls, C.W. (2016) *Evolving Agendas in European English-medium Higher Education: Interculturality, Multilingualism and Language Policy*. Basingstoke: Palgrave Macmillan.

Eurydice (2006) Content and language integrated learning at school in Europe. See https://op.europa.eu/en/publication-detail/-/publication/756ebdaa-f694-44e4-8409-21eef02c9b9b (accessed September 2019).

Frenzel, A.C., Goetz, T., Lüdtke, O., Pekrun, R. and Sutton, R.E. (2009) Emotional transmission in the classroom: Exploring the relationship between teacher and student enjoyment. *Journal of Educational Psychology* 101 (3), 705.

Ganzeboom, H.B. and Treiman, D.J. (1996) Internationally comparable measures of occupational status for the 1988 international standards classification of occupations. *Social Science Research* 25, 201–239.

Golden, L., Henly, J. and Lambert, S. (2013) Work schedule flexibility: A contributor to happiness? *Journal of Social Research and Policy* 4 (2), 107–135.

Gruber, M.-T., Lämmerer, A., Hofstadler, N. and Mercer, S. (2020) Flourishing or floundering? Factors contributing to CLIL primary teachers' wellbeing in Austria. *CLIL. Journal of Innovation and Research in Plurilingual and Pluricultural Education* 3 (1), 19–34.

Hattie, J.A.C. (2009) *Visible Learning. A Synthesis of Over 800 Metaanalyses Relating to Achievement.* London: Routledge.

Hofstadler, N., Talbot, K.R., Mercer, S.J. and Lämmerer, A. (2020) The thrills and ills of CLIL. In C. Gkonou, J.M. Dewaele and J. King (eds) *The Emotional Rollercoaster of Language Teaching* (pp. 13–30). Bristol: Multilingual Matters.

Ingersoll, R.M. (2006) *Who Controls Teachers' Work? Power and Accountability in America's Schools.* Cambridge, MA: Harvard University Press.

Johnson, S., Cooper, C., Cartwright, S., Donald, I., Taylor, P. and Millet, C. (2005) The experience of work-related stress across occupations. *Journal of Managerial Psychology* 20 (2), 178–187.

Kalimo, R., Pahkin, K., Mutanen, P. and Topipinen-Tanner, S. (2003) Staying well or burning out at work: Work characteristics and personal resources as long-term predictors. *Work & Stress* 17 (2), 109–122.

Klusmann, U., Kunter, M., Trautwein, U., Lüdtke, O. and Baumert, J. (2008) Teachers' occupational well-being and quality of instruction: The important role of self-regulatory patterns. *Journal of Educational Psychology* 100 (3), 702–715.

Kunter, M., Klusmann, U., Baumert, J., Richter, D., Voss, T. and Hachfeld, A. (2013) Professional competence of teachers: Effects on instructional quality and student development. *Journal of Educational Psychology* 105 (3), 805–820.

Li, M., Wang, Z., You, X. and Gao, J. (2015) Value congruence and teachers' work engagement: The mediating role of autonomous and controlled motivation. *Personality and Individual Differences* 80, 113–118.

Lyubomirsky, S., King, L. and Diener, E. (2005) The benefits of frequent positive affect: Does happiness lead to success? *Psychological Bulletin* 131 (6), 803–855.

Macaro, E., Curle, S., Pun, J., An, J. and Dearden, J. (2018) A systematic review of English medium instruction in higher education. *Language Teaching* 51 (1), 36–76.

Marsh, D. (ed.) (2002) *CLIL/EMILE. The European Dimension: Actions, Trends and Foresight Potential.* Public Services Contract.

Mercer, S., Oberdorfer, P. and Saleem, M. (2016) Helping language teachers to thrive: Using positive psychology to promote teachers' professional well-being. In D. Gabryś-Barker and D. Gałajda (eds) *Positive Psychology Perspectives on Foreign Language Learning and Teaching* (pp. 213–229). Cham: Springer.

Moate, J.M. (2011) The impact of foreign language mediated teaching on teachers' sense of professional integrity in the CLIL classroom. *European Journal of Teacher Education* 34 (3), 333–346.

Naidoo, V. (2006) International education: A tertiary-level industry update. *Journal of Research in International Education* 5 (3), 323–345.

Nikula, T. (2010) Effects of CLIL on a teacher's classroom language use. In C. Dalton-Puffer, T. Nikula and U. Smit (eds) *Language Use and Language Learning in CLIL Classrooms* (pp. 105–124). Amsterdam: John Benjamins Publishing Company.

OECD. (2005) *Teachers Matter: Attracting, Developing and Retaining Effective Teachers.* Paris, FR: OECD Publishing. See https://www.oecd.org/education/school/34990905.pdf (accessed September 2019).

Pappa, S., Moate, J., Ruohotie-Lyhty, M. and Eteläpelto, A. (2017) Teacher agency within the Finnish CLIL context: Tensions and resources. *International Journal of Bilingual Education and Bilingualism*, 1–21.

Pekrun, R., Goetz, T., Frenzel, A.C., Barchfeld, P. and Perry, R.P. (2011) Measuring emotions in students' learning and performance: The Achievement Emotions Questionnaire (AEQ). *Contemporary Educational Psychology* 36 (1), 36–48.

Sagiv, L. and Schwartz, S.H. (2000) Value priorities and subjective well-being: Direct relations and congruity effects. *European Journal of Social Psychology* 30, 177–198.

Skinnari, K., and Bovellan, E. (2016) CLIL teachers' beliefs about integration and about their professional roles: Perspectives from a European context. In T. Nikula, E. Dafouz, P. Moore and U. Smit (eds.) *Conceptualising Integration in CLIL and Multilingual Education* (pp. 145–170). Bristol: Multilingual Matters.

Smit, U. and Dafouz, E. (2012) Integrating content and language in higher education: An introduction to English-medium policies, conceptual issues and research practices across Europe. *AILA Review* 25, 1–12.

Smith, A., Brice, C., Collins, A., Matthews, V. and McNamara, R. (2000) *The Scale of Occupational Stress: A Further Analysis of the Impact of Demographic Factors and Type of Job*. Sudbury: Health and Safety Executive.

Spilt, J.L., Koomen, H.M.Y. and Thijs, J.T. (2011) Teacher wellbeing: The importance of teacher–student relationships. *Educational Psychology Review* 23 (4), 457–477.

Talbot, K. and Mercer, S. (2018) Exploring university ESL/EFL teachers' emotional well-being and emotional regulation in the United States, Japan, and Austria. *Chinese Journal of Applied Linguistics* 41 (4), 410–432.

Travers, C.J. (2017) Current knowledge on the nature, prevalence, sources and potential impact of teacher stress. In T.M. McIntyre, S.E. McIntyre and D.J. Francis (eds) *Educator Stress: An Occupational Health Perspective* (pp. 25–54). New York, NY: Springer Berlin Heidelberg.

Travers, C.J. and Cooper, C.L. (1996) *Teachers Under Pressure: Stress in the Teaching Profession*. New York, NY: Routledge.

Treiman, D.J. (1977) *Occupational Prestige in Comparative Perspective*. New York, NY: Academic Press.

Wächter, B. and Maiworm, F. (eds) (2014) *English-taught Programmes in European Higher Education: The State of Play in 2014*. Bonn: Lemmens Medien GmbH.

Williams, D. (2015) A systematic review of EMI and implications for the South Korean HE context. *ELT World Online*, 1–23.

10 'It Wasn't My Fault': Lecturers' Notes to Former Selves after Five Years of EMI Service

Antonio Jiménez Muñoz

Introduction: The Tense Transition Towards EMI

This study interviews university lecturers from around the world who are teaching a subject through English even though this is not their L1. It investigates these teachers' experiences, professional training histories, motivation, confidence (both the feeling they can successfully execute their tasks and that others may contribute to such success), self-ideation (i.e. how our experience is constructed in discourse) and other beliefs (i.e. a number of psychological assumptions, understandings about reality and propositions based on their own perceptions and interactions with their environment – see also Chapters 5, 6, 7 & 8) after five years of teaching through in this role. A quantitative-qualitative analysis of transcripts and their codifications is subsequently performed to evaluate which aspects cause greater concern. This is complemented by a corpus-based analysis of their notes to their former selves, a reflection exercise asking them to highlight what psychological and pedagogical aspects of their foreign-language teaching and learning they believe more relevant at present and wish they had known before. The two-pronged aim of such an approach is to discern which key psychological and practical issues remain unalleviated, and to anticipate ways in which early anxiety, negative self-ideation and fears of underperformance can be discussed, and hopefully avoided, in pre-service training programmes.

The widespread introduction of English as a Medium of Instruction (EMI), understood as the use of English to teach an academic subject in countries or regions where the first language (L1) of the majority of the population is not English, has been a major change in worldwide higher education (HE) in recent decades. The rapid growth of EMI in the vast majority of non-Anglophone universities worldwide has been propelled by the internationalisation of institutions, curricula and research, the attraction of foreign students, the intended improvement of the multicultural and linguistic competences of national graduates, increased university competition and the focus on employability within a highly globalised context (Doiz *et al.*, 2011). This convergence towards English on the part of HE institutions places language as an additional and incidental target for degree programmes, designed, paradoxically, with no specific room for language instruction. This is in line with the 'widespread belief that incorporating elements of English into the curriculum has the serendipitous effect of promoting incidental language learning' (Pecorari *et al.*, 2011: 58). That is, EMI provisions assume that, somehow, English will be learnt if students are exposed to it – with minimal or no curricular adaptation (Ali, 2013). Beyond internationalisation, researchers have argued that the main underlying motivation for English-taught programmes such as Content and Language Integrated Learning (CLIL) or EMI is to provide the 'added value' of learning both content and language, offering 'two for the price of one' (Bonnet, 2012: 66), without much evidence for such an expectation. At a bare minimum, EMI works assumes that content or skills will be acquired, and language proficiency would improve (Shohamy, 2013).

This assumption is also mirrored in the case of teaching: if lecturers are competent instructors in their subject and proficient in English, then they would be just as competent when teaching EMI classes. However, the reality is more complex: the reported findings on the overall effectiveness of EMI on student outcomes are mixed or inconclusive, which suggests that complex factors are at play. Two recent meta-studies (Graham *et al.*, 2018; Macaro *et al.*, 2018) have explored 83 and 25 articles respectively, to find that while some studies found slightly better performance in EMI cohorts, these improvements are not statistically significant. Furthermore, that content learning is not homogeneous: low-ability EMI students attained a lower level of achievement compared to those taught in their L1 and high-ability EMI students performed better than high-ability L1 learners (Graham *et al.*, 2018: 29). To complicate matters further, other studies have reported that EMI students slightly outperform L1 undergraduates, but higher bands or grades are harder for them to achieve (Hernandez-Nanclares & Jimenez-Munoz, 2017).

In most countries, the rapid and disparate adoption of EMI has entailed a major overhaul of academic life for lecturers and students. Especially for the former, it has become a source of tension (see also Chapters 3, 8 & 9), for several reasons. First, it has created a new, implicit division: EMI instructors have different needs, because their learners do. Secondly, the status of language as an inherent goal – and thus relevant to assessment criteria – is perceived as crucial by some lecturers, while most consider language not a learning target in itself

(Airey, 2013; Dearden, 2015; Wilkinson, 2013), or have even refused to pay any attention to students' English (Aguilar, 2017). Finally, when lecturers face EMI classrooms, problems and anxieties can start to arise because of tensions between structural expectations and the hard realities of teacher (Werther et al., 2014) and student (Tsui, 2018) limitations.

Instructors transitioning towards EMI have often complained about the challenge of teaching content through a foreign language and fear that their students may find it difficult to understand them or pick up deficient vocabulary or pronunciation (Pulcini & Campagna, 2015), both evidences of perceived and projected foreign-language anxiety, defined as negative emotional reactions towards L2 use (Horwitz, 2010). Thus, there is an implicit disjuncture between the institutional assumption that teaching subjects through English is identical to teaching in a L1 and teachers' first-hand experiences when teaching in this role. For instance, lecturers may find themselves needing to amend or cater to the linguistic needs of students progressing with insufficient English proficiency from secondary schools (Jimenez-Munoz, 2016), or using non-academic English to increase intelligibility. This has phenomenal implications: potentially underprepared students enter degrees taught in a foreign language, where neither faculty nor lecturers have made any adjustments to the design of pre-existing modules initially devised to be taught in the students' L1s (Halbach & Lázaro, 2015).

EMI Training: The Perfect Storm for Psychological Distress?

Modern curricular design in HE, in principle, moves away from the present paradigm in which the responsibility for students' English proficiency development lies with English lecturers and courses' (Ali, 2013: 75). However, in EMI it is crucial to understand how classroom practitioners may face tensions because of perceived or actual shortcomings on their part (see also Chapter 11), as well as those of their students. In non-Anglophone countries, students' 'school English' does not generally meet academic requirements when progressing to HE (Erling & Hilgendorf, 2006: 284). At the same time, English has been implicitly considered by universities as an entry 'requisite rather than an expressed learning outcome' (Dafouz et al., 2014: 3). However, the direct transition from L1 instruction to EMI is tremendously complex for students, not only in language terms, but also for teachers, who may experience 'teacher stress', defined as 'the experience by a teacher of unpleasant, negative emotions, such as anger, anxiety, tension, frustration or depression, resulting from some aspect of their work as a teacher' (Kyriacou, 2001: 28). Many EMI lecturers are experienced but new to teaching through a foreign language, so content lecturers, or lecturers who are teaching a non-linguistic subject such as physics or history, may additionally feel uncertain about who is really responsible for their students' language learning (Dearden, 2018). Hence, the dilemma for content-area instructors is not so much to teach through English – which can be a considerable challenge, particularly in areas less connected to research in English – but whether to become responsible, additionally, for the development of students' language proficiency as well as discipline-specific skills (Aguilar, 2017; Airey, 2011; see also Chapters 8 & 11).

Content lecturers teaching in non-linguistic degree programmes may feel inadequately trained for such a challenge, which can lead to language or personal anxiety, and even resistance to EMI (Ali & Hamid, 2018; Doiz *et al.*, 2011; Tange, 2012). The skills needed for the fostering, tracking and assessment of language skills largely exceed content lecturers' previous professional training. Classroom observations have generally revealed an essential disregard of language aspects in EMI lectures, seminars, assignments and assessment (Aguilar & Rodríguez, 2012; Cho, 2012; Costa & Coleman, 2013; Hu & Jun, 2014; Kuteeva & Airey, 2014; Li & Wu, 2018). Additionally, code-switching between the L1 and a foreign language is not automatic and thought processes in L2 are distinct from those in a L1 (Kong & Hoare, 2011). Even if these processes were similar, the question about which language proficiency standard to offer or require from students would still stand, with content teachers tending to overlook vocabulary and grammar aspects in feedback and assessment (Lasagabaster & Doiz, 2018). Consequently, such disregard for language can ultimately jeopardise student grades because of the interrelationship between content and language achievement; for instance, empirical studies on EMI have shown that both the grasp of theoretical content and the development of hand-on skills rely heavily on students' prior linguistic proficiency (Ament & Perez-Vidal, 2015; Hernandez-Nanclares & Jimenez-Munoz, 2017).

The uncertainty about the actual outcome of EMI likely has a detrimental effect on lecturer confidence and anxiety levels. As such, professional development should be considered as a means to potentially alleviate stress prior to starting EMI. However, most surveys of HE EMI training programmes in Europe and Asia reveal that they have been driven towards *ad hoc*, one-off lecturer accreditations rather than systematic teacher development (Lauridsen, 2017). Furthermore, the majority of these trainings have been devoted to improving lecturers' English language competence (Halbach & Lázaro, 2015) and not EMI-specific pedagogical skills (O'Dowd, 2018). Language requirements have been shown to vary greatly among EMI teaching staff and institutions (Aguilar & Rodríguez, 2012; Airey, 2011; Guarda & Helm, 2016), often with in-house or external language certification as the only requirement for lecturers who wish (or are compelled) to teach in English. Although there is no conclusive agreement on the minimum language level required for teaching EMI, lecturers' expected level of English after accreditation ranges from B2 to C1 (Dearden, 2018), although this varies greatly from country to country (Costa & Coleman, 2013).

There is, therefore, a very narrow approach to teacher training and professional development, as most training programmes merely aim at transferring pre-existing lecturer skills into merely transactional English. However, it must be noted that 'there may need to be some profound changes in EMI academics' linguistic awareness and pedagogical skills: a monologic, teacher-led pedagogy will not be sufficient' (Dearden, 2018: 325). In addition, there are psychological aspects to EMI teaching and learning that are often overlooked; not only do EMI teachers have to deal with their own language anxiety, but they also should attempt to 'lower learning anxiety of local students' (Huang, 2015: 77). Such expectations would not alleviate language stress; rather, these need to equip lecturers with tools and techniques to scaffold language into content learning, better support students in their language learning and to help content teachers include language targets into feedback and assessment (Pérez-Vidal, 2015; Valcke & Wilkinson, 2017). At the EMI classroom level, focusing on language objectives in addition to content objectives may require further lecturer training as more attention to language and metalinguistic sophistication has been shown to be beyond most lecturers' current skills or purview (Morton, 2018). In rare cases where more pedagogical training has been provided, these programmes have 'improved the teachers' self-efficacy by guiding them to think about the nature of EMI and its role in content learning, and by providing modelling and microteaching practice in a learning community' (Chen & Peng, 2019), which may help in lowering stress levels.

Despite foreign-language classroom anxiety being a long-established concept (Horwitz et al., 1986; Horwitz, 2010), it has been associated more with student performance rather than that of teaching staff (Hewitt & Stephenson, 2011; Horwitz, 1996). This is perhaps one possible reason why EMI policy in HE has not measured the psychological implications of such a paradigm shift for lecturers and has generally relied on L1 teaching experience and L1-L2 skills transference. The disregard for studies on the complexity of EMI classroom interaction (Fortanet & Ruiz Madrid, 2014; Haines, 2015; Molino, 2015; Pun & Macaro, 2019) has created a situation in which most EMI designs overlook teacher and learners' needs, thus creating the perfect storm for psychological distress (i.e. severe or sustained stress) in lecturers. This has been recently reported in both Asian and European in settings where teachers have lacked proficiency or have been compelled to teach EMI by their departments (Chou, 2018; Margić & Vodopija-Krstanović, 2018). Language anxiety has been shown to be heavily linked to self-perceptions of insufficient language proficiency in multilingual contexts (Bell, 2008; Sparks & Ganschow, 2007). While language anxiety in lecturers has generally been believed to lessen with experience, it must be noted that lecturers transitioning to EMI teaching typically come from situations where they are already experienced and confident in their expertise, classroom management and L1 language skills. When they shift to teaching their subject through English, in light of the above considerations, they may feel unprepared, unqualified and anxious about their performance or uncertain about what to expect or demand from students. This anxiety can be heightened by the fact that they may face experiences and feelings they thought they had overcome years or decades ago. This situation is worth exploring in detail; there is a marked lack of research on the psychological aspects of EMI teaching. With few exceptions (Kunt & Tum, 2010; Vu & Burns, 2014; Zacharias, 2013) the numerous studies on EMI teacher beliefs have generally overlooked this issue, and it is still 'safe to say that research focusing on teacher foreign language anxiety has remained in its infancy' (Tum, 2012: 2056). It would also be useful to align the potential lessening of anxiety not only with experience, but also with other relevant pedagogical aspects that should be covered by training. To attain evidence of this, it would be best to give voice to experienced EMI staff themselves, and to construct an interpretive model inductively, rather than presenting them within a number of predefined research questions. This inductive process uses in-depth interviewing, which may set general areas for discussion but it does not highlight any predefined issues, so that 'it would not inhibit participants' responses' while remaining 'highly responsive to participants' individual differences and the contextual transformations' (Liu, 2016: 132). Thus, response and comment variations, as well as off-topic or unexpected phenomena, can occur as prompted by participant responses.

The Study

Method

Data in this study consisted of semi-structured interviews of approximately one-hour with 60 EMI lecturers from 20 countries (Table 10.1). These interviews were conducted in English. The interview protocol was based off relevant literature and it asked about their experiences, professional training histories, motivation, confidence and other beliefs after five years of service as EMI instructors. Their answers to questions were transcribed manually and then inductively annotated and codified using MAXQDA 18 computer-assisted mixed methods text analysis software. Qualitative data was then prepared for statistical analysis, so that each contribution was associated to a number of codes. The resulting code dataset was then explored quantitatively with R software 3.6.0, using Pearson correlation coefficients to unearth the relations between potentially co-dependent variables, with a significance threshold of alpha 0.05. Additionally, lecturers were asked to write a 500-word note to their former selves, an unstructured reflection exercise asking them to highlight what aspects of EMI teaching and learning they believed to be more relevant after gaining experience and which they wished they had known at the start of their EMI teaching. Their notes were subsequently analysed through SEANCE 1.2.0 (Crossley *et al.*, 2017), a validated corpus-linguistics sentiment analysis tool that includes 1,254 indicators of feeling, emotion, social cognition and social order in natural language. The complex dataset was further analysed through correlations, as above, to establish common links among indicators.

Participants and their training programmes

After an initial enquiry with circa 500 EMI lecturers worldwide, 221 responded they had been in EMI service for five years or more at the same institution. Out of these, 178 expressed their willingness to be interviewed, recorded and subsequently transcribed. Informants were selected to keep a comparable number per country, as well as similar EMI teaching experience, making participants as homogeneous as possible; finally, 60 of these interviews were carried out, representing 20 different countries. In practice, this entails three informants per country; since EMI approaches are very varied even within the same country, the aim was not to achieve in-depth knowledge of a particular country, but to give a more comprehensive snapshot of EMI practice worldwide. A balance was sought between different universities and areas of knowledge, sexes and state-funded vs. private institutions.

To create a clearer picture of their EMI training, the initial 500 participants (i.e. before interviews) answered questions about whether their institutions had an accreditation system in place or not, the language level required to be an EMI teacher (based on the CEFR), and the length and nature of their EMI training programme (i.e. whether it included any pedagogical input) if it existed. Additionally, they were asked how EMI accreditation was achieved (via language tests or classroom observation, etc.) if this was required in their context. An outline of informant training programmes, grouped by country, shows stark differences in their training and background. Not all universities, not even those within the same country, required all of their staff to be accredited or to follow training before teaching EMI modules; similarly, language level, the amount of hours devoted to such training (when required), the weight of pedagogical aspects in the training syllabus, and whether lesson observations took place in order to assess EMI teaching skills vary greatly from country to country and institution to institution as shown in Table 10.1.

Table 10.1 Outline of EMI teacher-training programmes by country ($n = 500$)

Country	Accreditation required (%)	Min. CEFR	Training hours (avg.)	Pedagogical content in training programmes (%)	Language testing (%)	Lesson observation required (%)	Male	Female	Avg. age
Austria	75	C1	12	0	75	25	1	2	32
Brazil	25	B2	32	5	100	0	2	1	28.33
China	14.3	B1	62	0	64.3	21.4	1	2	30
Croatia	0	B2	0	0	100	0	1	2	26
Estonia	100	C1	55	8	100	25	2	1	35
Germany	0	N/A	0	0	0	0	2	1	41.33
Greece	100	B2	68	12	87.5	37.5	1	2	34
Hong Kong	92.9	B2	44	3	78.6	21.4	2	1	31
Hungary	100	B2	42	6	100	50	1	2	29.33
India	25	B1	12	0	25	0	2	1	31
Japan	100	C1	74	4	100	42.9	1	2	37
Poland	50	C1	20	0	50	50	1	2	29.33
Russia	28.6	C1	52	14	100	14.3	1	2	27.33
South Africa	0	N/A	0	0	0	0	2	1	37
South Korea	33.3	B1	45	0	100	0	2	1	39.33
Spain	88.9	B2	57	6	55.6	11.1	1	2	43
Taiwan	54.5	C1	62	2	90.9	18.2	2	1	31.33
Turkey	66.7	B1	74	7	75	16.7	2	1	33
Ukraine	66.7	B2	26	4	100	0	1	2	28.33
United States*	8.3	C1	0	0	16.7	75	2	1	27
Total (Avg.)	51.46	B2	36.85	3.55	70.93	20.43	30	30	32.5

* Universities in Spanish-speaking areas.

This snapshot of pre-service or in-service EMI training reveal great inconsistency in EMI training, with a potential impact on teacher anxiety. First, there is no coherence in accreditation standards for teachers across institutions; some countries (Croatia, Germany, South Africa, universities in Spanish-speaking areas in the United States) have no accreditation programmes in place and generally assume EMI preparedness to coincide with language proficiency, which varies from B1 in countries such as China or India to C1 in Austria, Russia or Taiwan. Secondly, EMI training programmes are generally short (average under 40 hours) but also vary greatly. The content devoted to EMI pedagogical skills is very limited; on average, just 3.55% of the training programmes. Finally, the weight of lesson observations in training programmes is low (20.43%), which reveals that universities do not always have actual classroom evaluation of hands-on command of the language and teaching skills of their lecturers. Table 10.1 show the lack of homogeneity and quality-assurance safeguards, which ultimately transfer the responsibility of providing EMI programmes almost entirely to the lecturers themselves. EMI is a recent development in most countries, and it is often the case that already-experienced lecturers take over the job of teaching through English; in this study, many alluded to a 'moral duty' and 'responsibility' when they were asked why they enacted EMI policies (Zacharias, 2013: 98). However, already experienced or not, it is usually their first time teaching in English; many lecturers report being thrown into EMI courses haphazardly (Airey, 2011), which can 'constitute a severe strain on lecturers who are not experienced EMI teachers' (Werther *et al.*, 2014: 454).

Interviews and notes to former selves

To construct the questions for the semi-structured interviews, six major areas were identified after interview piloting at two universities: experience, professional training, motivation, confidence, self-ideation and other beliefs. For each of these, a number or key questions were asked including questions about their experiences and roles as both researchers (which implicitly puts them in connection with larger English-speaking audiences) and lecturers. Informants were provided the opportunity to elaborate and digress, within reason, as long as they touched upon all of the topics, though not necessarily in the same order. The interview questions are shown in Table 10.2.

Qualitative codification of interview transcripts was inductive; i.e. there was no set of pre-defined themes, other than the areas covered by these questions. Rather, it was the reading and annotation of lecturer's interview transcripts that created a bottom-up list of active issues. A two-pass recodification was carried out once all of the transcripts had been processed, to accommodate emerging codes in all transcripts.

Table 10.2 EMI-related interview questions

Q1	What EMI modules have you taught?
Q2	Why did you decide to start teaching in English?
Q3	Did you feel prepared when you started teaching in English?
Q4	How confident are you in your teaching skills in English now?
Q5	Do you see yourself more as a researcher than a teacher?
Q6	Are you an active researcher (in English)?
Q7	Do you feel different from a L1 teacher?
Q8	What is your major motivation for staying in EMI?
Q9	What has been teaching EMI like for you, personally?
Q10	Do you feel you have been successful?
Q11	Do you have any particular concerns at present?
Q12	Do you think you could improve as an EMI lecturer? (If so, how?)

A total of 3764 codifications were annotated (n=60 participants, average 62.73 codifications per interview).

As a final question, informants were asked to write a not to their former selves. This was a creative-writing exercise designed as a reflection on their past experiences. They were provided one week in which to produce this note. It was explained they should focus on what they wished they had known at the beginning of their EMI teaching, or what they would say to their former selves if it were possible. They were given the following prompt to produce a 500-word text:

Dear Former Self,

I am writing to you from the future. I have been now teaching EMI for over 5 years and I would like to let you know that…

Results

Interviews

The analysis of interview codifications resulted in 42 distinct issues raised by interviewees, from considerations about the English language to concerns about student preparedness. Table 10.3 shows the most frequent codes, their relative weight in the codifications and how many participants commented on the issue.

These results reveal that English language is, by far, one of the most relevant concerns arising in the interviews (see also Chapters 3, 8, 10 & 11). This is not surprising, since it is a pivotal aspect of EMI provisions and research activities, such as presenting at conferences or interacting with other colleagues worldwide. However, lecturers seem to pay more attention to the English language as a separate entity than to their own

Table 10.3 Top 15 codes in interviews

Code	Frequency	Percentage of total codifications	Percentage of participants (total)
English_language_general	655	17.4	100 (60)
Training_negative	309	8.2	100 (60)
Nervousness_own	294	7.8	100 (60)
Content_negative	252	6.7	100 (60)
English_language_own	203	5.4	96.67 (58)
Interaction_classroom	184	4.9	90 (54)
English_language_student	166	4.4	86.67 (52)
Unpreparedness_student	117	3.1	70 (42)
Motivation_positive	102	2.7	68.33 (41)
Resources_positive	94	2.5	65 (39)
Internet_positive	87	2.3	58.33 (35)
Presenting_content	79	2.1	51.67 (31)
Time_neg	72	1.9	46.67 (28)
Writing_students_neg	68	1.8	46.67 (28)
Satisfaction_positive	60	1.6	45 (27)

linguistic performance or the language of their students. Although virtually all lecturers comment on language issues, the frequency of comments on English as an independent system double comments where lecturers reflect on actual language use. Also, for these teachers, it seems that the focus on their own English competence is more important for them, but closely followed by their concern about students' English and their preparedness for EMI. Other major anxiety factors (besides their own language proficiency) such as insufficient training, nervousness and worries about watered-down, oversimplified or excessively summarised content, uncertainty about which language standards to expect from students or complaints about lack of time for preparation and students' poor writing skills are also mentioned. On the other hand, positive aspects such as motivation, having ample resources and digital resources or general satisfaction are also relatively frequent.

The overall picture is one of great concern: if some codifications (i.e. English as a language, classroom interaction or presenting content, totalling 918 codifications) can be said to be neutral, most items raised in the interviews are related to negative aspects (language, content or learning concerns and shortcomings, 1198 codifications), which greatly outweigh positive connotations (such as motivation, having resources, 343 codifications). This presents, in principle, a bleak prospect. A more detailed snapshot of the balance and relevance of these positive and negative issues can be determined through an analysis of the bivariate correlations among them. When correlated, the following pairs were

Table 10.4 Top five bivariate correlations in interviews ($p = 0.038$)

Variable pair	R-squared	Adjusted R-squared
Training_negative ~ Nervousness_own	0.8557	0.8552
Satisfaction ~ Nervousness_own	0.7032	0.7028
English_language_student ~ Writing_students_neg	0.6538	0.6535
Satisfaction ~ Training_negative	0.5791	0.5789
Unpreparedness_student ~ Motivation_positive	0.5277	0.5274

shown to be significantly related (Table 10.4); i.e. that when one was mentioned by an interviewee, the other was also frequently mentioned as well.

The very strong relation (i.e. above 0.70) between the negative consideration of training as insufficient and self-perceived nervousness seems logical. It can be assumed that if lecturers were 'not given any indication about how to teach' (informant 14, hereafter as inf) during training, or were 'only required decent English' (inf 8) they would feel as nervous as when they 'started teaching, and that was 20 years ago!' (inf 47). Consequences include 'considerable anxiety' (inf 33), a 'tendency to overprepare' (inf 22) and a 'general sense of uncertainty about what to expect from students' (inf 54). Lecturers think that 'sometimes something works with a group and not with another' (inf 37), which 'does not usually happen teaching in my language' (inf 29). Similarly, complaints on students' English correlate highly (i.e. above 0.60) with concerns about their writing; although it is not uncommon to find lecturers who believe that 'their English is better than mine was at their age' (inf 8) or even 'better than my pronunciation' (inf 17), they complain that 'they speak better than they write' (inf 60) and they 'find it very hard not to be informal' (inf 45) or they write 'like they talk' (inf 47), so that 'they tell you a story, but this is an academic essay' (inf 12), which would suggest specific training in Academic English is needed before students enrol EMI degrees.

On the contrary, the strong link between positive and negative elements is more counterintuitive. When asked, interviewers who commented on both being 'generally satisfied' (inf 23) or 'happy with my lessons in English now' (inf 51) tended to also comment on being 'nervous for the whole year' (inf 23) when they started teaching through English and 'dreading about lessons' (inf 51). Similarly, those expressing that they give 'mostly good lessons' (inf 18) and 'it is clear that students learn' (inf 56) also complain more about the lack of training 'to learn how to help the students' (inf 18) or how to make that learning 'even better' (inf 56). Finally, lecturers who thought that students were 'not prepared for university' (inf 33) and 'lack basic skills' (inf 45) they should 'have learnt at high-school' (inf 18) also tend to perceive that students are 'more motivated' (inf 45) and 'work harder' (inf 18) than L1 students, because EMI requires 'much more dedication' (inf 33).

Notes to lecturers' former selves

The analysis of sentiment in teachers' notes to their former selves can offer an even more nuanced approach to these relations. As it is more unstructured and introspective, these notes are intended to complement the comments in the interviews, which were mainly aimed at the consideration of external factors (which, as discussed, were seen in mainly negative terms) such as language, institutions, training or students. The focus on personal experience might lead to a more relevant observation about the experience of teaching EMI by contrasting memories from the early stages with current performance and beliefs after relatively long experience, which is typically less influenced by anxiety (Hewitt & Stephenson, 2011; Horwitz, 1996). Indicators of sentiment in texts are usually created by using well-established emotion markers such as the *Affective Norms for English Words*, ANEW (Bradley & Lang, 1999) or the *Geneva Affect Label Coder*, GALC (Scherer, 2005) as well as more recent developments such as the *NRC Emotion Lexicon* (Mohammad & Turney, 2013). The latter contains over 1200 indicators of basic human emotions such as excitement, longing, anger, anxiety or boredom, also subcategorised by connotative nuances or part-of-speech. These emotions are flagged when a given string is found in the text. For example, GALC detects anxiety markers if the strings *afraid, alarm*, anguish*, anxi** or *apprehens** are present and works out its relevance, offering a normalised indicator. Advanced indices included in the study can find up to 14,000 words flagging different emotions or mental states.

When analysed through SEANCE (Crossley *et al.*, 2017), which calculates all the aforementioned indices, the notes to the lecturers' former selves (n = 60; avg. 476.03 words; SD 4.41%) showed the following emotion markers (Table 10.5) as the most prominent.

The exploration of these indices (see Kyle (2018) for further code marker references) reveals a very positive reflection, which contrasts with the fact that codifications in the interviews tended to reveal a negative outlook. Negative markers are infrequent in the notes, only partially appearing in the cases of *Arousal* (which can signal the awakening of affiliation or hostility) and *Vader_compound* (showing mixed emotions). This unearths three relevant findings:

- the essential mode for lecturers in these notes is emotional rather than cognitive or factual; when reminiscing, the relative weigh of *Valence* (level of positive or negative liking), *Dominance* (level of control) and *Polarity* (positive vs. negative values) account for the four most relevant indicators;

Table 10.5 Top 15 sentiment indicators in lecturers' notes

Marker	Meaning	Index source	Average
Valence	Expression of feeling	Bradley and Lang (1999)	24.16148474
Dominance	Expression of respect and power	Bradley and Lang (1999)	21.7796044
Arousal	Affiliation or hostility	Bradley and Lang (1999)	21.70418803
Polarity	Expression of emotions	Cambria et al. (2012)	6.097165992
Hu_liu_prop	Feeling over emotion	Hu and Liu (2005)	6.363743333
Joy_component	Positive emotions	Scherer (2005)	4.001285187
Vader_compound	Mixed emotions	Hutto and Gilbert (2014)	3.8719
Vader_neutral	Evaluation, assessment	Hutto and Gilbert (2014)	2.846
Hu_liu_pos_perc	Positive perception	Hu and Liu (2005)	2.566666667
Action_component	Active words	Stone and Hunt (1963)	2.526190476
Vader_positive_ adjectives	Positive emotions	Hutto and Gilbert (2014)	2.316837846
Positive_verbs_ component	Positive verbs	Scherer (2005)	2.205939035
Active_GI_verbs	Active verbs	Stone and Hunt (1963)	2.153
Strong_GI_adjectives	Word implying strength	Stone and Hunt (1963)	2.082282048
Virtue_GI_adjectives	Indication of approval	Stone and Hunt (1963)	1.988153153

- such a reflection on their past is essentially positive; lecturers tend to be compassionate, understanding or approving of their former selves, because they feel they rose to the challenge of EMI teaching;
- there is a clear contrast between current and past experiences, as indicated in the presence of mixed feelings and resentment towards past situations, but these mainly act as a catalyser for the more abundant positive comments.

To analyse the relations among indices, 242 primary emotion indicators were selected, leaving out those referring to a specific part-of-speech and those with empty values. When correlated, they confirmed such co-dependence (Table 10.6).

Table 10.6 Top five bivariate correlations in interviews ($p = 0.029$)

Variable pair	R-squared	Adjusted R-squared
Valence ~ Arousal	0.8134	0.8311
Valence ~ Dominance	0.7862	0.7859
Arousal ~ hu_liu_prop	0.7498	0.7496
Dominance ~ joy_component	0.7167	0.7165
Arousal ~ Virtue_GI	0.6967	0.6965

The strong link between *Valence* (feeling) and *Arousal* (affiliation or hostility) or *Dominance* (respect and power) helps interpret lecturers' standpoints when confronting their past. They did so from an emotional point of view, essentially recognising a sense of attachment and compassion for past anxieties. Such a standpoint is constructive: *Arousal* can indicate the presence of positive or negative comments, though here these are mainly positive perceptions, emotions or indications of approval. While some negative aspects appeared to be more prominent in interview codifications, these comments seem to be restricted here to their use for contrasting with current situations or suggestions. Teachers insisted that they 'needn't have worried so much' (inf 14) about their own performance and that they would 'be fine after all' (inf 28), although most recognised 'it was hard at first' (inf 49). Lecturers advised their former selves to 'focus on the students, on their learning' (inf 26) and 'their English' (inf 21) in 'any way you can' (inf 55). Most believed that students can 'learn in many ways outside the classroom' (inf 54) and that 'lectures should cover the basics' (inf 37) or 'just what is essential' (inf 29), so they can 'enjoy teaching' (inf 33). A revealing idea appears in some notes: the presence of EMI as a 'problem' (inf 38) rather than an opportunity, where lecturers feel the need to remind their former selves that they are part of the solution, and that they can 'feel proud' (inf 46). As one lecturer put it, 'It was traumatic. I tell myself: it wasn't me. I was not the problem; I was fine – I didn't know it then, but I was fine. It was the students, the problem; their English, their knowledge and the complexity of learning everything through English. But we got through' (inf 49).

Discussion and Conclusion

Results show how, while key sources of anxiety remain problematic after at least five years of EMI teaching (in light of the interview codifications), experience generally appeases anxiety, negative self-ideation and fears of underperformance. The emphasis on positive aspects or the diminishing of past negative experiences is a sign of current psychological well-being, in contrast with past anxieties. However, such an improvement is not propelled by experience only; as seen in the interviews and the analysis of the notes to their former selves, there is a link between anxiety relief and the displacement of pedagogical focus on student learning. The analyses of data make it manifest that experienced EMI lecturers implicitly highlight the need for resilience and a growth mindset in the face of adversity, which can also be crucial for their prospective students.

As reported by these successful lecturers, there seem to be important shortcomings in non-personalised training programmes, which may add to initial anxiety and pressure, on top of other aforementioned organisational aspects. Consequently, a number of vital progressive steps are suggested to ease the transition towards EMI: moving from pre-service, one-size-fits-all accreditation and training to a developmental professional development for EMI; including pedagogy and EMI-specific teaching micro-skills; introducing aspects of linguistic description and reflection for both instructors and their learners; promoting collaboration among EMI lecturers; and, finally, assessing students' linguistic competence before they begin EMI courses and offering them EAP (English for Academic Purposes) training as per their areas of specialisation. These components would result in better anticipation of EMI-specific problems and less uncertainty about what actually happens during EMI teaching and learning. Many lecturers in STEM (Science, Technology, Engineering and Mathematics) subjects (half of the sample in this study are STEM) are under the misapprehension that language requirements are minimal (Macaro & Dearden, 2016) beyond specialised vocabulary (Ruiz *et al.*, 2010). These assumptions greatly contrast with long-established views within Applied Linguistics, where successful undergraduates in immersion contexts have been known to require highly specialised forms of written and spoken discourses (Cummins, 2000) precisely because 'different types of scientific discourse make use of a variety of syntactic structures in differing proportions' (Carter-Thomas & Rowley-Jolivet, 2001: 19) and these are always subject to a 'disciplinary affordance that underpins appropriate holistic meaning-making' (Linder, 2013: 44). In other words, students do need not only subject-specific vocabulary and supporting syntax, but also academic and disciplinary communicative competences.

A number of limitations to this study have to be acknowledged. First, the corpus is small, particularly considering universities around the world participated, and it reports the comments of lecturers with many different backgrounds in several countries, with different language and professional development requirements (Table 10.1). Additionally, it encompasses lecturers who volunteered and had not dropped teaching EMI after at least five years, which implies a certain degree of success on their part. The results, however, display insights into successful EMI lecturers' present and former selves and their related feelings, which new entrants to EMI teaching can take as a useful benchmark. Most experienced lectures seem to have perceived the introduction of bilingual programmes as an opportunity for the revision of instructional design in order to make it more participative, inclusive and student-centred (Guarda & Helm, 2016) and the interviews and notes reveal that progress in this direction relieves teacher concerns. Such a pedagogical shift is indeed needed in the implementation of EMI and thus needs to be guaranteed by improved training programmes. The inclusion of more active pedagogies in better EMI training would not only affect teacher performance and self-perception, but also considerably alleviate lecturers' stress considerably, especially since EMI is still expanding fast to new countries, areas of knowledge – and lecturers.

Implications for Policy and Practice

In many respects, EMI lecturer responses in interviews are on par with comments and perceptions from those by foreign-language teachers (Brown, 2009), CLIL practitioners (Di Martino & Di Sabato, 2012) and other EMI studies (Aguilar & Rodríguez, 2012; Floris, 2014), both experienced and pre-service. Teachers' 'self-efficacy beliefs may decline when a high level of stress or anxiety is experienced' (Tsui, 2018: 107); consequently, suggested proposals for specific course components must be included in all professional development for EMI teachers and lecturers (as well as primary and secondary CLIL and foreign language teachers in general) particularly in the case new entrants to the profession. Lecturers who find themselves having to teach EMI without much preparation and perhaps with low levels of English, have feelings that other teachers who have to teach their subjects through English can identify with. To know in advance that stress and anxiety are commonplace, and that they usually alleviate with time, can help as a coping mechanism. Also, for EMI trainers it is worth noticing that individual beliefs and perceptions are heavily affected by organisational changes, which can highlight the need for better implementation of both professional development and immersion programmes in the directions summarised above. Furthermore, spreading the notion that when 'a university is going EMI then we would expect some important structural changes to be made' (Dearden, 2018: 336) can perhaps help lecturers understand they are not solely responsible for the success of EMI programmes: it must be a joint, well-supported and well-guided effort on the part of both academics *and* their institutions.

References

Aguilar, M. (2017) Engineering lecturers' views on CLIL and EMI. *International Journal of Bilingual Education and Bilingualism* 20 (6), 722–735.

Aguilar, M. and Rodríguez, R. (2012) Lecturer and student perceptions on CLIL at a Spanish university. *International Journal of Bilingual Education and Bilingualism* 15 (2), 183–197.

Airey, J. (2011) Talking about teaching in English: Swedish university lecturers' experiences of changing teaching language. *Iberica* 22, 35–54.

Airey, J. (2013) 'I don't teach language.' The linguistic attitudes of physics lecturers in Sweden. *AILA Review* 25, 64–79.

Ali, N.L. (2013) A changing paradigm in language planning: English-medium instruction policy at the tertiary level in Malaysia. *Current Issues in Language Planning* 14 (1), 73–92.

Ali, N.L. and Hamid, M.O. (2018) English-medium instruction and teacher agency in higher education: a case study. In C. Chua (ed.) *Un(intended) Language Planning in a Globalising World: Multiple Levels of Players at Work* (pp. 234–250). Berlin: De Gruyter.

Ament, R. and Perez-Vidal, C. (2015) Linguistic outcomes of English medium instruction programmes in higher education: A study on economics undergraduates at a Catalan university. *Higher Learning Research Communications* 5 (1), 47–68.

Bell, J. (2008) Statistics anxiety and business statistics. *Education* 129 (2), 282–286.

Bonnet, A. (2012) Towards an evidence base for CLIL: How to integrate qualitative and quantitative as well as process, product and participant perspectives in CLIL research. *International CLIL Research Journal* 1 (4), 65–78.

Bradley, M. and Lang, P. (1999) *Affective Norms for English Words (ANEW): Instruction Manual and Affective Ratings*. Miami, FL: University of Florida.

Brown, A.V. (2009) Students' and teachers' perceptions of effective foreign language teaching: A comparison of ideals. *The Modern Language Journal* 93 (1), 46–60.

Cambria, E., Havasi, C. and Hussain, A. (2012) SenticNet 2: a semantic and affective resource for opinion mining and sentiment analysis. *Proceedings of the 25th International Florida Artificial Intelligence Research Society Conference*, 202–207.

Carter-Thomas, S. and Rowley-Jolivet, E. (2001) Syntactic differences in oral and written scientific discourse: the role of information structure. *ASp* 31 (33), 19–37.

Chen, Y. and Peng, J. (2019) Continuing professional development of EMI teachers: A Chinese case study. *Journal of Education for Teaching* 45 (2), 219–222.

Cho, D.W. (2012) English-medium instruction in the university context of Korea: Tradeoff between teaching outcomes and media-initiated university ranking. *The Journal of Asia TEFL* 9 (12), 135–163.

Chou, M. (2018) Speaking anxiety and strategy use for learning English as a foreign language in full and partial English-medium instruction contexts. *TESOL Quarterly* 58 (2), 611–633.

Costa, F. and Coleman, J.A. (2013) A survey of English-medium instruction in Italian higher education. *International Journal of Bilingual Education and Bilingualism* 16 (1), 3–19.

Crossley, S., Kyle, K. and McNamara, D. (2017) Sentiment analysis and social cognition engine (SEANCE): An automatic tool for sentiment, social cognitionand social order analysis. *Behavior Research Methods* 49 (3), 803–821.

Cummins, J. (2000) *Language, Power and Pedagogy: Bilingual Children in the Crossfire*. Clevedon: Multilingual Matters.

Dafouz, E., Camacho, M. and Urquía, E. (2014) Surely they can't do as well: A comparison of business students' academic performance in English-medium and Spanish-as-first-language medium programmes. *Language and Education* 28 (3), 223–236.

Dearden, J. (2015) *English as a Medium of Instruction: A Growing Global Phenomenon*. London: British Council.

Dearden, J. (2018) The Changing roles of EMI academics and English language specialists. In Y. Kırkgöz and K. Dikilitaş (eds) *Key Issues in English for Specific Purposes in Higher Education* (pp. 323–333). New York, NY: Springer.

Di Martino, E. and Di Sabato, B. (2012) CLIL implementation in Italian schools: Can long-serving teachers be retrained effectively? The Italian protagonists' voice. *Latin American Journal of Content and Language Integrated Learning* 5 (2), 73–105.

Doiz, A., Lasagabaster, D. and Sierra, J.M. (2011) Internationalisation, multilingualism and English-medium instruction. *World Englishes* 20 (3), 345–359.

Erling, E. and Hilgendorf, S. (2006) Language policies in the context of German higher education. *Language Policy* 5, 267–292.

Floris, F.D. (2014) Learning subject matter through English as the medium of instruction: students' and teachers' perspectives. *Asian Englishes* 16 (1), 47–59.

Fortanet, I. and Ruiz Madrid, N. (2014) Multimodality for comprehensive communication in the classroom: Questions in guest lectures. *Iberica* 28, 203–224.

Graham, K., Choi, Y., Davoodi, A., Razmeh, S. and Dixonet, Q. (2018) Language and content outcomes of CLIL and EMI: A systematic review. *Latin American Journal of Content and Language Integrated Learning* 11 (1), 19–37.

Guarda, M. and Helm, F. (2016) 'I have discovered new teaching pathways': The link between language shift and teaching practice. *International Journal of Bilingual Education and Bilingualism* 20 (7), 897–913.

Haines, K. (2015) Purposeful interaction and the professional development of content teachers: Observations of small-group teaching and learning in the international classroom. In J. Valcke and R. Wilkinson (eds) *Integrating Content and Language in Higher Education* (pp. 39–58). Frankfurt am Main: Peter Lang.

Halbach, A. and Lázaro, A. (2015) *La acreditación del nivel de lengua inglesa en las universidades españolas*. Madrid, ES: British Council.

Hernandez-Nanclares, N. and Jimenez-Munoz, A. (2017) English as a medium of instruction: evidence for language and content targets in bilingual education in economics. *International Journal of Bilingual Education and Bilingualism* 20 (7), 883–896.

Hewitt, E. and Stephenson, J. (2011) Foreign language anxiety and oral exam performance: A replication of Phillips's MLJ study. *Modern Language Journal* 95, 1–20.

Horwitz, E. (1996) Even teachers get the blues: Recognizing and alleviating language teachers' feelings of foreign language anxiety. *Foreign Language Annals* 29 (3), 365–372.

Horwitz, E. (2010) Foreign and second language anxiety. *Language Teaching* 43, 154–167.

Horwitz, E., Horwitz, M. and Cope, J. (1986) Foreign language classroom anxiety. *Modern Language Journal* 70, 125–132.

Hu, G. and Jun, L. (2014) English-medium instruction in Chinese higher education: A case study. *Higher Education* 67 (5), 551–567.

Hu, M. and Liu, B. (2005) Mining and summarizing customer reviews. *Proceedings of the 10th Association for Computing Machinery Special Interest Group on Knowledge Discovery and Data Mining International Conference on Knowledge Discovery and Data Mining*, 168–177.

Huang, D.-F. (2015) Exploring and assessing effectiveness of English medium instruction courses: The students' perspectives. *Procedia-Social and Behavioral Sciences* 173, 71–78.

Hutto, C.J. and Gilbert, E. (2014) VADER: A Parsimonious Rule-Based Model for Sentiment Analysis of Social Media Text. *Proceedings of the Association for the Advancement of Artificial Intelligence Eighth International Conference on Weblogs and Social Media*, 216–225.

Jimenez-Munoz, A. (2016) Content and language: The impact of pedagogical designs on academic performance within tertiary English as a medium of instruction. *Porta Linguarum* M1, 111–125.

Kong, S. and Hoare, P. (2011) Cognitive content engagement in content-based language teaching. *Language Teaching Research* 15 (3), 307–324.

Kunt, S. and Tum, D.O. (2010) Non- feelings of foreign language anxiety. *Procedia Social and Behavioral Sciences* 2 (2), 4672–4676.

Kyle, K. (2018) SEANCE 1.2.1. index, database. See https://drive.google.com/file/d/1SUfSYNyuaWT2i4tQkiyr2rxVeqnh3cQe/view (accessed March 2019).

Kyriacou, C. (2001) Teacher stress: Directions for future research. *Educational Review* 53 (1), 27–35.

Kuteeva, M. and Airey, J. (2014) Disciplinary differences in the use of English in higher education: Reflections on recent language policy developments. *Higher Education* 67 (5), 533–549.

Lasagabaster, D. and Doiz, A. (2018) Language errors in an English-medium instruction university setting: How do language versus content teachers tackle them? *Porta Linguarum* 30, 131–148.

Lauridsen, K. (2017) Professional development of intenational classroom lecturers. In J. Valcke and R. Wilkinson (eds) *Integrating Content and Language in Higher Education* (pp. 25–37). Frankfurt am Main: Peter Lang.

Linder, C. (2013) Disciplinary discourse, representationand appresentation in the teaching and learning of science. *European Journal of Science and Mathematics Education* 1 (2), 43–49.

Li, N. and Wu, J. (2018) Exploring assessment for learning practices in the EMI classroom in the context of Taiwanese higher education. *Language Education & Assessment* 1 (1), 28–44.

Liu, L. (2016) Using generic inductive approach in qualitative educational research: A case study analysis. *Journal of Education and Learning* 5 (2), 129–135.

Macaro, E. and Dearden, J. (2016) Higher education teachers' attitudes towards English: A three country comparison. *Studies in Second Language Learning and Teaching* 6 (2), 3–34.

Macaro, E., Curle, S., Pun, J., An, J. and Dearden, J. (2018) A systematic review of English medium instruction in higher education. *Language Teaching* 51 (1), 36–76.

Margić, B. and Vodopija-Krstanović, I. (2018) Language development for English-medium instruction: Teachers' perceptions, reflections and learning. *Journal of English for Academic Purposes* 35, 31–41.

Mohammad, S. and Turney, P. (2013) Crowdsourcing a WordEmotion Association Lexicon. *Computational Intelligence* 29 (3), 436–465.

Molino, A. (2015) Comprehension and interaction in university lectures delivered in English. *Ricognizioni* 2 (4), 139–153.

Morton, T. (2018) Reconceptualizing and describing teachers' knowledge of language for content and language integrated learning (CLIL). *International Journal of Bilingual Education and Bilingualism* 21 (3), 275–286.

O'Dowd, R. (2018) The training and accreditation of teachers for English medium instruction: an overview of practice in European universities. *International Journal of Bilingual Education and Bilingualism* 21 (5), 553–563.

Pecorari, D., Shaw, P., Irvine, A. and Malmström, H. (2011) English for academic purposes at Swedish universities: Teachers' objectives and practices. *Iberica* 22, 55–78.

Pérez-Vidal, C. (2015) Languages for all in education: CLIL and ICLHE at the crossroads of multilingualism, mobility and internationalisation. In M. Juan-Garau and J. Salazar-Noguera (eds) *Content-based Language Learning in Multilingual Educational Environments* (pp. 31–50). New York, NY: Springer.

Pulcini, V. and Campagna, S. (2015) Internationalisation and the EMI controversy in Italian higher education. In S. Dimova, A.K. Hultgren and C. Jensen (eds) *English-Medium Instruction in European Higher Education* (pp. 65–87). Boston, MA: De Gruyter Mouton.

Pun, J. and Macaro, E. (2019) The effect of first and second language use on question types in English medium instruction science classrooms in Hong Kong. *International Journal of Bilingual Education and Bilingualism* 22 (1), 64–77.

Ruiz, M., Palmer, J. and Fortanet, I. (2010) *English for Professional and Academic Purposes.* Amsterdam: Rodopi.

Scherer, K. (2005) What are emotions? And how can they be measured? *Social Science Information* 44 (4), 695–729.

Shohamy, E. (2013) A critical perspective on the use of English as a medium of instruction at universities. In A. Doiz, D. Lasagabaster and J.M. Sierra (eds) *English-Medium Instructon at Universities: Global Challenges* (pp. 196–210). Bristol: Multilingual Matters.

Sparks, R. and Ganschow, L. (2007) Is the foreign language classroom anxiety scale measuring anxiety or language skills? *Foreign Language Annals* 40 (2), 260–286.

Stone, P.J. and Hunt, E.B. (1963) A computer approach to content analysis: Studies using the general inquirer system. *Proceedings of the American Federation of Information Processing Societies*, 241–256.

Tange, H. (2012) Organising language at the international university: Three principles of linguistic organisation. *Journal of Multilingual and Multicultural Development* 33, 287–300.

Tum, D.O. (2012) Feelings of language anxiety amongst non-native student teachers. *Procedia Social and Behavioral Sciences* 47, 2055–2059.

Tsui, C. (2018) Teacher efficacy: A case study of faculty beliefs in an English-medium Instruction training programme. *Taiwan Journal of TESOL* 5 (1), 121–128.

Valcke, J. and Wilkinson, R. (2017) *Integrating Content and Language in Higher Education: Perspectives on Professional Practice.* Frankfurt am Main: Peter Lang.

Vu, N.T.T. and Burns, A. (2014) English as a medium of instruction: Challenges for Vietnamese tertiary lecturers. *The Journal of Asia TEFL* 11 (3), 1–31.

Werther, C., Denver, L., Jensen, C. and Mees, I.M. (2014) Using English as a medium of instruction at university level in Denmark: The lecturer's perspective. *Journal of Multilingual and Multicultural Development* 35 (5), 443–462.

Wilkinson, R. (2013) English-medium instruction at a Dutch university: Challenges and pitfalls. In A. Doiz, D. Lasagabaster and J.M. Sierra (eds) *English-Medium Instruction at Universities: Global Challenges* (pp. 3–24). Bristol: Multilingual Matters.

Zacharias, N.T. (2013) Navigating through the English-medium-of-instruction policy: Voices from the field. *Current Issues in Language Planning* 14, 93–108.

11 L2 Confidence in CLIL Teaching: A Tale of Two Teachers

Erwin M. Gierlinger

Introduction

The central focus of this study is a question that has surfaced yet remained elusive in my previous fieldwork in content and language integrated learning (CLIL). How do teachers experience the transition to CLIL teaching that may take them out of their linguistic and pedagogical comfort zones, may put them in a deficit position linguistically and could perhaps undermine their teaching confidence (Bovellan, 2014; Gierlinger, 2007; Hüttner *et al.*, 2013)? In CLIL environments (i.e. educational contexts where subjects, or parts of subjects, are taught through a foreign language with a dual focus on content and language learning), content teachers, or teachers who are teaching non-linguistic subjects such as Geography or Biology, may lack specific training in foreign language pedagogy and L2 teaching experience. As such, feelings of linguistic insecurity are possible. This combined with a possible lack of linguistic pedagogical knowledge may adversely affect content teachers' L2 confidence working in CLIL programmes.

In general education contexts, there is an extensive literature showing a robust relationship between teachers' self-confidence and their well-being, job satisfaction and commitment (for a review, see Zee & Koomen, 2016). In this chapter, teacher self-confidence is understood as one's abilities to mobilise the motivation, cognitive resources or courses of action needed to successfully execute a specific task within a given context (Luthans & Youssef-Morgan, 2017). Understood in this way, a teacher's sense of self-confidence could increase from gaining classroom experience or having mastered particular activities (Snyder & Lopez, 2009).

Furthermore, there is also growing research on language teacher's self-confidence (see also Chapters 12 & 15) which emphasises its domain-specificity, fluidity, vulnerability and driving role for successful teaching (Swanson, 2014; Wyatt, 2018). However, research on CLIL teachers' self-confidence and how this relates to their teaching is still in its infancy. This study therefore aims to address this research gap by investigating CLIL teacher self-confidence working at the secondary level in Austria.

Theoretical Framing

Two conceptual frameworks appear particularly useful for exploring CLIL teachers' self-confidence. The first is Swain and Lapkin's (2013) languaging perspective. From this perspective, knowledge is co-constructed through discourse. That is, language functions as the agent, regulator and mediator of learning. The second perspective follows Luthans and Youssef-Morgan's (2017) understanding of the specific and contextualised nature of confidence. These perspectives appear useful in understanding how CLIL teachers may confidently and resiliently cope with a learning environment which, from a communicative point of view, puts them into a potential deficit position. One manifestation of self-confidence that is particularly relevant in CLIL classrooms is L2 confidence, which is understood in this chapter to be a subcomponent of teachers' general sense of self-confidence. This paper takes the position that CLIL teachers' L2 confidence can be investigated from three different angles. First, would be teachers' perceived confidence in communicating their subject in the TL, possibly supported by other languages. This is subject languaging confidence. Second, their perceived confidence in using the target language (TL) for general purposes, or TL languaging confidence. The last angle would be perceived confidence in teaching the TL, or TL teaching confidence. This paper considers subject languaging confidence, TL languaging confidence and TL teaching confidence all as relevant components of teachers' L2 confidence, but also of their senses of self-confidence more generally.

By following two content teachers as they implement CLIL in their subjects, this study aims to contribute to an understanding of how CLIL teachers' self-confidence and linguistic identities, informed by their L2 confidence, shape and affect their pedagogical understanding of CLIL.

CLIL in Austria

The context for CLIL implementations in Austria is rooted in the so-called 'push for foreign languages' (Fremdsprachenoffensive), which was promoted by the Austrian Ministry of Education in the early 1990s. It was primarily intended to be an initiative to further the learning of foreign languages at Austrian schools. It spelled out that a foreign language could be used as a linguistic vehicle for the teaching of subject specific content. As this new law did not lay out any detailed legal constraints or mandatory admission criteria, it led to an upsurge in CLIL projects which allowed individual schools to set up their locally focused and tailor-made CLIL programmes. Basically, these ranged from short project-based modules to grander schemes, in which English, or other languages, were used as a means of instruction for one or more subjects throughout the whole school year. Recently CLIL has been made compulsory in secondary technical colleges for 72 lessons per year beginning at around age seventeen (see also Chapter 6).

From a language proficiency point of view the Austrian Ministry of Education does not require CLIL teachers to have any further qualifications beyond their official qualified teacher status, although regional education boards may ask non-language teachers to provide evidence of their TL competence. Since Austria has a dual-specialisation system in which teachers in secondary education become dual-subject specialists (i.e. a secondary teacher would go on to teach two subjects in school, for example, History and Geography), most of the optional CLIL projects have been carried out by teachers with the TL as one of their subjects (Gierlinger, 2017a). This would mean that a teacher who had a dual specialisation in English and History may teach history through English. In this case, this teacher would have pedagogical training in English; for those teachers who do not specialise in a language subject, they would not have any pedagogical training in English.

Although the legal context for implementing CLIL in primary and secondary education in Austria could be considered benevolent and in technical colleges even highly encouraging, the CLIL research situation within the Austrian context is rather fragmented and certainly lacks a concerted approach on a governmental level.

Research Design and Methodology

Aim of study

The following research question will be investigated: how does a multilingual teaching environment, such as CLIL, affect teachers' L2 confidence? In order to answer this question, a longitudinal qualitative study was designed. This qualitative study was carried out during the school year 2012–2013. Data were gathered through reflective interviews and classroom observations. The study investigated two teachers' experiences of introducing CLIL into their subject classes and how this linked to their linguistic and pedagogical confidence. It is hoped that information gained from this study adds to the discussion about teacher L2 confidence and the psychological aspects of CLIL teaching more generally.

Data collection and participants

The teachers, who had an interest in CLIL, were approached by the researcher and took part voluntarily. Both teachers taught their subjects, history and chemistry, in CLIL and non-CLIL formats. T1 taught chemistry and his second subject was physics. T2 taught history and his second subject was German. This design allowed the researcher to compare their parallel CLIL and non-CLIL courses in the same subjects.

Data were gathered from two non-selective lower secondary comprehensive school classes (14 to 15-year-olds), where CLIL was introduced through modular projects. For example, the history teacher carried out a project on the American elections as part of the curriculum and some units (modules) of this project would be taught in the TL, others in students' L1. The selection of these modules was up to the teacher's discretion. For more on this modular CLIL approach see Krechel (2003).

The classroom observational data were gathered by video recording whereby the focus of the filming was on the teachers. Only the teacher-student interactions were transcribed by the researcher and in most cases, the teaching of both CLIL and non-CLIL classes took place on the same day. These lessons normally lasted for 50 minutes and occurred twice a week; however, in some cases, classes were back to back on the same day. Further data were collected through a combination of semi-structured interviews with the two teachers. These interviews included stimulated recall reflections (Barnard & Burns, 2012). Stimulated recall is a type of introspective research methodology that involves the verbalisation of cognition retrospectively rather than concurrently. The interviews were semi-structured in the sense that they were all stimulated by the same criteria which were observation notes, lesson transcripts and observational data. There was no specific protocol for the interviews as the data gathering was intended to build up a broad picture of the challenges CLIL teachers faced when implementing this approach in their teaching.

However, one focal point of the reflection sessions and interviews was the use of the TL and how this affected teachers' confidence in the CLIL classroom. This led to reflection questions concerning critical language incidents, such as communication breakdowns, clarification and comprehension problems, use of the L1 and behavioural incidents. Through this specific design of short reflective recall sessions immediately after the lessons, followed by longer and extra-scheduled reflection interviews, it was hoped that the resulting data would contain more revealing descriptions of teachers' beliefs about how their linguistic confidence shaped their pedagogical practices.

In all, 1343 minutes of recorded data were transcribed and evaluated. The reflective interviews for T1 were 12 in total and for T2 were 10 in total. For T1, this amounted to 252 minutes of data and, for T2, 310 minutes. The interviews with the teachers were carried out in German and translated by the author in close co-operation with an L1 user of English.

The CLIL classes followed identical curricular demands as non-CLIL classes. There were no specific regulations or recommendations for the amount of time to be used in the TL for these teachers in their CLIL classes.

Both teachers had significant experience teaching their subjects. T1 had been teaching physics and chemistry for 26 years. T2 had been teaching history and German for 15 years. Neither of them was an English language specialist and both had only minimal previous experiences with CLIL. They taught in a non-selective comprehensive school, with students spanning an age range from 10 to 15 years. In terms of English language proficiency, T1, the science teacher, was approximately of B1+ level, and T2, the history teacher, was approximately C1.

Coding was done inductively following Corbin and Strauss' (2008) processes for grounded theory. Major categories were identified through an iterative and comparative process using the qualitative software MAXQDA. Then, this was synthesised and supplemented by a review of the relevant literature on teacher identity, teacher confidence and CLIL teachers' beliefs. Aspects identified with respect to CLIL teachers' beliefs on their language use and their confidence in this were taken for a re-vision of the data and used to reappraise the coding. This reappraisal process as supplemented by the CLIL literature was primarily intended to be a confirmation backup for the coding categories evolving from the inductive data analysis. For example, concepts such as TL proficiency in CLIL (Guillamon-Suesta & Renau Renau, 2015), code-switching in CLIL (Hunt, 2011), incidental L2 learning in CLIL (Hüttner *et al.*, 2013) or CLIL teachers' understanding how language works to create meaning (Tan, 2011) became instructive in the understanding and categorisation of CLIL teachers' data within this project. Through this iterative inductive – deductive analysis the internal validity of the project was established and eventually three major categories were identified. These will be described in the following section.

CLIL teachers as confident L2 subject languagers (CT-CL2SL)

This category focuses on teachers' L2 subject languaging competence, which is teachers' perceived ability to confidently and successfully use their complete language repertoire for the meaning-making of subject content in a TL. In this respect, CLIL teachers may or may not language their subject knowledge in at least two languages.

CLIL teachers as confident L2 users (CT-CL2U)

This category focuses on teachers' L2 perceived confidence in using the target language. This category addresses teachers' foreign language learning histories and how they relate to their perceptions of their L2 competence.

CLIL teachers as confident L2 teachers (CT-CL2T)

This category addresses CLIL teachers' perceptions of their abilities to confidently use explicit and deliberate L2 pedagogy as part of their CLIL teaching. From a theoretical perspective, it is motivated by the assertion that an explicit focus on linguistic features will enhance learners' conceptual and linguistic learning (Heine, 2014). Dafouz-Milne (2011: 205) contends that 'it is of vital importance that CLIL classes are also language oriented and, specifically, that CLIL teachers incorporate explicit instructional plans in which language objectives are systematically integrated with academic objectives'.

Results and Discussion

The three major categories are presented and exemplified through classroom vignettes and teacher quotes.

CLIL teachers as confident subject languagers (CT-CL2SL)

In his reflective interview, T1, the chemistry teacher, expressed clear pedagogical beliefs about chemistry teaching. He also conveyed a strong belief about the utility of CLIL by arguing for its potential as a means of accumulating cultural capital for students (Bourdieu, 1977). Additionally, he voiced his personal interest in how 'chemistry as a subject happens in the Anglican world', and how he hoped to establish a more global perspective in his chemistry classrooms through the use of English. To him, only English was considered a cultural asset for his students; in fact, no other languages were named in this respect by either teacher regarding CLIL.

He emphasised the learning value of chemistry through CLIL by stating that the use of technical terms in the L2 allowed for deeper learning through what he believed to be more intensive networking in the brain:

Extract 1: Interview (T1)

As teacher and subject teacher, I was pleased. I think, and this is the essence for me, that the capacity to remember (Behaltekurve) has dramatically increased, I think this has to do with more intensive networking in the brain, well, the things one knows from brain research …

The belief that working with technical terms in a foreign language leads to better networking in the brain comes up several times in his data. He expressed this in a variety of metaphors, such as, 'you can literally hear (students') brains rattle along'. He also considered chemistry particularly suitable for CLIL, since in the 'concrete case of chemistry, all technical terms already come from the English language'. Furthermore, he argued that students' motivation for chemistry, especially in lower secondary education tended to wane quickly and he expected this attitude to be softened through the novelty value of CLIL.

One of his main pedagogical aims for his students was to be able to follow the thinking of chemistry experts and to be able to converse with these experts if given the chance. Thinking like a scientist was a recurring theme for him and meant learning to use language like a scientist would. On the other hand, he made it clear that since scientific thinking was his primary concern, having limited foreign language competence was not necessarily a major hindrance to comprehension, as the students could also use their L1s. He mentioned that scientific thinking differed markedly from what he called humanities' thinking. For him, scientific thinking was primarily a transformational process from everyday language to academic and subject-specific language. He insisted that students needed to recognise that, 'they will not get anything new from me, but the things that they already know in their language are transferred to a new context ... in my mother tongue I also switch between everyday language, educated language, and academic language'. He considered CLIL to be a bilingual approach including the L1 for students and the foreign language being subservient to subject learning.

T2 also considered his subject, history, to be highly appropriate for CLIL. For example, he described how a substantial number of topics in the Austrian history curriculum could be related to the history of the United Kingdom. He stated that CLIL would broaden his students' horizons and make the subject of history more interesting. He emphasised that using precise argumentative language was a necessary skill for students, independent of which language they used. He expected students to be already fairly familiar with a lot of the technical terms raised in his history projects, 'it was not that big of a challenge that they could not handle, as you often hear these things in the media, for example, primaries, the winner takes it all, that was already known to most of them'. Several times he pointed out the 'fundamental importance' for his students to become competent in English and emphasised a positive emotional attitude towards learning a foreign language. Generally speaking, teachers' emphasis on the high value and status of learning English through CLIL may positively affect their motivation and ultimately their persistence and self-confidence in this domain (Sahakyan *et al.*, 2018; Wyatt, 2018).

In respect to teachers' confidence as subject languagers through English, T1, despite his communicative optimism, began to voice a language deficit attitude after his first teaching experiences. In the subsequent reflective interviews, he regretted having problems with his teaching since English was not his L1. Generally, he felt much more at ease in the L1 chemistry class as the following quote demonstrates.

Extract 2: Interview (T1)

... from a teaching point of view, I make a lot more notes for the CLIL class than for the German [chemistry] class, which makes sense as I can hold the lesson without any preparation, but for the English CLIL class I need to prepare, I need the vocabulary and I take more notes and look at them, which doesn't happen in German [chemistry lessons], there I never consult my preparations.

He also regretted that his verbal 'quick-wittedness and spontaneity of word-play' was not the same in his CLIL class as compared to the non-CLIL class. In the observational data, T1 displayed a fair number of grammatical errors, hesitation markers, code-switching and problems with everyday register, however, the classroom data showed that he was perfectly able to communicate the subject content as evidenced by the low number of linguistic clarification requests of his students. This was also reflected in his assessment of his own subject teaching skills, for which he states that 'it would be very awkward and embarrassing, if after 27 years of teaching I discovered now through English the true facts of my subject', and 'the only thing I need to prepare are the right words, and yes I take more notes which I keep checking, which does not happen in German (his L1), there I never look through my notes'.

After a critical disruption incident with some students and a discussion about this with the researcher in one of the reflective interviews, he talked to the students and they told him 'in a very mature way that they had problems with the subject content and even more so in English and that's why they drifted away after 10 minutes'. He also told them how his own L2 language problems, 'English is not my mother tongue and I have struggled with it (as a learner)' affected his concentration in the CLIL class and made him probably more susceptible to some overreactions. After this talk, he decided to accept code-switching not as a deficit phenomenon but as an important teaching aid in the process of learning subject content and creating meaning (see also T1 Extract 4) (see Chapter 8).

Extract 3: Interview (T1)

Yes, I feel a lot more secure especially when code-switching. I noticed in the last lesson that because of my language deficits, I was not able to present content in the way I would have liked to do as native subject teacher, and the consequence for me was also in the preparation, when-ever I have the feeling I cannot bring home the point, then I code-switch and turn towards my mother tongue, and I feel fine and going back to English is now easier for me.

Extract 3 illustrates how, when this teacher began code-switching, he felt more secure and at ease teaching his subject through English which seemed to be related to his confidence in teaching chemistry content. Though he still acknowledges, what he perceives to be language deficits while teaching CLIL, code-switching allows him to shift into German instantly and, in his view, be more effective in his teaching and more capable to 'bring home the point' of his chemistry lessons.

Furthermore, he not only acknowledged the CLIL classroom as a multilingual learning space, but he also boosted his L2 teaching confidence by his capability to organise and execute a course of action that allowed him to confidently deal with his linguistic disruption problems. However, later repetitions of his perceived 'deficit and disruption' problem in further reflection interviews made it clear that changes in complex environments, such as CLIL, are not necessarily permanent and they may fluctuate over time.

He also mentioned his pride in being able to teach chemistry in English and described his colleagues' responses as, 'appreciation and the word impressed springs to mind, especially from an elderly colleague who is also a physics and chemistry teacher and he said he would never dare to do this from a language point of view'. His pride in his teaching skills through the foreign language seemingly demonstrates a positive and resilient L2 self-confidence.

T2, like T1, addressed the extra mental effort required to teach in English. He compared his command of English in the classroom to a rollercoaster where he sometimes felt fine and sometimes felt it was hard going. Although he was quite critical of his own language use by calling it 'not so elegant', 'gobbledegook', 'that was bumpy' and 'that was a bad mistake', his self-critiques appeared matter of fact. For instance, when discussing his ability to teach his subject through English, he acknowledged, '… not everything is perfect, but this is obvious, isn't it?'. This matter of fact, or seemingly blasé attitude was later explained by T2, 'how I'm doing with the language [L2]? … what I notice is that sometimes I say *wis* instead of *with* and the children notice this, and they start laughing because they know this is wrong, but I don't care'. This attitude seemed to affect his confidence in a sense that he perceived mistakes as a natural part when teaching his subject in English. Rather than sensing mistakes as damaging to his self-image as a history teacher, he described them as natural and a part of the process of teaching CLIL.

However, unlike T1 who conceded that his 'faulty' L2 competence might be a reason for students' lack of understanding, T2 considered his own perceived lack of verbal elegance not to be a cause for his students' comprehension problems. Instead, he noticed that students' poor command of English inhibited their understanding of the history content, which seemingly forced him to resort back to the L1. He explained:

Extract 1: Interview (T2)

[W]hen you talk to the kids, either they get it or they don't, you notice this from their body language, somewhere there is a question mark, a really massive question mark, and then you start code-switching [back to German]

The reflection data and especially the classroom recordings showed code-switching as a regular part of teachers' languaging processes in their CLIL courses mostly motivated by comprehension, behavioural and planning issues. The exact trigger for each teacher, however, appeared to be individually determined, and its strength or importance was typically motivated by a variety of domain-specific factors such as, safety in chemistry or topical relevance related to Austrian historical perspectives. For example, T1 explained in an interview that he would code-switch during the instructional preparation for students' chemical experiments, as he had to make absolutely sure they used the correct equipment properly to avoid any hazards. In another instance, T2 pointed out that certain global topics in history were better suited for teaching in English than were local Austrian topics. Whilst on a superficial level it may be argued that the choice of suitable topics for CLIL or code-switching, is hardly related to teachers' confidence as subject languagers, the data suggested that the CLIL teachers in this study had a fairly clear theory of mind as to why they would feel confident about using certain topics in CLIL or not. Given this, it will be argued that their personal beliefs strongly affect their confidence as subject languagers in CLIL.

Furthermore, they also mentioned at various times that irritations or disruptions such as student behaviour, technical problems, unexpected administrative incidents or misfired experiments appeared to affect their L2 confidence more significantly and more so than similar incidents happening in the L1 classroom. In T2's words, 'everything I want to say in German can be said in English but it is of course more difficult, it is of course more strenuous, it costs a lot of energy, but for me it is a positive energy and it is not a negative stress, it is a positive stress'.

CLIL teachers as confident L2 users: CT-CL2U

This construct refers to CLIL teachers as confident L2 users (CT-CL2U) and is typically associated with a lack of anxiety when communicating in the second language coupled with positive ratings of self-proficiency in that language. This category also related to teachers' foreign language learning histories and their perceived L2 competence.

When talking about their L2 language competence, both teachers related this to memories of their own language learning history. From the first interview on, T1 drew a very negative picture related to his own scholarly learning experiences with English. He used emotional language such as 'having been traumatised', and, 'having undergone very, very bad experiences in my English teaching'. In a later interview he mentioned 'being traumatised through my school biography, my school trauma'. However, although there had clearly been some negative experiences concerning his scholarly language learning, he did not adopt a pessimistic or self-blaming attitude. Quite the contrary, he externalised the blame by describing his English learning as heavily writing-biased which caused him serious problems but did not negatively affect his identity as an English speaker. He explained, 'I have been able to literally talk myself through re-examinations and in oral conversations I have never been shy'. He saw himself as a very good communicator who did not shy away from making mistakes but looked for opportunities to communicate in English. To illustrate this attitude, he recounted an incident at his school where he, in English, helped four ERASMUS (European Region Action Scheme for the Mobility of University Students) students to sort out some administrative problems 'and I served them quite well and we had a very good conversation, but I've always been like this'.

T2 implied that CLIL teaching meant using English as much as possible. He emphasised how his one year stay in the United Kingdom as a language assistant, albeit not as an EFL teacher, had been formative towards his interest in English. Reflecting on his own EFL history, he also pointed out various problems with his former language teachers. This resulted in him giving up his wish to study English in lower secondary education when he realised one of his former English teachers was also one of the lecturers at the college of education. Nevertheless, he explicitly rejected having been adversely affected by this:

Extract 2: Interview (T2)

Good lord, I definitely do not suffer from any trauma through this, quite the contrary, I have fun teaching in English … but I have had fun and you get into English again, you can practise the language and that is something beautiful and good.

He also described his belief that the learning of a new language necessitates a willingness to communicate and to not be self-conscious or embarrassed by speaking in the classroom. Accordingly, he emphasised that language use should be about having fun and being relaxed instead of form focused. His emphasis on the foreign language enjoyment factor (Dewaele & MacIntyre, 2016) was demonstrated by addressing the concept of 'fun in language learning' several times throughout the interviews.

All in all, both teachers expressed confidence in their status as TL users albeit showing different expectations and motivations regarding their self-image of the L2 user they would like to be in their CLIL contexts. For example, the history teacher, T2, mentioned several times in his interviews and in classroom incidents that, 'I am neither a trained English speaker (*Anglist*) nor English teacher, sometimes I'll lack the necessary vocabulary and I'll make mistakes, that's clear, on the other hand there is nothing bad about this'. In fact, both showed a more dynamic self-image that was open to change rather than a solely static and fixed L2 user concept. For example, T2's reflection on giving up on his initial ideal L2 self in a specific context (personal things and instructions) to adopt a flexible code-switching stance justified by whatever seemed to work best to him:

Extract 3: Interview (T2)

[Y]ou want to do everything in English but when it is about personal things, who has to do what to get the kids going, then you resort to the mother tongue, but actually in the end I reproached somebody in English, so, it's more a kind of backwards and forwards.

It is also interesting to notice how T1 displayed a similar transition from his initial belief in wanting to be a predominantly TL user in his CLIL classroom, towards being a bilingual language user. This complex adaptive process appears to align with Dörnyei and Ryan's (2015) conceptualising of the ideal L2 self as a moving picture rather than a fixed target.

CLIL teachers as confident L2 teachers: CT-CL2T

This category covers CLIL teachers' confidence in using explicit and deliberate L2 teaching measures as part of their subject teaching. Both teachers made it clear to their students and in their interviews that their teaching role did not imply being an English teacher. They expressed a clear perception of themselves as enthusiastic L2 users but not L1-like language users; a status, they associated with EFL teachers. However, they both did not see this as a deficit aspect in their teaching role, but rather as a feature that allowed them to communicate with their students in a different way. T2 described this sentiment explicitly several times in his classroom, '[I]t doesn't matter if you make mistakes. I am not [word emphasised] an English teacher so I will not correct you, you can talk, as much as you can, that's the most important thing', or as a response to a student who addressed him in German, 'I would say try it first in English, I'm totally convinced that you will manage this'. By creating a communicative space mostly unaffected by corrective language feedback, the teacher intended to establish a language-encouraging atmosphere. For example, see the following classroom extract:

Extract 4: Classroom observation (T1)

T1: yes and this is what we have in the lab, usually a filter, (ahm) and some (ahm), (ahm), (ahm), (.) (shows a funnel, body language shows uncertainty)

S: Trichter [*funnel*]

T: Trichter, [*funnel*] and what we have to do with the round filter is to (.) (folds it)

P: knick [*fold*] it

PP: knicking [*folding*]

T: knicking, [*folding*] thank you for the word, I do not know if it's right, but it sounds good

S: it's fold

SS: knicking

S: you fold it

T: I fold it

S: knicking (laughter)

T: many times and then I can make it for our **Trichter**, [*funnel*] shall we try to find the word (walks over to his laptop) I have opened my dictionary, what's the word for **Trichter**, (types it into his laptop), and ahm (.) funnel, it's the word funnel, it's for me (writes it down on the board)

In this incident, the teacher set up a lab procedure which involved separating and purifying mixed substances such as dirty and salty water. While trying to set up this procedure, various hesitation markers, short pauses and an obvious 'I don't know' that was displayed by his body language, was accompanied by showing the object to the students. This language problem prompted a student to provide the L1 word 'Trichter'. The teacher picked it up without any comment or hesitation and continued presenting and describing what he needed to do with it. While folding the paper, he signalled again visually and linguistically (but without code-switching) a problem with the desired word 'fold/bend'. This prompted a student to provide him with the word 'knick' which originates from the Germanic word 'knicken' (bend). This was immediately taken up by other learners and by the teacher, even though, another student voiced her doubts by suggesting the correct word 'fold'. However, it was repeated and accepted by the teacher who continued his demonstration and who also quickly became aware that his first problem of the naming of the object had not yet been solved. Although he still code-switched and mentioned the German word, he simultaneously provided a successful language learning model by using his laptop to look up the word online. The students could follow this, as his computer was linked to the overhead projector. He then decided to make this term even more salient by repeating it, writing it on the board and telling them to write it into their study notes. The turns overlapped throughout this learning conversation and it did not take longer than 90 seconds.

However, both teachers were insistent in not integrating any pre-planned or deliberate language teaching measures. For example, discussions about CLIL methodology where the researcher suggested introducing a set of keywords on hand outs were quickly abandoned. Both teachers felt this turned them into foreign language teachers, which they did not want to be and felt underqualified for. Also, they considered language teaching measures to be too time consuming.

Although T2 initially appeared a little more receptive about the introduction of keywords, he changed his mind later by saying that although teaching keywords may be useful:

Extract 4: Interview (T2)

[T]hese keywords will be introduced again and again and then the whole thing goes automatically, it will be picked up by the kids ... it is automatic and sometimes because of the various repetitions it is there, automatically without their conscious awareness.

Both teachers deemed this implicit learning-through-speaking approach to be enough for CLIL L2 teaching. As T1-Extract 4 shows, there were no pre-planned language teaching measures. Instead, language teaching took the form of occasionally drawing learners' attention towards vocabulary (see also Chapter 3). In some instances, when the teachers appeared to notice some lexical problems, they initiated a comprehension check and, if necessary, provided the item's translation. All in all, even though both teachers used a broad variety of general and subject-specific didactic measures in their CLIL classrooms such as group-work, project work, enquiry-based learning, autonomous learning, web-based learning, multi-modal learning, etc., deliberate language-focused teaching measures other than code-switching were non-existent. The teachers themselves did not consider this to be a disadvantage.

Conclusion

This study set out to contribute to an understanding of teachers' senses of linguistic confidence and teacher self-confidence in CLIL settings by longitudinally investigating the beliefs and languaging practices of two teachers' classroom behaviours and procedures. The findings of this qualitative study reveal tension for CLIL teachers who are experts in their subjects but find themselves teaching in a second language. These teachers are subject didactic professionals but language subject didactic amateurs. Whilst this has been noticed by other research (Bovellan, 2014; Hüttner et al., 2013; Lasagabaster, 2013; Morton, 2012), the longitudinal design of this study allowed not only revealing incidents of their classroom struggles but also showed in greater granularity teachers' development through CLIL teaching. From this, it emerged that teachers' L2 confidence was a complex, unstable and domain-sensitive phenomenon that cannot be pinned to a simple and stable cause-and-effect model. For example, recall T2's 'roller-coaster' metaphor for his teaching through English or T1's changing attitude towards code-switching in his CLIL classroom. All in all, both teachers' languaging confidence was contingent on their interpretation of contextual factors such as student feedback, emotional and behavioural issues, subject-specific language issues and content coverage among other situated factors.

Furthermore, by eventually moving from an ideal self towards a more feasible self (Sahakyan *et al.*, 2018), both teachers developed a sense of L2 confidence that allowed them to work more resiliently and optimistically in this environment that can be challenging linguistically.

These findings contribute to a deeper understanding of the complexity of teachers' L2 confidence in a CLIL environment. In particular, the findings caution against an adoption of a simplistic EFL training competency model for CLIL teacher education, since L2 competence is likely to be supportive for teachers' confidence but does not appear to be sufficient because other beliefs including their subject teaching and pedagogical confidence, the cultural value of the TL, or teachers' perception of successful communication exert a powerful impact. The findings, therefore, point to a broader knowledge base for CLIL teacher education which not only enhances teachers' TL competence but also addresses their pedagogical CLIL competence, sense of self-confidence and how L2 confidence affects this and well-being. This knowledge base needs to help CLIL teachers in their attempts to explicitly scaffold the learning of new content through pedagogical measures that utilise the students' complete linguistic repertoires in order to learn content and the target language successfully in the CLIL classroom.

This study has also presented a more realistic picture of the languaging challenges involved for novice CLIL teachers. These challenges include teachers' use of the target language for socialising purposes in the classroom, for instructional and behavioural issues and, above all, for mediating domain-specific content. This study has pointed out that the pedagogical use of their language resources affects teachers' L2 confidence in complex ways. In particular, the longitudinal data have highlighted that this confidence is not a linear and cumulative phenomenon but a highly contextually sensitive one, which is deeply affected by teachers' interpretations and perceptions of their local contexts. It has also been evidenced that this emergent and fluid linguistic confidence is reflected in and consistent with teachers' choice of pedagogical interventions. Furthermore, in this study, deficit perceptions with respect to L2 confidence in CLIL led to stressful and critical incidents in the classroom but they also led to incidents of more participatory learning. It appeared as if a complex and reciprocal interplay between teachers' beliefs, their assessments of the situations and ensuing actions and students' reactions triggered the difference between teachers' perception of being more or less confident L2 users and their perception of whether they were flourishing or failing as CLIL teachers.

The construct of L2 confidence, therefore, needs to be seriously addressed and investigated as an important psycho-linguistic reality in the CLIL classroom by any CLIL teacher education programme. In other words, CLIL teacher education courses that fail to incorporate a module on L2 confidence in their curriculum may not adequately prepare teachers for this content and language learning approach. T1's comment on the importance of having self-confidence in CLIL may thus provide an important pointer for future studies:

Extract 5: Interview (T1)

I think this CLIL project needs teacher personalities with both feet in the classroom. It is a challenge, that is, I acknowledge my weaknesses (*he had commented on his L2 struggles a few minutes earlier*), and this takes strength.

Limitations and Future Studies

Although the two teachers were accompanied for more than a year and a rich dataset was collected, this study is limited by several factors. First, the students did not have a choice related to their project participation. In a learning environment this can be potentially face-threatening and high risk through possible L2 classroom anxiety (Dewaele, 2017). Introducing CLIL needs sensitive participation choices in order to not trigger resistance behaviour (Mehisto & Genesee, 2015). Secondly, the decisive influence of subject-specific factors on CLIL teachers' languaging practice shows the need for other subject studies to be able to draw conclusions on a broader basis. Certainly, a future study would also benefit from a broader population and a wider gender base.

The limitations of this study also point at directions for future research. If similar case studies were carried out, they would need a careful assessment of teachers' language skills. This would allow for a more fine-grained analysis of their L2 confidence needs. An interpretation of these needs would also be strengthened by an initial and final quantitative assessment of their confidence towards CLIL.

Implications for Policy and Practice

In terms of pedagogical implications, the L2 confidence coding scheme discussed in this paper may be utilised for a tri perspectival CLIL teacher education programme which follows the conceptualisation of CLIL teachers as confident subject languagers, as confident L2 teachers and as confident L2 users in its training modules. Any such training programme should be motivated by reflective action or lesson study cycles with a strong component on L2 teaching and learning strategies and resilience and awareness activities that allow for a much more realistic preparation for this at times challenging context. Attempts that go beyond a 'classical' language competence CLIL teacher education syllabus towards a syllabus promoting positive pedagogical languaging are gaining prominence (Genesee & Hamayan, 2016; Gierlinger, 2017b; Meyer *et al.*, 2015). Gierlinger's (2015) SALT model for teaching CLIL appears helpful in this respect as it evolved as a practical methodological tool from numerous CLIL courses. The letters S-A-L-T stand for four key dimensions of instructed and deliberate CLIL languaging. The first dimension of SALT, 'S', focuses on the teaching and learning of content through **strategic** languaging in the CLIL classroom. The dimension 'A' investigates the use of **all** languages available in the classroom for the benefits of CLIL. The third dimension, 'L', considers the different **literacies** of knowledge representation and meaning making in CLIL. The fourth dimension 'T' focuses on the **target** language in CLIL and its crucial role in the learning of subject knowledge. These dimensions are operationalised into methodological interventions and are put into pedagogical procedures by the teacher as the local expert. Furthermore, SALT was also designed as a mindfulness tool to boost teachers' languaging confidence for their local CLIL implementations.

On a school-based level, official measures such as preparatory courses for the CLIL classes, closer and institutionalised cooperation between L2 specialists and CLIL teachers, extra planning time, easy access to CLIL relevant resources (materials, books, media) etc. would all be important support measures to enable CLIL teachers' to flourish in their new linguistic roles.

References

Barnard, R. and Burns, A. (eds) (2012) *Researching Language Teacher Cognition and Practice: International Case Studies*. Bristol: Multilingual Matters.

Bourdieu, P. (1977) *Outline of a Theory of Practice*. Cambridge: Cambridge University Press.

Bovellan, E. (2014) Teachers' beliefs about learning and language as reflected in their views of teaching materials for content and language integrated learning (CLIL). Unpublished PhD thesis, Jyväskylä: University of Jyväskylä.

Corbin, J.M. and Strauss, A.C. (2008) *Basics of Qualitative Research: Techniques and Procedures for Developing Grounded Theory* (3rd edn). London: Sage.

Dafouz-Milne, E. (2011) English as the medium of instruction in Spanish contexts: A look at teacher discourses. In Y. Ruiz de Zarobe, M. Sierra and F. Gallardo del Puerto (eds) *Content and Foreign Language Integrated Learning: Contributions to Multilingualism in European Contexts*, (pp. 189–209). Frankfurt: Peter Lang.

Dewaele, J.-M. (2017) Psychological dimensions and foreign language anxiety. In S. Loewen and M. Sato (eds) *The Routledge Handbook of Instructed Second Language Acquisition* (pp. 453–471). New York, NY: Routledge.

Dewaele, J.-M. and MacIntyre, P.D. (2016) Foreign language enjoyment and foreign language classroom anxiety: The right and left feet of the language learner. In P.D. MacIntyre, T. Gregersen and S. Mercer (eds) *Positive Psychology in SLA* (pp. 215–235). Bristol: Multilingual Matters.

Dörnyei, Z. and Ryan, S. (2015) *The Psychology of the Language Learner Revisited*. New York, NY: Routledge.

Genesee, F. and Hamayan, E. (2016) *CLIL in Context- Practical: Guidance for Educators*. Cambridge: Cambridge University Press.

Gierlinger, E.M. (2007) Modular CLIL in lower secondary education: Some insights from a research project in Austria. In C. Dalton-Puffer and U. Smit (eds) *Empirical Perspectives on Classroom Discourse* (pp. 79–118). Frankfurt: Peter Lang.

Gierlinger, E.M. (2015) 'You can speak German, sir': On the complexity of teachers' L1 use in CLIL. *Language and Education* 29 (4), 347–368.

Gierlinger, E.M. (2017a) The challenging interplay of content, context, and community for CLIL implementations and a didactic model to cope with CLIL's hybrid pedagogy. *English as a Global Language Education (EaGLE) Journal* 3 (1), 63–88.

Gierlinger, E.M. (2017b) Teaching CLIL? Yes, but with a pinch of SALT. *Journal of Immersion and Content-Based Language Education* 5 (2), 188–215.

Guillamón-Suesta, F. and Renau Renau, M.L. (2015) A critical vision of the CLIL approach in secondary education: A study in the Valencian Community in Spain. *LACLIL* 8 (1), 1–12.

Heine, L. (2014) Models of the bilingual lexicon and their theoretical implications for CLIL. *The Language Learning Journal* 42 (2), 225–237.

Hunt, M. (2011) UK teachers' and Learners' experiences of CLIL resulting from the EU-funded project ECLILT. *Latin American Journal of Content and Language Integrated Learning* 4 (1), 27–39.

Hüttner, J., Dalton-Puffer, C. and Smit, U. (2013) The power of beliefs: Lay theories and their influence on the implementation of CLIL programmes. *International Journal of Bilingual Education and Bilingualism* 16 (3), 267–284.

Krechel, H.-L. (2003) Bilingual modules. In M. Wildhage and E. Otten (eds) *Praxis des bilingualen Unterrichts* (pp. 194–215). Berlin: Cornelsen.

Lasagabaster, D. (2013) The use of the L1 in CLIL classes: The teachers' perspective. *LACLIL* 6 (2), 1–21.

Luthans, F. and Youssef-Morgan, C.M. (2017) Psychological capital: An evidence-based positive approach. *Annual Review of Organizational Psychology and Organizational Behavior* 4 (1), 339–366.

Mehisto, P. and Genesee, F. (2015) *Building Bilingual Education Systems: Forces, Mechanisms and Counterweights*. Cambridge: Cambridge University Press.

Meyer, O., Coyle, D., Halbach, A., Schuck, K. and Ting, T. (2015) A pluriliteracies approach to content and language integrated learning – mapping learner progressions in knowledge construction and meaning-making. *Language, Culture and Curriculum* 28 (1), 41–57.

Morton, T. (2012) *Teachers' Knowledge About Language and Classroom Interaction in Content and Language Integrated Learning*. Madrid: Universidad Autonoma de Madrid.

Sahakyan, T., Lamb, M. and Chambers, G. (2018) Language teacher motivation: From the Ideal Self to the Feasible Self. In S. Mercer and A. Kostoulas (eds) *Language Teacher Psychology*. Bristol: Multilingual Matters.

Snyder, C.R. and Lopez, S.J. (2009) *Oxford Handbook of Positive Psychology*. Oxford: Oxford University Press.

Swain, M. and Lapkin, S. (2013) A Vygotskian sociocultural perspective on immersion education: The L1/L2 debate. *JICB* 1, 101–129. doi:10.1075/jicb.

Swanson, P. (2014) Confidence is essential for language teachers. *Contact* 40 (3), 34–39.

Tan, M. (2011) Mathematics and science teachers' beliefs and practices regarding the teaching of language in content learning. *Language Teaching Research* 15 (3), 325–342.

Wyatt, M. (2018) Language teachers' self-efficacy beliefs: An Introduction. In S. Mercer and A. Kostoulas (eds) *Language Teacher Psychology* (pp. 122–140). Bristol: Multilingual Matters.

Zee, M. and Koomen, H.M.Y. (2016) Teacher self-Efficacy and its effects on classroom processes, student academic adjustment, and teacher well-being. *Review of Educational Research* 86 (4), 981–1015.

12 Addressing Teacher Confidence as a Barrier to Bilingual Classroom Transmission Practices in Wales

Nia Mererid Parry and Enlli Môn Thomas

Introduction

The history of the Welsh language over the past century has been very much a history of decline, with numbers decreasing from nearly 900,000 speakers (54.4% of the population) in 1891 (Aitchison & Carter, 1993) to 19% of the population in 2011 (Stats Wales, 2012). Welsh currently totals just over 500,000 speakers, with around 250,000 of those using Welsh as a daily language (Stats Wales, 2012). However, contrary to the decline in numbers, the history of Welsh-medium and bilingual education represents a pattern of growth and success and is widely recognised to be 'one of the most remarkable developments in Wales' education system during the second half of the twentieth century' (Welsh Government, 2010: 4). Wales therefore boasts a highly successful bilingual and Welsh-medium education system that implements a variety of teaching strategies to develop pupils' Welsh and English skills (Welsh Government, 2010).

However, despite the success of various bilingual and/or Welsh-medium instructional methods, transmitting Welsh as an L2 in English-medium schools has not received the same levels of success (Davies, 2012). This is often due to its confinement to Welsh (as a subject) lessons (WJEC, 2015), but also due to a lack of pupil engagement with learning Welsh as an L2 (Davies, 2012). In light of Welsh Government's goals of reaching a million speakers of Welsh by 2050, and increasing the number of speakers using it as a daily language in the process (Welsh Government, 2017), there is a clear expectation that schools, regardless of their medium of instruction, support these goals. Ultimately, these goals require improved methods of delivering Welsh as an L2 subject but also a more systemic approach to normalising the use of Welsh across subjects in schools, involving Welsh in all aspects of school life.

One particular approach that has been introduced into the secondary school sector to address these concerns is *Cymraeg bob Dydd* 'Incidental Welsh' (henceforth IW) (Davies, 2012). IW is a model for normalising the use of Welsh in English-medium secondary schools beyond the designated Welsh subject lessons. IW requires teachers, native speakers and learners alike, to deliver everyday Welsh vocabulary and phrases as part of their subject lesson, whatever the subject of the lesson may be. Whilst such an approach provides additional exposure to Welsh for the pupils and in varied educational domains, and exposure is crucial for language development (Gathercole & Thomas, 2009), implementing this model poses a challenge for the English-medium sector for a number of reasons, not least for the fact that English-medium schools employ a large number of non-Welsh-speaking staff:

> Recruiting staff who are confident and capable of teaching their subjects through the medium of Welsh is a challenge across many areas of Wales. Attracting well-qualified Welsh specialists is a particular challenge for many English-medium secondary schools. (Estyn, 2017: 40)

Integrating language and content for the purpose of linguistic vitality therefore poses an additional challenge to the non-Welsh-speaking teacher's role. Whether L2 learners are willing to use their developing L2 language in any given situation is determined by a complex interaction of internal (affective) and external (contextual) factors, including self-perceived communicative competence, anxiety and the ideal L2 self, with one of the strongest predictors being an individual's perceived self-confidence in their L2 (Mystkowska-Wiertelak & Pawlak, 2017). In a minority language context where access to the minority language is limited, such as is the case in Wales, it is necessary to provide sufficient language support for staff in order to increase confidence and reduce anxieties around using Welsh so that they are able to contribute effectively to linguistic models such as IW.

This chapter explores current practices in the implementation of IW across schools in Wales. It evaluates the effectiveness of a programme of Welsh language support that was developed to support teachers working in the secondary school sector who declared minimal knowledge of, or who lacked confidence in using Welsh. Drawing on data from classroom observations, questionnaires and focus groups, the study presented in this chapter explores (i) L2 teacher confidence, that is self-confidence, characterised by a speaker's levels of competence and anxiety (Clément, 1980, 1986; see also Chapters 10, 11 & 15) in using Welsh in the classroom,

(ii) current practices in the implementation of IW across the curriculum and (iii) the impact of formal language support sessions, tailored to individual teacher needs, on raising teacher confidence in implementing IW. The chapter begins with an overview of the main challenge in increasing exposure to Welsh in English-medium schools, followed by a short introduction to IW and the barriers to its implementation. It goes on to present the research methodology employed followed by the results obtained from three phases of data collection. Pedagogical implications arising from the findings are presented at the end.

The Linguistic Nature of English-Medium Schools in Wales: Teacher Competence

In the secondary sector, which is the focus of the present study, 1772 teachers (17.3%) teach through the medium of Welsh, while 421 (4.1%) are qualified to teach through the medium of Welsh but do not do so and 8051 (78.6%) are currently not qualified to teach through the medium of Welsh and, therefore, do not currently deliver any Welsh when teaching or engaging with their pupils (Stats Wales, 2018). Despite not being able to teach through the medium of Welsh, and in most cases with no basic knowledge of the language, those 8000+ teachers are expected to contribute to Welsh Government's goal of increasing speaker numbers and encourage the use of Welsh among pupils via the implementation of IW.

Incidental Welsh

Learning Welsh is compulsory in Wales up to age 16. In Welsh-medium schools, Welsh is typically taught as an L1. In English-medium schools, Welsh is typically taught as an L2. In both cases, the two languages are largely segregated within the classroom. However, over many years, the Welsh Joint Education Committee (WJEC), as have others, have raised concerns that despite years of Welsh lessons, L2 pupils are leaving school unable to form sentences and unaware of basic Welsh vocabulary (Estyn, 2007).

In response to these concerns, Davies (2012) conducted an evaluation of Welsh L2 in Wales and presented the Welsh Government with a set of recommendations. One of these recommendations was to implement Incidental Welsh (IW) in all subject lessons in English-medium schools. Incidental language is defined as being a non-instructional method of delivering language in which learners can acquire the words implicitly without the need to make a conscious effort to learn the language (Barcroft, 2009). IW allows both languages to share the same space in a natural and supportive way as a medium of language integration rather than language segregation. This involves integrating both language and content within a given context of learning (García, 2009). Although explicit methods are known to be more effective among older children (Spada & Tomita, 2010), this pedagogical approach operates under the principle that additional exposure to the language, albeit incidental (implicit) rather than purposeful (explicit), leads to the following outcomes: continued learning of Welsh outside the Welsh lesson, which is critical in forming a base for continued language development; it allows pupils to expand on what they learn formally (and explicitly) in their Welsh lessons, in an informal (more implicit) and less effortful way (Saffran *et al.*, 1997); Welsh becomes normalised across the curriculum and not restricted to the Welsh lesson; Welsh becomes normalised to everyday life via its use for general language interaction and not purely for subject content (cf. BICS [Basic Interpersonal Communicative Skills] vs. CALP [Cognitive Academic Language Proficiency] – Cummins, 2008); and teachers are able to repeat vocabulary and phrases for different contexts (e.g. addressing whole class vs. addressing individuals), and this repetition influences how well individuals remember these utterances (Huckin & Coady, 1999).

Whilst there is no official syllabus that outlines expectations relating to the content and implementation of IW, instruction and support is largely *ad hoc*, often developed by Welsh teachers within the school. However, it is largely understood by teachers to involve simple everyday words such as greetings, basic commands and praise (see results below, Parry & Thomas, in preparation; Thomas *et al.*, 2018). For those with little or no previous knowledge of Welsh, there may be a number of barriers that could hinder their ability to engage effectively with this challenge and understanding what these barriers are and how teachers feel about the challenge is critical in order to offer appropriate support.

Barriers to the implementation of Incidental Welsh

One clear barrier to the successful implementation of IW, as noted above, has to do with teachers' minimal knowledge of Welsh. On a global level, almost all teachers, regardless of their subject expertise, are now expected to be language teachers, and motivated to deliver language in addition to subject knowledge (Fan, 2013). In contexts of linguistic revitalisation, however, this expectation goes beyond addressing L1 language skills and involves the introduction of L2 terms and phrases in a naturalistic way. This poses a challenge, not only for the teacher who needs to acquire the language, but also for the education sector as a whole in terms of how best to support non-Welsh-speaking staff to be able to use some Welsh in their teaching. However, in order for this to happen, we first need to understand the barriers L2 teachers may face. Some known barriers are outlined below:

First, teachers who are not at what Medgyes (2001) refers to as a threshold level of proficiency in order to be able to teach effectively are more likely to be dependent on resources (e.g. textbooks, worksheets and teacher guides) and less likely to be creative and improvise in their teaching (Dewaele, 2015). Creativity and improvisation are known to sustain pupils' motivation (Piccardo, 2013), and particularly so in language learning classrooms (Arnold, 1999). Teachers who are not confident in speaking or teaching Welsh are therefore likely to experience changes to their teaching styles that are not necessarily intended. Similarly, bilinguals often report that they feel different when speaking one language or another and may not always feel like themselves (Dewaele & Nakano, 2012). In contexts of Higher Education, L2 English-speaking lecturers delivering courses through the medium of English are often perceived as being dry, too technical and lacking spark (Wilkinson, 2005), less lively, less expressive and less fluent than L1 speaking teachers. They are also often perceived as having slower speech rates, issues with pronunciation and often limited in their understanding of new terminology (Klaassen, 2001). L2 English-speaking teachers can therefore experience unintended changes to how they are perceived as a consequence of using their L2. Since these changes to a teacher's teaching style and persona do not often go unnoticed, they may lead to unintended consequences for the speaker. Within the context of integrating language and content, having a weak grasp of the target language may lead to reduced levels of self-confidence and increased levels of anxiety in delivering that language in the classroom (Seidlhofer, 1999):

> Self-perceived communication confidence can be viewed as an important predictor of communicative behaviour, mainly because learners' decision to speak is based on their own evaluation of their L2 proficiency level. (Mystkowska-Wiertelelak & Pawlak, 2017: 37)

A second barrier therefore has to do with affective factors, most notably language anxiety – the feeling of fear and apprehension when having to use a language in which the speaker is not proficient (Du, 2009). While a wealth of research has identified teachers' role in supporting children's mental health and well-being (Askell-Williams & Lawson, 2013; Brooker, 2009; Ekornes et al., 2012; Graham et al., 2011; Mazzer & Rickwook, 2013, 2015), surprisingly little is known about issues relating to teachers' own mental health, despite suggestions that teachers' mental health can be of greater importance than their subject knowledge or the teaching method employed (Mundia, 2013; Smith, 1968). Forty-seven percent of educational professionals recently reported that they had experienced depression, anxiety and panic attacks due to their work (Education Support Partnership, 2018), which are conditions that are closely linked to an individual's levels of self-esteem (Sowislo & Orth, 2013). All teachers experience stress at some point or another. However, dealing with any stressor is much easier when using an L1 than when using an L2 (Brown, 2000). Given that teachers who have low levels of confidence and high anxiety levels are more vulnerable to difficulties relating to the delivery of their teaching (Schwarzer & Hallum, 2008), understanding what causes these internal states in various external contexts is important. It has also been shown that teachers are not immune from foreign language anxiety (Horwitz, 1996). Reducing language anxiety and increasing self-confidence are therefore crucial to the success of any pedagogical models promoting increased language use, particularly when the teacher delivering the provision in their second language (see also Chapters 10 & 13).

Methodology

The current study explored teacher confidence in using Welsh in the classroom, their current engagement with IW, and the impact of formal language support sessions, tailored to individual teacher needs, on raising teacher confidence in implementing Welsh across the curriculum. Drawing on a mixed methods design, this study was conducted in three parts. Part 1 involved teacher questionnaires disseminated among teachers teaching in English-medium secondary schools in Wales that had not received any formal support in delivering IW. This was in order to explore current practices in the delivery of IW based on the current minimal support given. The questionnaire focused on teachers' use of, training in and knowledge of Welsh. Part 2 involved classroom observations conducted in two different contexts: (i) a context where specific, personalised support had been offered to teachers, and (ii) a context where no such formal individualised support had been provided. Part 3 involved questionnaires and focus groups with those who had received personalised language support in order to explore how they engaged with and felt about the experience they gained through that support. All three parts of the study were approved by the School of Education and Human Development Ethics Board, Bangor University, and the procedures developed were fully compliant with the ethical protocol, including informed consent and ensuring anonymity. All questions were prepared bilingually, and teachers were able to answer using whichever language felt most comfortable to them. Where responses were provided in Welsh, they were translated into English by the L1 Welsh-speaking first author.

Part 1: Teacher questionnaire

An online questionnaire was created to capture trends in secondary teachers' Welsh language abilities, their Welsh language use and Welsh language training needs. The questionnaire, along with a cover letter and a participant information sheet, was emailed to all English-medium schools in Wales. The questionnaire invited responses to a series of background questions (e.g. 'How long had they been teaching in Wales?'), followed by a series of language specific questions that were designed around four themes: (i) teachers' Welsh language abilities (e.g. 'What is your proficiency in Welsh?'); (ii) their use of Welsh within their classrooms (e.g. 'Do you use any Welsh in your lessons?'); (iii) their confidence levels (e.g. 'How confident are you to use Welsh?'); and (iv) their training needs (e.g. 'What support, if any, do you get to develop your Welsh language skills and confidence?'). In each case, participants were given an opportunity to elaborate on their responses. The questionnaire therefore contained a mixture of closed (yes/no, 6-point Likert Scale) and open-ended questions.

All teachers who took part in Part 1 ($n = 47$) were working in English-medium schools in Wales. The majority of teachers originally came from Wales (75%), with a minority coming from England (21%) and only a small number (4%) originating from outside the United Kingdom. Of the 47 questionnaires that were returned, the majority of teachers (67%) worked in schools in north Wales, 19% in mid Wales and 17% in south east Wales, and covered a wide breadth of subject fields, primarily mathematics and science (26%) and language (24%), but also humanities (15%), arts (13%) and 'other' (22%). The sample contained teachers with a range of years of teaching experience, from 0 to 5 years' experience (24%), 6 to 10 years (21%), 11 to 15 years (19%), 16 to 20 years (21%) to 20+ years (15%). While the number of respondents was low due to low take-up rates of email surveys among schools, the patterns obtained within the sample are interesting and provide valuable insights alongside the data obtained from Parts 2 and 3.

Part 2: Classroom observations

Condition 1 of the observations involved a series of 25 classroom observations that were conducted in four English-medium secondary schools in north Wales. A day was spent at each of the four schools, following Year 8 students (age 12 to 13 years), and included attending all of their lessons for that day. The 25 teachers observed in these schools had received no formal, personalised Welsh language support, and the length of the observations varied from 50 minutes each to an hour (depending on the school). In Condition 2 of the observations, the three teachers observed had received specific, personalised, one-to-one Welsh language support that was organised by the local educational consortia. While the school is a bilingual secondary school catering for around 20% of children from homes where at least one parent speaks Welsh, the majority of staff are non-Welsh-speaking and are therefore currently only engaged with teaching through the medium of English.

This training took the form of weekly group and a personalised one-to-one session with a Welsh Language Tutor for a period of six weeks. It involved vocabulary learning, sentence construction, pronunciation exercises and resource development support. The observations that took place within these lessons lasted an hour each.

The observation methodology focused mainly on teachers' implementation of IW – how Welsh was used, when, for what purpose and how often. This information was recorded on a purposefully designed observation schedule, where each instance of IW was recorded and quoted, as appropriate. None of the classes were recorded in video or audio form due to the small-scale nature of the study and in order to reduce the possible anxieties experienced by the teachers. Given the paucity of examples of Welsh observed within each of the 25 classrooms in Condition 1, the data presented here constitute a composite analysis of the minimal Welsh that was observed across all four schools.

Part 3: Teacher focus groups

In order to further explore teachers' experience of the specific, personalised Welsh language support received, the three teachers who had received the training were given a short questionnaire to complete followed by a subsequent focus group interview to provide opportunities to elaborate further on their responses. All three teachers had volunteered to receive the training and consented to their participation in the focus group and questionnaire. Teachers were asked about their confidence and proficiency, the Welsh language learning sessions with the Welsh tutors and how they implemented what they learned from the training in their lessons. The focus group lasted around 40 minutes in total.

The findings of each part are presented and discussed below. In all cases, both verbal and written responses are noted verbatim in text.

Findings and Discussion

Part 1: Teacher questionnaires

As noted above, almost all teachers who returned the questionnaires reported at least some basic level of Welsh. Only 2% of the sample ($n = 1$) reported that they had no Welsh at all. Most of the informants (85% of the sample) reported using at least some Welsh in their lessons, although, even for one native Welsh speaking teacher, teaching in an English-medium school made it easy to forget to use Welsh: 'It's strange, being fluent when I'm teaching an English class as I am now in an English school I forget to use it'.

In describing where, when and how they used Welsh, most of the teachers (41/50 of the examples given) either referred explicitly to the term IW or provided a list of the types of activities that are typical within the delivery of IW. These were:

(1) the use of Welsh greetings;
(2) the use of Welsh commands;
(3) praising children in Welsh;
(4) eliciting Welsh responses to the class register;
(5) the use of everyday/basic phrases in Welsh;
(6) introducing colours and numbers in Welsh;
(7) conducting classroom routines in Welsh;
(8) using Welsh praises when marking pupils' work; and
(9) some questioning in Welsh.

Three further comments that were made were related to teachers' use of Welsh to enhance subject knowledge and to introduce subject-specific terms and definitions, and only one teacher mentioned the combination of Welsh and English in a bilingual manner.

In addition to these responses, a further two teachers reported purposeful differentiation in their use of Welsh, based on the linguistic capabilities of their pupils. One teacher explained that they: 'Siarad Cymraeg gyda'r plant iaith gyntaf, Incidental Welsh gyda'r gweddill/ Speak Welsh with first language children, Incidental Welsh with the others'. Such use of Welsh may increase pupils' exposure to Welsh in contexts beyond their Welsh lessons. However, unless teachers have a clearly defined developmental strategy in place, pupils (and the teacher) are unlikely to progress in their learning beyond the static terms and phrases that they use (Dickinson, 1992).

In terms of the type of support currently offered to teachers offering IW, in many cases (in 17 of the 43 responses returned; 4 teachers did not answer), teachers reported receiving support from members of the Welsh department and colleagues within their school. Many ($n = 9$) also benefitted from a variety of resources that were available at school, such as crib sheets, themes/words for the weeks, comment cards, language placemats, posters and PowerPoints. Some teachers ($n = 7$) had been to Welsh language courses, two of which commented on the provision of time given to support this. One respondent mentioned that they received 'too much' Welsh language support. However, the remaining teachers that provided an answer ($n = 11$) reported no or insufficient support in their schools, leading them to look for support elsewhere, e.g.:

None. I have looked into taking part in Welsh lessons for adult learners at my local university, but, financial constraints meant I can't take part. Within school there has been one or two CPD (Continuing Professional Development) sessions on Welsh, but it is not taught or followed up. All the Welsh I have learned I have picked up from hearing in assemblies or meetings.

Of the 85% ($n = 40$) who reported that they did deliver some form of Welsh in their lessons, 32.5% ($n = 13$) reported very little or no confidence in doing so, 37.5% ($n = 15$) reported middling confidence, and only 30% ($n = 12$) reported that they were 'quite' or 'very' confident in doing so. Beyond the descriptions of teachers' use of Welsh in the classroom noted above, one teacher mentioned their lack of confidence, particularly around making mistakes in front of pupils: 'Not confident and pupils pick up on any mistakes'. Interestingly, a series of Chi square analysis revealed that while there was no relationship between confidence and where in Wales they teach (χ^2 (8, $n = 47$) = 7.767, $p > 0.05$), where they were born (χ^2(8, $n = 47$) = 6.286, $p > 0.05$), or years of service (χ^2 (16, $n = 47$) = 16.289, $p > 0.05$), there was a relationship between confidence level and their subject (χ^2 (16, $n = 46$) = 35.022, $p < 0.05$) and, unsurprisingly perhaps, between confidence and whether they use Welsh or not (χ^2 (4, $n = 47$) = 11.498, $p < 0.05$). Supporting staff to use Welsh in the secondary sector may therefore require differentiated training, a different focus and different expectations in order to increase teacher confidence across all subjects of the curriculum.

In line with the previous literature outlining the links between self-competence and use (e.g. Mystkowska-Wiertelak & Pawlak, 2017), one teacher mentioned their awareness of their limited knowledge of Welsh as a reason for their patterns of use: 'I don't know enough to confidently use it'. Such beliefs about one's abilities can limit the extent of Welsh one is able to or is willing to use, as a different teacher mentions:

'No more than that as I don't know more'.

However, despite the fact that approximately two thirds of the sample reported middling, little or no confidence in delivering Welsh, of those who responded to the question regarding whether or not they would like to receive more support ($n = 45$), only 57.8% ($n = 26$) reported that they would, with 42% ($n = 19$) declaring that they would not. In those cases where they would not like to receive more support, the reasons provided focused around a sense of already knowing who to approach for help – 'I know where to go and who to approach should I need additional support' – suggesting that to many, they were happy delivering the level of Welsh they were accustomed to and not necessarily looking to expand on that. However, 73.7% of the beginners ($n = 14$), and 75% of those with basic words ($n = 9$) (and 1 respondent each from the intermediate, nearly fluent and fluent categories) reported that they would like more support for reasons such as a desire to increase confidence, improve pronunciation, to improve conversational Welsh, for subject specific vocabulary and sentence structure and to be able to create resources.

In summary, most of the teachers were engaged with the use of Welsh in some form or another, but, in most cases, that use was confined to specific terms or phrases that teachers felt most comfortable in delivering. However, unless developed appropriately, such use will do little to increase pupils' or teachers' learning and do little in terms of increasing self-confidence and use in the long term.

Part 2 looked at the potential differences in the delivery of IW among teachers who had received additional support and those who had not.

Part 2: Classroom observations

Observations were carried out in five schools: four where no personalised Welsh language support had been provided to the teachers (Condition 1), and one school where personalised Welsh language support had been provided for a period of six weeks prior to the observation (Condition 2).

In Condition 1 (no personalised Welsh language support), very little Welsh was heard during the four days of observations across the four schools, with many lessons containing no use of Welsh at all. However, the types of contexts where Welsh was heard were similar across all four schools and fell under one of five themes: framing of the lesson (e.g. *bore da* – 'good morning', *dewch i mewn* – 'come in'), eliciting set expressions (e.g. eliciting *yma* 'here/resent' in response to the reading out of the classroom register), classroom management (e.g. *tri, dau, un ... tawelwch* – 'three, two, one ... silence', *da iawn* – 'very good'), code-switching (e.g. *go into* chwech o grwps – 'go into six groups') and visual aids (e.g. posters displaying a range of different Welsh vocabulary and set phrases including days of the week, months of the year, colours, question forms and subject-specific vocabulary) (for more detailed information, see Parry & Thomas, in preparation). With the exception of code-switching, which was delivered by Welsh language teachers who were clearly fluent in Welsh, the Welsh that pupils heard from 25 teachers within the four schools was very limited. When it did occur, it took a very structured form and did very little to elicit pupils' use of Welsh. In sum, the delivery of Welsh by each of the teachers (and the responses by pupils) can be categorised as minimal.

In Condition 2 (personalised Welsh language support) three teachers who received personalised one-to-one support from a Welsh tutor on a weekly basis for 6 weeks were observed teaching in their classroom environments. Teacher 1 was already nearly fluent in Welsh but lacked confidence in using it, but Teachers 2 and 3 were beginners. These same teachers were subsequently interviewed about their experiences of the course and how it had impacted on their delivery of Welsh (if at all) (see Phase 3 below). All three teachers were observed to be using Welsh, but to different degrees, depending on the pupils' language skills and the subject being taught. In the case of two of the teachers (one of which included the near-fluent teacher), the Welsh that was observed went

Table 12.1 A representation of the overall language that was heard during the observations in Condition 2

	Teacher language	Pupil language
Teacher 1 (fluent)	Mixture of Welsh (instructions) and English (content)	Minimal use of Welsh
Teacher 2 (beginner)	Minimal use of Welsh (low ability children)	No Welsh
Teacher 3 (beginner)	Mixture of Welsh (instructions) and English (content)	Minimal use of Welsh

beyond the traditional types of expressions that are usually aligned to IW (as outlined in Phase 1) using more elaborate expressions such as *gwaith cartref os gwelwch yn dda* – 'homework please', *Gobeithio bod chi i gyd wedi gorffen labelu nawr* – 'Hope you have all finished labelling now' or *paid a siarad efo fo mae ganddo fo waith i'w wneud* 'don't talk to him, he has work to do'. The type of Welsh used by the remaining teacher tended to be more confined to the typical IW forms (*da iawn* – very good, *dau funud i fynd* - two minutes to go, etc.).

In two classrooms, children were presented with bilingual information on the walls, and the classrooms housed Welsh-medium textbooks and worksheets. In one mathematics lesson, the initial slides presented to the class were bilingual, with the remainder of the tasks presented in Welsh only. In sum, the delivery of Welsh by each of the three teachers (and the responses by pupils) can be categorised as follows (see Table 12.1).

What these results show is that all teachers – Conditions 1 and 2 – tend to approach IW in a similar way in terms of how, when and where they introduce Welsh into the classroom as shown by overlapping themes such as greetings, classroom management and bilingual discourses etc. However, those who had received personalised Welsh language support training went a little further in their use of Welsh, exploring more advanced concepts around codeswitching and using more elaborative language patterns. However, the fact that teachers may have used more Welsh and in wider variety of ways does not necessarily mean that those teachers were more confident in their delivery. Phase 3 explore the extent to which the additional support provided impacted on teachers' confidence in delivering IW.

Part 3: Teacher focus groups and questionnaires

The three teachers observed in Condition 2 of Part 2 (teachers that had received personalised support) were given a questionnaire and took part in a subsequent focus group interview about their experiences both during and after receiving the training. When asked to reflect on their own engagement with and use of Welsh after the programme, all teachers reported that they were more able and willing to use Welsh in their classrooms. For example, Teacher 1 stated: 'Yes, yeah I do. I do with the younger ones, the year 7 especially and year 8, I've started talking to them a lot more in Welsh even though the lessons are through the medium of English'. Teacher 2 explained that they used Welsh a little bit more than before the training: 'I think probably a little bit, the odd word here and there in the staff room and a bit more of "*gwaith dosbarth*" [classwork] and things like that'. Teacher 3 further explained that she is more confident to use more Welsh after the training, and felt that 'the pupils are supportive' while Teacher 1 noticed that: 'the kids, they, especially the year 7 class, [...] have started embracing their Welsh a bit more'. This notion of support from the pupils was noted by two teachers. Teacher 3 mentioned classes that she perceived as supportive:

> I'm not with the older classes but I do use a lot of Welsh resources and bilingual resources anyway, therefore, I don't have to speak as much but I am doing more incidental stuff particularly with the more supportive younger classes who are nice about it ... .

Having the support of the pupils was significant for the teachers. As noted before in this chapter (e.g. Horwitz *et al.*, 1986), fear of being judged impacts learners' confidence to use the language, and therefore having the support of their pupils meant that the teacher felt more confident in using Welsh. In fact, given that being evaluated by others is one of the top 10 sources of stress reported by teachers (Kyriacou, 2000), it is not surprising that L2 speakers of a language may feel this way.

All three teachers found the programme resources and the one-to-one nature of the training very useful, and this was facilitated by the fact that the training happened within their school. For example, in the questionnaire, Teacher 2 wrote: 'A good scheme. It's possible to improve my Welsh whilst still being present in school for my classes'.

Teachers made frequent references, both in the questionnaire and in the focus groups, to the fact that the programme of support was helpful in raising their confidence: (i) in using Welsh in general; (ii) in delivering IW; (iii) in delivering subject specific knowledge in Welsh; and, (iv) in creating Welsh classroom resources. Example responses are presented below:

First, in terms of their confidence to use Welsh in general, all three teachers noted in the questionnaire that the programme, albeit only a short intervention, had reportedly increased their confidence around using Welsh. Teacher 1 explained: '*Mae'r cynllun wedi bod yn ddefnyddiol i mi ffeindio'r hyder i ddysgu drwy'r Gymraeg*/the programme has been useful for me to find the confidence to teach through Welsh'. Teacher 2 echoed this claim and said that they feel, 'more confident in using snippets of Welsh whilst teaching'. And Teacher 3 felt more confident in speaking Welsh: 'It has built up my confidence to use more spoken Welsh'. For Teacher 1 in particular, who was already fluent in Welsh, the programme helped build her confidence around specific structures of Welsh, such as the mutation system, that are highly complex to master (Thomas & Mayr, 2010):

> … my writing in Welsh isn't as strong as my spoken so we did a lot of written tasks and *treiglo* [mutation] and things that I need as a professional in order to provide documentation and emails and stuff in Welsh.

One key component of the programme that led to increased confidence for this teacher, as detailed in the questionnaire, was the realisation that spoken language did not have to be perfect: '*Deall does dim rhaid iddo fod yn berffaith bob tro* / Understand that it doesn't always have to be perfect each time'. This links to the notion of the ideal L2 self (Yashima, 2009) or the so-called 'native speaker fallacy' (Phillipson, 1992), where L2 speakers often assume L1 speaker norms as the ideal. Understanding that L2 (and L1 speakers) have their own idiolects as well as shared expressions that may divert from prescriptive norms can help increase learners' ratings of self-competence, that can lead to increased confidence and reduced anxiety (Winograd, 2005).

Second, the main purpose of the programme was to increase teachers' confidence in delivering IW, particularly among teachers who had basic or very low knowledge of Welsh. Teacher 3 was clearly affected positively by the programme. In the questionnaire, she stated that she 'enjoyed taking part in this scheme. It has built up [her] confidence to use more spoken Welsh (IW) in the classroom'. In the focus group, Teacher 3 explained that she listens 'to spoken Welsh more which is what [she] wasn't able to do in the staff room'.

Third, in terms of confidence in delivering subject-specific knowledge in Welsh, all three teachers felt that teaching subject specific content in Welsh was a challenge. However, Teacher 1 felt that the course had helped with raising her confidence in using subject-specific terms in Welsh and was something she would like more training in: 'teaching science through the medium of Welsh, that's where my confidence was lacking'.

Finally, in terms of confidence in creating Welsh classroom resources, even though Teacher 1 was already fluent in Welsh, it was clear that she lacked confidence in her knowledge of Welsh, particularly in relation to the written form (as noted under (i) above). Following the course, however, she had reportedly regained her confidence and was actively producing more bilingual resources: '*Rwyf wedi dechrau geirfa a datblygu llyfrau gwaith ddwyieithog* [sic] / I have started vocabulary and developing bilingual workbooks'.

This impact was not only seen in relation to Teacher 1 but also in relation to Teacher 3, who, as a beginner learner of Welsh, was actively developing bilingual resources: 'All my KS3 (key stage 3) resources are now bilingual'.

It is clear, therefore that, in line with the observations described in Part 2, the course seemed to have impacted the teachers differently, although for all three teachers, the course, albeit short-term in its delivery as a pilot project, did increase their engagement with the language in one way or another:

> I think that I feel more encouraged to produce more things bilingually following the course and it did give me confidence ... (teacher 1)

> I don't know really if it had any impact at all. I mean enjoyable but I don't find myself speaking Welsh ... I suppose that I listen a little bit more intently in the staff room setting. I pick up on a few more words now and I understand a little bit more of what's being said but delivery wise, it's not really affected that (teacher 2)

> I listen to spoken Welsh more which is what I wasn't able to do in the staff Room ... Pupils who speak to me in Welsh but then suddenly change to English, I'm you know, getting them to repeat it so that they just don't just assume ... (teacher 3)

Conclusion

This chapter explored teacher confidence in integrating language and content as experienced by teachers delivering IW in secondary schools in Wales. More specifically, it focused on the implementation and impact of a one-to-one pilot Welsh language support scheme, geared towards developing teacher confidence in using Welsh with pupils. As the Welsh language support sessions were delivered over the course of six weeks, they were not expected to reverse the linguistic situation in any given context; however, they did resulted in some interesting – and largely positive – outcomes that are worthy of further discussion, and that have important implications for training and support, as noted below.

First, it was clear, particularly from the findings of Phases 1 and 3, that reluctance to use Welsh is often linked to low levels of confidence. These low levels of confidence seemed to be fuelled by the teacher's fear of being wrong, as judged by other teachers and by the pupils in their immediate environment. Respondents in Phase 3 noted quite clearly how the one-to-one Welsh language support sessions helped break down that confidence barrier, making it possible to feel free to make mistakes in a supportive environment. Ensuring that there is a whole-school approach to supporting teachers who are reluctant speakers of Welsh, or at the beginner stage of learning, is thus critical to the success of any such intervention. This not only relates to colleagues within the school but also to the pupils themselves who can feel empowered in their abilities to support the teacher's journey as an L2 learner, as indicated by Teacher 3 in Phase 3. This could be achieved through collaborative activities that promote the use of Welsh in the school, where pupils gain recognition for the support and guidance they provide. While the one-to-one support was geared towards increasing teachers' ability to deliver IW, the experiences gained through receiving the one-to-one support led to increased engagement with, and use of Welsh, in general (in class, with colleagues in the staff room), increased delivery of subject specific knowledge in Welsh (unless deemed inappropriate to do so – e.g. with lower ability maths groups) and creating Welsh/bilingual classroom learning resources. These findings suggest that such an intervention – even if delivered in short phases – can impact positively on teachers' willingness and ability to expand their engagement with and use of Welsh, provided that the teacher is a willing participator in the process.

Second, there were clear differences in the use of Welsh as observed by those who had received one-to-one language support and by those who had not. Across the 25 different teachers who had not received any specific Welsh language support training, the use of Welsh was minimal (albeit part of the Welsh curriculum), and, where used, was presented largely in the form of simple set statements that did little to elicit Welsh responses from pupils or to expand on and/or develop pupils' knowledge of Welsh (see 12). Conversely, across the three teachers who had received the one-to-one Welsh language support sessions, the use of Welsh was much more prominent, featuring more elaborated forms and utterances that could serve to provide more varied structures in the input to pupils and elicit more open responses from them. However, in all cases, the use of Welsh tended to veer towards set phrases and structures (framing the lesson; classroom management; etc.), which, by themselves, serve to normalise the use of Welsh outside the Welsh as a subject lesson, but, unless developed, lessens the opportunities for dyadic interactions between the teacher and pupil or opportunities to elicit spoken forms. This suggests that more training is needed both for teachers, and for those supporting their linguistic development, in terms of the purpose of IW and the opportunities it affords to develop both teachers' and pupils' knowledge and use of Welsh. In a similar vein, the results of Phase 2 observations show the lack of consistency in the delivery of IW, not only across schools and regions, but also within schools within specific regions, across teachers, subjects and age groups.

Implications for Policy and Practice

There is a clear need for a more consistent approach to IW at a policy level, with clear guidance for the expected outcomes in order that schools can plan effectively for its implementation. Together, these findings suggest that even short-term, one-to-one language training can support teachers who are currently unable or unwilling to use Welsh in the classroom to gain confidence to start using at least some of the language in their teaching. Such interventions need strategic support at school level in order that teachers are given the time and opportunity to increase their knowledge of Welsh. However, clearer guidelines are needed on the purpose and aims of IW in order that schools' investment in teacher time help lead to increased teacher and pupil confidence in using Welsh, fulfilling the Welsh Government goals of achieving a million speakers of Welsh by 2050.

References

Aitchison, J.W. and Carter, H. (1993) The Welsh Language in 1991: A broken heart and a new beginning. *Planet* 97, 3–10.

Arnold, J. (1999) *Affect in Language Learning*. Cambridge: Cambridge University Press.

Askell-Williams, H. and Lawson, M.J. (2013) Teachers' knowledge and confidence for promoting positive mental health in primary school communities. *Asia-Pacific Journal of Teacher Education* 41 (2), 126–143.

Barcroft, J. (2009) Effects of synonym generation on incidental and intentional L2 vocabulary learning during reading. *TESOL Quarterly* 43 (1), 79–103.

Brooker, C. (2009) The national continuous quality improvement tool for mental health education: Results of targeted and supported implementation in England. *Journal of Interprofessional Care* 20 (3), 276–289.

Brown, H.D. (2000) *Principles of Language Learning and Teaching*. New York, NY: Longman.

Clément, R. (1980) Ethnicity, contact, and communicative competence in a second language. In H.M. Giles, W.P. Robinson and P.M. Smith (eds) *Language: Social Psychological Perspectives* (pp. 147–154). Oxford: Pergamon.

Clément, R. (1986) Second language proficiency and acculturation: An investigation of the effects of language status and individual characteristics. *Journal of Language & Social Psychology* 5, 271–290.

Cummins, J. (2008) BICS and CALP. In B. Street and N. Hornberger (eds) *Encyclopaedia of Language and Education* (pp. 71–83). New York, NY: Springer.

Davies, S. (2012) *One Language for All: A Review of Welsh Second Language at Key Stages 3 and 4*. Cardiff: Welsh Government.

Dewaele, J.M. (2015) On emotions in foreign language learning and use. *The Language Teacher* 39, 13–15.

Dewaele. J.M. and Nakano, S. (2012) Multilinguals' perceptions of feeling different when switching languages. *Journal of Multilingual and Multicultural Development* 34 (2), 107–120.

Dickinson, L. (1992) Learner Training for Language Learning. Dublin: Authentik.

Du, X. (2009) The affective filter in second language teaching. *Asian Social Science* 5 (8), 162–166.

Education Support Partnership (2018) Teacher wellbeing index 2018, 22 October. See https://www.educationsupportpartnership.org.uk/about-us/press-centre/teacher-wellbeing-index-2018-highlights-stress-epidemic-and-rising-mental (accessed March 2019).

Ekornes, S., Hauge, T.E. and Lund, I. (2012) Teachers as mental health promoters: A study of teachers' understanding of the concept of mental health. *International Journal of Mental Health Promotion* 14 (5), 289–310.

Estyn (2007) *An Evaluation of the GCSE Welsh Second Language Short Course*. Cardiff: Publication Section Estyn.

Estyn (2017) *An Evaluation of the GCSE Welsh Second Language Short Course*. Cardiff: Publication Section Estyn.

Fan, Y. (2013) Every teacher is a language teacher: Preparing teacher candidates for English language learners through service-learning. *Gateways: International Journal of Community Research and Engagement* 6, 77–92.

García, O. (2009) *Bilingual Education in the 21st Century: A Global Perspective*. Chichester: Wiley-Blackwell.

Gathercole, V.C.M. and Thomas, E.M. (2009) Bilingual first-language development: Dominant language takeover, threatened minority language take-up. *Bilingualism: Language and Cognition* 12 (2), 213–237.

Graham, A., Phelps, R., Maddison, C. and Fitzgerald, R. (2011) Supporting children's mental health in schools: Teacher views. *Teachers and Teaching* 17 (4), 479–496.

Horwitz, E.K. (1996) Even teachers get the blues: Recognizing and alleviating non-native teaches' feelings of foreign language anxiety. *Foreign Language Annals* 29, 365–372.

Horwitz, E.K., Horwitz, M.B. and Cope, J. (1986) Foreign language classroom anxiety. *Modern Language Journal* 70, 125–132.

Huckin, T. and Coady, J. (1999) Incidental vocabulary acquisition in a second language: A review. *Studies in Second Language Acquisition* 21, 181–93.

Klaassen, R.G. (2001) *The International University Curriculum: Challenges in English-Medium Engineering Education*. Delft University of Technology.

Kyriacou, C. (2000) *Stress-Busting for Teachers*. Cheltenham: Stanley Thornes Publishers.

Mazzer, K.R. and Rickwood, D.J. (2013) Community-based roles promoting youth mental health: comparing the roles of teachers and coaches in promotion, prevention and early intervention. *International Journal of Mental Health Promotion* 15 (1), 29–42.

Mazzer, K.R. and Rickwood, D.J. (2015) Teachers' role breadth and perceived efficacy in supporting student mental health. *Advances in School Mental Health Promotion* 8 (1), 29–41.

Medgyes, P. (2001) When the teacher is a non-native speaker. In M. Celcie-Murcia (ed.) *Teaching English as a Second or Foreign Language* (pp. 415–427) (3rd edn). Boston, MA: Heinle & Heinle.

Mundia, L. (2013) Relationship between mental health and teaching. *International Journal of Mental Health* 42 (2–3), 73–98.

Mystkowska-Wiertelak, A. and Pawlak, M. (2017) *Willingness to Communicate in Instructed Second Language Acquisition: Combining a Macro- and Micro-Perspective*. Bristol: Multilingual Matters.

Parry, N.M. and Thomas, E.M. (forthcoming) An evaluation of the effectiveness of Welsh second language across the curriculum in English Medium schools in North Wales.

Phillipson, R. (1992) *Linguistic Imperialism*. Oxford: Oxford University Press.

Piccardo, E. (2013) Epistemological evolution in language didactics: The hidden face of emotions. *Lidil* 48, 17–36.

Saffran, J.R., Newport, E.L., Aslin, R.N., Tunick, R.A. and Barrueco, S. (1997) Incidental language learning: Listening (and learning) out of the corner of your ear. *American Psychological Society* 8 (2), 101–105.

Schwarzer, R. and Hallum, S. (2008) Perceived teacher self-efficacy as a predictor of job stress and burnout: Mediation Analyses. *Applied Psychology* 57, 152–171.

Seidlhofer, B. (1999) Double standards: Teacher education in the expanding circle. *World Englishes* 18 (2), 223–245.

Smith, B.O. (1968) *Teachers for the Real World*. Washington, DC: American Association of Colleges for Teacher Education.

Sowislo, J.F. and Orth, U. (2013) Does low self-esteem predict depression and anxiety? A meta-analysis of longitudinal studies. *Psychological Bulletin* 139 (1) 213–240.

Spada, N. and Tomita, Y. (2010) Interactions between type of instruction and type of language feature: A meta-analysis. *Language Learning* 60 (2), 263–308.

Stats Wales (2012) Welsh speakers by local authority and broader age groups, 2001 and 2011 census. [Homepage of Welsh Government]. See https://statswales.gov.wales/

Catalogue/Welsh-Language/welshspeakers-by-la-broaderage-2001and2011census (accessed January 2019).

Stats Wales (2018) Teaching of Welsh in primary, middle and secondary schools by local authority, region and category [Homepage of Welsh Government]. See https://statswales.gov.wales/Catalogue/Education-and-Skills/Schools-and-Teachers/teachers-and-support-staff/School-Staff/teachingwelshprimarymiddlesecondaryschools-by-localauthorityregion-category (accessed March 2019).

Thomas, E.M. and Mayr, R. (2010) Children's acquisition of Welsh in a bilingual setting: A psycholinguistic perspective. In D. Morris (ed.) *Welsh in the 21st Century* (pp. 99–118). Cardiff: Cardiff University Press.

Thomas, E., Apolloni, D. and Parry, N. (2018) *Dulliau Addysg Dwyieithog: cyfeilyfr cyflym i addysgwyr*. Bangor: GwE.

Welsh Government (2010) *Welsh-medium Education Strategy*. Cardiff: Welsh Government.

Welsh Government (2017) *Cymraeg 2050: Miliwn o siaradwyr*. Cardiff: Welsh Government.

Wilkinson, K.M. (2005) Disambiguation and mapping of new word meanings by individuals with intellectual/developmental disabilities. *American Journal on Mental Retardation* 110, 71–86.

Winograd, K. (2005) *Good Day, Bad Day. Teaching as a High-Wire Act*. Lanham: Rowman & Littlefield Education.

WJEC. (2015) *GCSE Final Results*. Cardiff: WJEC CBAC Ltd.

Yashima, T. (2009) International posture and the ideal L2 self in the Japanese EFL context. In Z. Dörnyei and E. Ushioda (eds) *Motivation, Language Identity and the L2 Self* (pp. 144–163). Bristol: Multilingual Matters.

13 Professional Development in Action: Teachers' Experiences in Learning to Bridge Language and Content

Victor Arshad and Roy Lyster

Introduction

As the popularity of content-based instruction (CBI) programmes continues to rise around the world and across educational levels, it is ever more vital for teachers who teach in such programmes to be equipped with effective strategies to bridge language and content instruction. Calls for teacher professional development (PD) to provide guidance have been widespread (e.g. Cammarata & Tedick, 2012; Fortune *et al.*, 2008) but research into what type of support would be beneficial remains scarce, and the voices of teachers themselves are often absent from the literature. In order to fill this gap, this chapter explores the lived experiences of eight teachers at the elementary and secondary levels who teach social studies in French to mainly English-speaking students. Conducted during the first year of a three-year PD partnership in Québec with the goal of providing insight into how the eight teachers responded to and interpreted the PD support, the present study documents their affective trajectories as they designed and implemented instructional units with a language focus.

Background

CBI programmes, where the target language may be a second, foreign, regional, heritage or indigenous language, are implemented worldwide in a myriad of styles with an equal myriad of terminology, such as content-based language teaching (CBLT), content and language integrated learning (CLIL) as well as various forms of immersion education. Despite such variability, the essential philosophy underlying CBI as a pedagogical approach remains the same: to provide exposure to, and engagement with, the target language via subject-matter instruction, which affords learners a motivational basis for purposeful communication and a cognitive basis for target language learning.

The positive development of student academic achievement, as well as indicators such as motivation and self-confidence within CBI programmes have been well documented (e.g. Serra, 2007; Turnbull et al., 2001). At the same time, studies have revealed weaknesses in student proficiency in the target language, such as a lack of grammatical accuracy, lexical richness, sociolinguistic appropriateness and substantial interference from the mother tongue (e.g. Harley, 1992; Kong & Hoare, 2012). There is now consensus that, in order for an additional language to be learned effectively through CBI, a greater focus on language must be integrated into the content-driven curriculum (e.g. Dalton-Puffer et al., 2010; Lyster, 2007). Exposure to content on its own is not sufficient to produce proficient speakers of a target language; an integrated approach in which both language objectives and content objectives are prioritised together must be implemented. Teachers in CBI programmes are at the forefront of this endeavour but, despite the availability of strategies and frameworks for the integration of content and language (e.g. Ball et al., 2016; Echevarría et al., 2008), there is a significant gap in research on the application of these models.

The existing literature has explored teacher knowledge and teacher collaboration within CBI contexts. Surveys of immersion teachers' perceptions about their teacher training found that many felt their pre-service education and any in-service PD opportunities were insufficient or inadequate (Day & Shapson, 1996; Kong et al., 2011). Most felt unprepared to teach content-based classes in the target language and much less able to integrate specific language objectives into the curriculum. A recurring theme experienced by many CBI teachers is that of an increasing sense of isolation due to a lack of support from colleagues or school districts (Cammarata & Tedick, 2012) and rigid school culture, hierarchies, and policies that inhibit collaboration (Kong, 2014). Yet the literature on PD in education has underscored the importance of collaborative planning and sharing in order for teachers to become active agents in their own learning (e.g. Borko, 2004). In limited cases when collaboration does occur, CBI teachers typically report that most instances of cross-linguistic and cross-curricular planning are incidental (Lyster et al., 2009) or effective only when structured and guided through PD (Lyster et al., 2013).

Calls for PD in CBI programmes have remained consistent yet there are few studies with CBI teachers' experiences during PD initiatives as a central focus barring two notable exceptions. The first is a study by Cammarata and Haley (2018), which reported on 15 French immersion teachers in a PD project undertaken to support them in appropriating and implementing a content-language-literacy integrated curricular planning framework. Findings indicated that sustained PD interventions organised around collaborative work had a positive effect on the participating teachers' ability to counterbalance content and language/literacy instruction.

The second study, by Tedick and Zilmer (2018), focused on 75 immersion teachers' perceptions of the PD they received on language-focused content instruction in the context of online courses designed for that purpose. The researchers found that the teachers appreciated PD experiences that were relevant to their practice, led to observable changes in student learning and provided opportunities for feedback, enactment, collaboration and reflection. Tedick and Zilmer acknowledged the limitations of findings based solely on self-report and teacher perceptions, and concluded with a call for research on what they characterised as *PD in action*:

> We need research that involves observing teachers in their classrooms and interacting with them as they engage in PD experiences – observing PD in action. Video recordings of teachers enacting new practices and reflecting on them would not only serve as important data for analysis but could also potentially serve as important material for future PD. (Tedick & Zilmer, 2018: 290)

The Present Study

Building on Fullan's (2015) emphasis on the need to better understand teachers' subjective experiences in order to promote sustainable change, the present study focused on answering the following research question to capture *PD in action*: what are CBI teachers' lived experiences during a PD initiative focusing on improving CBI pedagogy?

To support teachers in implementing a counterbalanced approach that gives content and language objectives complementary status while shifting students' attention between language and content (Lyster, 2007, 2016), a three-year PD initiative was undertaken between McGill University and the Eastern Townships School Board (ETSB), an English-language school board in Québec, a Canadian province in which the dominant language is French. The ETSB's course offerings are mainly in English and serve predominantly English-speaking communities that also consist of some French-speaking families. It offers its social studies course in French in addition to a French as a second language (L2) course to both elementary and secondary students; learning social studies through the medium of an L2 is especially rich and complex due to the dense nature of the material and the wide-ranging linguistic repertoire required (Schleppergell & de Oliveria, 2006). Consequently, this was an ideal setting to provide teachers with strategies to enrich students' L2 learning through the integration of content and language.

The initiative was funded by the Québec ministry responsible for education to support partnerships between universities and school boards. Only Year 1 of the three-year initiative was the object of a detailed analysis of teachers' affective experiences, the full results of which are reported in the first author's MA thesis (Shahsavar-Arshad, 2016) and encapsulated here; what transpired in Years 2 and 3 will be briefly summarised at end of the chapter.

Participants

The eight teacher participants were female. Seven of the teachers taught at the elementary level and one teacher taught at the secondary level (Grade 7 in Québec); the majority were teaching a separate French L2 class in addition to the social studies course. Some had training in L2 pedagogy while others did not. All teachers indicated that they rarely or never participated in any type of PD or collaboration with other teachers. The teachers are identified by pseudonyms in Table 13.1 along with other relevant participant characteristics.

Project design

The eight teachers in Year 1 participated in five daylong PD sessions throughout the school year, a timeline of which is described below:

(1) October – Workshop 1: the ETSB provided an overview of the provincial social studies curriculum and relevant instructional strategies. Teachers then began to choose a content-specific theme for their instructional units.
(2) November – Workshop 2: McGill University gave a presentation on the challenges and benefits of a dual focus on language and content.

Table 13.1 Study participants

Teacher	Mother tongue	Years of teaching experience	Teaching French L2 and Social Studies	Background in L2 teaching	Grade level
Beatrice	French	33	No	Yes	6
Chantal	French	21	Yes	Yes	1, 2
Corinne	French	5	Yes	Yes	4
Delphine	French	11	Yes	Yes	4, 5, 6
Danielle	French	20	Yes	No	6
Gabrielle	French	12	Yes	Yes	6
Sandrine	French	27	No	No	7
Vanessa	English/ French	15	Yes	No	4

Teachers then began to choose a language element to integrate within their content-specific theme for their instructional units. An instructional model comprising four phases – Contextualisation, Awareness, Practice, Autonomy – and thus called the CAPA sequence (Lyster, 2019; Tedick & Lyster, 2020), was provided to teachers to follow in designing their integrated units:

(i)   Contextualisation: establishes a meaningful context related to content by means of a text that has been adapted to make specific target features appear salient and frequent.

(ii) Awareness: encourages students to reflect on the target features in a way that helps them to discover the patterns governing their use in the text.

(iii) Practice: provides opportunities for students to use the target features in a meaningful yet controlled context and to receive feedback.

(iv) Autonomy: returns to the content area to help students develop fluency and confidence as they use the target features in a discipline-specific or thematic context.

Figure 13.1 was presented to illustrate how the CAPA sequence begins with a primary focus on social studies during the Contextualisation phase, then zooms in on language during the Awareness phase and Practice phase. During the Autonomy phase, the instructional focus is again on the social studies content that served as the starting point. The figure was described as an hourglass to illustrate which phases focus more on content and which focus more on language but does not represent this proportionally in terms of time or importance. An instructional unit following the sequence is described in more detail in the Year 1 Results section of the chapter, under Collaboration.

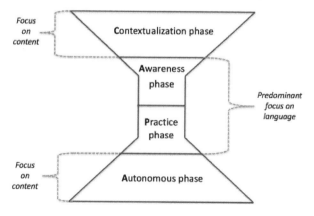

Figure 13.1 The CAPA sequence (adapted from Lyster, 2016)

(3) December – Workshop 3: entirely devoted to further developing the instructional units with support from both peers and the project team.

(4) January – Workshop 4: included time for completion of the instructional units, but began with a short presentation by McGill University about questioning techniques and corrective feedback.

(5) February and March – Implementation: teachers implemented their units in their respective classrooms while being video recorded.

(6) April – Workshop 5: teachers participated in stimulated recall sessions, viewing video clips of each other's instructional units in the classroom and reflecting on the process of planning and implementation.

Data collection and analysis

Data were gathered through the following sources:

(1) Survey 1: all teachers completed an online survey prior to Workshop 1 to gather background and contextual information.

(2) Interview 1: after either Workshop 1 or 2, all teachers took part in audio-recorded, semi-structured interviews with open-ended questions designed to elicit their thoughts on teaching social studies in French to predominantly non-francophone students.

(3) Close observations of as well as personal discussions with the teachers during all workshops, which contributed to a holistic perspective of their experiences.

(4) Visits to the schools in order to become familiar with the teachers' daily realities in addition to the visits during the filming of their instructional units.

(5) Survey 2: after viewing the recordings of their teaching during Workshop 5, all teachers completed a second online survey, which asked them to rate certain aspects of the PD and to gauge their perceptions regarding its effectiveness.

(6) Interview 2: all teachers participated in a second audio-recorded, semi-structured interview designed to elicit descriptions of lived experiences, allowing them to expand on notions covered in Survey 2 as well as to speak freely through open dialogue.

The data were analysed using elements of the hermeneutic phenomenological paradigm (van Manen, 1997), which in social science and educational research concerns the essence, or nature, of lived experiences for participants in a given study; the inner, intuitive world of participants' day-to-day experience becomes an empirical source of knowledge and meaning (Barnacle, 2004). Data analysis within the phenomenological paradigm requires an ability to be reflective, with the end goal of determining core constituents that define a particular experience through thematic analysis. Repeated themes, phrases, patterns and commonalities across multiple teacher responses were considered as core constituents.

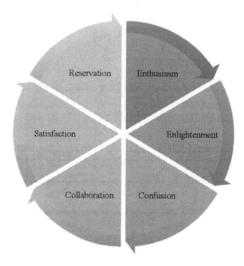

Figure 13.2 Directional and interconnected representation of teachers' experiences

Year 1 Results

The lived experiences of the eight teachers were categorised into six core constituents: enthusiasm, enlightenment, confusion, collaboration, satisfaction and reservation. The core constituents follow a chronological and cyclical pattern, more or less mirroring the structure of the PD initiative. They capture the progression of the teachers' affective trajectory as they unfolded, yet they remain continuous and overlap to form a whole, as reflected in Figure 13.2. Each core constituent will be presented with a representative quote from the participants and is supported by data translated into English from the original French.

Enthusiasm: 'Yes, it's possible!'

All the teachers were highly eager to embark on the initiative to receive help to attend to language in the classroom more productively (see also Chapter 12); they believed they lacked the pedagogical knowledge, appropriate resources and time to do so. They were enthusiastic to get PD support as all had indicated low levels of student comprehension as a major obstacle. When asked if she incorporated language into her lessons during Interview 1, Danielle responded as follows:

Danielle: Not yet. That's why I am here [laughter].

Researcher: OK. Do you think that it's important?

Danielle: Absolutely. Actually, I limit myself to vocabulary. Just maybe difficult words related to content, that's maybe not where the priority should be. I understand pretty well now and I think I'm happy to be here.

During classroom observations prior to the implementation of units, no systematic attention was paid to language by any of the teachers while they taught; any type of focus was either incidental or spontaneous. Lessons that were observed consisted of discussions, dialogues, presentations and other communicative activities that did not have a specific focus on the language needed by students to express themselves. As a result, student errors were quite common, but rarely corrected due to their frequency. All teachers acknowledged the importance of attending to language forms but indicated they continued to be stuck on precisely how to draw attention to them. The PD initiative was thus regarded as a bearer of much needed assistance and served as an opportunity to receive concrete training. The following exchange with Vanessa, Delphine and Corinne captures the positive energy with which all the teachers approached their involvement:

Vanessa:	I find that for us, just the fact that we are able to sit together and discuss, it's going to really change the way we do things, because we are going to concentrate, give ourselves the time; we said that time was something that we didn't have.
Delphine:	Exactly. Me personally, after two days, my vision has already changed and I have confidence in myself and the fact of saying, yes it's possible! And having ideas to do things, to create things so that finally it will all be easier.
Corinne:	And the training, I think. It's this workshop that's giving us the opportunity, that's giving us the ideas and the opportunity to sit down together. Most of the teachers who teach social studies are not properly trained to do it, we are the living proof. Most of the time it's, go on, figure it out, fly with your own wings but you have to give them training as well I think. It would be the key aspect, a fundamental key aspect. Professional development.
Vanessa:	And to have a day in the month of January or April, one whole day to work on it is rare. Really rare.

Enlightenment: 'Aha!'

Teachers expressed feelings of enlightenment at two pivotal moments. From the social studies perspective, the teachers believed that all content prescribed in the curriculum had to be completed in a single academic year; this was a primary source of stress. A major 'aha' moment, as described by Corinne, occurred during Workshop 1 when an educational consultant from the ETSB presented a detailed curriculum map displaying which topics, skills and competencies are to be covered at what levels. She explained that teachers were not expected to cover all the curricular topics and could instead use the curriculum map as a guide, giving competencies and skills priority over topics. Upon this announcement, there was a collective sigh of relief in the air. Workshop 1 was the first official clarification regarding the social studies curriculum that the teachers had had; they had lamented the lack of time to attend to language partly due to the amount of content material they thought they needed to cover.

With regard to language, Figure 13.2, the four-phase CAPA sequence, proved to be a crucial aid for teachers to visualise the when and how of language and content integration, and thus proved to be indispensable, as reiterated throughout the participants' surveys and interviews. The visual representation became a concrete, accessible tool for them to plan their lessons, as described by Delphine in Survey 2:

> **Delphine:**   I really remembered and loved the hourglass with the four steps to integrate the teaching of French and social studies. This way of integrating the two subjects is simple to understand and renders it all really easy to accomplish.

Confusion: 'You have to swim in the mud to be able to swim in water'

Although the teachers experienced various enlightening moments, a sense of confusion remained present, generated particularly during the planning process when specific steps needed to be taken to bring students' attention to language. The CAPA sequence served as a practical guide but the teachers continued to feel unsure how to proceed, as stated by Danielle and Sandrine in their respective Interview 2:

> **Danielle:**   Listen, the only thing I can say is that at the beginning, OK, the presentation was clear. I know what I'm doing. Then, I sit down with pen and paper, try to pick a topic. And I spent a lot of time swimming in the dark. At a certain time, I started to choose going down one path and then ... When I unblocked it was really fast. But I spent a lot of time swimming in the dark at the beginning. I can't really say what it was. I think that at a given moment you have to work, how should I say, you have to swim in the mud to be able to swim in water, if I can use that image.
>
> **Sandrine:**   I was really lost in the beginning, I didn't know which way to turn, I wasn't sure if I followed the contextualisation activity, the awareness activity, the guided practice and all that ... I didn't really know where I was going.

The CAPA sequence had helped shape teachers' thinking, but the workshops did not seem to provide a sufficient variety of concrete examples to conceptualise an effective lesson. There remained a lack of clarity and insecurity throughout the planning process. None of the teachers had ever designed a lesson within social studies that systematically focused on language, which led to an initial swim in the dark; a messy, muddy experience.

Collaboration: 'L'équipe fait la force!'

The PD initiative served as an occasion for productive collaborative sharing, which was a key ingredient in the finalisation of teachers' units. None had reported any type of collaboration with either social studies or French L2 teachers prior to the initiative. The teachers often saw their teaching contexts as a lonely and self-guided affair. There was no organisational structure within individual schools or through the school board to facilitate the sharing of resources. A partnered environment and a supportive network during the PD helped to alleviate initial fears regarding planning, especially in the case of Delphine, Corinne and Vanessa, three teachers that taught the same grade at the same school. The trio had never planned together and had been unable to meet prior to the PD sessions due to their schedules; this was their first opportunity to sit together and plan as a team.

They chose to integrate a focus on the use of *avoir* and être as auxiliary verbs in the *passé composé*, one of the past tense forms in French, within their unit on the explorer Jacques Cartier. During the Contextualisation phase, students watched a narrated, time-lapsed, animated biographical video of Cartier that Corinne had produced which mapped out key exploits in the explorer's life. The narrative was replete with instances of the *passé composé* using both auxiliary verbs. After watching the video, the content focus stayed in the foreground as students discussed the main points surrounding Cartier's voyages.

During the Awareness phase, the text of the video's narration was projected on the interactive whiteboard, with instances of the *passé composé* in bold. Students were asked first to identify the verbs in the *passé composé* and then, together with metalinguistic support from their teacher, to create a list of verbs that use *avoir* and those that use être as auxiliaries. During the Practice phase, each student received one of five images illustrating an important event or place related to Cartier and wrote a description using verbs in the *passé composé*. They then mingled with other students to find those with the same image, and together in small groups they synthesised their descriptions to create an historical account based on the images, which they then conveyed orally to the whole class, thus giving the teacher an opportunity to provide corrective feedback as necessary. For the Autonomy phase, students produced an illustrated timeline in small groups depicting some of the landmark events in Cartier's career, including a legend for each event using the *passé composé* to portray a trajectory of his experiences as an explorer.

The trio noted that their collaborative experience was at the core of their planning, having benefited from the experience of designing the task together, but also to validate and reassure one another regarding their practice. In response to the question, 'What was the most beneficial aspect of working as a team?' Delphine summarised the experience during Interview 2:

> **Delphine:** Sharing resources, sharing the work. We really said to each other, you, you do the photocopies, you, you write the text, you, you're going to find the verbs. I think we tripled what we were capable of doing in a short amount of time. We tripled the ideas as well; brainstorming ideas by three is a lot more efficient than alone. And to believe what we were doing was good, to validate our ideas because when you're alone, you always question yourself: Is this right? Is this not right? ...

The notion of collaboration to alleviate doubt, anxiety, confusion and uncertainty (see also Chapter 2) was consistently noted by the trio, with multiple voices during the planning process allowing for a more effective approach to developing curriculum.

All the teachers appreciated the collaborative atmosphere of the workshops. However, Corinne, Vanessa and Delphine were the only group who taught the same level at the same school and were able to design, plan and implement all aspects of their unit together. The other five teachers were from different schools. Chantal was particularly vocal in seeking support, whereas Beatrice, Sandrine, Gabrielle and Danielle were more inclined to work independently, asking questions or requesting guidance more sparingly. These teachers' sense of confusion during the planning process was more acute. The teachers who were more independent noted that they would have preferred to work with a colleague and stressed in the surveys that teachers should be paired with colleagues from their own schools in future initiatives. Upon seeing the video prepared by the trio, Beatrice remarked, '*L'équipe fait la force!*' (literally translated as 'The team makes strength!').

Satisfaction: 'The ship has sailed and it should be a great journey'

All teachers exhibited a sense of profound satisfaction regarding both the process and the outcome of their participation in the PD initiative. Their fulfilment was attributable to two important factors. First, they enjoyed the reflective and collaborative process which the initiative permitted. Second, they were able to see first-hand, thanks to the implementation of their units, the results and benefits of adopting an approach that integrated language and content. Chantal expressed the following on Survey 2:

> **Chantal:**   The project introduced us to new concepts, it gave us time to discuss, to digest the approach and, finally, the project gave us an opportunity to try what we had just learned by offering us both support and direction. What else is there to say? The ship has sailed and it should be a great journey.

The implementation phase proved to be a vital component in their assessment of the benefits of the initiative and of integrating language and content. In Interview 2, Vanessa described her realisation that the project had been a success:

> **Vanessa:**   It would probably be at the end of the project, when my students presented their timeline. There are some students who have a lot of difficulty in French who were able to really do well in terms of grammar in French but also on the life of Jacques Cartier and I think it's the fact of repeating often, always manipulating the same information even if we focused on French and sometimes history, it really, really, helped a lot.

The teachers were able to see that there was light at the end of the dark tunnel that formed during the planning process through implementation. All teachers expressed approval towards the integration of language and content as they saw its effects on their students and indicated a strong desire to continue applying the principles they had learned during the PD to their teaching.

Reservation: 'Now what's missing is the time'

The teachers experienced the PD positively and with unanimous satisfaction, yet before, during and after, a sense of reservation remained. There were two major concerns that continued to permeate their realities as CBI teachers: lack of suitable resources and lack of planning time. Resources used were typically meant for native speakers of French, which were too difficult for students to manipulate and comprehend. The teachers were therefore always required to adapt materials in order to render them comprehensible, requiring a considerable amount of time. In order to follow the CAPA sequence, all teachers had to first find material, adapt it to their students' level, then adapt it further to create an additional focus on language.

While all teachers expressed interest in continuing to apply the notions from the PD, they were also aware that it was the PD which allowed them three afternoons and one full day of planning time to generate their units.

Vanessa, Delphine and Corinne, all acknowledged they did not have any time to meet during school hours, and it was solely due to the workshops that they were able to collaborate. The lack of adequate planning time to find suitable resources and material to integrate language and content effectively was an external hurdle that the PD could not rectify in the long term. Many teachers expressed their frustration about the lack of appropriate resources and lack of time as reflected in this comment from Interview 2:

Delphine: The biggest difficulty I find, and I repeated it often in the questionnaire, it's really the resources in a second language. Maybe it was an expectation that I had that was too high to leave with resources already made. Because that's often a big challenge. I find that now I have a better understanding, I really loved the hourglass with four steps. Now what's missing is the time, it's always the biggest challenge, the time to create these resources. It becomes even frustrating when we know what we have to do, but we're not able to put it in our schedule to be able to do it.

The teachers also indicated that they wanted more specific ideas for units integrating content and language that they could use in the future. They wanted to continue to implement a counterbalanced CBI approach, but needed more sustained and long-term guidance, materials and time to do so. While many expressed the desire for future opportunities for PD relating to CBI, the same concerns that existed at the onset before their participation and which led them to begin the initiative with enthusiasm remained.

Years 2 and 3

Similar to Year 1, there were eight teachers participating in Year 2, including two teachers who had participated in Year 1 and thus served as lead teachers. Year 2 of the project also proceeded with five daylong workshops addressing similar themes, but in a more intensive manner during a two-month period as opposed to seven months. The participating teachers in Year 2 completed the same online surveys at the beginning and end of the PD but, unlike Year 1, participants were not interviewed. Analysis of the Year 2 surveys revealed that teachers reported less confusion, which we interpreted as attributable to three major factors: (a) the more intensive schedule with sessions closer together, (b) the mentorship of the lead teachers from the previous year and (c) the greater number of concrete examples of instructional units in the form of those created by teachers in Year 1. In addition, teachers in Year 2 were particularly enthusiastic about benefiting from viewing the videos of one another, with one remarking on Survey 2, 'Theory is good but seeing teachers in action in the videos is precious!'

Finally, in Year 3 of the project, four teachers from Years 1 and 2 chose to attend from one to three planning days to refine their instructional units and to continue developing an integrated social studies curriculum. The project finale entailed a daylong workshop to which all social studies/French L2 teachers at the ETSB were invited. A counterbalanced approach to content and language integration was presented, drawing on the video clips of the participating teachers from Years 1 and 2, and the seven participating teachers in attendance were available to share their units with their colleagues in small-group sessions. Some examples included 'Jacques Cartier and the *passé composé*', 'Pirates and prepositions', 'Iroquoian villages and grammatical gender' and 'Indigenous cultures and third-person plural verbs'. At the same time, we officially launched the French-language website that was designed for this project (https://mcgill.ca/etsb/), which is currently home to eight instructional sequences for other teachers to access.

Discussion and Implications for Policy and Practice

The results of Year 1 are reminiscent of those reported by Tedick and Zilmer (2018) who found that teachers appreciate PD experiences that are meaningful, lead to observable changes in student learning and provide opportunities for collaboration, feedback, enactment and reflection. With a view to shedding light on the practical implications of the present study in order to help enhance future instances of PD in CBI programmes, the discussion is organised according to the four benefits that participating teachers identified as the most satisfying through their experiences.

An integrated approach

The PD aimed consistently to raise the teachers' awareness of three essential and interrelated components of effective CBI: curricular content, L2 pedagogy and the integration of the two. First, the teachers needed and appreciated clarification of the social studies curriculum as there was considerable inconsistency reported: What content needs to be covered? What competencies and skills are priority? Knowledge of the content curriculum is the foundation upon which lesson planning occurs and it is critical for this foundation to be firmly conceptualised in the minds of CBI teachers. Secondly, teachers were given an overview of corrective feedback strategies and oral scaffolding techniques that optimise conditions for L2 learning (Lyster *et al.*, 2013). Teachers were highly receptive to this as it was a realisation and a reminder of the constant language needs of their students. And finally, the integration of content and language was emphasised with a specific framework that served as a blueprint for designing lessons. This integrated approach seemed to alleviate some anxiety and aided in the comprehension of CBI as a more concrete rather than an abstract approach.

A visual and sequential guide

The CAPA sequence proved to be an effective resource for teachers to begin to conceptualise how the integration of language and content can be achieved. The teachers appreciated a visual and sequential model that guided them in their planning but this did not fully alleviate difficult experiences while planning. They require even more specialised guidance during the planning process, replete with ample examples of tangible, practical and ready-to-go instructional units in order to begin creating their own. Concrete ideas for CBI units, tailored to the realities of CBI teachers, would allow them to envision what they could also create and implement within their individual school contexts, thereby alleviating initial anxiety, confusion and doubt. A focus on language while teaching content is a new concept for many teachers and a guided progression through all the stages of planning is vital.

A collaborative and supportive network

The PD brought multi-level actors such as teachers, educational consultants and researchers together to work towards strengthening CBI pedagogy to improve learning outcomes. Collaboration across the education spectrum has been documented as being a contributing factor to the positive experience of teachers (Maeroff, 1988). Within the context of the present study, the multilateral partnership created a professional learning community (Dufour *et al.*, 2008) in which the teachers found meaning through collaborative support and co-constructed learning. This proved to be a crucial element for the completion of the CBI curricular units as the teachers were able to overcome a pervasive feeling of isolation, a common experience of CBI teachers. They were able to discuss their doubts with team members and pushed each other forward. Collective and collaborative teacher experiences during PD are primordial for success and change (e.g. Cammarata & Haley, 2018; Smith, 2015).

The teachers also felt satisfaction with the initiative as it met the prerequisites for effective collegial collaboration:

- an institutional structure that provided the time and space for collaboration;
- a team of different types of educators collaborating;
- workshops were spaced out across the academic year to allow adequate time for planning, collaboration and implementation;

- all team members were enthusiastically committed to the project;
- an adequate amount of time was allotted to share and reflect on the experience as a whole (Lieberman, 1986).

PD is also likely to be more effective if teachers from the same school, department, area or grade level collaborate together (Wayne *et al.*, 2008). In this particular case, all the teachers participated in a collaborative environment yet those that were recruited from separate schools indicated more confusion and more feelings of isolation than the group of teachers working as a team from the same school and teaching the same grade level.

Implementing an effective sharing method, such as an online repository of which the website created at the end of Year 3 is an example, allows teachers to distribute their work and re-use other units developed for different grade levels. This can somewhat mitigate the reservations expressed by teachers in regard to lack of planning time during the regular academic year and, thus, lack of time to adapt material.

An implementation phase

Instrumental in teachers reporting satisfying experiences during the initiative was the implementation of the instructional units they had designed themselves. This enacting phase gave them first-hand experience in integrating language and content in the classroom, enabling them to perceive a positive change in their students' progress. If PD provides teachers with an opportunity to test and change practices in the classroom, thereby enabling them to notice or see a change in student learning outcomes, there is more likely to be a change in teachers' beliefs and attitudes (Guskey, 2002).

Despite the stress that participating teachers expressed at the thought of being video recorded and then having to watch themselves in the company of peers, there was a collective sigh of relief after watching the videos and unanimity in giving consent to have the videos shown for future PD purposes. The teachers expressed pride in their accomplishments, a sense of professional growth and a willingness to share with others.

Conclusion

The present study focused on eight social studies teachers during the first year of a three-year PD initiative comprising five full-day sessions. Because PD initiatives need to be tailored to suit local needs and contexts, what teachers experienced in this case may not be the same as teachers in other contexts. However, given the relative scarcity of CBI teacher voices during *PD in action*, this study can serve as a steppingstone to understanding the meaning that certain CBI teachers attribute to the help they receive. It brings to the fore their perspectives, and future studies of the same nature will provide further insight into how to create effective PD for effective CBI.

Improvements must also be made to the curriculum and material available for CBI programmes. Teachers continue to be bound by challenging and restrictive external factors that hinder their abilities to teach CBI effectively. On the one hand, CBI programmes are often based solely on a content curriculum, with no language objectives embedded within the curriculum itself; on the other, high-quality CBI resources are scarce for L2 learners, particularly in the Québec context. To compound these two matters, CBI teachers are given limited planning time despite being expected to target both language and content simultaneously, without appropriate resources or clear curriculum guidelines to do so. Such fundamental reforms are critically needed along with improved pre-service and in-service teacher guidance to sustain the effectiveness of CBI in the future.

References

Ball, P., Kelly, K. and Clegg, J. (2016) *Oxford Handbooks for Language Teachers: Putting CLIL into Practice.* Oxford: Oxford University Press.

Barnacle, R. (2004) Reflection on lived experience in educational research. *Educational Philosophy and Theory* 36 (1), 57–67.

Borko, H. (2004) Professional development and teacher learning: Mapping the terrain. *Educational Researcher* 33 (8), 3–15.

Cammarata, L. and Haley, C. (2018) Integrated content, language and literacy instruction in a Canadian French immersion context: A professional development journey. *International Journal of Bilingual Education and Bilingualism* 21 (3), 332–348.

Cammarata, L. and Tedick, D. (2012) Balancing content and language in instruction: The experience of immersion teachers. *The Modern Language Review* 96 (2), 251–269.

Dalton-Puffer, C., Nikula, T. and Smit, U. (2010) *Language Use and Language Learning in CLIL Classrooms.* Amsterdam: John Benjamins.

Day, E. and Shapson, S. (1996) A national survey: French immersion teachers' preparation and their professional development needs. *The Canadian Modern Language Review* 52 (1), 248–270.

Dufour, R., Dufour, R. and Eaker, R. (2008) *Revisiting Professional Learning Communities at Work: New Insights for Improving Schools.* Bloomington, IN: Solution Tree.

Echevarría, J., Vogt, M. and Short, D. (2008) *Making Content Comprehensible for English Learners: the SIOP Model.* Boston, MA: Pearson Education.

Fortune, T., Tedick, D. and Walker, C. (2008) Integrated language and content teaching: insights from the immersion classroom. In T. Fortune and D. Tedick (eds) *Pathways to Multilingualism: Evolving Perspectives on Immersion Education.* Clevedon: Multilingual Matters.

Fullan, M. (2015) *The New Meaning of Educational Change* (5th edn). New York, NY: Teachers College Press.

Guskey, T. (2002) Professional development and teacher change. *Teachers and Teaching: Theory and Practice* 8 (3), 381–391.

Harley, B. (1992) Patterns of second language development in French immersion. *Journal of French Language Studies* 2, 159–183.

Kong, S. (2014) Collaboration between content and language specialists in late immersion. *The Canadian Modern Language Review* 70 (1), 103–122.

Kong, S. and Hoare, P. (2012) The development of academic language proficiency: Challenges for middle school immersion in Hong Kong and Xi'an. *International Education* 41 (2), 88–109.

Kong, S., Hoare, P. and Chi, Y. (2011) Immersion education in China: Teachers' perspectives. *Frontiers of Education in China* 6 (1), 68–91.

Lieberman, A. (1986) Collaborative work. *Educational Leadership* 43 (5), 4–8.

Lyster, R. (2007) *Learning and Teaching Languages through Content: A Counterbalanced Approach*. Amsterdam: John Benjamins.

Lyster, R. (2016) *Vers une approche intégrée en immersion [Towards an Integrated Approach in Immersion]*. Montréal: Les Éditions CEC.

Lyster, R. (2019) Making research on instructed SLA relevant for teachers through professional development. *Language Teaching Research* 23 (4), 494–513.

Lyster, R., Collins, L. and Ballinger, S. (2009) Linking languages through a bilingual read-aloud project. *Language Awareness* 18 (3–4), 366–383.

Lyster, R., Quiroga, J. and Ballinger, S. (2013) The effects of biliteracy instruction on morphological awareness. *Journal of Immersion and Content-Based Language Education* 1 (2), 169–197.

Lyster, R., Saito, K. and Sato, M. (2013) Oral corrective feedback in second language classrooms. *Language Teaching* 46 (1), 1–40.

Maeroff, G. (1988) *The Empowerment of Teachers*. New York, NY: Teachers College Press.

Schleppergell, M. and de Oliveira, L. (2006) An integrated language and content approach for history teachers. *Journal of English for Academic Purposes* 5, 254–268.

Serra, C. (2007) Assessing CLIL at primary school: A longitudinal study. *International Journal of Bilingual Education and Bilingualism* 10, 582–602.

Shahsavar-Arshad, V. (2016) Learning to bridge language and content: Teachers' experiences during a professional development initiative on content-based instruction. Unpublished MA thesis, McGill University.

Smith, G. (2015) The impact of a professional development programme on primary teachers' classroom practice and pupils' attitudes to science. *Research in Science Education* 45 (2), 215–239.

Tedick, D. and Lyster, R. (2020) *Scaffolding Language Development in Immersion and Dual Language Classrooms*. New York, NY: Routledge.

Tedick, D. and Zilmer, C. (2018) Teacher perceptions of immersion professional development experiences emphasizing language-focused content instruction. *Journal of Immersion and Content-Based Language Education* 6 (2), 269–294.

Turnbull, M. Lapkin, S., and Hart, D. (2001) Grade 3 immersion students' performance in literacy and mathematics: Province-wide results from Ontario (1998–1999). *The Canadian Modern Language Review* 58, 9–26.

van Manen, M. (1997) *Researching Lived Experience: Human Science for an Action Sensitive Pedagogy*. London, ON: Althouse Press.

Wayne, A., Yoon, K., Zhu, P., Cronen, S. and Garet, M. (2008) Experimenting with teacher professional development: Motives and methods. *Educational Researcher* 37 (8), 469–479.

14 A Longitudinal Study of Japanese Tertiary Students' Motivation, Perceived Competency and Classroom Dynamics in Soft-CLIL

Rieko Nishida

Introduction

This chapter reports on one part of a larger study which aimed to investigate possible changes in tertiary students' motivation, perceived language competency and perceptions of classroom dynamics during a one-semester English language course in Japan. This course integrated content and language by taking a Soft-CLIL approach. In Soft-CLIL courses, content is integrated from the curriculum as part of the language course. To investigate students' motivation, perceived competence and perceptions of their classroom dynamics, a questionnaire was administered to 128 first- and second-year university students in Japan at three intervals during the course of one semester. The results of this study showed increases in intrinsic motivation, as well as listening, speaking and reading perceived competency that were statistically significant. Though this study showed increases in these measurements over the course of one semester, this study design cannot attribute the changes to the Soft-CLIL implementation alone. However, the chapter argues why the Soft-CLIL approach could have contributed to these changes. It is hoped that this study can add to the developing body of knowledge about different forms of integrated content and language programs at the tertiary level and the role of psychological factors in such contexts.

Development of CLIL in Japan

Against the backdrop of globalisation, the Japanese Ministry of Education, Culture, Sports, Science and Technology (MEXT) (2014a) has called for improvements in students' English proficiency levels from elementary school to university level. MEXT (2014a) has announced 'The English Education Reform Plan Responding to Rapid Globalisation' which is due to be implemented in 2020. The new reform plan will be implemented at all educational levels in Japan. According to MEXT (2014a), the aim is for Japanese people to achieve the highest level of English proficiency in Asia. For this reason, many Japanese governmental initiatives and university programmes are promoting English as a means of instruction. Among these is Global 30 (G30), which is a project that aims to establish a university network for internationalisation (MEXT, 2017a). G30 has three primary purposes. The first goal of G30 is to ensure that students from outside of Japan are able to start and complete degree programmes in English in Japan. Second, G30 has a goal of recruiting international faculty for job openings. Last, G30 has the goal of promoting strategic international cooperation. An additional aim is to expand international student programmes that would promote inter-university exchange agreements (MEXT, 2009). However, for this to be implemented, fundamental changes in university systems across Japan are necessary. To address the aims of G30, specifically in terms of increasing English language proficiency in Japan, MEXT (2014b) has encouraged the integration of content and language and, as such, many Japanese institutes have begun to implement CLIL (Sugita McEown *et al.*, 2017). CLIL is often defined as 'a dual-focused educational approach in which an additional language is used for the learning and teaching of both content and language' (Coyle *et al.*, 2010: 1); however, CLIL can take various forms and this study looks specifically at one type of CLIL known as Soft-CLIL (Bentley, 2010).

What is Soft-CLIL and why in Japan?

According to Bentley (2010), CLIL has been variously implemented and may be applied flexibly depending on local needs. Bentley (2010: 6) states that 'CLIL is a term used to cover a range of contexts and models. Some schools teach topics from the curriculum as part of a language course. This is called soft CLIL'. Ball *et al.* (2016: 27) emphasise that 'Soft-CLIL has specific linguistic objectives, whereas "hard" CLIL typically has content objectives only'. Ikeda (2013: 32) explains that 'Soft-CLIL is a type of content and language integrated instruction taught by trained CLIL language teachers to help learners develop their target language competency as a primary aim and their subject/ theme/ topic knowledge as a secondary aim'. According to Ikeda (2013: 41), 'for CLIL to take root solidly in the Japanese educational climate, the "soft" version of CLIL should be recognised as an adapted, contextualised breed while, at the same time, its authentic, universal model (i.e. European CLIL) is pursued as the norm'. In other words, while Ikeda (2013) recommends European-style CLIL as a means for CLIL to 'take root' in the Japanese contexts, he notes that a soft form of CLIL, or Soft-CLIL, can be implemented in specific contexts when appropriate.

In the present study, Soft-CLIL was implemented in students' English classes. These classes fulfilled students' undergraduate requirements in English. These courses were distinct from other EFL courses on offer as their syllabi were specifically designed to be relevant for students' university specialisations or degree programmes. In each of these Soft-CLIL courses, all the students were from the same discipline e.g. engineering. Therefore, in the context of this study, Soft-CLIL for the students from the School of Engineering meant these students had syllabi designed around engineering themes in English (see the nature of Soft-CLIL for undergraduate courses for details).

Motivation

CLIL has drawn interest in many parts of Japan and has been adopted by several institutes at the tertiary level (e.g. Irie, 2018; Kashiwagi, 2015; Nishida, 2019; Sasajima, 2011; Sugita McEown & McEown, 2019; Watanabe *et al.*, 2011). However, few studies have investigated how CLIL programmes in Japan affect students' motivation. A previous study by the first author, Nishida (2019), explored how the integration of content and language impacted students' motivation in the tertiary context. The findings provided initial evidence of the connection between motivation and language learning in the CLIL context. Other research has also suggested that CLIL is linked to learner motivation (Coyle *et al.*, 2010; Lasagabaster, 2011; Thompson & Sylvéin, 2019; see also Chapters 4, 10, 11 & 15). For example, Lasagabaster (2011) investigated that students' interest and instrumental orientation, attitude towards learning situation and effort were higher in CLIL than EFL.

This study also aims at understanding learner motivation in the Soft-CLIL context. To operationalise motivation, the study drew on Deci and Ryan's self-determination theory (SDT) (1985, 2002). According to SDT, motivation is conceptualised as stretching along a continuum between intrinsic and extrinsic motivation, which are, respectively, more or less self-determined. When learners exhibit intrinsic motivation, they find activities more interesting and enjoyable, which can lead to growth in learning (Deci & Ryan, 1985). To measure motivation, this study employed the Language Learning Orientations Scale (LLOS) (Noels *et al.*,

1999, 2000). Specifically, this study used the Japanese version of the LLOS used in Yashima *et al.* (2009).

The LLOS is based on a conceptualisation of motivation along three subscales: (1) intrinsic motivation – knowledge (IMK), (2) intrinsic motivation – accomplishment (IMA) and (3) intrinsic motivation – stimulation (IMS). Using this measure of intrinsic motivation (IMK, IMA, IMS), Noels *et al.* (1999, 2000) conducted a study exploring the relationships between teachers' communication styles and students' intrinsic and extrinsic motivation. In their study, a correlation analysis showed that intrinsic motivation was related to positive language learning outcomes with greater motivational intensity and also the self-assessment of perceived competence. In the Japanese context, Yashima *et al.* (2009) conducted a study using the same intrinsic motivation measurement with Japanese tertiary students. In their study, intrinsic motivation was correlated with anxiety about not understanding everything taught in class ($r = 0.48$, $p = 0.01$). In this study, the scales are used to investigate the motivation of students attending the Soft-CLIL course.

Perceived Competence

Similar to motivation, perceived communication competence has been suggested to affect language learning positively (Nishida, 2019). Indeed, according to Yashima (2002), perceived competency is argued to be the single most vital factor fostering positive attitude toward communication (willingness to communicate). It is clear that feeling competent is a critical component of motivation in SDT theory and is central to successful language learning. Therefore, this study also sought to understand how learners perceived their competence in diverse skill areas in the Soft-CLIL classes. According to MacIntyre *et al.* (1998: 551), perceived communicative competence refers to 'the overall belief in being able to communicate in the L2 in an adaptive and efficient manner'. Cognitive and affective components are indicated in his definition of perceived communicative competence. The cognitive component is 'the self-evaluation of L2 skills, a judgement made by the speaker about the degree of mastery achieved in the L2', while the affective corresponds to 'language anxiety; specifically, the discomfort experience when using a L2' (MacIntyre *et al.*, 1998: 551). To measure perceived communication competency, the study used questionnaire items from Eiken Foundation of Japan (EIKEN). EIKEN produces and administers English-proficiency tests with the backing of the Japanese Ministry (MEXT). EIKEN also produces the items for self-assessment of perceived communication competence based upon the English-proficiency test (EIKEN, 2006). In this study, the items from EIKEN were asked to measure students' perceived communication competency.

Group Dynamics

In the Soft-CLIL courses which are the focus on this study, a key component of the teaching design is working on collaborative projects with peers. As collaborative work is encouraged by MEXT (2017b), students' experience in the classroom and positive forms of group dynamics are encouraged and necessary. In language teaching specifically, group dynamics may play an especially important role given the need for learners to engage in pair or group work which lie at the heart of many communicative language teaching approaches and be willing to speak up in the foreign language in front of the group (Dörnyei, 2001; Dörnyei & Murphey, 2003; see also Chapter 15). Additionally, group dynamics within the social unit of the classroom can be a key contributory factor in motivating students in the language classroom (Tanaka, 2018, 2019). In the Japanese context, Imai (2017) also showed that group work has a positive influence on students' learning in the classroom situation in CLIL. Therefore, in order to measure group dynamics, a tool was used in this study which uses items from Nishida and Ikemoto (2019), which has already been employed in a comparable context. Their study found that group dynamics was high throughout the semester.

Research Question

The present study was conducted to see how Japanese tertiary-level students' motivation, perceived competency and group dynamics would change, if at all, through exposure to a semester of a Soft-CLIL class at university. This study addresses the following research questions:

(1) In what ways do students' motivation and perceived competence in speaking, listening, reading and writing change during one semester of a Soft-CLIL approach, if all?
(2) In what ways do group dynamics develop during one semester of a Soft-CLIL approach, if at all?
(3) How do students experience a Soft-CLIL class in general?

The Empirical Study

Procedure

This chapter reports on one part of a larger study which took place during the fall semester of 2016–2017. This phase involved administering the Japanese version of the LLOS (Noels *et al.*, 1999, 2000; Yashima *et al.*, 2009), the EIKEN and select items from a group dynamics survey by Nishida and Ikemoto (2019) to students in four different classes.

The questionnaires were given to students at three intervals every seven weeks throughout the semester. This questionnaire was designed to elicit information about intrinsic motivation based upon the SDT framework (Noels *et al.*, 1999, 2000; Yashima *et al.*, 2009). Additionally, the survey aimed to assess perceived competence in listening, speaking, reading and writing (EIKEN STEP 2 modified by the author) and group dynamics (Nishida & Ikemoto, 2019). The present study focuses on data collected in the fall semester of 2016–2017.

Participants

A total of 128 students participated in this study. The students were between 19 and 21 years old. Four classes were chosen to participate; the author was the teacher in each of these four classes. One class was from the School of Engineering, two classes were from the School of Engineering Science, and one class was a combined group made up of students from the School of Law and the School of Economics. In each class, the syllabi were similar in design with the exception of the content objectives, which were distinct and represented the subject-specific character of each course.

The nature of Soft-CLIL for undergraduate courses

In practice, a variety of courses are taught in English at Osaka University and the university offers various credit courses in English in both undergraduate programs and graduate courses. To fulfil undergraduate requirements for English courses, Soft-CLIL classes called Content Class are one type of course offered. These courses are offered to the first- and second-year undergraduate students. At this university, students are expected to take 6 to 8 credits of English courses in total, depending on their department.

In these students' Soft-CLIL classes, there were three educational aims. Firstly, in terms of content, for the School of Engineering students, the syllabus included the ethics of Artificial Intelligence (AI), issues on singularity, deep learning technology, smart phones and robots in engineering. Secondly, all the lessons also aimed to enhance students' critical perspectives and global perspectives as global citizens. Finally, the students also focused on language objectives in a similar manner to a traditional EFL course.

The Soft-CLIL course in the present study was designed around two content-based research projects during the semester. These research projects were based on students' degree programmes. These research projects were collaborative, and, after completion, the students presented their research projects in groups. A reward of extra points was given for the best group performance which was decided by the students.

Ethical considerations

In terms of ethics, the students were told that the questionnaires were not part of their exam or assessment for the course. The students were assured that their participation would not affect their grades for the course in any way. Students were asked to participate voluntarily. The data were treated confidentially.

Materials

In the motivation questionnaire, the Japanese version (Yashima *et al.*, 2009) of the LLOS was employed (Noels *et al.*, 1999, 2000); items were related to intrinsic motivation-knowledge, intrinsic-accomplishment and intrinsic-stimulation (Noels *et al.*, 1999, 2000; Yashima *et al.*, 2009). In terms of perceived communication competence, I adopted the items from EIKEN STEP 2 Cando List, including perceived competence in speaking, listening, reading and writing (EIKEN, 2006). In addition, items related to group dynamics were also included (Nishida & Ikemoto, 2019). The questionnaires were not adapted in any specific ways for the Soft-CLIL context.

The questionnaires were written in Japanese and distributed to students in the class at evenly spaced intervals throughout the semester (i.e. Time 1: Week 1; Time 2: Week 8; Time 3: Week 15). There were 15 lessons total during the semester. Right before Time 2 (week 8) and Time 3 (week 15), the midterm research project and the final research project were conducted, respectively (Table 14.1).

Table 14.1 Timeline for questionnaire

	Syllabus	Timeline for Research	
Week 1	Orientation	Time 1	Questionnaire 1
Week 2	Standard class – content-related		
Week 3	Standard class – content-related		
Week 4	Standard class – content-related		
Week 5	Standard class – content-related		
Week 6	Standard class – content-related		
Week 7	Presentation		
Week 8	Presentation	Time 2	Questionnaire 2
Week 9	Standard class – content-related		
Week 10	Standard class – content-related		
Week 11	Standard class – content-related		
Week 12	Standard class – content-related		
Week 13	Standard class – content-related		
Week 14	Presentation		
Week 15	Presentation	Time 3	Questionnaire 3, Open-ended comment

Table 14.2 Cronbach's' Alphas for questionnaire items

	Time 1	Time 2	Time 3
Group Dynamics	α. 921	α. 924	α. 921
IM-Knowledge	α. 836	α. 899	α. 858
IM-Accomplishment	α. 788	α. 868	α. 931
IM-Stimulation	α. 896	α. 903	α. 924
Perceived Competency (Listening)	α. 855	α. 862	α. 879
Perceived Competency (Speaking)	α. 876	α. 893	α. 920
Perceived Competency (Reading)	α. 937	α. 926	α. 940
Perceived Competency (Writing)	α. 940	α. 946	α. 941

Questions were answered on a five-point Likert scale and ranged from 1 (strong disagreement) to 5 (strong agreement). SPSS ver.24 was used for multivariate statistical analysis. For further analysis, Cronbach's Alphas were calculated, and all items maintained high Alphas (Table 14.2). Intrinsic motivation (knowledge) (from Noels *et al.*, 1999, 2000; Yashima *et al.*, 2009; 3 items, $\alpha = -.84–.90$), intrinsic motivation (accomplishment) (from Noels *et al.*, 1999, 2000; Yashima *et al.*, 2009; 3 items, $\alpha = 0.79–0.93$), intrinsic motivation (stimulation) (from Noels *et al.*, 1999, 2000; Yashima *et al.*, 2009; 3 items, $\alpha = 0.90–0.92$), perceived competence in reading (from EIKEN, 2006; 3 items, $\alpha = 0.93–0.94$), perceived competency in listening (from EIKEN, 2006; 3 items, $\alpha = 0.86–0.88$), perceived competency in speaking (from EIKEN, 2006; 3 items, $\alpha = 0.88–0.92$), perceived competence in writing (from EIKEN, 2006; 3 items, $\alpha = 0.94–0.95$) and group dynamics (from Nishida & Ikemoto, 2019; 4 items, $\alpha = 0.92$). Additionally, descriptive statistics were carried out including mean and standard deviation and repeated measurement of analysis of variances (ANOVA) were conducted. Then, descriptive statistics and repeated measurement of analysis of variance were used to show changes through the course (Figures 14.1 & 14.2, Tables 14.3 & 14.4).

In order to support the quantitative data, students also had an opportunity to answer an open-ended question at the end of the semester during the third questionnaire ('Please indicate what you thought about this English class this semester'). A total of 121 students responded to the open-ended questions in Japanese and 183 total descriptions in Japanese were obtained. Qualitative data were transcribed for analysis. Grounded theory approach guided the analysis (Strauss & Corbin, 1990) and the qualitative data were open-coded. Then the descriptions identified from open-coding were categorised and grouped into higher-order categories that represented six different categories. In the coding process, the descriptions were coded in Japanese, then after coding, were translated into English.

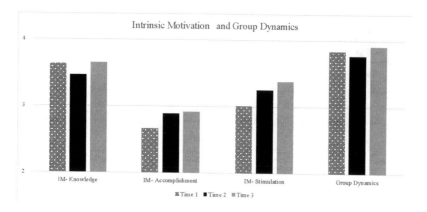

Figure 14.1 Students' changes in motivation and classroom dynamics in Soft-CLIL

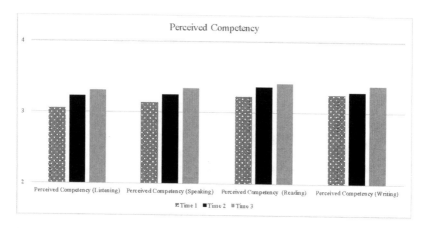

Figure 14.2 Students' changes in perceived communication competency in Soft-CLIL

Table 14.3 Descriptive statistics

	Time 1		Time 2		Time 3	
	M	**sd**	**M**	**sd**	**M**	**sd**
Group Dynamics	3.84	0.80	3.77	0.78	3.91	0.79
IM-Knowledge	3.63	0.86	3.47	0.95	3.65	0.86
IM-Accomplishment	2.66	0.87	2.89	0.95	2.92	1.02
IM-Stimulation	3.01	1.05	3.25	1.03	3.38	1.03
Perceived Competency (Listening)	3.06	0.77	3.23	0.76	3.31	0.74
Perceived Competency (Speaking)	3.14	0.89	3.25	0.80	3.34	0.80
Perceived Competency (Reading)	3.23	0.77	3.37	0.71	3.41	0.71
Perceived Competency (Writing)	3.26	0.84	3.29	0.83	3.38	0.77

Table 14.4 Students' changes in motivation, perceived competency and group dynamics

	Type III Sum of Square	df	Mean Square	F	p	η^2	Post-hoc
Group Dynamics	1.271	2, 254	0.635	2.150	0.119	0.017	N/A
IM-Knowledge	2.429	2, 254	1.214	3.726	0.025	0.028	2–3
IM-Accomplishment	5.112	1.878, 238.56	2.721	5.063	0.008	0.038	1–2, 1–3
IM-Stimulation	8.909	2, 254	4.454	15.049	0.000	0.106	1–2, 1–3
Perceived Competency (Listening)	4.324	2, 254	2.162	12.536	0.000	0.090	1–2, 1–3
Perceived Competency (Speaking)	2.574	1.876, 238.30	1.287	5.325	0.005	0.040	1–3
Perceived Competency (Reading)	2.215	1.854, 235.40	1.108	6.348	0.002	0.048	1–2, 1–3
Perceived Competency (Writing)	1.047	2, 254	0.523	2.144	0.119	0.017	N/A

Results

First, Cronbach's alphas for questionnaire items were calculated (Table 14.2) and then descriptive statistics were carried out including average and standard deviation for Time 1 (Week 1), Time 2 (Week 8) and Time 3 (Week 15) (see Figure 14.1, Figure 14.2 & Table 14.3). Then, repeated measurement of analysis of variance was conducted (Table 14.4). For repeated measurement of analysis, sphericity was checked by Mauchly's test; sphericity was assumed to have significance if $p > 0.05$ (Oshio, 2004). Sphericity was not an issue for group dynamics, IM-knowledge, IM-stimulation or perceived competency in listening and writing. The Greenhouse-Geisser was used for IM-accomplishment, perceived competency in reading and speaking (see Table 14.4). Results showed statistical significance and increases in intrinsic motivation-stimulation: $F(2,254) = 15.049$, $p < 0.01$, $\eta^2 = 0.106$ and intrinsic motivation-accomplishment: $F(1.878, 238.56) = 5.063$, $p < 0.01$, $\eta^2 = 0.038$, perceived competency in reading: $F(1.854, 235.40) = 6.348$, $p < 0.01$, $\eta^2 = 0.048$, perceived competency in listening: $F(2,254) = 12.536$, $p < 0.01$, $\eta^2 = 0.090$ and perceived competency in speaking: $F(1.876, 238.30) = 5.325$, $p < 0.01$, $\eta^2 = 0.040$ that were statistically significant. One subcomponent of the intrinsic motivation scale, also knowledge, showed a tendency to increase, although it did not reach a significant level after Bonferroni's adjustment. In particular, intrinsic motivation (stimulation) and perceived competency in listening showed increasing tendencies toward the end of the semester. Group dynamics did not increase but remained stable throughout the course.

Result of the Open-ended Question

Students' comments were analysed and six different categories were identified including group research project (positive), improvement of English, relationships with other students, positive impact on content learning, increase in perceived competency and autonomous participation in the class. In their responses they responded as 'group research presentation (positive)' (49% of the responses), 'having a good relationship with other students' (20% of the responses), 'improvement of English' (18% of the responses), 'positive impact on content learning' (10% of the responses), 'increase in perceived competency' (2% of the responses) and 'autonomous participation in the class' (1% of the responses) (see Table 14.5). All comments were nearly able to fit into these 6 categories, except for one. One of the students showed a negative comment about English in general. They wrote positive comments such as: 'I enjoyed working with other students', 'I had to work with other students in the class, and it was fun!' and 'Group presentation made me nervous but it was really a good experience for me'. In addition to these comments, one of the students included comments such as 'I was pleased I enrolled on this course, because the content was related to my subject study!'. Others wrote comments such as 'The research project was certainly stimulating, as it induced my curiosity in the field of my expertise', 'I thought of my future at an academic conference. In the future, I will have to do a presentation in English at academic conferences, so this course made me think of my future

Table 14.5 Students' general comments about CLIL class responses

Category	Students' descriptions	Responses	Percentage
Group research presentation (positive)	'Research project and group presentation were fun as I had to think about a research topic'. 'Group presentation made me nervous but it was really a good experience for me'.	89	49%
Having a good relationship with other students	'I had to work with other students in the class, and it was fun'. 'Group research project was good for me to work with other students in the class.'	36	20%
Improvement of English	'I think my Engish has been impoved. I've got a good score on the quiz'. 'My English pronounciation is better than before.'	33	18%
Positive impact on content learning	'Content was stimulating in the class, so I enjoyed it'. 'I am glad that content was very close to my major'.	18	10%
Increase in perceived competency	'I feel I accomplished a lot in this class.' 'After I did a research presentation, I felt I accomplished a lot'.	5	2%
Autonomous participation in the class	'I actively participated in this class.' 'I participated autonomously in this class'.	2	1%
	Total of Responses	**183**	**100%**

self'. Students seemed to appreciate and be stimulated by the integration of content and language, suggesting CLIL can be effective for tertiary students in this context.

Discussion

The current study has yielded a number of findings concerning motivation, perceived competency and classroom dynamics in the four classes throughout a semester-long English language course with a Soft-CLIL implementation.

First, CLIL has drawn considerable interest in many parts of the world and in Japan, but the empirical research concerning CLIL in respect to motivation is still very limited in number (for exceptions, see Lasagabaster, 2011; Thompson & Sylvén, 2019). In the current study, the intrinsic motivation of the learners seemed to increase during the course. In this study, there was no control group so it is difficult to assign the reasons for this to the Soft-CLIL approach; however, some comments from the qualitative data suggest that the approach may be part of the reason for this finding.

The second finding in this study was that perceived competency in speaking and listening, showed a significant increase toward the end of the semester. Although perceived competency was not too high at the beginning of the term, toward the end of the semester, their perceived competency in speaking, listening and reading seemed to have increased. One possible reason for this improvement could be the numerous opportunities to use the language, as the qualitative data showed that improvement of English. One student indicated that his English is better than before and similar comments were obtained from the other students, too.

The third finding in this study concerned the group dynamics. The group dynamics remained stable throughout the semester according to the quantitative data. And the qualitative data showed that students seemed to enjoy group research presentation, and nearly a half the responses showed positive responses on a group research presentation. Also, many students stated that they had a good relationship with others in the class, and they enjoyed working with their classmates. Working in a group or in a pair, and to form group dynamics therefore seemed to have a positive impact upon the Soft-CLIL class.

A limitation of this paper is that the measurements were not adapted to ask students specifically about the Soft-CLIL approach. In reality, a multitude of situated and contextually relevant factors could affect change such as relationship to peers, the teacher, the classroom design and with Soft-CLIL being only one of the variables. Future research could attempt to isolate these variables and adapt measurements to foreground the Soft-CLIL setting in order to learn more about the specific impact of taking such an approach in this context at university. However, the qualitative data offers some valuable insights which suggest the merits for teaching in this way. For example, students seemed to enjoy group research presentation, have a good relationship with other students, improvement of English, having a positive impact on content learning, increase in perceived competency and autonomous participation in the class, as shown in the qualitative data.

Finally, according to Ikeda (2013), in order take root in the Japanese educational system, a Soft-CLIL approach should be recognised as an adapted form of European style CLIL that can be suited to the Japanese EFL context. As the Japanese educational policy and system is different from the European context, CLIL needs to fit into the Japanese context and educational expectations and needs. In this current study, the Soft-CLIL approach seemed to be well adopted by learners and the data shows that in this setting, the learners appeared at least to improve in terms of motivation and their sense of competence. Although this cannot be directly attributed to the Soft-CLIL approach, it at least implies that in this particular course, the learners did not suffer any negative effects of the approach in regard to these psychological variables. Given the insights from the qualitative data, there is reason to be optimistic that this approach may suit learners at the tertiary level in Japan and further research needs to examine what about this approach is valuable for the learners.

Empirical studies of motivation and other psychological factors in CLIL remain very limited globally and also in Japan specifically (Irie, 2019; Nishida, 2019; Sugita McEown & McEown, 2019). The present study therefore is an initial empirical contribution to understanding the nature of a Soft-CLIL context in Japan from the learner perspective. Further research, however, is still needed to compare CLIL and non-CLIL environments combined with control group and experimental designs incorporating baseline measures in order to capture a more complete picture of CLIL in the Japanese tertiary context.

Implications for Policy and Practice

The approach taken in this course was generally appreciated by the students as illustrated by their open-ended comments. In particular, students highlighted the importance of having content related to their respective programmes of study. For instance, one student commented, 'I was pleased I enrolled on this course, because the content was related to my subject study!'. For the students in this study, being able to conduct a project with an explicit focus on content from their field of expertise was a reported source of motivation for many students. One student explained 'The research project was certainly stimulating, as it induced my curiosity in the field of my expertise'. Comments like these suggest the value of bringing in content which is relevant for their studies and future careers.

In these Soft-CLIL courses, the use of content materials was carefully chosen, a syllabus and lesson plans were well organised. In order to adopt CLIL in the Japanese tertiary setting, it is vital for teachers to find appropriate teaching materials for students in relation to their course of studies. Naturally, sourcing materials that are specific to particular educational designs, such as the course design in this study, is often not easier said than done. Such material may not be readily available and may need to be adapted, translated or scaffolded in order to fit local needs. In some cases, this may imply extra work for teachers to prepare suitable materials and feel comfortable with the content of the students' course of studies. To successfully implement CLIL in Japan, the workloads of teachers who are responsible for its implementation need to be recognised. Therefore, a possible concern in this context might be the impact of a potentially heavier workload on teachers' well-being due to the extra materials generation and preparation time that may be necessary. That said, many teachers often enjoy the creative elements of materials generation and are likely to enjoy learning more and interacting about students' interests. One possible way that teachers could be supported is through supportive teacher networks. These networks could facilitate the sharing of materials, teaching methods and could also help support each other's well-being as they adjust to teaching in new contexts.

In addition, in this Soft-CLIL course, the participating students were encouraged to participate in collaborative learning. This is not a feature unique to CLIL teaching; however, the focus on shared content interests facilitated a fruitful climate of collaboration among the students. This occurred naturally as the students became the content experts as they were often the ones most familiar with the topic at hand. In such settings which are student centred, group dynamics are extremely important and teachers and students need to work together to create a comfortable and supportive classroom environment, so that students feel comfortable and secure in using the language with and among their peers.

Conclusion

Due to higher levels of connectivity and globalisation, an increasing number of educational settings are adopting CLIL; Japan is no exception to this trend. This is occurring at multiple levels, from the primary to the tertiary level. The goal in implementing these programmes is to enhance the English language skills of Japanese citizens as English is an official requirement from MEXT. Given the saliency of this approach throughout Japan, we need a systematic programme of research to understand the effects such teaching designs have on learners' motivation, perceived competence and actual levels of proficiency across skill areas. We also need to understand the effects on language teachers, who are sometimes being expected to teach content from areas beyond their own personal fields of expertise. My own experiences in this particular course were positive. Furthermore, the learners in this study also reported to have positive experiences in this course. This has led me to believe that Soft-CLIL is one possible way to motivate learners and empower them to open up their minds for a more globalised future while simultaneously equipping them with language skills and relevant content knowledge that they will need for their future careers.

Acknowledgements

This work was supported by JSPS Grant-in-Aid for Scientific Research (B), KAKENHI Grant Number 17H02359. We all appreciated the support given by the JSPS grant. I would like to show my appreciation to Dr Imao Yasuhiro at Osaka University for his statistical advice.

References

Ball, P., Kelly, K. and Clegg, J. (2016) *Putting CLIL into Practice.* Oxford: Oxford University Press.
Bentley, K. (2010) *The TKT Course CLIL Module.* Cambridge: Cambridge University Press.
Coyle, D., Hood, P. and Marsh, D. (2010) *C.L.I.L. Content and Language Integrated Learning.* Cambridge: Cambridge University Press.
Deci, E.L. and Ryan, R.M. (1985) *Intrinsic Motivation and Self-determination in Human Behavior.* New York: Plenum.
Deci, E.L. and Ryan, R.M. (2002) *Handbook of Self-determination.* Rochester, MN: University of Rochester Press.
Dörnyei, Z. (2001) *Motivation Strategies in the Language Classroom.* Cambridge: Cambridge University Press.
Dörnyei, Z and Murphey, T. (2003) *Group Dynamics in the Language Classroom.* Cambridge: Cambridge University Press.
EIKEN (2006) Self-perceptions list. See https://www.eiken.or.jp/eiken/exam/cando/pdf/Eiken_CandoList_translation.pdf (accessed February 2019).
Ikeda, M. (2013) Does CLIL work for Japanese secondary school students? Potential for the 'weak' version of CLIL. *International CLIL Research Journal* 2, 30–34.
Imai, J. (2017) Teaching writing through content language integrated learning: Content analysis of student essays and group discussions. *Junendo Global Kyoikuronshu* 2, 80–86.
Irie, K. (2018) CLIL as a bridge to EMI: Autonomy-fostering curriculum. *KAKENHI symposium*, Osaka, Japan.
Irie, K. (2019) Transition or integration? EAP, CLIL, and EMI. *KAKENHI symposium*, Osaka, Japan.
Kashiwagi, K. (2015) How CLIL classes exert a positive influence on teaching style in student centered language learning through overseas teacher training in Sweden and Finland. *Procedia- Social and Behavioral Science* 173, 79–84.
Lasagabaster, D. (2011) English achievement and student motivation in CLIL and EFL settings. *Innovation in Language Learning and Teaching* 5, 3–18.
MacIntyre, P.D., Clément, R., Dörneyi, Z. and Noels, K. (1998) Conceptualizing willingness to communicate in a L2: A situated model of confidence and affiliation. *The Modern Language Journal* 82, 545–562.

MEXT (2009) Higher education in Japan. See http://www.mext.go.jp/en/policy/education/highered/title03/detail03/__icsFiles/afieldfile/2012/06/19/1302653_1.pdf (accessed October 2019).

MEXT (2014a) English education reform plan corresponding to globalization. See http://www.mext.go.jp/en/news/topics/detail/__icsFiles/afieldfile/2014/01/23/1343591_1.pdf (accessed February 2019).

MEXT (2014b) *Eigo Kyouiku no arikata ni kansuru yuusikisya kaigi (no.6).* [Experts' meeting for English education in Japan]. See http://www.mext.go.jp/b_menu/shingi/chousa/shotou/102/shiryo/attach/1350327.htm (acessed October 2019).

MEXT (2017a) G30 project toha? [What is G30 project?]. See http://www.mext.go.jp/a_menu/koutou/kaikaku/1383342.htm (accessed October 2019).

MEXT (2017b) *Atarashii Gakushuusidouyouryou ga mezasu sugata.* [New educational guideline]. See http://www.mext.go.jp/b_menu/shingi/chukyo/chukyo3/siryo/attach/1364316.htm (accessed October 2019).

Nishida, R. (2019) The integration of content in the language classroom to enhance students' motivation in language learning. *Gengobunka Kenkyu Project* 12–22.

Nishida, R. and Ikemoto, M. (2019) *Nihonjin Eigo gakushusya niokeru CLIL to doukizuke [Integration of content and language to motive students in language learning in the Japanese EFL context]* (mimeo) *and Technology* 46, 151–170.

Noels, K.A., Clément, R. and Pelletier, L.G. (1999) Perceptions of teachers' communicative style and students' intrinsic and extrinsic motivation. *The Modern Language Journal* 83, 23–34.

Noels, K.A., Pelletier, L.G. and Vallerand, R.J. (2000) Why are you learning a second language? Motivational orientations and self-determination theory. *Language Learning* 50, 57–85.

Oshio, S. (2004) *Kenkyujireidemanabu SPSS to AMOS niyoru shinricyousa datakaiseki [SPSS and AMOS for the data analysis]* Tokyo Shoseki: Tokyo.

Sasajima, S. (2011) *CLIL: Content and Language Integrated Learning.* Tokyo: Sanshusa.

Strauss, A.L. and Cobin, J. (1990) *Basics of Qualitative Research: Grounded Theory Procedures and Techniques.* Newbury Park: Sage.

Sugita McEown, M. and McEown, K. (2019) Self-regulatory processes among Japanese EFL learners in CLIL course contexts. *3rd International Conference on Situating Strategy Use*, Osaka, Japan.

Sugita McEown, M., Sawaki, Y. and Harada, T. (2017) Foreign language learning motivation in the Japanese context: Social and political influences on self. *Modern Language Journal* 101, 533–547.

Tanaka, M. (2018) Individual perceptions of group work environment and L2 learning Motivation. *3rd international Psychology of Language Learning conference*, Tokyo, Japan.

Tanaka, M. (2019) Effects of group work environment on motivation and learning outcomes. *TESOL 2019 International Convention & English Language Expo*, Atlanta, GA, USA.

Thompson, S.A. and Sylvén, L.K. (2019) CLIL and motivation revisited: A longitudinal perspective. In L.K. Sylvén (ed.) *Investigating Content and Language Integrated Learning: Insights from Swedish High Schools* (pp. 76–97). Bristol: Multilingual Matters.

Watanabe, Y., Ikeda, M. and Izumi, S. (2011) *CLIL (Content and Language Integrated Learning). Volume 1. Principles and Methodologies.* Tokyo: Sophia University Press.

Yashima, T. (2002) Willingness to communicate in a second language: The Japanese EFL context. *Modern Language Journal* 86, 55–66.

Yashima, T., Noels, K., Shizuka, T., Takuchi O., Yamane, S. and Yoshizawa, K. (2009) The interplay of classroom anxiety, intrinsic motivation and gender in the Japanese EFL context. *Journal of Foreign Language Education and Research* 17, 41–64.

15 Motivations and Synergy on a Sociolinguistics Module in Language Teacher Education in Argentina

Darío Luis Banegas and Richard S. Pinner

Introduction

This chapter discusses the impact of a Sociolinguistics module on motivation at a four-year initial English language teacher education (IELTE) programme in Esquel, a city in southern Argentina. In analysing the module, we concentrated on the interplay between two psychological constructs, motivation and self-confidence and content and language integrated learning (CLIL) as a teaching approach.

Within a sociocultural and critical framework for language teacher education (Banegas, 2017a; Golombek & Johnson, 2019), CLIL informs the sociolinguistics module under investigation. CLIL can be defined as an educational approach or pedagogical model (Morton & Llinares, 2017) with the dual purpose of teaching academic content and an additional language holistically. In CLIL, discrete language skills such as speaking, listening, reading and writing are developed together with cognitive skills, grammar and vocabulary through input and activities that are based on communication (Genesee & Hamayan, 2016). CLIL gives attention to meaning and form from a systemic functional grammar perspective (McCabe, 2017) and authenticity of materials, tasks, purposes and audience (Pinner, 2013).

In the context of this study we asked ourselves: how does a CLIL-driven sociolinguistics module impact on student-teachers' and tutor's motivation and sense of self-confidence?

266

Motivational Synergy

Motivation, as a fluctuating and complex construct, is arguably one of the most active areas of psychological research in language acquisition (Boo *et al.*, 2015; Dörnyei & Ryan, 2015; Ushioda & Dörnyei, 2017; see also Chapter 14). Framed in relational views of motivation which examine language learners' possible selves, recent work on motivation in language education has shed light on the importance of the relationship between learners and teachers. For example, Henry and Thorsten (2018) highlight that positive relationships and fruitful contact moments between teachers and learners exert positive effects on learner motivation and learning. In reviewing the literature, the authors argue that when teachers provide emotional and academic support to students through balanced feedback, encouragement, promotion of learners' self-confidence and a positive attitude towards their own professional role, learners experience a motivational boost. These teachers' attitudes help construct positive relationships with their students at both individual and group levels. Such relations foreground the importance of group dynamics and ecological flows in the motivational context of teaching and learning.

Building on Ushioda's person-in-context relational view of motivation (2009), Pinner (2019) approaches relational motivation as an exchange in energy, which must be mutually enriching for both students and teachers in order to be truly effective. Pinner suggests that both teachers and students can naturally become (and often are already) aware of how people in a group feel. Due to humans' hardwired capacity for empathy, social groups, in this case a teacher and learners, generally are able to perceive what other individuals are feeling and will pick up on even very subtly occurring cues (Iacoboni, 2009). This capacity for empathy is linked with social and emotional intelligence. As Gkonou and Mercer (2017) have shown, social and emotional intelligence is not only vital for language teaching, but it is also something that improves with a teacher's experience. This is important, as in-service teachers generally have only a small bank of professional experience to draw on. Furthermore, due to emotional contagion (Hatfield *et al.*, 1993), the predominant feelings or emotions in a group can spread to other individuals, making group dynamics vitally important for understanding the motivation of a class of learners (Dörnyei & Murphey, 2003; Murphey *et al.*, 2012). These dynamics naturally involve the teacher and as the teacher plays a central role in classroom motivation and generally has the most power and authority in a classroom setting, the overall reactions between a group of learners and the teacher are of vital importance when looking at classroom motivation.

When a class works together as a group, and both the students' and the teacher's aims for the class are aligned, then this can be seen as motivational synergy. Such synergy arises only when there is a shared sense of congruence in the learning aims of members of the class, which

Pinner (following van Lier, 1996) labels as social authentication. Put simply, when students and teachers are working together towards shared aims and their *actions* in the class match their *beliefs* about what they should be doing in the class, this creates a shared sense of motivational synergy – a feedback loop of reciprocal energy that helps keep the students motivated while simultaneously validating the teachers' efforts. This is a class-wide motivational phenomenon, formed at the link between student and teacher. However, this link can be 'either positively or negatively synergistic', as Deci *et al.* (1997: 68) first observed.

CLIL is appraised as being an inherently authentic and motivating model for language instruction, due to what Coyle *et al.* (2010) label as authenticity of purpose. In other words, CLIL classes achieve authenticity through the relevance of the content to the students' lives and such a feature leads to a positive impact on motivation (e.g. Lasagabaster & Doiz, 2017). In the case of IELTE, a CLIL approach has been found to raise student-teachers' motivation, English language proficiency and sense of self-confidence as future teachers (Banegas, 2020).

The motivational synergy arising from learner-teacher interactions in an educational environment may lead to stronger levels of self-confidence in both learners and teachers. In this chapter we conceptualise self-confidence as the belief in one's ability to complete a task effectively and take on challenges (see also Chapters 11). This is akin to discussions of self-efficacy (Wyatt, 2018) and self-concept (Lohbeck *et al.*, 2018; see also Chapter 4). Applied to (future) teachers, self-confidence refers to their trust in their own professional and personal abilities, which entail the ability to promote and develop knowledge engagement through content mastery and teaching skills (Maclellan, 2014; Nolan & Molla, 2017). In IELTE, both student teachers and tutors are reflected in this definition, but we should add that both developing and helping develop content mastery and English language proficiency are mutually dependent and central in building the confidence of future teachers of English and their tutors respectively. In the teaching domain, self-confidence is concomitant with notions of teacher effectiveness and self-efficacy; while we acknowledge their centrality, these two constructs exceed the scope of the present chapter.

Context

In Argentina, teachers are typically trained through a combination of an applied-science model with reflection. Modules delivered in English do not usually provide language support, and therefore, the focus is entirely on content with the expectation that the student teachers operate at high proficiency levels (Banegas, 2020). This is the reason why our experience stands out as it includes support in terms of both content and language.

The IELTE programme in which this chapter is set is organised around three broad areas: (1) general education (delivered in Spanish), (2) subject-matter education (delivered in English) and (3) professional practice (delivered in Spanish and English). Upon completion, teachers are qualified to teach English as a foreign language in kindergarten, primary and secondary education.

The Sociolinguistics module is mandatory and located in the second semester of Year 3, with three hours of instruction each week for sixteen weeks. By the time the student teachers enrol in the module they have already taken other related modules such as Introduction to Linguistics, Descriptive Grammar, Phonetics and Phonology, English Language Improvement and Psycholinguistics. The aims of the Sociolinguistics module are to: (1) reflect on linguistic diversity and strategies for effective communication in teaching and learning, (2) improve English language proficiency at the academic level, (3) foster metalinguistic and intercultural reflection and (4) establish links with topics from other modules in the programme.

The module has the following content organised in three units:

- Unit 1: Diachronic and synchronic linguistics. Key concepts: accent, dialect, register, style, gender, age, conversational analysis, politeness, multilingualism and plurilingualism. How varieties are represented in Argentinian curricular guidelines, and language teaching materials.
- Unit 2: Language and culture. English-speaking communities and variations: linguistic diversity and Standard English. Idiolects, sociolects and chronolects. Lavender linguistics. Inclusive language. Contact languages and linguistic issues: bilingualism and diglossia. Changes. Pidgins and creoles. Englishes. Linguistic and cultural representations. Interculturality and global citizenship education.
- Unit 3: Attitudes towards linguistic diversity. Identity, self and otherness. Criteria for communicative adjustment. Language awareness. Superdiversity.

The mandatory readings are:

- Holmes, J. (2013) *An Introduction to Sociolinguistics* (4th edn). London/New York, NY: Routledge.
- Montgomery, M. (2008) *An Introduction to Language and Society* (3rd edn). London/New York, NY: Routledge.
- Stockwell, P. (2007) *Sociolinguistics: A Resource Book for Students*. London/New York, NY: Routledge. Sections A and B.
- Yule, G. (2017) *The Study of Language* (6th edn). Cambridge: Cambridge University Press. Chapters 18–20.

The module is taught through CLIL where sociolinguistics is the content, and academic English, particularly following CALP (cognitive academic language proficiency) applied to CLIL is the language

(Anderson, 2011; Lorenzo & Rodríguez, 2014). Because the programme focuses on educating future teachers of English, several modules are delivered in English and adopt a CLIL approach to offer student teachers the opportunity to develop content knowledge together with English language proficiency. While it could be argued that the experience is closer to English Medium Instruction (EMI), we maintain it is CLIL given the systematic language support built in in each module.

The Study

In this study we adopted a teacher research perspective (Borg & Sanchez, 2015) as it is research carried out by teachers to understand their immediate context. Such a framework differs from the primarily interventionist/transformational intent of action research and it allows educators to examine in detail the processes that people undergo in small groups and the motivational synergy that emanates from specific teaching and learning processes.

We collected data from two cohorts. Cohort 1 from 2017 was composed of 20 L1 Spanish-speaking student teachers, with ages ranging between 20 and 45. There were 19 females and one male; four of the females had between one and five years of teaching experience. Cohort 2 from 2018 consisted of 12 L1 Spanish-speaking student teachers, with an age range from 20 to 32. In this group, there were nine females and three males, with no teaching experience. However, in the sections that follow we treat both cohorts as one group of student teachers since their perceptions of the module were similar.

As we wished to conduct our study in a manner that combined teaching, learning and researching, a qualitative (Ritchie & Lewis, 2003) and ecological research perspective was employed as we collected data from each cohort. Thus, Darío kept a journal for the whole duration of the module. More importantly, data from the student teachers came from tasks completed in pairs which acted like interviews, evidence of their learning such as exams, assignments and feedback on group presentations and a final whole class discussion at the end of the module with each cohort. While preliminary data provided Darío with insights and support for improving teaching and overall module delivery, we engaged in final data analysis in early 2019 aided by thematic analysis (Terry, 2015), which entailed an iterative process which included individual (each author) open-ended inductive coding followed by the generation of axial coding and unifying themes to strengthen connections. When discrepancies emerged, we discussed them to reach consensus. Once a codebook was agreed upon, the data sets were re-analysed to ensure transparency and confirmability.

In compliance with ethical aspects of research, the student teachers had a choice in participating in this study. They were assured that lack of participation or withdrawing from the study at a later stage would not affect their grades. All the student teachers involved in the module agreed to take part in the investigation. Confidentiality and anonymity were agreed, and the student teachers selected the pseudonyms used below.

Findings and Discussion

This section is organised around three interdependent dimensions: (1) student-teachers' initial expectations, (2) student-teachers' revisited expectations and final perceptions and (3) the tutor's perceptions. These three dimensions reflect the main summarised findings of the data and can be used to examine how motivational synergy was experienced or perceived from both the participants and tutor's points of view.

Student-teachers' initial expectations

At the beginning of the module, the student teachers ($n = 32$) were asked to share their expectations about the Sociolinguistics module through a pair-work activity (Figure 15.1).

Thematic analysis of the student-teachers' answers provided hints about their initial motivations and personal investment in this CLIL-based Sociolinguistics module. Without any discrepant data, three clear categories emerged: (1) positive prior experiences with other modules, (2) interest in specific Sociolinguistics topics and (3) interest in finding connections between Sociolinguistics and English language teaching. It should be mentioned that all student teachers showed expectations which belonged to two or even three of these categories.

Concerning student-teachers' prior experiences, the participants concurred that the learning outcomes of two modules, Introduction to Linguistics and Psycholinguistics, generated positive expectations given the CLIL approach also used in them. The following extracts attest to this category:

Extract 1: Clarisa

Last term I learnt so much in Psycholinguistics that I'm eager to learn more about the social aspect of language. I enjoyed the module because I learnt both let's say the module and improved my English.

1.	Individually, think and jot down your expectations.
2.	Share them with a partner.
3.	Summarise your conversation and hand it in. I may ask you to elaborate on your answers. I will audio-record this bit of the session.

Figure 15.1 Activity on student-teachers' expectations

Extract 2: María & Esther

We enjoyed Introduction to Linguistics a lot because of all the activities we did and how they were always connected to teaching, and they helped us with language improvement. We did read a little bit on Sociolinguistics, so our expectations are about learning more about it with a similar learning approach to Intro to Linguistics.

It seems that the teaching and learning processes behind Introduction to Linguistics and Psycholinguistics had left positive memories in the student-teachers' trajectories and therefore their expectations on this new module were motivated by such memories. Positive experiences definitely play an important role not just for language acquisition (Oxford, 2016) but also for developing novice teachers (Hiver, 2016). Through CLIL, both aspects are covered holistically and therefore CLIL finds traction among student teachers when they realise that language and content are learnt in tandem. As such, this experience exerts a positive influence on affective factors such as motivation.

As regards specific Sociolinguistics topics, 30 student teachers mentioned that they expected to learn about different topics. Table 15.1 condenses these topics and their frequency in student-teachers' responses.

When they were provided with the module syllabus after the activity described in Figure 15.1, Darío asked them to compare their expected topics with the syllabus to help them notice that some of their expectations were already included in the module. Furthermore, Darío took this opportunity to emphasise that CLIL would be adopted.

Last, student-teachers' expectations were motivated by an apparent lack of internal programme congruence. Out of 32, 25 student teachers expected the module to offer explicit links and support for two modules, ELT Didactics for Secondary School Learners and Professional Practice and the Practicum, which were also offered in the third year of the programme. When Darío asked them to elaborate on this expectation, one student teacher said:

Extract 3: Marisa

It'd be great if every module in the programme could help us become better teachers. Sometimes, some modules are only about English as a

Table 15.1 Student-teachers' expected topics

Expected topic	Frequency
Language and cultures	24
Varieties of English	21
Social functions of language	17
Language change	9
Societal influence on individual language use	5

system, as a language, but there are no connections to teaching. I'd like to find in Sociolinguistics tools to improve my teaching, to improve my English of course, but above all, to offer my students better classes and opportunities for learning.

Such expectations proved extremely fruitful in strengthening the module and combining student teachers' needs and wants with the aims Darío had set for the module. As Pinner (2019) has discussed, congruent learning aims are prerequisites for achieving motivational synergy. This also led to strengthening the CLIL aspects of the entire IELTE programme as more of the modules were able to find common ground in terms of both content and language aims.

Student-teachers' final perceptions

Towards the end of the module, two activities helped gather data from the student teachers: (1) a pair-work task to revisit their initial expectations and (2) a whole-group discussion followed by some time for individual reflective writing.

In the pair-work task, the student teachers said that the module had met their expectations even though they would have liked to have a two-term module as they felt some topics needed more time and depth. In the second activity they expanded their perceptions. In supporting their positive attitude to the congruence between their expectations and the module, their answers could be understood around two major themes: (1) growth through language awareness and (2) learning as a result of motivational synergy.

By growth through language awareness, we mean those answers which indicated student-teachers' empowerment and commitment beyond the IELTE programme as they developed higher levels of language awareness triggered by learning about dialects and accents:

Extract 4: Lara

I have had so many situations where I've seen myself making fun of people's way of speaking, or passing judgement to friends on the way others talk. Like we sometimes tend to mock those from Buenos Aires, or those from northern Argentina, or I just roll my eyes when some students with a Mapuche origin speak so gaucho-like. Now, I have learnt to be more reflective and deconstruct my own prejudices. And this is not about English. It's about me as a person, and then as an inclusive and understanding teacher.

Extract 5: Teresa

Coming from San Juan, another region different to the Spanish spoken in Patagonia, I sometimes felt ashamed or too much self-conscious of my own Spanish. By looking at Englishes, dialects, accents and drawing comparisons with the linguistic landscape in Argentina, I have become proud of my dialect, and proud of the reasons behind it.

While Lara learnt to embrace varieties of Spanish, Teresa, learnt to embrace her own identity as a Spanish-speaker with a different accent which described the region where she had been born and raised. In both cases, a focus on content encouraged not only a collective sense of language awareness as, in the case of Lara and Teresa, student teachers developed contextual linguistic awareness, but also an individual sense of language use and identity represented through the linguistic choices speakers can make. This also came up later when discussing register and style:

Extract 6: Denise

I really enjoyed the activities in which we had to say or teach the same thing adjusting our language according to the context, audience, etc. That helped me become aware of the plasticity and flexibility we as teachers need to have.

In this way, the CLIL Sociolinguistics module helped the developing teachers to see themselves not only as future teachers, but also to look objectively at their future role in society as teachers, giving them an improved sense of awareness of other people and their perceptions. Arguably, this would also imply that many are more attuned to factors that contribute to motivational synergy, in that they seemed to have shown development in their emotional intelligence. As discussed earlier, with only a limited amount of professional experience, new teachers may struggle to manage such phenomena in their classes at first. However, by learning about how language affects people's perceptions of others in society, the student teachers were able to apply existing and developing personal experience to their future professional setting.

The second theme, learning as a result of motivational synergy, conflates all those comments which signalled that the module had met and exceeded their expectations because not only had they learnt what they expected regarding specific topics, but also, because they had developed their English language proficiency and strategies for English language teaching.

In their contributions, the student teachers associated the impact of the module to their motivation and sense of self-confidence. For example, on the English language proficiency dimension, they expressed:

Extract 7: Teresa

I enjoyed the group presentations because thanks to them I've become more fluent, like my speaking skills are better now. Sometimes we don't have many opportunities for speaking without interruptions or longer contributions.

Extract 8: Toti

The writing assignments were wonderful. The instructions were clear, there was helpful and balanced feedback, and I could improve my writing skills a lot. When I wrote the assignment on South African English, I learned to write more formally, to pay more attention to sentences, cohesion and coherence. Then I felt more motivated to write the final essay because I could see that my writing had improved a lot.

As we discussed at the start of this chapter, the module has dual focused aims in terms of content knowledge and language proficiency. It was heartening to see that the CLIL module was successful in these aims and that many of the student teachers felt an increase in linguistic competence as their understanding of certain sociolinguistic concepts improved. This would suggest that content topics which deal with language in society are a good fit within the CLIL approach as the dual aims mesh well together through the nature of the content (see also Chapter 14). In addition, Extract 7 and Extract 8 also reveal the participants' empowerment and commitment in relation to the module outcomes.

Concerning pedagogical content knowledge as a part of professional learning, the student-teachers' responses indicate a positive impact as they could build bridges between sociolinguistics topics and English language teaching. A common pattern across their justifications was the presence of motivational synergy, which materialised either in different spheres of the tutor's practices or in how certain topics had been addressed. The extracts reveal the multiple-faceted success of CLIL concerning language, content, motivation and self-confidence. For example, regarding Darío's practices, a student teacher stressed the vitality of the relationship between Darío and herself and highlighted the role of tutor feedback:

Extract 9: Estefanía

I think the most significant impact came from you [Darío]. You were always eager to help us, giving us ideas through the activities, giving us positive feedback and encouragement when we had too much on our plates.

In other cases, the student teachers imagined their future teacher selves and predicted the kind of relationship they would have. For example, two studentteachers commented:

Extract 10: Corina

Having learnt about different Englishes has been awesome. I can't help thinking about how I can introduce different Englishes in my lessons so that I help students become aware of the diversity there is out there. You exposed us through different speakers, with different Englishes, although they were always professionals, so by the time we focused on Englishes we had already been exposed to some varieties.

Extract 11: Manchi

Learning about IRE and IC has made me become aware of the importance of the types of questions I will ask learners to help them think. The activity in which we had to record and analyse lesson bits was illuminating as it motivated me to pay more attention to questions we ask and are asked in teaching situations.

The tutor's perceptions

This section is based on Darío's journal. Between 2017 and 2018, he wrote 32 entries, totalling a number of 5344 words. There was an entry for every lesson taught and lessons which mostly consisted of student-teachers' group presentations on assigned topics. In the entries, there was a tendency to structure each entry into two parts: a descriptive summary of the lesson and personal reflections on it.

Thematic analysis offered four categories: (1) student – tutor motivation, (2) congruent practices, (3) student-teachers' English language proficiency and (4) self-confidence. Below, we expand each category and include supporting data.

By far, the most prevalent category was that of student – tutor motivation. Darío's main concern was that of motivating and sustaining motivation among the student teachers in both cohorts. The entries show what aspects of the lesson motivated the student teachers and how such motivation impacted on the tutor's contribution to motivational synergy. For example, in Extract 17, which corresponds to the entry written on Lesson 1 in August 2017, we find:

Extract 12: Tutor's journal

I'm happy to see that the students enjoyed the role-play activity on being researchers and members of a new community. I saw them super engaged, and how that helped them make sense of the role of ethnography and classroom ethnography in ELT. Seeing them so enthusiastic about the module is an engine to drive me to think of similar tasks to explore other concepts.

In October 2017, a similar entry reveals:

Extract 13: Tutor's journal

The video on the difference between IRE [initiation-response-evaluation] and IC [instructional conversation] attracted them a lot to deal with conversational analysis from a social perspective. I'm glad I chose that video. They came up with hundreds of amazing examples about their own learning when young or classroom situations they've observed. I think I'll exploit this a lot more next week and I'll ask them to audio-record bits of actual lessons for analysis. For 2018 I'll also ask students to role-play situations to show the difference.

Extracts 12 and 13 illustrate a common pattern across the entries which describe the connections between student-teacher motivation and tutor motivation as seen from the tutor's eyes. According to the entries, the topics activities proposed became a source of growth for student-teachers' engagement, empowerment and commitment (also Extracts 4–5 and 7–8). Furthermore, their proactive behaviour, in turn, acted as a drive that helped the tutor maximise those pedagogical strategies that were assessed as positive judging by the student teachers' involvement.

Entries usually included tutor's concerns with congruent practice, i.e. coherence between language pedagogies taught in the programme and expected to be found in the student-teachers' practicum and the tutors' own teaching practices. These concerns, often coded as questions, are found both in 2017 and 2018 perhaps triggered by student-teachers' expectations about the links between the Sociolinguistics module and language teaching support within a CLIL approach. For example, one entry from 2017 and one from 2018 illustrate this category:

Extract 14: Tutor's journal

Could they see this lesson followed a TBL approach [task-based learning] as regards organisation? I know I need to show them with my teaching how we want them to teach. How can I make sure of that every single lesson? I can't offer this intermittently. I'm not some Xmas lights! Perhaps I should start including five minutes at the end of each session where we reflect on how the lesson went, to raise their awareness? Decisions decisions decisions.

Extract 15: Tutor's journal

Sometimes I see that my lessons are too teacher-centred and that's exactly the opposite of what we teach them. Or like today, there were several language issues in the wrap-up and I failed to do something about that. I need to work more on my helping them reflect on their own use of English.

While Extract 14 shows the tutor's concerns with his own teaching practices as exemplars, Extract 15 also reveals the third category: student-teachers' English language proficiency. Following a CLIL approach, Sociolinguistics was aimed at developing content knowledge and English language skills. Entries in this category show frustration and concerns around student-teachers' identity as teachers in the future.

Only two entries, written after the student teachers submitted their final assignments and delivered group presentations, transmit a more positive attitude:

Extract 16: Tutor's journal

I had them last year and I'm not sure I see much change. Same mistakes, same vocab, same language level. Same code-switching behaviour in [student-teacher's name]. perhaps they just don't bother to look up words in the dictionary. It drives me crazy. I tell them to check words, to use the dictionary, and some just write and speak as if they were teenage students. Next year, they're graduating, how are the students going to see them? Other colleagues?

Extract 17: Tutor's journal

Wow! You see? When they study, and prepare their slides and rehearse, results are so much different! They sounded confident, fluent, accurate, I only gave them constructive feedback on how defined creoles, but other than that, there were no problems with their English. I congratulated them on this so that they see that it does make a difference on the audience.

Issues around student-teachers' development regarding content knowledge, transferences to pedagogical modules and English language proficiency were concomitant to tutor self-confidence in his understanding and implementation of CLIL. Entries tended to include this category both at the beginning and at the end of each academic year:

Extract 18: Tutor's journal, 14 August 2018

If they don't learn, it's 50-50. I'm getting paid so that they learn and become better teachers and model users of English to their students. It's my responsibility to find ways of scaffolding and supporting them.

Extract 19: Tutor's journal, 13 November 2018

I'm proud of them. Their essays were impeccable. They managed to integrate several sources so my work paid off finally after I insisted so much in class, and with examples and all on how to organise their essays, what to include, how to analyse each bit, how to include examples for the assertions they make. It's awesome to see them include and discuss central concepts through careful language use.

In addition, Extract 19 shows planes that overlap around the axis provided by motivation. Once again, Darío refers to the motivational synergy between student teachers and himself, particularly with high levels of self-confidence in both the tutor and the student teachers. In relation to CLIL, the extract supports the idea that motivation and confidence enhancement can be positive outcomes of having content and language aims. In this case, the quality Darío found in the student-teachers' essays is the product of both content appropriation and language proficiency.

When contrasting the student-teachers' views with those of Darío as encoded in his journal entries, Extracts 4–11 confirm the impact that the module had on the student teachers lives at the intersection between the tutor's practices, his own motivation and the integration of content and language learning. If we understand these extracts in light of the tutor's journal, we can see motivational synergy between the tutor's perceptions and lived experiences while teaching the module and the student teachers' own experiences. Both student teachers and tutor seemingly generated a spiral in which their motivations and sense of self-confidence acted as drives to sustain or enhance motivation even when there were challenges.

Implications for Policy and Practice

The experience reported in this chapter provides implications not only for linguistics-related modules in IELTE but also for the different areas that constitute IELTE programmes. Implications may be related to psychological aspects as well as teaching practice aspects.

Knowing student-teachers' expectations helped the tutor gain insights into their beliefs and imagined future selves as teachers of English. Knowing their wants and needs contributed to calibrating the module so that there was a stronger connection between the IELTE curriculum and student-teachers' needs. In this regard, tutors can find out about their expectations through pair-work tasks that act as warm-up to the module content and provide data which can be used for teacher research. Tutors can then keep student-teachers' answers and examine them at the end of the module retrospectively to understand student-teachers' progress and encourage awareness, reflection and self-assessment. Tutors can even create an online forum to promote asynchronous student-teacher interaction for the discussion of expectations, realities and overall student-teachers' trajectories and identities as future teachers. We believe that the more calibrated and aligned student-teachers' and tutors' expectations are, the stronger chances of generating motivational synergy. When there is sustainable motivational synergy, the classroom becomes a powerhouse which boosts student teachers' as well as tutors' potential and effectiveness.

It is also of paramount importance to frame module contents so that they are directly linked to language teaching. IELTE programmes are not expected to educate future linguists initially, but language teachers and therefore tutors must make every effort to link linguistics topics to situated language teaching and learning. To achieve this aim, student teachers can be asked, in agreement with other modules such as the practicum, to observe, record and analyse authentic classroom interactions and to, examine school syllabi and teaching materials such as coursebooks or other multimodal materials teachers can employ. In so doing, Sociolinguistics, or other branches of linguistics, can contribute to student-teacher's professional awareness about language as a meaning making system in and outside of the classroom. This chapter has shown that motivational synergy is enhanced when student teachers can make connections between studying language as social practice and English language teaching. In turn, motivation leads student teachers to develop a stronger sense of self-confidence in their identity construction as future teachers.

Framing IELTE modules in a CLIL approach helps student teachers become more cognisant of not only subject-matter knowledge but also academic language. Tutors can mobilise knowledge through materials, activities and balanced feedback. In so doing, they may allow student teachers to develop their English language proficiency through guided practice, language awareness and opportunities for using the language critically and with authentic purposes. For example, before having student teachers write an essay, they could navigate published articles in ELT and identify general as well as subject-specific academic vocabulary that will help them aim higher. When student teachers become aware of improvement in their content knowledge and English language proficiency, their motivation rises and so does their awareness of how educational approaches such as CLIL operate in practice.

In-service teachers may also benefit from developing sociolinguistic understanding, particularly in the areas of language change and variation, in language education in order to create context-responsive materials and classroom situations which promote interculturalism and plurilingualism. In addition, becoming aware of language change and variation (e.g. Englishes) can enhance their self-confidence in using their L1 as well as English or other languages they speak (e.g. heritage languages) more confidently.

Conclusion

In this chapter we have discussed how a CLIL-driven Sociolinguistics module can impact on student-teachers' and tutor's motivation and sense of self-confidence. Given the motivational synergy that emerged between student teachers and their tutor, we would like to invite teacher educators to energise their teaching practices by adopting a CLIL framework which also includes student-teachers' perceptions, expectations and professional future selves. Psychological aspects such as motivation and self-confidence deeply affect learning even in higher education, and thus, it seems almost crass to point out that learning, no matter the education level, is still holistic and it involves emotions and personal relations.

References

Anderson, C.E. (2011) CLIL for CALP in the multilingual, pluricultural, globalized knowledge society: Experiences and backgrounds to L2 English usage among Latin American L1 Spanish users. *Latin American Journal of Content & Language Integrated Learning* 4 (2), 51–66.

Banegas, D.L. (2017a) Introduction. In D.L. Banegas (ed.) *Initial English Language Teacher Education: International Perspectives on Research, Curriculum and Practice* (pp. 1–11). New York, NY: Bloomsbury.

Banegas, D.L. (2020) Teaching linguistics to low-level English language users in a teacher education programme: An action research study. *The Language Learning Journal* 48, 148–161

Boo, Z., Dörnyei, Z. and Ryan, S. (2015) L2 motivation research 2005–2014: Understanding a publication surge and a changing landscape. *System* 55, 145–157.

Borg, S. and Sanchez, H.S. (eds) (2015) *International Perspectives on Teacher Research*. Basingstoke: Palgrave.

Coyle, D., Hood, P. and Marsh, D. (2010) *CLIL: Content and Language Integrated Learning*. Cambridge: Cambridge University Press.

Deci, E.L., Kasser, T. and Ryan, R.M. (1997) Self-determined teaching: Opportunities and obstacles. In J.L. Bess (ed.) *Teaching Well and Liking It: Motivating Faculty to Teach Effectively* (pp. 57–71). Baltimore, MD: Johns Hopkins University Press.

Dörnyei, Z. and Murphey, T. (2003) *Group Dynamics in the Language Classroom*. Cambridge: Cambridge University Press.

Dörnyei, Z. and Ryan, S. (2015) *The Psychology of the Language Learner Revisited*. Abingdon: Routledge.

Genesee, F. and Hamayan, E. (2016) *CLIL in Context: Practical Guidance for Educators*. Cambridge: Cambridge University Press.

Gkonou, C. and Mercer, S. (2017) *Understanding Emotional and Social Intelligence among English Language Teachers*. London: The British Council.

Golombek, P.R. and Johnson, K.E. (2019) Materializing a Vygotskian-inspired language teacher education pedagogy. In S. Walsh and S. Mann (eds) *The Routledge Handbook of English Language Teacher Education* (pp. 25–37). New York, NY: Routledge.

Hatfield, E., Cacioppo, J.T. and Rapson, R.L. (1993) Emotional contagion. *Current Directions in Psychological Science* 2 (3), 96–100.

Henry, A. and Thorsten, C. (2018) Teacher–student relationships and L2 motivation. *Modern Language Journal* 102, 218–241.

Hiver, P. (2016) The triumph over experience: Hope and hardiness in novice L2 teachers. In P.D. MacIntyre, T. Gregersen and S. Mercer (eds) *Positive Psychology in SLA* (pp. 168–179). Bristol: Multilingual Matters.

Iacoboni, M. (2009) *Mirroring People: The Science of Empathy and How We Connect with Others*. New York, NY: Picador.

Lasagabaster, D. and Doiz, A. (2017) A longitudinal study on the impact of CLIL on affective factors. *Applied Linguistics* 38 (5), 688–712.

Lohbeck, A., Hagenauer, G. and Frenzel, A.C. (2018) Teachers' self-concepts and emotions: Conceptualizations and relations. *Teaching and Teacher Education* 70, 111–120.

Lorenzo, F. and Rodríguez, L. (2014) Onset and expansion of L2 cognitive academic language proficiency in bilingual settings: CALP in CLIL. *System* 47, 64–72.

Maclellan, E. (2014) How might teachers enable learner self-confidence? A review study. *Educational Review* 66 (1), 59–74.

McCabe, A. (2017) Systemic functional linguistics and language teaching. In T. Bartlett and G. O'Grady (eds) *The Routledge Handbook of Systemic Functional Linguistics* (pp. 591–604). New York, NY: Routledge.

Morton, T. and Llinares, A. (2017) Content and language integrated learning (CLIL): Type of programme or pedagogical model? In A. Llinares and T. Morton (eds) *Applied Linguistics Perspectives on CLIL* (pp. 1–16). Amsterdam: John Benjamins.

Murphey, T., Falout, J., Fukada, Y. and Fukuda, T. (2012) Group dynamics: Collaborative agency in present communities of imagination. In S. Mercer, S. Ryan and M. Williams (eds) *Psychology for Language Learning: Insights from Research, Theory and Practice* (pp. 220–238). London: Palgrave Macmillan.

Nolan, A. and Molla, T. (2017) Teacher confidence and professional capital. *Teaching and Teacher Education* 62, 10–18.

Oxford, R.L. (2016) Toward a psychology of well-being for language learners: The 'EMPATHICS' vision. In P.D. MacIntyre, T. Gregersen and S. Mercer (eds) *Positive Psychology in SLA* (pp. 10–87). Bristol: Multilingual Matters.

Pinner, R.S. (2013) Authenticity and CLIL: Examining authenticity from an international CLIL perspective. *International CLIL Research Journal* 2 (1), 44–54.

Pinner, R.S. (2019) *Authenticity and Teacher-Student Motivational Synergy: A Narrative of Language Teaching*. New York, NY: Routledge.

Ritchie, J. and Lewis, J. (eds) (2003) *Qualitative Research Practice: A Guide for Social Science Students and Researchers*. Thousand Oaks, CA: Sage.

Terry, G. (2015) Doing thematic analysis. In E. Lyons and A. Coyle (eds) *Analysing Qualitative Data in Psychology* (2nd edn) (pp. 104–118). London: Sage.

Ushioda, E. (2009) A person-in-context relational view of emergent motivation, self and identity. In Z. Dörnyei and E. Ushioda (eds) *Motivation, Language Identity and the L2 Self* (pp. 215–228). Bristol: Multilingual Matters.

Ushioda, E. and Dörnyei, Z. (2017) Beyond global English: Motivation to learn languages in a multicultural world: Introduction to the special issue. *Modern Language Journal* 101, 451–454.

van Lier, L. (1996) *Interaction in the Language Curriculum: Awareness, Autonomy and Authenticity*. London: Longman.

Wyatt, M. (2018) Language teachers' self-efficacy beliefs: A review of the literature (2005–2016). *Australian Journal of Teacher Education* 43 (4), 92–120.

16 Conclusion: Challenges, Opportunities, Implications and Future Directions

Kyle Read Talbot and Marie-Theres Gruber

It was a tremendous privilege editing these chapters and we are grateful to have had the opportunity. As we near the end of this edited collection, we would like to reflect on lessons learned from the contributions and highlight some possible directions for future research.

Challenges

The chapters in this collection have foregrounded challenges that both teachers and learners experience in integrated content and language (ICL) settings. One theme that many of the teacher-related studies in this collection share is the perception that teaching in such settings implies a heavier workload, higher cognitive expenditures or increased time costs (see also Aguilar, 2017; Gefaell & Unterberger, 2010; Infante *et al.*, 2009). The notion of perceiving a heavier workload was highlighted in seven of the 12 teacher-related chapters (Pappa, Chapter 2; Polat & Mahalingappa, Chapter 5; Dafouz, Chapter 8; Talbot *et al.*, Chapter 9; Jiménez Muñoz, Chapter 10; Gierlinger, Chapter 11; Arshad & Lyster, Chapter 13). Reasons for this included a lack of relevant material or a need to customise material specifically for integrating content and language, insufficient planning time, linguistic challenges, rigid curriculum restraints, balancing content and language objectives as well as generally feeling a sense of time pressure.

The fact that teachers in ICL contexts may often feel as if they are obliged to do more work or that a higher workload is implicit in the adoption of ICL teaching approaches needs to be reflected on by those responsible for the growth and spread of such initiatives. Teaching is widely known as a stressful profession (Johnson *et al.*, 2005; McIntyre *et al.*, 2017) and it is generally accepted that teachers' workloads are increasing across educational levels and types (Bovellan, 2014). As such, it is of crucial importance to ensure that teachers are not even more unduly burdened by the implementation of ICL programmes. Naturally, how to offset this workload or reward teachers for their extra efforts warrants further attention from educational researchers and policy makers. Gefaell and Unterberger (2010), for instance, explain that teachers' enthusiasm for CLIL teaching can be dampened due to the considerable workload and suggest dedicated time for planning lessons, targeted training programmes that address didactic and pedagogic skills and collaborative teacher networks to alleviate this. Pappa (Chapter 2: 22) similarly suggested how supportive teacher networks can be a means to coping with the challenges of teaching in CLIL contexts, explaining that how collegial relationships afforded her teacher participants 'support, guidance, collaboration and encouragement'.

One difference noted was at the tertiary-level. Many teachers at this level did not perceive materials generation as burdensome (Jin *et al.*, Chapter 3; Talbot *et al.*, Chapter 9), as many of these teachers pointed out that the language of their discipline was English which made classroom materials relatively easier to obtain. It is worth reflecting on whether teachers integrating content and language through languages other than English would have different experiences or perceive the same availability of resources. In other settings at the tertiary level, teachers found themselves investing considerable time and effort adapting materials (Dafouz, Chapter 8). While Nishida (Chapter 14) primarily focuses on tertiary-level students in Japan, she also addresses materials generation in ICL contexts. She suggests that it may add to a teachers' workload to create or adapt new materials for ICL settings, but points out that many teachers enjoy the creative aspects of materials generation.

We also noted a strong focus on self and linguistic confidence and possible threats to this in several chapters (Pappa, Chapter 2; Dalton-Puffer *et al.*, Chapter, 6; Dafouz, Chapter 8; Talbot *et al.*, Chapter 9; Jiménez Muñoz, Chapter 10; Gierlinger, Chapter 11; Parry & Thomas, Chapter 12; Arshad & Lyster, Chapter 13; Banegas & Pinner, Chapter 15). Indeed, a number of studies have pointed out that the experience of linguistic insecurity and/or linguistic challenges can be a concern for teachers (Aguilar, 2017; Bovellan, 2014; Doiz & Lasagabaster, 2018; Fernández & Halbach, 2011; Moate, 2011) and learners in ICL contexts (Dalton-Puffer *et al.*, Chapter 6).

Many chapters also highlight the difficulties that teachers in ICL settings may face, including challenges to their professional integrity. For instance, in the Welsh secondary setting, Parry and Thomas (Chapter 12) reflected on how teachers' reluctance to use Welsh was linked to low confidence. This was in part fueled by the 'teacher's fear of being wrong, as judged by other teachers and by the pupils' (Chapter 12: 227).

Fortunately, their study demonstrated that even a short-term intervention could make a meaningful difference for teachers. Naturally, the efficacy of such interventions should be explored further in other contexts and with other populations and languages. In at least one study, feeling more prepared to teach in ICL settings (in this case CLIL/EMI) reported a more positive sense of well-being than their colleagues who did not (Hessel et al., 2020). Studies such as this offer hope that effective interventions and training programmes can bolster teachers' confidence and well-being.

An implementation challenge related to a secondary Austrian CLIL setting was pointed out by Dalton-Puffer et al. (Chapter 6). In their chapter, they highlighted the tension between a more flexible or more top-down implementation of CLIL; particularly, the possible tension that exists when teachers take agency in how CLIL is implemented locally in both obligatory and optional settings in Austrian secondary education. While they reflected on how this 'might well ensure a manageable level of challenge and reduce negative emotions [...] and foster an inclusive environment' for teachers and learners alike, they argued that 'this cannot be the final stage of a sustainable and effective CLIL practice' (Chapter 6: 108). What they highlight is a grey area in which an *ad hoc* implementation of CLIL allows teachers the freedom to interpret CLIL in ways that they and their students might find comfortable; yet, they argue that this needs to be balanced with research and stakeholder feedback in order to 'optimise the potential of CLIL and avoid the risk of having too low expectations of what is achievable' (Chapter 6: 108). Similarly, Talbot et al. (Chapter 9), also in the Austrian setting, pointed out in their comparison of CLIL/EMI across educational levels, that the *ad hoc* implementation of CLIL/EMI allowed teachers flexibility and an opportunity to express their creativity, but at the same time, for some teachers a lack of clarity was disorienting. As both Dalton-Puffer et al. (Chapter 6) and Talbot et al. (Chapter 9) share a setting, this may be an indication of a contextual peculiarity. Further research initiatives could explore whether this may apply to other settings and what mediates the sense of autonomy and freedom against a sense of aimlessness.

Though more chapters related to the experiences of teachers in ICL settings than learners overall, several chapters also highlighted learner-specific challenges. For instance, Dalton-Puffer et al. (Chapter 6) point out that students in their study questioned their own competence related to both English and the content of their CLIL courses (see also, Cho, 2012; Ellili-Cherif & Alkhateeb, 2015). For many student participants in their study, the content in CLIL courses was reported as being sufficiently difficult in German and learning through English made this even more difficult. The authors point out that, in their context, students described this in 'emotionally coloured' terms expressing anxiety and frustration, especially those who were new to CLIL (Chapter 6: 106).

Notably, students were not only concerned with their own language competence, they pointed out that it could be a challenge if their teachers were not prepared to teach content in English. For both teachers and students in their study, demands were perceived positively or negatively depending how participants viewed the threshold level of the challenges they faced.

Milla and García Mayo (Chapter 7) highlighted another possible learner-related challenge linked to student expectations of their CLIL classrooms. In their study, they pointed out that CLIL students expected oral corrective feedback (OCF); in other words, CLIL students wanted feedback on their language. Though unstated in their chapter, it stands to reason that when students' expectations do not match the reality of their situation, this has the potential to create a feeling of cognitive dissonance, as has been shown in other studies (Goldschmidt & Seifried, 2008; Maloshonok & Terentev, 2017).

Opportunities

Despite the existence of challenges, contributions in this volume also presented an optimistic view of the possible positive benefits to be found accompanying ICL programmes. For instance, the notion of translanguaging as a means of coping with anxieties and boosting confidence for both students and teachers emerged as a theme and was generally perceived as a benefit in five chapters (Jin et al., Chapter 3; Dalton-Puffer et al., Chapter 6; Dafouz, Chapter 8; Talbot et al., Chapter 9; Gierlinger, Chapter 11). One example was highlighted by Gierlinger (Chapter 11) who pointed out that the teachers in his study felt more comfortable and secure knowing they could switch between English and German when needed and that this enhanced their sense of efficacy. Dalton-Puffer et al. (Chapter 6) suggested that translanguaging on the part of the teacher often acted to support students' confidence in the classroom. Encouraging both teachers and students to access their full linguistic repertoires in ICL settings may impact their confidence positively (cf. Kuteeva, 2019). Future studies focusing explicitly on the role of translanguaging in various ICL settings would be a valuable addition to this specific research area (see also, Anderson & Lightfoot, 2018; Lin, 2018; Macaro, 2018), particularly, its relationship to linguistic and self-confidence and well-being.

Another positive theme to emerge from these contributions was the role of teaching experience and how this alleviated teachers' anxieties over time, which, arguably would impact learners positively, too. Gaining teaching experience in these settings prompted teachers to feel more comfortable and efficacious (see also Moate, 2011). One example of this can be found in Jiménez Muñoz' chapter (Chapter 10). He pointed out, that while some anxiety-inducing challenges remained after five years of experience with the teachers in his study, that, 'experience generally appeases anxiety, negative-self-ideation and fears of underperformance' (Chapter 10: 188). Similarly, Dafouz (Chapter 8) points out that teachers' early struggles tend to wear off as they become more experienced and confident. As many new teachers feel overwhelmed when they perceive discrepancies between what they expected teaching to be like and their actual classroom experience (Ingersoll & Smith, 2004; Kim & Cho, 2014), it is essential to prepare early career stage teachers, or teachers new to ICL settings, so that their expectations of life as a teacher in such contexts are realistic. One such example was found in Arshad and Lyster' contribution (Chapter 13). In this chapter, the authors outline a professional development (PD) initiative with one specific component focusing on the challenges and benefits of a dual focus on content and language. In terms of teaching experience specifically, PD initiatives could aim to imbue teachers with a sense of hope that much of the negativity experienced as an early career stage teacher tends to diminish over time.

A further benefit was highlighted in Banegas and Pinner's chapter (Chapter 15) who highlight the potential of utilising language-focused content modules to integrate content and language. They reflected on how 'motivational synergy is enhanced when student-teachers can make connections between studying language as a social practice and English language teaching' (Chapter 15: 280). With their sample of pre-service English language teachers, Banegas and Pinner (Chapter 15) pointed out that employing a Sociolinguistics module, contributed to these students 'professional awareness' (Chapter 15: 280). They explained, 'Sociolinguistics, or other branches of linguistics, can contribute to student teacher's professional awareness about language as a meaning making system in and outside of the classroom' (Chapter 15: 280).

Speaking to the learner experience specifically, opportunities were found in meeting and overcoming challenges related to learning in ICL programmes. Dalton-Puffer et al. (Chapter 6: 103), for instance, showed how 'working through complex engineering content in a second language increases the cognitive demand on learners', but, in the Austrian HTL CLIL context, rather than being perceived negatively, students tended to understand this increased cognitive engagement as motivating and enriching. They point out that for both learners and teachers, it is often the perception of whether the demands are suitable or excessive that is indicative of positive or negative experiences.

Learner psychology

Although more contributions in this edited collection centred on teachers, there were also lessons to be learned about the psychological experiences of learners in this volume. Two chapters (Roiha & Mäntylä,

Chapter 4; Nishida, Chapter 14) focused on learners' views exclusively, two chapters on teachers and learners in combination (Dalton-Puffer *et al.*, Chapter 6; Milla & García Mayo, Chapter 7) and one chapter looked at pre-service language teachers and their classroom teacher in combination (Banegas & Pinner, Chapter 15). One example demonstrating learners' views can be found in Roiha and Mäntylä's contribution (Chapter 4). In their case study exploring the life course of one student, they discussed how his experiences with CLIL contributed to the development of his positive self-concept. The effect of CLIL on his English language self-concept was, according to the chapter authors, an essential factor in the development of his positive relationship with English. Student beliefs were also foregrounded in Chapter 7 in which, Milla and García Mayo elaborated on how the beliefs of students in a CLIL context in Spain were similar to those in EFL contexts. They explored teacher and learners' beliefs about oral corrective feedback (OCF) in CLIL and EFL contexts in Spain. In their study, CLIL students viewed OCF in much the same way that EFL students view OCF, as a necessary and important part of their CLIL lessons. Understanding that some students may want explicit language feedback is an important consideration that CLIL teachers should recognise, especially considering the mixed findings about teachers' language-related practices in CLIL and other ICL classrooms (Costa, 2012; Hu & Gao, 2020; van Kampen *et al.*, 2018). Naturally, future research initiatives should further explore students' beliefs about language feedback and other factors in ICL settings and investigate whether their expectations match teachers' actual language-related practices and feedback. Teachers could also conduct research in their own classrooms to learn about the expectations of their students when it comes to this approach to teaching and learning. For example, Banegas and Pinner (Chapter 15) reflected on how becoming familiar with learners' expectations would allow teachers to calibrate these with their own expectations; this, they argue, would be motivating for the teacher and learners alike.

Finally, another point worth reflecting on relates to how the language of instruction is perceived by students. The students in Dalton-Puffer *et al.*'s (Chapter 6) took a pragmatic and 'emotionally neutral' (Chapter 6: 100) view towards English use in the Austrian technical secondary setting. For them, it seemed that this was an inevitability and consequence of an increasingly globalised world, and an essential skill needed for future employability. From this perspective, they viewed CLIL, in English, as a suitable response to this reality. Dalton-Puffer *et al.* (Chapter 6) reflected on what they referred to as the 'normalising of CLIL' in this very particular setting. They argued, 'obligatory CLIL works if and only if it is in English, reflecting the sociolinguistic reality of "globalised bilingualism"' (Chapter 6: 106). The importance of how the language of instruction is perceived is also highlighted in Roiha and Mäntylä's (Chapter 4) contribution. They describe how their participant's positive relationship with English affected his language use, and further, how his somewhat negative view towards other languages seemingly acted to reinforce his positive relationship with English which stemmed, at least in part, from using it meaningfully in supportive settings, such as he experienced with CLIL.

Teacher psychology

The number of contributions in this volume focusing on teachers is worth noting. Mercer and Kostoulas (2018: 2) pointed out that, 'When compared with the diversity, depth and breadth of research available on learner psychology, there is a notable scarcity of comparable studies examining a wide range of psychological constructs in teachers'. As such, it is refreshing to see the number of contributions in this volume focusing on the psychological experiences of teachers. In fact, 12 of the 14 chapters focused on teachers although the call for papers was intended to cover research on all possible stakeholders. Of the 12 chapters focusing on teachers, nine focused exclusively on teachers (Pappa, Chapter 2; Jin *et al.*, Chapter 3; Polat & Mahalingappa, Chapter 5; Dafouz, Chapter 8; Talbot *et al.*, Chapter 9; Jiménez Muñoz, Chapter 10; Gierlinger, Chapter 11; Parry & Thomas, Chapter 12; Arshad & Lyster, Chapter 13).

Several contributions in this volume reflected on teachers' senses of identity and professional integrity (Pappa, Chapter 2; Jin *et al.*, Chapter 3; Gierlinger, Chapter 11). For instance, Pappa (Chapter 2) suggested that many Finnish teachers persist in offering CLIL 'despite the decrease in schools providing CLIL instruction and the persistence of challenges that teachers deemed responsible for the considerable decline in enthusiasm for CLIL' (Chapter 2: 17). What she referred to as a 'grassroots initiative' demonstrated how some teachers were willing to embrace roles as both non-language subject and language teachers. Interestingly, she outlined how the conflicts and tensions experienced by teachers in ICL settings can function as sites of growth for teachers' relational identities. This occurred through bonding over the tensions they experienced collectively. Yet, whereas Pappa mentioned that many teachers embraced their role as content teachers and as language teachers in her chapter, Jin *et al.* (Chapter 3) reflected on how the tertiary-level EMI teachers in their sample in Austria were more reluctant to embrace playing a language teaching role, a finding which has been supported in other EMI contexts (Aguilar, 2017; Doiz & Lasagabaster, 2018). Exploring further how, why and under what conditions teachers embrace roles as content and language teachers, or just content teachers, as well as how this impacts how they feel about their teaching will be an essential avenue for researchers to explore further. Though research into teacher identity is important to better understand the dynamism of teaching and what it means to be a teacher, it is arguably even more important during periods of intensive changes or educational reforms (Day & Kington, 2008), such as what we see in ICL contexts.

Collaboration and supportive networks also influenced stakeholders' psychological experiences (Pappa, Chapter 2; Dafouz, Chapter 8; Parry & Thomas, Chapter 12; Arshad & Lyster, Chapter 13; Banegas & Pinner, Chapter 15). For instance, Banegas and Pinner (Chapter 15) reflected on the synergistic effects that can be created when aims between teachers and students are aligned within the classroom; they describe this as creating a 'feedback loop of reciprocal energy that helps keep the students motivated while simultaneously validating the teachers' efforts' (Chapter 15: 268). Whereas Banegas and Pinner looked at the effects of teacher-student synergy, Pappa (Chapter 2) explored how shared aims and mutual support between teachers within CLIL programmes can support a positive workplace culture and support teachers who doubt their efficacy. This type of positive office culture was also addressed in the Parry and Thomas (Chapter 12) contribution. They discussed the efficacy of a 'whole-school approach' (Chapter 12: 227) to supporting teachers and argued that this type of approach was necessary in designing interventions to aid teachers. Collaboration was also a key element and source of enjoyment for teachers undergoing a professional development initiative in the CBI context (Arshad & Lyster, Chapter 13). The in-service teachers in Arshad and Lyster's study (Chapter 13: 241) saw the PD initiative as 'an occasion for productive collaborative sharing'.

It was also encouraging that the notion of teacher well-being was reflected in several chapters in this collection (Pappa, Chapter 2; Jin et al., Chapter 3; Talbot et al., Chapter 9; Jiménez Muñoz, Chapter 10; Gierlinger, Chapter 11; Parry & Thomas, Chapter 12; Banegas & Pinner, Chapter 15). Parry and Thomas (Chapter 12), for instance, consider how a wealth of research explores how teachers are fundamental in supporting students' well-being but less is focused on the teachers' well-being and mental health. Hopefully, the prevalence with which well-being was addressed within these chapters reflects increased recognition of the importance for teacher well-being more generally. Talbot and Mercer (2018: 425) argued that, 'teachers who enjoy high levels of well-being are more likely to be successful teachers, more engaged with their language teaching practice, and better able to face challenges that occur along the way'. This argument extends to teachers teaching in ICL contexts that, as we have seen in this collection, often encounter both opportunities and challenges that teachers in other settings may not face.

Implications for research

A range of methodological approaches are represented in this volume. This includes qualitative interview and focus group designs (e.g. Pappa, Chapter 2; Jin et al., Chapter 3; Dafouz, Chapter 8; Talbot et al.,

Chapter 9), survey studies (Nishida, Chapter 14), as well as mixed-method designs (e.g. Dalton-Puffer *et al.*, Chapter 6; Milla & García Mayo, Chapter 7; Parry & Thomas, Chapter 12) and teacher research (Banegas & Pinner, Chapter 15). Though this edited collection includes more qualitative than quantitative contributions, there was creative variety in the research designs and types of analyses utilised in the qualitative studies. For instance, one study combined thematic and narrative analysis of an 'individual life course' interview (Roiha & Mäntylä, Chapter 4). This methodology allowed the authors to look at the data from various perspectives and to separate their participant's life into epochs. Polat and Mahalingappa (Chapter 8) used multiple sources of data in conjunction. Their participants wrote about the challenges and opportunities of implementing features from a teaching protocol in their lessons, this data then shaped the course of subsequent interviews with the teacher participants. In Chapter 6, Dalton-Puffer *et al.* conducted a secondary data analysis from two data sets to compare the psychological experiences of teachers and students in voluntary versus mandatory CLIL in Austrian upper secondary schools. The collection also features longitudinal designs (Gierlinger, Chapter 11; Arshad & Lyster, Chapter 13; Nishida, Chapter 14). For example, Gierlinger utilised multiple interviews, classroom observations, videotaped lessons and stimulated recall sessions over the course of one school year. Arshad and Lyster (Chapter 13) also presented a longitudinal study, their chapter reports on the first-year results of a three-year teacher professional development initiative.

Novel methodological designs were also featured in this collection. For instance, Jiménez Muñoz (Chapter 10) employed a quantitative-qualitative analysis of interview transcripts with an international sample of experienced EMI educators. This allowed him to combine inductive coding methods as well as frequency counts of the codifications and their correlates. His participants were also asked to write a note to their former selves which served as a reflection task for what they wish they would have known about teaching EMI that they know now. Analysis of this task was completed through 'a validated corpus-linguistics sentiment analysis tool that includes 1254 indicators of feeling, emotion, social cognition and social order in natural language' (Chapter 10: 180).

In examining the chapters, we also noticed a theme related to sampling. It was clear that many of the teachers who participated were teachers who were excited to be teaching in ICL settings and generally felt confident and successful in doing so. Notably, in Chapter 3, Jin *et al.* reflect on how one of their teacher participants in the Austrian tertiary-level EMI context reflected on how there are teachers that feel uncomfortable teaching their subjects in English but would hesitate to admit this publicly. Certainly, knowledge about resilient and successful teachers in these settings is important. By tracing their paths of success, these teachers can potentially serve as benchmarks for those who are new or struggling in these settings; however, it will also be important for future researchers to try to gain access to those who are compelled to participate involuntarily and/or do not feel confident in their ability to teach within such programmes. Reaching this hard to access group will be essential in outlining a more complete picture of the psychological experiences of all types of classroom stakeholders.

Many of the studies in this collection highlight individual case studies and explore smaller samples with a high degree of granularity and nuance. At the same time, we believe there is room for larger scale investigations about the psychological experiences of both learners and teachers in future research explorations that could help illustrate larger trends. One such example can be found in Hessel *et al.* (2020) who compare the well-being and job satisfaction of CLIL teachers at the secondary and EMI at the tertiary level in Austria. They find that in general, secondary teachers score lower on key well-being measures than do their tertiary level counterparts. Yet, the differences in job satisfaction between the cohorts are less significant. It will be important to look at the psychological experiences of stakeholders in ICL contexts from multiple angles and with a diversity of methodological approaches to generate a clearer picture of their experiences and perceptions in such settings.

Finally, in order to understand the experiences of key stakeholders more clearly in ICL settings, there is also a need to learn more about the reactions and reflections of learners and teachers based on outcomes. For instance, it would be a worthy endeavour to explore how teachers reflect and react to student content and language outcomes in ICL programmes. Outcome-based research would add a fascinating new perspective to the experiences that teachers and learners have in these settings.

Implications for professional development

A major theme presented in this edited collection was the importance of self-confidence for teachers in these settings (Pappa, Chapter 2; Dalton-Puffer *et al.*, Chapter, 6; Dafouz, Chapter 8; Talbot *et al.*, Chapter 9; Jiménez Muñoz, Chapter 10; Gierlinger, Chapter 11; Parry & Thomas, Chapter 12; Arshad & Lyster, Chapter 13; Banegas & Pinner, Chapter 15). One such avenue for PD was mentioned by Gierlinger (Chapter 11). He advocated for PD programmes to address teacher confidence in ICL settings along three dimensions: (1) helping teachers become confident to use their entire linguistic repertoire in their classes, (2) helping teachers become confident in using the target language and (3) helping teachers become confident in language teaching pedagogy. From this perspective, bolstering teacher confidence in any of these directions may benefit the teacher's holistic sense of self-confidence overall. Parry and Thomas (Chapter 12) also reflected on a PD intervention to bolster teachers' self-confidence in speaking Welsh in their classrooms and even a short intervention seemed to impact the self-confidence of the teachers in their study positively. In terms of future research initiatives, teacher confidence in any of these directions could be further explored with teachers in various ICL contexts worldwide. Ideally, this would involve teachers at various stages of their careers and with differing levels of teaching experience generally and in respect to ICL. Notably, these PD initiatives may also hold value for experienced teachers who are stepping into ICL settings for the first time. Of course, the existence of challenges in these settings is not the only reason why such PD initiatives are valuable. Understanding and aiming to bolster the self-efficacy of teachers is valuable in its own right and is relevant for their experience of job satisfaction (Klassen & Chiu, 2010) and well-being (Zee & Koomen, 2016).

Another interesting point related to PD is made by Arshad and Lyster's (Chapter 13) who answer Tedick and Zilmer's (2018: 290) call for research on *PD in action*, or 'research that involves observing teachers in their classrooms and interacting with them as they engage in PD experiences'. The cohort of CBI teachers undertaking their *PD in action* initiative all reported being satisfied with the initiative and planned to apply the knowledge they gained to their future teaching; however, 'they were also aware that it was the PD which allowed them three afternoons and one full day of planning time to generate their units' (Chapter 13: 243). Balancing teachers perceived lack of time with the need for meaningful PD that fits the challenges and needs of teachers in their situated settings should be a central concern for educational researchers and policy makers going forward. This point was further emphasised by Jiménez Muñoz (Chapter 10) who pointed out that one-size-fits-all approaches to assist teachers in the transition to ICL setting dominates and that a more contextualised approach is needed.

Implications for practice

Relevant practical considerations for teachers' practice and classrooms were articulated in several of the chapters in this collection. For instance, in Chapter 2, Pappa suggests that teachers reflect on their identity and emotions and learn to see them as accessible and integral parts of their teaching. She points out that by regulating emotions in a constructive way, teachers can come to a deeper understanding of the reasons why they have chosen to teach within CLIL programmes. Pragmatically, teachers can talk with their learners about the various emotions they will likely experience in their ICL classes to normalise their experience of various classroom feelings by pointing out that experiencing both positive and negative emotions is part of the learning experience.

Jin *et al.* (Chapter 3) also focused on teacher identities. They highlight the potential of translanguaging as a pedagogical tool for teachers, and point out that it has been shown to be effective in a variety of contexts. Translanguaging may allow both teachers and learners to tap into more of their linguistic resources and can facilitate 'problem solving and knowledge construction' (Chapter 3: 51). Teachers can reflect on their identities as multilinguals and attempt to balance this with the guidelines of their respective programmes. For some teachers, tapping into their broader linguistics repertoires, and encouraging students to do the same, may act to release pressure and tension in the event of misunderstandings or when feeling cognitively overburdened.

Roiha and Mäntylä (Chapter 4) show how important authentic language use was for their case study participant, Kimmo. In the view of Kimmo, CLIL classes were considered sites of authentic communication. Roiha and Mäntylä suggest that facilitating a safe environment where learners feel comfortable and supported to communicate freely and take risks in the target language would go a long way towards promoting authentic communication in ICL classrooms.

Polat and Mahalingappa (Chapter 5: 90) reflect on an important point related to selecting curriculum for the integration of content and language, pointing out that this 'requires utmost attention' as the effectiveness of curriculum implementations depend on many factors such as the teacher, the discipline, the population of students and the curriculum itself. They also highlight how a 'one-size-fits-all' approach to instructional models or curricula may be 'fundamentally flawed'. Pragmatically, this suggests the need for context-appropriate and local accommodations for both instructional models and curricula. It also suggests the need to support teachers as they adapt to make things more appropriate for their own classrooms.

A practical consideration noted in Dalton-Puffer et al.'s (Chapter 6) contribution relates to what they labelled as 'safety nets' (Chapter 6: 106) for CLIL teachers. These are strategies that teachers employ, consciously or unconsciously, to reduce feeling cognitively overburdened in their CLIL classes. Such safety nets included choosing which subjects or topics to teach in English and which to teach in German, depending on how the teachers perceived their complexity, and the ability of their students. Dalton-Puffer et al. point out how teachers and students alike would move to German to avoid a communication breakdown or language issue. One takeaway message from their chapter is that teachers in a variety of settings may benefit from consciously reflecting on 'safety nets' that would allow them to reduce their own cognitive burden and better flourish in their own settings.

Several implications relevant for teachers' practice were considered in Milla and García Mayo's (Chapter 7) contribution. Notably, they discussed how a convergence of teachers' beliefs and practices can benefit teachers. One strategy suggested by Milla and García Mayo (Chapter 7: 126), specifically related to OCF, would be to 'include actual video-recordings of their behaviour in different content classes in such a way that they could observe the frequency (or lack thereof) with which they use OCF and the most frequent types in their repertoire' in CLIL training programmes. Notably, in Chapter 11 (Arshad & Lyster), such an approach was used as part of a CBI PD initiative. Arshad and Lyster pointed out that although the teachers that took part were initially apprehensive to be filmed, they ultimately expressed pride in their accomplishments as they watched themselves teach.

Another way for teachers to address a potential mismatch between what students may expect in their ICL classes is to level with students about what they expect from such courses. At the same time, depending on the goals of the programme or teacher, clarifying what students should expect in terms of language feedback and instruction, or lack thereof, may help teachers and students get on the same page about their classes. Such a strategy was reflected on by one teacher participant in Jin et al.'s (Chapter 3: 48) chapter. Their participant pointed out how at their university, they 'try to prepare students for the fact that we are not a language university'. Such clarifications may help bridge potential mismatches between expectations and reality for both students and teachers in ICL programmes. An example of this was found in Banegas and Pinner's contribution to this volume (Chapter 15). The authors highlighted how learning about pre-service students' expectations helped their teacher educator in 'calibrating the module so that there was a stronger connection between the IETE curriculum and student-teachers' needs' (Chapter 15: 279).

In Chapter 8, Dafouz points to the relationship between explicit teacher preparation for ICL programmes and their chances for success in such settings. In her view, feeling supported in such settings is consequential for teachers in terms of their efficacy and professional integrity. Furthermore, she suggests that this is arguably even more important for experienced teachers as they might be forced to reevaluate their 'long-standing teaching practices and psychological beliefs to new realities that may demand different skills and competences' (Chapter 8: 150). A similar conclusion about the need for greater support for teachers was reached in Chapter 9 (Talbot et al.) and Chapter 11 (Gierlinger). Talbot et al. suggest that a clear implication from their study is that teachers need to be supported in ICL programmes, not only for their teaching, but for their well-being more generally. Particularly, they suggest that self-care and the prioritisation of well-being should not be viewed as a triviality for teachers, but rather as 'a key building block for effective practice' (Chapter 9: 170). Similarly, Gierlinger in Chapter 11 highlights the specific need to address teacher confidence to help teachers feel more comfortable and efficacious in their CLIL teaching. For Gierlinger, addressing teacher confidence is directly relevant to teachers' practice and perception of well-being more generally. Addressing teacher confidence was also at the centre of Parry and Thomas'

(Chapter 12) contribution. Their study offers hope that even short-term interventions can act to address teachers' confidence to use the target language in ICL classrooms.

Jiménez Muñoz (Chapter 10) points out that for teachers in ICL programmes, it is important to recognise that feeling imbalanced in the process of acclimating to educational change is normal and that this recognition will likely have a positive effect on teachers. Particularly, he suggests that 'to know in advance that stress and anxiety are commonplace, and that they usually alleviate with time, can help as a coping mechanism' (Chapter 10: 190). A practical consideration that may be worth considering in some contexts would be to facilitate mentor pairings with teachers who are new to ICL teaching with teachers who are more experienced in such settings.

Chapter 14 (Nishida) also has clear practical classroom implications. She points out that for her student participants, 'being able to conduct a project with an explicit focus on content from their field of expertise was a reported source of motivation for many students' (Chapter 14: 262). This is likely to occur naturally in higher education and in job-oriented secondary schools given the focus of such programmes, yet Nishida's chapter is an explicit reminder of how taking students' specific interests into account can be a motivating force in ICL classrooms.

Closing thoughts

We hope this collection serves to spark more interest and awareness about the experiences of various stakeholders in ICL contexts. Though we have done our best to include a wide range of ICL programmes, geographical settings, methodological approaches, educational levels and languages, what we have been able to gather here is just a sample of the diversity that exists in these areas. As such, many questions remain; with this, come opportunities and avenues for future research initiatives.

Without question, the psychological experiences of the stakeholders matter a great deal to the success of ICL programmes, and how, why and to what degree stakeholders invest in them. One area in need of future exploration relates to how best to facilitate conversations between policy makers and classroom stakeholders. Classroom stakeholders are often not consulted about the spread of ICL programmes nor which classes this takes place in (Dearden & Macaro, 2016; Macaro et al., 2018). One notion to emerge from this collection is that conversations that involve classroom stakeholders may provide them with a greater sense of ownership in how these programmes are implemented and may help policy makers ensure they are able to understand and meet their needs more effectively. Ensuring that there are ample and on-going opportunities for dialogue between policy makers, university and school managers and classroom stakeholders would help disambiguate what the aims of such programmes are and allow teachers and students to express their needs for support as they embrace their new roles by involving them in defining and researching their perspectives. Day and Kington (2008: 22) argue, 'it is important, then, for policy-makers and school leaders, if they really want the implementation of system-wide school and curriculum change and improvement agendas to meet with success, to factor into their planning the potential effects upon teachers' professional identities'. Indeed, if the implementation of ICL programmes are seen through the lens of educational reform, the success of such reforms depend in large part on the psychological experiences of the stakeholders involved; their identities, experiences, emotions, reactions, senses of investment, commitment, well-being beliefs, attitudes, self-efficacy and ability to cope with challenges are all factors that relate to the stability or instability teachers and learners perceive as they progress through their professional lives and educational journeys respectively.

References

Aguilar, M. (2017) Engineering lecturers' views on CLIL and EMI. *International Journal of Bilingual Education and Bilingualism* 20 (6), 722–735.

Anderson, J. and Lightfoot, A. (2018) Translingual practices in English classrooms in India: Current perceptions and future possibilities. *International Journal of Bilingual Education and Bilingualism*, 1–22.

Bovellan, E. (2014) Teachers' beliefs about learning and language as reflected in their views of teaching materials for content and language integrated learning (CLIL). Unpublished dissertation, Jyväskylä: University of Jyväskylä.

Cho, D.W. (2012) English-medium instruction in the university context of Korea: Tradeoff between teaching outcomes and media-initiated university ranking. *Journal of Asia TEFL* 9 (4).

Costa, F. (2012) Focus on form in ICLHE lectures in Italy: Evidence from English-medium science lectures by native speakers of Italian. *AILA Review* 25 (1), 30–47.

Day, C. and Kington, A. (2008) Identity, well-being and effectiveness: The emotional contexts of teaching. *Pedagogy, Culture & Society* 16 (1), 7–23.

Dearden, J. and Macaro, E. (2016) Higher education teachers' attitudes towards English medium instruction: A three-country comparison. *Studies in Second Language Learning and Teaching* 6 (3), 455.

Doiz, A. and Lasagabaster, D. (2018) Teachers' and students' second language motivational self system in English-medium instruction: A qualitative approach. *TESOL Quarterly* 52 (3), 657–679.

Ellili-Cherif, M. and Alkhateeb, H. (2015) College students' attitude toward the medium of instruction: Arabic versus English dilemma. *Universal Journal of Educational Research* 3.3, 207–213.

Fernandez, R. and Halbach, A. (2011) Analysing the situation of teachers in the Madrid bilingual project after four years of implementation. In Y. Ruiz de Zarobe, J.M. Sierra and F. Gallardo del Puerto (eds) *Content and Foreign Language Integrated Learning* (pp. 241–270). Frankfurt am Main: Peter Lang.

Gefaell, C. and Unterberger, B. (2010) CLIL programme evaluation: Deriving implementation guidelines from stakeholder perspectives. *Vienna English Working Papers* 19 (3), 29–35.

Goldschmidt, M.M. and Seifried, T. (2008) Mismatched expectations among developmental ESL students in higher education. *Research and Teaching in Developmental Education*, 27–38.

Hessel, G., Talbot, K., Gruber, M.-T. and Mercer, S. (2020) The well-being and hob satisfaction of Secondary CLIL and Tertiary EMI teachers [Special Issue]. *Journal for the Psychology of Language Learning* 2 (2), 73–90.

Hu, J. and Gao, X. (Andy) (2020) Understanding subject teachers' language-related pedagogical practices in content and language integrated learning classrooms. *Language Awareness*, 1–20.

Johnson, S., Cooper, C., Cartwright, S., Donald, I., Taylor, P. and Millet, C. (2005) The experience of work-related stress across occupations. *Journal of Managerial Psychology* 20 (2), 178–187.

Infante, D., Benvenuto, G. and Lastrucci, E. (2009) The effects of CLIL from the perspective of experienced teachers. In D. Marsh, P. Mehisto, D. Wolff, R. Aliaga, T. Asikainen, M.J. Frigols-Martín, S. Hughes and G. Langé (eds) *CLIL Practice: Perspectives from the Field* (pp. 156–163). Jyväskylä: University of Jyväskylä.

Ingersoll, R.M. and Smith, T.M. (2004) Do teacher induction and mentoring matter? *NASSP Bulletin* 88, 28–40.

Kim, H. and Cho, Y. (2014) Pre-service teachers' motivation, sense of teaching efficacy, and expectation of reality shock. *Asia-Pacific Journal of Teacher Education* 42 (1), 67–81.

Klassen, R.M. and Chiu, M.M. (2010) Effects on teachers' self-efficacy and job satisfaction: Teacher gender, years of experience, and job stress. *Journal of Educational Psychology*, 102 (3), 741–756.

Kuteeva, M. (2019) Revisiting the 'E' in EMI: Students' perceptions of standard English, lingua franca and translingual practices. *International Journal of Bilingual Education and Bilingualism* 23 (3), 287–300.

Lin, A.M.Y. (2018) Theories of trans/languaging and trans-semiotizing: Implications for content-based education classrooms. *International Journal of Bilingual Education and Bilingualism* 22 (1), 5–16.

Macaro, E. (2018) *English Medium Instruction: Content and Language in Policy and Practice*. Oxford: Oxford University Press.

Macaro, E., Curle, S., Pun, J., An, J. and Dearden, J. (2018) A systematic review of English medium instruction in higher education. *Language Teaching* 51 (1), 36–76.

Maloshonok, N. and Terentev, E. (2017) The mismatch between student educational expectations and realities: Prevalence, causes, and consequences. *European Journal of Higher Education* 7 (4), 356–372.

McIntyre, T.M., McIntyre, S.E. and Francis, D.J. (eds) (2017) *Educator Stress: An Occupational Health Perspective*. New York, NY: Springer Berlin Heidelberg.

Mercer, S. and Kostoulas, A. (2018) *Language Teacher Psychology*. Bristol: Multilingual Matters.

Moate, J.M. (2011) The impact of foreign language mediated teaching on teachers' sense of professional integrity in the CLIL classroom. *European Journal of Teacher Education*, 34 (3), 333–346.

Talbot, K. and Mercer, S. (2018) Exploring university ESL/EFL teachers' emotional well-being and emotional regulation in the United States, Japan, and Austria. *Chinese Journal of Applied Linguistics* 41 (4), 410–432.

Tedick, D. and Zilmer, C. (2018) Teacher perceptions of immersion professional development experiences emphasizing language-focused content instruction. *Journal of Immersion and Content-Based Language Education* 6 (2), 269–294.

van Kampen, E., Admiraal, W. and Berry, A. (2018) Content and language integrated learning in the Netherlands: Teachers' self-reported pedagogical practices. *International Journal of Bilingual Education and Bilingualism* 21 (2), 222–236.

Zee, M. and Koomen, H.M.Y. (2016) Teacher self-efficacy and its effects on classroom processes, student academic adjustment, and teacher well-being: A synthesis of 40 years of research. *Review of Educational Research* 86 (4), 981–1015.

Index